The Blackwell Guide to

Feminist Philosophy

MW01087273

—— Blackwell Philosophy Guides ——

Series Editor: Steven M. Cahn, City University of New York Graduate School

Written by an international assembly of distinguished philosophers, the *Blackwell Philosophy Guides* create a groundbreaking student resource – a complete critical survey of the central themes and issues of philosophy today. Focusing and advancing key arguments throughout, each essay incorporates essential background material serving to clarify the history and logic of the relevant topic. Accordingly, these volumes will be a valuable resource for a broad range of students and readers, including professional philosophers.

The Blackwell Guide to
Feminist Philosophy

Edited by
Linda Martín Alcoff and Eva Feder Kittay

Blackwell
Publishing

© 2007 by Blackwell Publishing Ltd

BLACKWELL PUBLISHING
350 Main Street, Malden, MA 02148-5020, USA
9600 Garsington Road, Oxford OX4 2DQ, UK
550 Swanston Street, Carlton, Victoria 3053, Australia

First published 2007 by Blackwell Publishing Ltd

1   2007

Library of Congress Cataloging-in-Publication Data

The Blackwell guide to feminist philosophy / edited by Linda Martín Alcoff
and Eva Feder Kittay.
p.   cm.—(Blackwell philosophy guides; 20)
Includes bibliographical references and index.
ISBN-13: 978-0-631-22427-3 (hardcover: alk. paper)
ISBN-10: 0-631-22427-0 (hardcover: alk. paper)
ISBN-13: 978-0-631-22428-0 (pbk: alk. paper)
ISBN-10: 0-631-22428-9 (pbk: alk. paper)
1. Feminist theory. 2. Women philosophers. I. Alcoff, Linda.
II. Kittay, Eva Feder. III. Series
HQ1190.B575 2006
305.4201—dc22   2006015949

A catalogue record for this title is available from the British Library

Set in 10/13 pt Galliard
by The Running Head Limited, Cambridge
Printed and bound in Singapore
by Markono Print Media Pte Ltd

The publisher's policy is to use permanent paper from mills that operate a sustainable
forestry policy, and which has been manufactured from pulp processed using acid-free and
elementary chlorine-free practices. Furthermore, the publisher ensures that the text paper
and cover board used have met acceptable environmental accreditation standards.

For further information on
Blackwell Publishing, visit our website:
www.blackwellpublishing.com

Contents

Acknowledgments

We dedicate this volume to all our philosophical foremothers whose work and courage have informed and inspired us.

We would like to thank the editors at Blackwell for encouraging and helping to shepherd this project to its completion. We also wish to thank our contributors for their patience and cooperativeness. Finally we want to thank Karen Burke and Chad Kautzer for their excellent assistance.

Linda Martín Alcoff
Eva Feder Kittay

July 2006

Notes on Contributors

Linda Martín Alcoff is Professor of Philosophy and Women's Studies at Syracuse University. Her books and anthologies include *Visible Identities: Race, Gender, and the Self* (2006), *Real Knowing: New Versions of the Coherence Theory of Knowledge* (1996), *Singing in the Fire: Tales of Women in Philosophy* (2003), and the co-edited collection *Feminist Epistemologies* (1993).

Angela Bolte teaches philosophy at the University of Nevada-Reno. She has published in the areas of philosophy of law, autonomy, and the philosophy of emotions.

Peg Brand teaches gender studies and philosophy at Indiana University in Bloomington. She is co-editor of *Feminism and Tradition in Aesthetics* (1995) and editor of *Beauty Matters* (2000).

Cheshire Calhoun is Charles A. Dana Professor of Philosophy at Colby College. Her books include *Feminism, the Family, and the Politics of the Closet: Lesbian and Gay Displacement* (2000), and *Setting the Moral Compass: Essays by Women Philosophers* (2003).

Lorraine Code is Distinguished Research Professor of Philosophy at York University in Toronto, Canada. Her books include *What Can She Know? Feminist Theory and the Construction of Knowledge* (1991), *Rhetorical Spaces: Essays on (Gendered) Locations* (1995), and *Ecological Thinking: The Politics of Epistemic Location* (2006).

Marilyn Friedman is Professor of Philosophy at Washington University in St Louis. Her books include *What Are Friends For? Feminist Perspectives on Personal Relationships and Moral Theory* (1993), *Political Correctness: For and Against* (1995), *Autonomy, Gender, Politics* (2003), and *Women and Citizenship* (2005).

Nancy J. Hirschmann is Professor of Political Science at The University of Pennsylvania. Her most recent books are *The Subject of Liberty: Toward a Feminist Theory of Freedom* (2003), and *On Freedom: Gender, Class, and Political Theory* (forthcoming).

Eva Feder Kittay is Professor of Philosophy at Stony Brook University. Her books include *Love's Labor: Essays on Women, Equality, and Dependency* (1999) and co-edited collections *The Subject of Care: Feminist Theoretical Perspectives on Dependency* (2002) and *Women and Moral Theory* (1987). She is working on a collection of her essays tentatively entitled: *A Humbler Philosophy: Rethinking Key Concepts in Light of Severe Cognitive Impairment.*

Hilde Lindemann is Associate Professor of Philosophy at Michigan State University. She is the editor of *Hypatia: A Journal of Feminist Philosophy*. Her books include *An Invitation to Feminist Ethics* (2005) and (as Hilde Lindemann Nelson) *Damaged Identities, Narrative Repair* (2001).

Tamsin Lorraine is an Associate Professor of Philosophy at Swarthmore College. She is the author of *Irigaray and Deleuze: Experiments in Visceral Philosophy* (1999) and is currently at work on a book tentatively titled *Feminism and Deleuzian Subjectivity.*

Eileen O'Neill is Professor of Philosophy at the University of Massachusetts at Amherst. Her previous publications include *Early Modern Philosophy: Mind, Matter, and Metaphysics* (2005) and the entries on "Marie de Gournay" and "Women in the History of Philosophy," in *The Encyclopedia of Philosophy*, Supplement (1996).

Elizabeth Potter is Alice Andrews Quigley Professor of Women's Studies at Mills College. Her recent publications *include Feminism and Philosophy of Science* (forthcoming) and *Gender and Boyle's Law of Gases* (2001).

Robin May Schott is Associate Professor of Philosophy at The Danish University of Education. She is the author of *Discovering Feminist Philosophy* (2003), *Cognition and Eros* (2004), and the editor of the Hypatia book, *Feminist Philosophy and the Problem of Evil* (forthcoming).

Ofelia Schutte is Professor of Philosophy at the University of South Florida in Tampa. Her publications include "Cultural Alterity: Cross-Cultural Communication and Feminist Thought in North-South Dialogue" *Hypatia: A Journal of Feminist Philosophy* 13 (2) (2000), and *Cultural Identity and Social Liberation in Latin American Thought* (1993).

Anita Silvers is Professor of Philosophy at San Francisco State University. Her books include *Disability, Difference, and Discrimination* (1998), *Blackwell's Guide to Medical Ethics* (forthcoming), and *Medicine and Social Justice: Essays on the Distribution of Health Care* (2002).

Shannon Sullivan is Head of the Department of Philosophy and Associate Professor of Philosophy and Women's Studies at Pennsylvania State University. Her publications include *Living Across and Through Skins: Transactional Bodies, Pragmatism, and Feminism* (2001), *Revealing Whiteness: The Unconscious Habits of Racial Privilege* (2006), and a co-edited collection on *Race and Epistemologies of Ignorance* (forthcoming).

Margaret Urban Walker is Lincoln Professor of Ethics at Arizona State University. She is author of *Moral Understandings: A Feminist Study in Ethics* (1998), *Moral Contexts* (2003), and *Moral Repair: Reconstructing Moral Relations After Wrongdoing* (forthcoming). She is editor of *Mother Time: Women, Aging, and Ethics* (1999) and *Moral Psychology: Feminist Ethics and Social Theory* (2004) with Peggy DesAutels.

Naomi Zack is Professor of Philosophy at the University of Oregon. She is the author of: *Race and Mixed Race* (1993), *Bachelors of Science* (1996), *Philosophy of Science and Race* (2002), *Inclusive Feminism* (2005), and *Thinking About Race* (2nd edition 2005). Zack is also the editor of *American Mixed Race* (1995), *RACE/SEX* (1997), and *Women of Color in Philosophy* (2002).

Defining Feminist Philosophy

Linda Martín Alcoff and Eva Feder Kittay

> [The] project of philosophy and that of feminist thinking have a fundamental struc-
> ture in common, an art of fighting fire with fire and looks with looks, of objectifying
> and analyzing surrounding thought, of regarding beliefs as objects that must be scru-
> tinized, when the supposedly normal attitude is to submit to what social life erects as
> doctrine. Nothing goes without saying, including what people think about the roles
> which have come down to men and women.
>
> (Michele Le Doeuff 1989: 29)[1]

Over the past thirty years, philosophy has become a vital arena for feminists. They
have scrutinized social beliefs about gender, human nature, familial duties, sexual
ethics, epistemic credibility, and even rationality. Philosophy has provided vital
means, such as methods of conceptual analysis and traditions of critique that have
allowed feminist scholars to subject cultural traditions and dogma about gender
identity and gender relations to objective, fair, but uncompromising examination.
In pursuing this work, feminist philosophers have also developed new methods of
analysis and critique, defined new lines of inquiry, and reinvigorated some of the
central areas of philosophy.

The growth and interest in feminist philosophy have been dramatic. At the end
of the 1970s one could count the volumes in print on women and philosophy on
two hands: there was the monumental *Second Sex*, by Simone de Beauvoir,[2] a few
books on women and philosophical topics written by women in previous centuries,
a few works questioning the tradition of political philosophy, and five collections of
essays specifically devoted to feminism and philosophy. Today, the volumes written
by contemporary authors are too many to enumerate and rival those produced
in other areas of philosophy. In a matter of a few decades, feminist philosophy
has emerged as a distinctive field, with a distinct literature including a journal
devoted exclusively to feminist philosophy. Essays in feminist philosophy appear,
if still infrequently, in mainstream journals. Feminist philosophy is taught at the
undergraduate and graduate levels, and has been the explicit (and implicit) focus of
doctoral dissertations. Job descriptions now include it as an area of specialization.

And its importance has been reflected in several Presidential Addresses in the American Philosophical Association and in the developments in other philosophical specializations, such as those that are represented in this volume: political philosophy (see Hirschmann), ethics (Friedman and Bolte), epistemology (Code), philosophy of science (Potter), aesthetics (Brand), history of philosophy (Schott), among others. The area is already vast and growing so quickly that a volume such as this cannot do justice to all the creativity and insights generated by feminist philosophical inquiry.

This anthology provides but a sample of many of the central areas to which feminist philosophers have made contributions that have advanced the field. It also includes feminist work in relatively new areas of philosophy, such as medical ethics (Lindemann), moral epistemology (Walker), the philosophy of race (Zack), lesbian philosophy (Calhoun), postcolonial philosophy (Schutte), and philosophy of disability (Silvers). The essays collected here are not, however, intended to be merely summaries of these fields over the decades. We have assembled some of the best and most influential feminist philosophers in a variety of areas and asked them to critically reflect on the field as well as to write about recent debates "in their own voice." Thus, readers will find essays here in which authors are taking positions and offering substantive arguments rather than attempting to write in a "voice from nowhere."

In the spirit of that assignment, in this introduction we, the editors, will offer our own view of the field of feminist philosophy and take our own position on debates over the nature of feminist philosophy, its relation to the field of philosophy as a whole, and its political content given the current climate of criticism of liberal politics in the academy. First, however, it is important to note that the topic of gender and the relation between gender and justice are not new to philosophy.

Gender in Canonical Philosophical Writings

Writings about women by philosophers such as Aristotle, Rousseau, Kant, Hegel, and Nietzsche for example, were arguably not motivated toward justice for women, as Mill or Wollstonecraft were (Plato is a more complicated figure as what he has to say about women in the *Republic* and in the *Laws* are arguably at odds with one another). Assertions about women and the proper or natural gender relations are sometimes included as asides. At other times, they are part of explicit claims about the nature or natural condition of women, which are intended to justify or explain women's subordination. Assumptions about women's inferior (although similar) or distinct (but still inferior) capacities also come to figure in larger arguments about the right order of social, ethical, or political life, or as part of arguments about the true nature of mankind. Often these claims were not well developed or carefully argued or developed through a consideration of contrary points of view. Indeed, as Michèle Le Doeuff has pointed out, "where women are concerned the learned utter, and institutions let them utter, words which fall clearly below their own usual standards of validation."[3] When opining about women, the philosophers who rank among the accepted luminaries of "the canon," (with some notable exceptions such as Condorcet and John Stuart Mill) largely manifest the tendency to accept these lowered standards. In this they mirrored and did not challenge the accepted opinions of their day. In fact, at times they represented the most conservative accepted views of women's capacities and place in life. Kant wrote notoriously that a woman with her "head full of Greek, like Mme Dacier, or [one who] carries on fundamental controversies about mechanics, like the Marquise de Chatelet, might as well even have a beard; for perhaps that would express more obviously the mien of profundity for which she strives."[4] Thus, the ultimate aim of unpacking the story of sexism in the history of philosophy, as Robin Schott argues in her essay for this volume, is to "help philosophy do its job better."

It is also true that we can turn to almost any age in philosophy to find feminist arguments, from Ancient Greece (notably Plato), through the Middle Ages (such as Christine de Pisan), into the era of Cartesian philosophy and the later Enlightenment (see O'Neill's discussion of Marie de Gournay, this volume). There are specific feminist philosophical writings, such as those of Sor Juana Ines de la Cruz (1648–95)[5] in the seventeenth century, Mary Wollstonecraft (1759–97) in the eighteenth century, John Stuart Mill (1806–73) and Charlotte Perkins Gilman (1860–1935) in the nineteenth century, and of course there are the influential writings of Simone de Beauvoir, in the mid-twentieth century. It is noteworthy that many of those mentioned are frequently not included within lists of philosophers. As Eileen O'Neill remarks, "If we utilize that method of historiography known as 'historical reconstruction,' we will take as central those issues deemed by the philosophers of the past to be the central ones; and we will count past figures to be philosophers just in case they were so deemed by their contemporaries." To the extent that the content of their works was not among those deemed to be central issues for philosophers of the past, they fail to be counted as philosophers in contemporary compendiums. Nonetheless, these writers were to have a profound effect on contemporary feminist philosophers, for whom the content of their works is decidedly central.

The Emergence of Contemporary Feminist Philosophy

A significant amount of feminist philosophy might fairly be characterized as an application of philosophical methods and approaches to feminist concerns. Mary Wollstonecraft's rational arguments in her animadversions directed at Rousseau's denigration of women; John Stuart Mill's logical argumentation in laying bare the fallacies of those who deny the equality of women; Simone de Beauvoir's deployment of existential philosophy in analyzing the restricted existential domain of women are prominent examples. One of the principal areas of debate among feminist philosophers concerns the utility, or disutility, of various philosophical approaches for the elucidation of women's oppression and for developing effective solutions. Some argue, for example, that feminist philosophy, with its doubled focus on theory and practice, will find its strongest resources in pragmatism (see Sullivan, in this volume). Others argue that poststructuralist approaches to conceptualizing identity and the self can best address the issue of differences among women (see Lorraine, in this volume).

If one is tempted by such examples to characterize feminist philosophy as the application of neutral philosophical means (which are untouched by feminist aims) to feminist topics of concern, this may be motivated by the desire to show that feminism affects only the choice of questions. On such a view, the answers to these questions are pursued with detachment and impartiality and have the same objectivity as any other philosophical investigation. Yet such a view does not adequately characterize feminist philosophy as a whole, nor, arguably, any field of inquiry within philosophy. This is because method and subject matter cannot really be made as distinct as this characterization presupposes: certain questions at times give birth to new methods. And new methods in turn, will highlight some questions, obscure others, and render still others unintelligible. There are questions that only arise once a new methodology has been introduced. We have seen such a process operative in metaphysics. Philosophy has only recently developed modal approaches as a way to adjudicate between competing intuitions about thought experiments. These modal considerations about possible worlds have themselves yielded new questions, such as questions about the nature of possibility. This last reflexive turn highlights a feature of philosophy that has helped to shape the emergence, nature, and trajectory of feminist philosophy.

For what is new in the more recent period of feminist work in philosophy is a greater self-consciousness about precisely the relationship between feminism and philosophy, and a questioning of philosophy itself as understood through the canonical works. The existing canons in both the Anglo-American and the Continental traditions in philosophy have been contested for their exclusions of women, as well as for viewing the women who wrote philosophy as mere chroniclers rather than original theorists and disputants (see O'Neill, this volume). These moves have been facilitated by the powerful liberatory movement of women that has very quickly changed the default assumption from "women are inferior to and ought to be subjugated to men" to "women and men are equals." Even conservatives find that they have to make arguments differentiating women's roles by arguing from the assumption of women's equality.

Earlier feminists had to develop arguments to show that women have the requisite capacities for self-governance, for rational thought, for the pursuit of knowledge, etc. Then as women slowly have come to be accepted as equals, the persistent absence of women in the canon of philosophy puts the onus on philosophers, rather than on women, to explain themselves. Why were the writings of so many female philosophers systematically excluded? Why were the writings on women by so many of the great male philosophers so obviously riddled by distorted logic and personal bias? As Code argues in her essay here, the persistence and ubiquity of such biases have led feminist epistemologists to explore the "normative conceptions of epistemic subjectivity" that have masked privilege and vested interest in the operations of philosophy itself.

This shift can be observed in one of the earliest, and arguably still one of the most audacious pieces of feminist philosophy, Marilyn Frye's now classic collection of essays, *The Politics of Reality*.[6] Frye, trained in the area of philosophy which favors conceptual and linguistic analysis of important terms, utilizes the method of conceptual analysis in exploring feminist concerns. But at the same time she gives birth to a new philosophical approach. Using standard conceptual analysis, Frye endeavors to clarify newly created feminist terms such as "sexism," "male chauvinism," and the startling application of "oppression" in conjunction with traditional female roles. Frye examines the meaning of these terms, giving them the coherence and intelligibility necessary before we can evaluate whether they refer to real phenomena. But in considering the meanings of these terms she makes reference to the concrete experiences of a group, namely women, rather than experiences that are presumed to be universal. Like J.L. Austin, she appeals to usage in the general language to establish meaning but her experience is not abstracted from its particularity in gender and culture. Implicit in her modification of conceptual analysis is, therefore, a critique of the putative universality of philosophical claims and the putative neutrality of philosophical methods.

If philosophy is to include the lives and experiences of women, it must own up to its false universalization of men's experiences. In the title essay of the book, Frye argues that those who possess power also possess the means to define their own reality, a reality that excludes the experiences and sometimes even the existence of those who make their own lives possible. Philosophy, as created by men who are dominant over women, has created a philosophical "reality" that scarcely recognizes women or their experiences. Women, she remarks in one essay, are the stagehands behind the world stage in which both the actors and the audience are men. But this "reality" is as illusory as that of Plato's cave. And it is for women philosophers to expose the errors of philosophy itself.

The process of exposing such errors has yielded important feminist investigations into standard issues of philosophy, but they are considered now in a new light. For example, the nature of rationality is explored with reference to the gendering of reason as masculine and the emotions as feminine; the mind–body problem is revisited with reference to the idea that we are first and foremost embodied and thus dependent beings; accepted notions of justice are criticized for their reliance on an understanding of human relations based on models of interactions between men; and so forth.

Reflexive Critique within Philosophy

In all of this work just described, it is clear that feminist philosophy has a particularly strong reflexive engagement with philosophy as a field. One might imagine that philosophers would welcome such an intense reflexive scrutiny of the field's founding assumptions, given the general level of respect which self-scrutiny is accorded and the general level of intensity with which it is pursued. Much of feminist philosophy naturally raises such metaphilosophical questions in regard to how deeply androcentrism is integrated into the philosophical enterprise itself.

One place to raise the question about androcentrism concerns the presumption that philosophy should deal only with universal non-contingent matters. Differences in the bodies of persons, or their different social conditions have been seen as contingent factors in light of the preeminent importance of a shared human capacity to reason. It is the presumed universality of what is essential to being that has permitted western philosophy to hold that valid answers to its inquiries are valid universally. Questions about the nature of the good (or the true, the beautiful, the just, etc.) have been presumed to be about what the good is (or the true, beautiful, just, etc.) regardless of *whose* good is in question. (Aristotle, recognizing that the good in itself may be different for different individuals, wrote "that we should pray that the good in itself be good for us."[7]) To ask, as some feminist philosophers have insisted doing, whether what has been spoken of as "the" good actually applies to women is an odd question under the presumption of universality. But feminist philosophers have shown that when men in traditional philosophical writings have used the term Man, presumably in the generic, they have really had in mind "man" used in a gender-specific way.

A careful look at historical texts reveals the occasional reference to women that betrays the presumed universality of the conclusions about (generic) Man. In particular, women's embodiment, their presumed deficiency in reason, and their inferior social status have rendered them deficient and falling out of the scope of the "universal." For Aristotle, only free men possessed all the elements needed for fully rational deliberation and action.[8] Women had the capacity to deliberate, but lacked the capacity to act on the results of their rational deliberation – their rational faculty lacked the requisite authority. Kant's sublime was an experience reserved for men, who alone could revere the power of the rational, while women's aesthetic capacities were limited to the sensuous pleasures of beauty.[9] Rousseau, who argued so eloquently for man's freedom and for man's autonomy, argued at the same time in favor of an education for Sophie (Emile's helpmeet and female counterpart) that would make her docile, and subservient, and Emile, her husband and master.[10] The servility that Emile was to escape by a proper education was the very aim of Sophie's upbringing. And as Susan Okin[11] demonstrated, even Rawls in *A Theory of Justice*[12] made the parties to the original position "heads of households," a term which in contrast to "female head of household" is gendered masculine. The putative universality of much of philosophy has been revealed to have a limited scope, one which is confined to men (and then, only to some men). This raises a serious question about whether or not the putative universality of philosophical claims should simply be extended to women, or whether those claims are in reality irreducibly and irrevocably particular, in which case philosophy needs to reconsider its attachment to universalistic arguments.

The insistence that the topics and results of philosophical inquiry have a universal scope has not only masked ways in which women were excluded from its midst, it also precluded asking about gender-specific phenomena such as contraception, abortion, pregnancy, and childbearing. This insularity was pierced in the 1960s and 1970s when philosophers entered debates on the permissibility or impermissibility of abortion. The literature on abortion by philosophers now fills volumes. Even this relatively conservative application of philosophical analysis to concerns important to women challenges any assumption that philosophy is a discipline whose boundaries are fixed and stable, or that philosophy is only about questions that know no gender or other distinctions among humans. And yet much of the philosophical literature on this gendered issue focuses on the status of the non-gendered fetus and on the rights and duties of (genderless) persons, not on the specific burdens and responsibilities a pregnancy imposes on *women*.

Subsequent feminist philosophers have asked still other questions about abortion and more generally about the way in which the woman's embodiment and her existential situation can be the subject of philosophical investigation. Might men and women view, and reason, about abortion differently? Being pregnant is a unique experience of being a singular individual who, at the same time, in*corpo*rates another entirely dependent being. Might a woman's perspective of having been pregnant, or anticipating the possibility, give her a relationship to the fetus and to abortion that is not readily available to men? If women had originally been the world's philosophers rather than men, might we not expect a great deal of theorizing about pregnancy (including the individuation problems posed by pregnancy) and might not a woman's right to abortion already be a nearly settled question?

In their pursuit of answers to such questions, feminist philosophers have had little motivation to follow the regulatory customs of philosophy, which have separated analytic from Continental approaches, and which have segregated the domains of value inquiry from ontological inquiry as well as from epistemological inquiry. We must accept the possibility that feminist philosophy will put pressure on philosophy itself, will expand its current boundaries, challenge unquestioned assumptions, and invent new methods. Many other fields recently developed within philosophy have had similar stretching effects. Consider the impact of naturalized epistemology on epistemology, or the influence of moral psychology on moral philosophy, or the sway of philosophical work in cognitive science on the philosophy of mind. There is no consensus about the proper effects of these new fields on existing problematics, but there have certainly been some dramatic proposals. So too in feminist philosophy.

Reflexive Critique within Feminist Philosophy

Just as philosophy needs to examine and reconsider its assumptions and methods in the face of feminist scrutiny, so feminist philosophy must itself be open to reflexive critique and its challenges. This means that feminist philosophy should neither be limited to the application of philosophical methods to feminist concerns, nor should it be characterized as the application of feminism or feminist methods to philosophy. How feminist philosophy defines itself, its subject matter, and its methods needs to be open to self-scrutiny, no less than philosophy itself must be. Many feminist philosophers have recognized that we ourselves must take care to avoid generating false universalisms. As Zack argues forcefully in this volume, we must diligently examine our own starting points and privileges. Otherwise they may be blind to the ways we fashion our reality and our philosophy around our limited experience (if not our interests). Feminist philosophy must remain self-aware that, as it purports to speak on behalf of women in the male-dominated world of philosophy, it does not occlude the experiences of those women who have not been sufficiently privileged to have a philosophical training. Feminist philosophers like Zack and Schutte in this volume have brought questions of racial identity and the ongoing legacy of colonialism to the forefront of any analysis of women's situation, disrupting any easy generalizations about female subjectivity. Cheshire Calhoun brings to the fore the importance of considering a woman's sexuality, while Anita Silvers underscores ways in which presumptions about ability and disability have (mis)shaped philosophical studies among feminist and non-feminist philosophy alike. At the same time, many of the advances of feminist scholarship have opened possibilities for considering various forms of embodiment and social situation. Still we must ask when, if ever, does feminist philosophy speak for all women? If it ought not to presume to speak for all women, what is feminist about it?

Feminist Philosophy as a Research Program

How then are we to define feminist philosophy in a way that is at once inclusive and critical? If we were to define feminist philosophy by reference to a number of substantive commitments about the nature of women's oppression and the nature of the solution, such commitments would help demarcate the field. But defining the field in this way would also risk dogmatism insofar as there is not much agreement on either the nature of the problem or the solution to whatever problems are identified. On the other hand, if we refuse to define feminist philosophy at all, how can we demarcate the field?

We suggest that feminist philosophy can be characterized as a research program or area of inquiry within philosophy that consists of a set of questions rather than commitments. In this way it is analogous to nearly every other research area within the discipline. Like other areas, feminist philosophy sets out to pursue inquiry about a specific area, but it remains open to the conceptualization of that area, its relation to other areas, even to its very existence. Epistemology pursues inquiry into knowledge, but there is no consensus over how to define knowledge, and many epistemologists have been busily deflating truth (which one might think is the object of knowledge). Still others have seriously considered the possibility that the skeptics are right and there is no knowledge after all. Yet most epistemologists believe philosophers can contribute to an understanding of what knowledge is (or is not). Similarly within political philosophy and ethics, one can assume that every contributor considers "justice" or "the good" to have value, but what one philosopher considers justice another considers the height of injustice. Some argue that justice is unattainable but can act only as an ideal, and postmodernists argue that the claim that justice has been reached, even about the most local event, is to invite injustice! Thus, research areas within philosophy do share some very minimal concerns or aims but they leave open the way those concerns and aims are pursued, conceptualized, and defined. And it is also possible, and not infrequent, that a major participant within a research area declares the whole project bankrupt.

Feminist philosophy has followed a similar trajectory. Minimally, feminist philosophers might be said to be those concerned with questions concerning gender. As the term "feminist" connotes the social movement of women for gender justice, it suggests that "feminist" philosophy carries with it such a political appeal as well. But there is no agreement on what gender means, whether gender is a legitimate category, even whether women can be truly said "to exist," that is, whether there is a single category that includes all and only those who should be, or generally are, categorized as women. (Here incidentally, is an area of inquiry not imagined prior to feminist probing, namely "the philosophy – or ontology or metaphysics – of gender.") All this is just as it should be, given the necessity of philosophy to be as uncompromising in its self-scrutiny as it is in scrutinizing the assumptions of others.

We also suggest that feminist philosophy is very broadly concerned with issues of justice for women – that is why it is *feminist* and not *feminine*. This suggests that it is an area of philosophy that has a political agenda. That it might have such an agenda is, in many philosophical circles, suspect. How can philosophical investigation be rigorous and objective if it has a political mission? But to say that it is an area of philosophy concerned with justice *for women* is just to say that it is an area concerned with justice, but one which rules out only such antediluvian positions as the claim that it is legitimate to treat women unjustly, as mere means to others' ends, as simple commodities, or that women should remain politically subordinate to men. It otherwise embraces a wide variety of positions concerning the nature of justice as well as the nature of gender, and in this regard is no more prone to adopting any one political stance as a favored position than does any other area of philosophy that concerns itself with justice and matters of value.

The disagreement within the field of feminist philosophy is as much a sign of philosophical vigor as it is of unsettled philosophical questions. It is true that to give such a minimal characterization of feminist philosophy as we have will result in including a very wide variety of views and concerns. Still there are some ways of doing philosophy that are excluded. Not included would be those which consider the question of women's status relative to men to be an issue which remains unsettled, that is, positions that still entertain the possibility that one sex, namely woman, is inherently inferior and needs to be subjugated to another, man. Aside from such an exclusion, feminist philosophy must either concern matters related to gender in some form, or must approach a problem with lessons learned from considering the ways gender has been philosophically investigated. Thus, to characterize feminist philosophy as a research area or sub-field that pursues questions related to gender justice is to give it no more, or less, political unity than that which exists in political philosophy or ethics or other sub-fields. And it also avoids a dogmatism that would shield political values or commitments from analysis.

Feminist Philosophy as Transformative

As a research program, feminist philosophy then has the potential not only to add to the list of traditional philosophical questions, but also to transform philosophy itself by introducing new approaches to traditional questions. This transformative effect of feminist philosophy is more developed in some areas than in others. Two of the most advanced areas are ethics and epistemology, and the insights gleaned have both influenced and in some cases been drawn from the sub-areas of the respective fields. They have also been influential on and influenced by related areas. Represented in this volume is the area of ethics, for example, but also bioethics, moral psychology, and the related area of political philosophy. We will consider first the case of ethics and then epistemology.

If any area of philosophy is amenable to exposing the false universalizing of traditional western philosophy it is in one that discusses the nature of how we should conduct our lives and organize our social world. For it is clear that in everyday life, men and women have traditionally occupied two separate worlds. Women's world, whatever else it may look like, has been occupied by children and others who are more or less inherently dependent on caring labor. And women's relationships to men have been defined in large part in terms of care. The ethical concerns of women importantly have been shaped by these constraints, while men's ethical concerns have featured relations with other adults, other ethical subjects, each of whom is independent of every other. The moral psychology that arises in these different contexts is marked as well and plays an important role in the way in which moral concepts are undertood in overarching theories as well as in applied areas such as bioethics (see Walker and Lindemann, this volume). Much of ethical theory joins political philosophy in taking the public space largely occupied by adult men as its sphere of inquiry and so it appears that ethical issues arise only among equal and independent adults (see Hirschmann, this volume). But this picture poorly reflects women's daily experiences, which often have been dominated by relations with dependents, i.e., with those who are not their equals. Feminist philosophers have argued convincingly that concerns reflected in the ethical theories developed by men rarely speak to ethical realities that women confront.

The development of an ethics of care has been the consequence of considerations such as these. Care ethics, like the conceptual analysis employed by Frye, has similarly performed a double duty in both addressing itself to specific ethical questions and in stretching the boundaries of ethics. Care ethics takes the paradigm case of human experience to be embedded in familial and dependent relationships, rather than in those of autonomous individuals, and it emerged in part from feminist philosophers' knowledge of caring relationships. But the virtues and conceptions of self, ethical decision-making, and goals of ethical deliberation discerned in the practice of caring for dependents appear to be of importance beyond the confines of the domestic sphere in which they play their major role. A care ethics postulates the importance of a concept of self that is always in-relationship, a self with somewhat permeable ego boundaries that sees itself connected to others. Care ethics reveals the limits of rational deduction as a method of ethical deliberation, and emphasizes the role of empathy, of responsiveness, and attunement to the other. And where much of traditional ethics emphasizes the importance of non-interference with another's plan of life, care ethics emphasizes the importance of maintaining connections with others in a manner that is neither violent nor injurious. Values and conceptions such as these have importance outside the domestic sphere, for example in health care, welfare policies, social organization, peace politics, and global concerns. In expanding our understanding of the ethical to include the concept of care which has a wide applicability in human affairs, care ethics has a transformative potential in both political and ethical theory.

Feminist epistemology began with questions coming from the sciences and the social sciences, about why, and how, women had been excluded from the sciences and how the many blatantly biased theories about women produced in both the natural and social sciences had achieved credence. This led feminist epistemologists to the more general question of why, and how, have women all over the world been epistemically disauthorized as knowers. Was this disauthorization justified? If not, what theories of justification provided an alibi for this general disauthorization? Feminist values of equality and inclusiveness have led to better empirical methods in the social sciences, correcting theories dependent on an evidentiary base that ignored women's experiences or women's interpretations of their experiences. Therefore, feminist epistemologists have argued that contextual values – that is, values beyond the usual list of parsimony, breadth, and simplicity to include such social values as democracy and egalitarianism – are useful guides of inquiry, not biases to be left behind, and that the epistemic effects of various value commitments can be judged and compared. One of the critical debates this has in turn engendered among feminist epistemologists and feminist philosophers of science is whether empiricism needs to be abandoned, or whether it can be reformed, a topic discussed by Potter in this volume.

While we have limited our discussion to feminist ethics and epistemology, we find similar transformations in other sub-disciplines. And the reach of feminism in philosophy has also impacted areas such as pragmatism, phenomenology, critical theory, postmodernism, race theory and postcolonial studies, among others. New fields have also been spawned including the metaphysics of sex and gender, and lesbian philosophy, areas in which the fundamental terms of sex and gender have been questioned, as well as the nature of oppression or injustice that requires a response (see Calhoun, this volume).

Although there is no consensus on major issues, there are a number of strong threads that run throughout feminist philosophy's diverse sub-fields. These include an emphasis on relationality, on the social context of life and thought, on the use of personal narrative, and a breakdown of rigid borders between rationality and the emotions. Thus, in epistemology feminists have emphasized the importance of testimony and of epistemic communities (see Code), and in ethics feminists have emphasized family obligations and validated emotional attachments (see Friedman and Bolte, and Walker). The epistemic themes are prominent in the ethical concerns as well. As Hilde Lindemann points out, the question of what counts as epistemic legitimacy and who has epistemic authority has a profound impact on the care provided by the medical profession. Similarly, feminist philosophers of science and epistemologists have taken the role of our emotional and relational lives into consideration when discussing the production and reception of knowledge. Feminist philosophers have then pointed to the broad impact a relational understanding of the self and subjectivity can have on philosophical matters. This revised understanding of subjectivity and connectedness has underscored the relevance of narrative accounts of the self and of social identity that portray the self as necessarily emerging out of dialogical contexts beyond the borders of any sub-discipline.

Any one of these emphases is not unique to feminist philosophy. Take for instance, the use of first-person experiences: other philosophers use first-person experiences to jog our intuitions or concretize a type of problem. For feminists, however, the importance of using first-person examples comes from more than the need for illustration but from a different understanding of how philosophy is connected, and responsible, to everyday life and to the silenced experiences of women. We suggest that it is these common threads – of relationality, of the importance of experience, and of a kind of pragmatic connection to the everyday – that have helped the field of feminist philosophy to cross borders that have long characterized, and limited, philosophy, borders such as the analytic and Continental divide in philosophy and disciplinary borders within and beyond philosophy.

In expanding the scope, method, and vision of philosophy, in allowing for a permeability of disciplinary boundaries, and in the active engagement of reflexive critique, the work of feminist philosophers has begun to overhaul our understanding of philosophy, even as it remains undeniably philosophical. The essays in this volume cover only a portion of this transformative literature. But we hope that they will be sufficiently provocative to make the reader want to explore further and stimulating enough to invite more voices into this vibrant conversation.

Notes

1 Michèle Le Doeuff, *Hipparchia's Choice: An Essay Concerning Women, Philosophy, Etc.*, translated by Trista Selous (Cambridge, MA: Blackwell, 1991).
2 Simone de Beauvoir, *The Second Sex*, 1949, tr. H.M. Parshley (London: Penguin, 1972).

3 Le Doeuff, *Hipparchia's Choice*, p. 29.

4 Immanuel Kant, *Observations on the Feeling of the Beautiful and the Sublime*, tr. John T. Goldthwait (Berkeley: University of California Press, 1960), p. 78.

5 An electronic edition of her complete works based on the text of Adolfo Méndez Plancarte and Alberto G. Salceda can be located at http://www.dartmouth.edu/sorjuana/

6 Marilyn Frye, *The Politics of Reality: Essays in Feminist Theory*, Trumansburg NY: The Crossing Press, 1983.

7 Aristotle, *The Nichomachean Ethics*, tr. A.K. Thomson (London: Penguin Books, 1976), p. 114.

8 Aristotle writes: "For the slave has no deliberative faculty at all; the woman has, but it is without authority, and the child has, but it is immature." Aristotle, *Politics,* translated by Benjamin Jowett, New York: Dover Publications, 2000, Book 1 Part XIII 1260a12–14.

9 See Kant, *Observations*, p. 76ff.

10 Rousseau, *Emile or On Education*, tr. Alan Bloom (New York: Basic Books, 1979).

11 Susan Moller Okin, *Justice, Gender, and the Family* (New York: Basic Books, 1989).

12 John Rawls, *A Theory of Justice* (Oxford: Oxford University Press, 1971, 1999).

Part I

Women and the Philosophical Canon

Chapter 1

Justifying the Inclusion of Women in Our Histories of Philosophy

The Case of Marie de Gournay

Eileen O'Neill

Introduction

In the past twenty years or more, feminism has influenced the history of philosophy in numerous ways. Feminist scholars, such as Genevieve Lloyd, Michèle Le Doeuff, Luce Irigaray, Prudence Allen, Andrea Nye, Nancy Tuana, Elizabeth Spelman, Penelope Deutscher, Moira Gatens, and Karen Green, have examined the changing conceptions of woman's nature, and of the feminine gender and its exclusions, in the history of western philosophy.[1] The contributors to *Feminism and Ancient Philosophy*, edited by Julie Ward, and to *Engendering Origins: Critical Feminist Readings in Plato and Aristotle*, edited by Bat-Ami Bar On, have brought feminist perspectives to bear upon their readings of Socrates, Plato, Aristotle, Lucretius, and the Stoics.[2] The Re-Reading the Canon series, published by The Pennsylvania State University Press, under the editorship of Nancy Tuana, has offered individual volumes of feminist essays, each devoted to reinterpreting the work of a single major thinker, such as Plato, Aristotle, Descartes, Kant, Hegel, Kierkegaard, or Nietzsche.[3]

Some scholars have used feminism as a lens through which to re-examine classic ethical theories, e.g., those of Aristotle, Hume, and Kant. Among these scholars are Nancy Sherman, Annette Baier, Robin May Schott, and Barbara Herman, to name just a few.[4] Feminists such as Carolyn Merchant and Evelyn Fox Keller have challenged the standard histories of the philosophy of science, and have re-examined the interrelations between women, gender, and the rise of early modern science.[5] Scholars, including Susan Okin and Carole Pateman, have also challenged traditional histories of social and political philosophy from a feminist perspective.[6] Important contributions on this topic have been made by the authors included in the collections of essays edited by Lorenne Clark and Lynda Lange, Carole Pateman and Elizabeth Gross, and Ellen Kennedy and Susan Mendus.[7]

Over the past twenty years or so, feminist historians of philosophy have also begun to pose for our own discipline the question that Linda Nochlin had raised a decade earlier for art history: Were there any pre-twentieth-century women who significantly contributed to philosophy? Scholars have found scores of earlier women philosophers. Many of these women corresponded with major male figures about detailed philosophical issues. And in the early modern period, more than fifty of the women published on a wide range of philosophical topics: morals and the passions, natural philosophy, metaphysics, rational theology, epistemology, philosophy of education, ethics, political philosophy, and aesthetics.

There is no question but that there has been a flurry of scholarly activity on this topic. We now have the groundbreaking *A History of Women Philosophers*, in four volumes, completed under the general editorship of Mary Ellen Waithe.[8] Several collections of essays on women philosophers, and collections of essays on individual women philosophers have also seen their way into print, and I am aware of collections that are now in progress.[9] The feminist series, Re-Reading the Canon, under the general editorship of Nancy Tuana, has published volumes on the work of Simone de Beauvoir, Hannah Arendt, Mary Wollstonecraft, and Ayn Rand.

The primary source materials are finally becoming available in modern editions – many of which are suitable for classroom use. In particular, I have in mind the editions that Broadview Press has released and will publish, e.g., works by Margaret Cavendish, Mary Astell, Mary Wollstonecraft, and Catharine Trotter Cockburn; the volumes in Cambridge Texts in the History of Philosophy, e.g. works by Margaret Cavendish and Anne Conway; the texts by Mary Astell, Margaret Cavendish, Christine de Pisan and Mary Wollstonecraft in Cambridge Texts in the History of Political Thought; The University of Chicago's series, The Other Voice in Early Modern Europe, which has released and will publish translations of works by Lucrezia Marinella, Marie de Gournay, Anna Maria van Schurman, and Jacqueline Pascal, Princess Elisabeth of Bohemia, Gabrielle Suchon, Madeleine de Scudéry, Oliva Sabuco de Nantes Barrera, Françoise de Maintenon and Emilie du Châtelet; Oxford University Press' series Women Writers in English 1350–1850 includes texts by Mary Chudleigh and Judith Sargent Murray; and Penguin Books' collections of writings by Sor Juana Inés de la Cruz and Margaret Cavendish. Finally, there are the hardcover editions, sometimes multi-volume ones, which Ashgate Publishing Company, Garland Press, and Thoemmes Press have produced; they have given us modern editions of the texts of Catharine Macaulay, Margaret Cavendish, Catherine Ward Beecher, Mary Shepherd, and Damaris Masham. There are also several anthologies of short selections from the texts of women philosophers, including Margaret Atherton's collection, which focuses on seventeenth- and eighteenth-century women, and Mary Warnock's, which includes women from the seventeenth through twenty-first centuries.[10]

While there was once a dearth of scholarship on early modern women philosophers, articles on them appear with some regularity in such journals as *Hypatia*,

British Journal for the History of Philosophy, Journal of the History of Philosophy, Australasian Journal of Philosophy, and *Journal of the History of Ideas*. And books on a wide range of topics related to women philosophers have also been published. There are now book-length treatments of seventeenth-century women philosophers,[11] women Cartesians,[12] Princess Elisabeth's correspondence with Descartes,[13] Queen Christina of Sweden and her circle,[14] women moralists of the French Neoclassical salons,[15] the philosophy of education of Catharine Macaulay,[16] and the relation of form and content in the moral writing of certain women philosophers[17] – to mention just a few examples. Biographies and book-length treatments have appeared dealing with figures such as Marie de Gournay, Margaret Cavendish, Catharine Macaulay, Mary Astell, Mary Wollstonecraft, Marie-Jeanne Roland, Sophie de Condorcet, Stéphanie-Félicité de Genlis, Louise d'Epinay, Germaine de Staël-Holstein, and Emilie du Châtelet.

Given the number of women who published high-quality philosophy in the early modern period, the range of the topics they treated, the recognition they received in the journals of the period, and the interest shown in reprinting and translating their work, the virtual absence of these women in nineteenth- and twentieth-century histories of philosophy has become a source of puzzlement. I should also add that historians of philosophy from the seventeenth and eighteenth centuries often did recognize the accomplishments of the women philosopher: in the seventeenth century, Gilles Menages, Jean de La Forge and Marguerite Buffet produced doxographies of women philosophers; and one of the most widely read histories of philosophy, that by Thomas Stanley, contains a discussion of twenty-four women philosophers from the ancient world. In the nineteenth century, Mathurin de Lescure, Alexander Foucher de Careil, and Victor Cousin wrote books on such figures as Princess Elisabeth of Bohemia, Emilie du Châtelet, Madeleine de Scudéry and Madeleine de Sablé. But when it comes to the general histories of philosophy of the eighteenth and nineteenth centuries only a handful of token women, largely "mystics" – who are not taken to be real philosophers – are mentioned. No woman is anywhere described as a significant, original contributor to early modern philosophy. Feminist scholars have recently attempted to provide reasons, both internal and external to philosophy, that explain women's absence from our histories.[18]

Despite the scholarly efforts of feminist scholars, the inclusion of women in our histories of philosophy has proven difficult to achieve. Take, for example, the case of Marie de Gournay. She was one of only nine women philosophers to have an entry in the supplement to the *Macmillan Encyclopedia of Philosophy*; she was also included in Waithe's *A History of Women Philosophers*; and she had a bio-bibliography in *The Cambridge History of Seventeenth-Century Philosophy*. Despite this, Gournay remains a much-neglected figure in general histories of philosophy. In the remainder of this chapter, I will focus on Gournay, and I will examine the methodological challenges, and the interpretive and evaluative problems that face a historian who is trying to justify the inclusion of a woman in the history of early modern philosophy.

Methodological Challenges to Justifying the Inclusion of Specific Women in Our Histories of Philosophy: The Case of Marie de Gournay

If we utilize that method of historiography known as "historical reconstruction," we will take as central those issues deemed by the philosophers of the past to be the central ones; and we will count past figures to be philosophers just in case they were so deemed by their contemporaries. Notice that given this method, it is not likely that the history of philosophy will include Gournay, since she is mainly important for her contribution to the "quarrel about women." And those deemed to be philosophers by their contemporaries in the seventeenth century did not, for the most part, take this "woman question" to be a serious philosophical issue.

On the other hand, if we utilize the method of historiography known as "rational reconstruction," the issues in a past era that are philosophically central will be those which most closely match our current philosophical concerns, or which causally have led to our coming to have our current concerns. There is certainly exciting work being done currently, by historians of feminist philosophy, which is uncovering foreshadowings of contemporary feminist issues and arguments in the work of newly rediscovered female philosophers of the past. But for all that, I think that we need to be careful in utilizing the method of rational reconstruction. For while it can give us philosophical forebears, it frequently does so at the price of distorting the views of past philosophers. It attempts to fit the complex reasoning of the past, which only partly and haphazardly overlaps with current interests, into a contemporary mold. A beautiful example of the unveiling of the distortion of rational reconstructions is Patricia Springborg's recent work on Astell's views about marriage.[19] She has shown that, far from sharing modern liberal feminist views about the right of women to revolt within marriage if the terms of the marriage contract are not upheld, Astell drew parallels between contracts in the domestic and public spheres precisely in order to criticize the contractarian view of the state. In short, Astell was not a liberal political theoretician, but a High-Church, Tory conservative who upheld the divine right of kings in the polis and the sanctity of marriage in the private sphere. Similarly, I think that to rationally reconstruct Gournay as providing arguments *in support* of the thesis of the intellectual and moral equality of men and women is to distort her views, by failing to attend to the historical setting in which her text is located.

Marie de Gournay (Paris, 1565–1645) is best known for her editorial work on the first, complete edition of the *Essays* (1595) of her mentor Montaigne, and for the preface to that work in which she defends it against contemporary criticisms.[20] In recent decades, feminist scholars have rediscovered her text, *Egalité des hommes et des femmes* [*The Equality of Men and Women*] (1622), which was influential in the development of feminist thought. But Gournay continues to be a much-neglected figure in the history of philosophy, in part, because in the scant literature on her there has been considerable debate about the philosophical significance of this text.

In what follows, I will attempt (1) to situate Gournay's text within the context of sixteenth- and seventeenth-century discussions about women's moral and intellectual capacities, and to explain why it is understandable that scholars have not, so far, taken this text seriously as a work of philosophy; (2) I will provide a new understanding of Gournay's method, which can solve interpretive problems that have been plaguing the commentators; and (3) I will highlight the philosophical significance of her text via an examination of some of the main arguments. In this way, I hope to provide a detailed example of the kind of work that needs to continue, if we are to make the case for the inclusion of women in our histories of philosophy.

Gournay's Text and the *Querelle des Femmes*

In the late Middle Ages and the Renaissance, we find in Europe numerous literary texts focusing on the relative merits of men and women. On the one hand, there are defenses of women's virtue that are influenced by the chivalrous courtly love tradition, as well as popularized versions of Platonism; and these texts have as their counterpart clerical satires, and secular bourgeois invectives against women. On the other hand, there is another tradition, which is at its high point from the fifteenth to seventeenth centuries. Here the focus is such things as women's right to men's respect, and appeals for women's education, as well as for a more active role in society. It is the confluence of these two traditions that gives rise to the genre known as the *Querelle des femmes*, or Quarrel About Women.

Some of the more famous early examples of the genre include Jean de Meung's invectives against women, and mockery of courtly love, in his 1277 contribution to the *Roman de la Rose* [*Romance of the Rose*]. Christine de Pisan responded to Meung and defended women in, among other works, her *Livre de la cité des dames* [*Book of the City of Ladies*] (circulated c. 1405). The formal characteristics of the genre include: compilations of biographies of illustrious women – often derived from Boccaccio's *De claris mulieribus* [*On Famous Women*] (1355–9) – appeals to authorities, and bits of argumentation that are sometimes presented within the form of a dialogue. The texts typically discuss the same set of historical facts and personages, and they gloss the same Biblical passages.

Critics have found the reasoning presented in this genre to be, at best, less than convincing, since imprecise generalizations about society, anatomy, and psychology, as well as facile comparisons with nature, are typically relied upon. In fact, the reasoning is sometimes so far-fetched and the Biblical glosses so unlikely, that the *Querelle* has sometimes been described as a genre written more to amuse than to persuade readers.[21] Consider Agrippa's *De nobilitate et praecellentia foeminei sexus . . . declamatio [Declamation on the Nobility and Preeminence of the Female Sex]* (1529) where he describes the following as an "argument": "The most noble part of the human body, that by which we are different from the brute beasts and by which we judge our nature divine, is the head . . . But the head of man is disfigured by baldness, while nature accords woman the great privilege of not becoming bald."[22] So much for rationally persuading us of the moral and intellectual dignity of women. And Castiglione, in his *Il Cortegiano* [*The Book of the Courtier*] (1528), certainly includes both attacks on and defenses of women with as much of an eye to the construction of a witty dialogue as to convincing the readers of the pro-woman arguments with which he seems to side.

Numerous women in the sixteenth and seventeenth centuries contributed to the *Querelle* literature, such as Hélisenne de Crenne, Louise Labé and Marie de Romieu in France; Lucrezia Marinella and Arcangela Tarabotti in Italy; and Anna Maria van Schurman in the Netherlands – to name just a very few.[23] The level of seriousness in these women's texts differs dramatically from woman to woman. For example, the mere rhetoric in Romieu's poem is a far cry from the rigorous syllogisms of Schurman, which utilize Aristotelian scholastic assumptions. Scholars have no evidence that Gournay read Christine de Pisan or any of the other French female contributors to the *Querelle*. She was a correspondent of Schurman, and we do know that Schurman read Marinella, but there is no evidence that Gournay was influenced by Marinella's text. On the other hand, two of the main influences on Gournay, as I will show in what follows, are Agrippa and Castiglione. And some scholars have suggested that Gournay's immediate reason for writing her text was as a response to the publication of the *Querelle* text by Alexis Trousset, *Alphabet de l'imperfection et malice des femmes* [*Alphabet of the Imperfection and Malice of Women*] (1617). So, Gournay's text is both motivated and influenced by the *Querelle des femmes* tradition: no wonder philosophers have been reluctant to take the work seriously.

Gournay's Method

But there is an additional problem that would seem to block any attempt to view Gournay's treatise as philosophy, namely her own description of her method. Having already told the readers that her "thesis" is "that of the equality of men and women," she goes on to explain:

> And while I think very highly of both the dignity and ability of the ladies, I do not claim, at this time, to be able to prove this by means of reasoning since the opinion-ated can always dispute this; nor by examples, since they are too common; thus only by the authority of God himself and of the pillars of his Church and of the great men who have served as the guiding light of the World. Let us place these glorious witnesses right at the start and reserve God and the holy Church Fathers for further on, like a treasure.[24]

How can Gournay's text be a philosophical one if she explicitly rejects the use of argument to prove her thesis? She appears to be saying that for any argument she can produce, those who have already made up their minds differently on the matter will provide other arguments for the negation of her thesis. And for each example of a wise and virtuous woman she can provide, her opponents will proffer examples of women lacking in the moral and intellectual virtues. Gournay appears to claim that she will prove her thesis by appeal to divine authority, as witnessed by the Early Fathers of the Church and as seen by the great pagan philosophers – albeit through a glass darkly. From this description of her method, one might surmise that the text will not include any arguments, or any mention of exemplary women. In fact, this is not the case. Furthermore, near the end of the treatise she explicitly asks the reader to consider "the examples, authorities, and reasons noted in this discourse, by which the equality of God's favors and kindness toward the two . . . sexes, indeed their very unity, has been proven."

Commentators have had a tortuous time attempting to understand what Gournay's method amounts to, and how it could possibly yield justifications for the thesis of the moral and intellectual equality of women and men. Mary Rowan holds that although Gournay's method was not uncommon in the Renaissance, it is unacceptable given modern views about rational argument:

> [Marie de Gournay] exercised a conscious eclecticism . . . drawing from her sources only those arguments appropriate to her cause. She often twisted even these to better suit her purpose. Even though she must have been aware that she quoted many of her authorities out of context, she persisted in using this outmoded exegetical technique.[25]

Rowan also thinks that Gournay's distortion of the eclectically chosen sources fails to yield a consistent case for the equality of men and women. She argues that Gournay's text is filled with "logical weaknesses and internal contradictions." Another Gournay scholar, Maya Bijvoet, similarly concludes that the effect of Gournay's "already-quite-conventional arguments is indeed muted by obvious contradictions."[26]

In a recent article, Douglas Lewis has offered a quite different reading of Gournay's method. According to him, Gournay believes that any argument she can provide – even those based on the authorities – "will be discounted so long as women have a subordinate rank in the world and do not manifest accomplishments comparable to those of men."[27] On his reading, the appeals to the authorities are simply meant to get readers to grant women's perceptions, including Gournay's, the natural authority they truly have. And it is such things as her "knowledge from her experience as well as her reading of women's accomplishments and of social arrangements different from her own" that provide the "principal evidence for her thesis."[28]

This is a strange method, indeed. According to it, the arguments do not provide the justification for the thesis; they simply play a psychological role in getting the women readers to see that their a posteriori knowledge about women's abilities can itself justify the thesis of the equality of men and women. But if the arguments play no justificatory role, and if, in the end, the justification of the thesis is ultimately a matter of empirical observation, it is hard to see why Gournay's treatise should be considered a philosophical text. Lewis concedes this: "Gournay's appeals to the authorities must have some evidential import in the context of her argument for equality, or otherwise her method and, along with it, her argument will contain little of philosophical interest."[29] But once it is admitted that the arguments play some justificatory role, Lewis' reading of Gournay's method faces the problems of Gournay's inconsistencies that Rowan and Bijvoet noted. And, in fact, Lewis does suggest that Gournay's use of Aristotle and St Paul as sources constitutes an indefensibly selective interpretation of their texts, and introduces serious tensions in her essay.

I want to offer a radically different understanding of Gournay's method than those that I have just described. As backdrop to my interpretation, recall that Gournay spent years studying and editing Montaigne's *Essais*, through which she would have learned of the ancient Pyrrhonean arguments. The scope of Pyrrhonean doubt – the range of propositions about which the skeptic suspends judgment – and related issues about how wide the scope *could* be, before it would be unclear how the skeptic could live, have recently come in for lively discussion.[30] In the case of Montaigne, I think Myles Burnyeat may have the correct reading: It is solely reason's judgments about the underlying structure of things – as we find them in scientific and philosophical theories – that are the target of Montaigne's brand of Pyrrhonism.[31] Montaigne claims that he consistently finds equipollent arguments both for and against assenting to philosophical claims, such as those about the nature of God and the immortality of the soul, to take just two examples. But the non-theoretical judgments of ordinary life, such as "This cart is about to hit me" or "It's sunny this morning" are insulated from the skepticism. In this way, the skeptic can live her life in accordance with the appearances, while escaping from the vanity of dogmatizing about the true natures of things.[32] But Montaigne differs dramatically from the ancient Pyrrhoneans in that there is another set of propositions that are also insulated from his skepticism – another range of propositions to which he will assent – namely, the articles of faith as God has revealed them in Scripture. As a fideist, he holds that faith requires no justification from reason, and that faith is known with greater certitude than anything else, for our only access to truth is through God's revelation. Thus, any knowledge that we have of the nature of God, or of our soul's immortality, we know only because God has revealed it to us.[33] In addition, as a *Catholic* fideistic skeptic, Montaigne's view seems to be that by abandoning the vanity of reason which has given rise to all of the theological disputes and fissures within Christianity, and by falling back into the tradition of the Catholic faith, in much the same way as the pagan skeptic submits to the appearances and the customs of ordinary life, fideistic skeptics attain something comparable, but superior, to the Pyrrhoneans' state of tranquility.[34]

If my characterization of Montaigne's fideistic skepticism is not entirely accurate, it is, I think, an accurate portrait of *Gournay's* skepticism. And Montaigne's own views are close enough to hers for us to take him to be Gournay's main source. I see Gournay's method as informed by this fideistic Pyrrhonism. And if this is correct, we can now formulate a reading of the claims she makes about her method that initially appeared inconsistent. When she states that she will not prove her thesis of equality "by means of reasoning, since the opinionated can always dispute this," she is voicing Pyrrhonean doubts about reason's ability to assent in the face of equipollent arguments. When she says that she will prove this "only by the authority of God himself," "the pillars of his Church," and the "glorious witnesses" of the ancient world, she is, on the one hand, signaling her Catholic fideism: our knowledge of woman's true nature cannot be known by reason, but only through divine revelation. On the other hand, as we will see shortly, the early Fathers of the Church and the pagan philosophers will only play the skeptical role of putting us in a position to see the futility of reason in attempting to access the thesis of equality.

In the remainder of this chapter, I will reconstruct four of Gournay's main arguments. I will argue that the arguments are not justifications for her thesis of equality. They are, rather, skeptical arguments meant to show the vanity of reason.

The Skeptical Challenge of Nurture to the Argument from Nature

Women surely achieve a high degree of excellence less often than men do, but it is a marvel that the lack of good instruction, and even the abundance of bad speech and teaching, does not make matters worse by keeping them from achieving excellence at all. Is there a greater difference between men and women than among women themselves, depending on the education they have had, depending on whether they were reared in the city or in a village, or depending on their National origin? And why couldn't an education or diet in practical affairs and Letters, equal to that of men, fill in the gap which usually appears between the minds of men and their own? For, nurture is so important that even a single branch of culture, that is to say, social interaction, which French and English women have abundant opportunities to engage in, while Italian women have none, is such that the latter are, by and large, far surpassed by the former. I say "by and large" because in particular cases Italian ladies sometimes prevail: we did take from them two Queens, to whose wisdom France is greatly obliged. Why, really, couldn't nurture make a decisive contribution to filling in the gap that we perceive between the intellectual faculties of men and of women, considering that in this example the worst surpasses the best with the assistance of a single part, namely, as I said, social interaction and conversation? For, in nature the Italian air is more subtle and suitable for refining the mind, as is clear in the case of their men when compared with Frenchmen and Englishmen.

(Gournay, *The Equality of Men and Women*)

Gournay notes that some of her dogmatic opponents cite Xenophon's *Symposium* as evidence that Socrates is critical of women's practical wisdom in comparison with that of men. She suggests a counter-reading of that text according to which Socrates either sees women "in light of the ignorance and inexperience in which they were nurtured" or, "in the worst case, he takes women's abilities in general to be less than that of men, leaving frequent and ample place for exceptions." But she distinguishes both of these positions from that of her interlocutors, who hold that all women are irremediably and by nature intellectually inferior to men. In her first main argument, Gournay attempts to raise skeptical doubts in the minds of her interlocutors about whether what they hold to be due to nature is not instead due to custom, environment, or education. Here is the argument:

1   Italian men display an intellectual superiority to Frenchmen and Englishmen.
2   Thus, national origin may be an important factor in determining one's intellectual performance and ranking in relation to others.

But Gournay wonders whether those who reason in this way might not accept the following:

3   But French and English women are given abundant opportunities to engage in social interaction, while most Italian women are given virtually none.
4   Italian women, by and large, display an intellectual inferiority to French and English women.
5   However, some Italian women (those who have received education and experience in social interaction, e.g., the Medici queens) display an intellectual superiority to French and English women.
6   Therefore, those whom we would expect to be ranked lower, with respect to the display of intellect [Italian women] sometimes surpass those whom we would expect to be ranked higher [French and English women], by means of the assistance of a single type of cultural nourishment: education and experience in social interaction.

Given that this reasoning is possible, Gournay has skeptical worries about the justification for the following thesis: The gap between the displays of intelligence of members of different nationalities is irremediable.
     Gournay now considers this parallel argument:

1*   Men display an intellectual superiority to women.
2*   Therefore, gender may be an important factor in determining one's intellectual performance and ranking in relation to others.

Again, Gournay wonders whether those who reason in this way might not accept the following:

3*   Men receive a wide range of educational and cultural experiences, while most women receive none.
4*   Women, by and large, display an intellectual inferiority to many men.
5*   However, some women [who have received a wide range of educational and cultural experiences] display an intellectual superiority to many men.

6* Therefore, those whom we would expect to be ranked lower with respect to the display of intellect [women] sometimes surpass those whom we would expect to be ranked higher [men], by means of the assistance of a wide range of educational and cultural experiences.

Given that this reasoning is possible, Gournay has skeptical worries about the justification for the following thesis: The gap between the displays of intelligence of members of different genders is irremediable. She challenges her interlocutors to show why education and other cultural experiences could not help to narrow the gap between the intellectual rankings of men and women.

Arguments that attempt to show that it is the lack of an intellectually stimulating environment, the lack of education, and the lack of experience in the world that account for women's poorer intellectual performance in comparison with men's go back at least as far as Christine de Pisan. But Gournay has fashioned an original form of the nature vs. nurture argument.[35] And what is most interesting about it is its status as a skeptical argument. As such, it avoids the specious and patently false claims that some of the earlier nature vs. nurture proponents had made about the mental capacities that women have by nature. For example, Christine de Pisan had claimed that "just as women have more delicate bodies than men, weaker and less able to perform many tasks, so do they have minds that are freer and sharper whenever they apply themselves."[36] Centuries later, Castiglione has the Magnifico tell us – perhaps facetiously – that it is a "proposition held in philosophy" that "those who are weak in body are able in mind" from which he concludes that "being weaker in body women are abler in mind and more capable of speculative thought than men."[37] Gournay's argument not only avoids hypotheses about which capacities women have by nature, it also draws no dogmatic conclusion about the specific roles that education, experience or environment might play in producing displays of intellectual excellence.[38] The role of the argument is simply to challenge her interlocutors' inference from the empirical observation – that men typically outstrip women in intellectual performance – to the conclusion that this is best explained by the fact that women have a distinct, and intellectually inferior nature to men's. Gournay attempts to get the interlocutors to resist this inference through the consideration of an alternative explanation – nurture – which they already find unobjectionable in the parallel case of Italian men's superior intellectual display over Frenchmen's, and which may equally be at play in the cases where women are compared to other women.

Having addressed the commonplace argument in the *Querelle des femmes* tradition that women's subordination to men is due to men's natural *intellectual* superiority to women, Gournay now attempts to address the equally common argument that women's subordination is due to men's natural *physical* superiority to women.

The Skeptical Challenge to the "Might Makes Right" Argument

And when men in many places would rob our sex of its share of the best advantages, inequality in physical force, rather than in spiritual powers or moral worth, can easily be the cause of the larceny and suffering. Physical force is such a low virtue that while men surpass women in this respect, animals far surpass men in the same respect. And if this same Latin Historiographer teaches us that where force reigns, equity, probity and modesty itself are the attributes of the conqueror, will we be surprised to see that competence and the virtues in general are those of our men, thus depriving women of them?

(Gournay, *The Equality of Men and Women*)

Gournay begins by rehearsing her interlocutors' argument from physical force, which utilizes the "might makes right" thesis, and then provides a parallel skeptical argument:

1 Men have the physical force to dominate women.
2 Might makes right: those who have the physical force to dominate others are justified in doing so, and the qualities of the dominators rightly constitute what is virtuous.
3 Therefore, by (1) and (2), men are justified in dominating women, and men's qualities rightly constitute what is virtuous.

Gournay's Parallel Argument:

1* Certain beasts have the physical force to dominate human beings.
2* Might makes right: those who have the physical force to dominate others are justified in doing so, and the qualities of the dominators rightly constitute what is virtuous.
3* Therefore, those beasts are justified in dominating human beings, and the beasts' qualities rightly constitute what is virtuous.

The view – that physical force or strength is a lowly virtue, and as such cannot justify the subordination of women to men – was not an uncommon one in the *Querelle* literature. For example, Castiglione notes that if one argues that man is more perfect than woman

because man is more robust, more quick and agile, and more able to endure toil, I say that this is an argument of very little validity since among men themselves those who possess these qualities more than others are not more highly regarded on that account; and even in warfare, when for the most part the work to be done demands exertion and strength, the strongest are not the most highly esteemed.[39]

But I think that the source for Gournay's comparison of powerful men to powerful beasts may ultimately be traced to St Augustine. In *On the Free Choice of the Will*,

Augustine says: "Since it is obvious that man is easily surpassed by many beasts in strength and other bodily faculties; in what thing does man excel, so that no beast can rule him, while he on the other hand can rule many of them? Is it not that very thing that we call reason or understanding?"[40] But once again, the originality and force of Gournay's argument is that she draws no dogmatic conclusion – in this case, from her animal comparison. One might think that Gournay sees that (3*) is obviously false, and that this, together with the empirical truth of (1*) in this valid argument, leaves only the falsity of the "might makes right" thesis to account for the argument's lack of soundness. But that would be the strategy of a dogmatist: someone who attempts to prove the falsity of a claim by means of argument. Gournay, on the other hand, has been influenced by the many considerations in Montaigne's "Apology for Raymond Sebond," in the *Essays*, that provide evidence against the common view of animals' inferiority to man. Montaigne's examples are aimed at showing that animals have faculties physically and intellectually superior to humans', and that they have psychological capacities, such as self-control and prudence, that often surpass those of human beings. Thus, Gournay would not claim to know that (3*) is false, nor is it her aim to demonstrate by argument that the "might makes right claim" is false. Her aim is the production of an equipollent argument for each of the arguments of the dogmatists. As a Pyrrhonean, she hopes that her interlocutors will find that the parallel argument gives them reason to doubt the truth of the "might makes right" thesis. But as for herself, a skeptic about philosophical theories – about what we can know on the basis of reason about the true natures of things that lie beyond appearances – Gournay assents to no view. She holds no position about which quality or qualities the possession of which would justify one creature in dominating another. Reason does not reach this far; it cannot uncover metaphysical or scientific truths about the nature of things, nor can it uncover moral truths.

The Skeptical Challenge to the Argument from Woman's Creation

To be exact, moreover, the human animal is neither man nor woman, the sexes having been created not as ends in themselves but *secundum quid*, as the School says, that is, solely for the purpose of propagation. The unique form and differentia of this animal, consists only in the human soul. And if we are permitted to jest in passing, the little joke that teaches us will not be inappropriate: nothing resembles a male cat on the window ledge more than a female cat. Man and woman are one to such a degree that if man is more than woman, then woman is more than man. Man was created male and female, the Scriptures say, reckoning the two as only one. For which reason Jesus Christ is called 'the Son of Man', even though he is only the son of a woman. Thus, the great Saint Basil later said: "Virtue in man and in woman is the same, since God has bestowed upon them the same creation and the same honor; *masculum et foeminam fecit eos*." Now in those who have the same Nature, their actions are likewise the same, and whenever their works are the same, they will be esteemed and valued the same in consequence. That, then, is the opinion of this powerful pillar and venerable witness of the Church. Concerning this point, it is timely to remember that certain ancient quibblers went so far with their foolish arrogance as to contest that the female sex, as opposed to the male sex, is made in the image of God, which image they must have taken to be in the beard, according to my understanding.

(Gournay, *The Equality of Men and Women*)

The question left at the end of the skeptical challenge to the "Might Makes Right Argument" was this: Should we be surprised that where force rather than right determines values, the conquerors will take themselves to be capable of virtue, but will deny that those in submission are capable of it? In the next, central section of her text, Gournay refers to one line of reasoning for women's diminished capacity for moral and intellectual virtue that derived from an interpretation of Scripture's account of woman's creation. Gournay notes that certain "ancient quibblers" were so arrogant as to "contest that the female sex, as opposed to the male sex, is made in the image of God."

The view that women are not made in the image of God appears to have been an uncommon one in the earlier theological literature, arising when it did surface from a misreading of Pauline texts.[41] Perhaps the best-known statement of this view is in an objection in *Summa Theologica* 1.93.4.1: "It would seem that the image of God is not found in every man. For the Apostle says that 'man is the image of God, but woman is the image (Vul., 'glory') of man' (1 Cor. 11: 7). Therefore, as woman is an individual of the human species, it is clear that every individual is not an image of God." St Thomas responds to this objection by correcting the reading of the Pauline passage. St Thomas argues that the view is unsupported by Scripture, saying: "The image of God, in its principal signification, namely the intellectual nature, is found both in man and in woman. Hence after the words 'To the image of God He created him,' it is added, 'Male and female He created them' (Gen. 1:27)."

Gournay sets out a similar, divinely inspired understanding of Scripture regarding woman's creation, namely that of St Basil. She indicates that what follows from St Basil's reading is that, far from the ancient quibblers' position, women and men are equally made in the image of God.

1   Forms/souls of creatures specify the properties essential to being a member of a particular species. (Teaching of the schools, which the opponents hold.)

2   Gender-specific properties are only essential for procreation; they are not essential for being a member of a species, and so are not specified by the Forms/souls. (Teaching of the schools, which the opponents hold.)

3   God created human males and females in a single act of creation, endowing them with the human Form/soul. (View of St Basil and traditional view of the Catholic Church.)

4   Therefore, human males and females have the same human Form/soul. (By 3.)

5   Therefore, human males and females are members of the same species. (By 1 and 4.)

6   The "image of God" refers to the human Form/soul. (Traditional view of the Catholic Church.)

7   Therefore, human males and females are both made in the image of God. (By 4 and 6.)

In response to the ancient quibblers' rejection of (7) for the claim that "only human males, not females, are made in the image of God," Gournay raises a skeptical worry about what this "image" could be, if not the human Form/soul – with the ironic remark that it must "be in the beard." Gournay is skeptical that any gender-specific property could account for being in God's image, since the sole purpose of these properties is procreative, even according to the opponents. But it is precisely this skeptical gesture which unveils the astounding implication of her opponents' views: To deny that women are made in God's image, would (as St Thomas would agree) seem to deny (3): that women share the same Form/soul as men. And this is to deny that women are human. St Thomas' opponent, of course, would have recoiled at this theologically and philosophically repulsive implication. After all, the opponent had aimed at showing that not all *members of the human species* are an image of God.

It is important to see that, once again, this is not an argument for a positive claim, namely that women are made in God's image and share in the human Form. Gournay's aim is once more skeptical and therapeutic: She is attempting to show her interlocutors their hubris in rejecting the Early Church Fathers' divinely inspired gloss on the account of woman's creation in Genesis I, and in believing that they can use reason to reinterpret St Paul and to prove that women's souls are inferior to men's.

It is important to see that, once again, this is not an argument for a positive claim, namely that women, as made in God's image and sharing in the human Form, will be judged according to the same standards as men in the afterlife. Gournay's aim is once more skeptical and therapeutic: She is attempting to show her interlocutors their hubris in rejecting the Early Church Fathers' divinely inspired gloss on the account of woman's creation in Genesis I, and in believing that they can use reason to reinterpret St Paul and to prove that women's souls are inferior to men's.

As it turns out, an anonymous treatise was published in 1595 entitled, *Disputatio nova contra mulieres, qua probatur eas homines non esse* [A New Disputation against Women, in which it is proved that they are not human beings].[42] While modern scholars disagree about the extent to which the text is merely a satire of the Anabaptists' literal Biblical interpretations, it was taken quite seriously in its own time. Among those who responded to it were Simon Gedik, a Lutheran theologian, the jurist J. U. Wolff, and the feminist nun Arcangela Tarabotti.[43]

It is not clear whether Gournay was aware of this treatise. But it would simply have been further grist for her mill – further evidence of the vanity of human reason. Independently of faith, and the authority and tradition of the Church, we struggle to find something that we can know beyond the appearances. Men may use reason to argue that women are not made in God's image, and they may even argue that women lack the human Form/soul. But there are equipollent arguments for the negations of these claims.

Gournay's skeptical challenge to the "argument from woman's creation" bears comparison with similar reasoning by Castiglione. The latter has one of his characters rehearse the view of "very learned men" (presumably Aristotelians) who have held that "since Nature always plans and aims at absolute perfection she would, if possible, constantly bring forth men; and when a woman is born this is a mistake or defect, and contrary to Nature's wishes."[44] This is taken to be evidence for the position that women "are of less dignity than men and incapable of practicing the virtues practiced by men."[45] This argument does not, of course, appear in Aristotle. And Castiglione may be attempting to show why Aristotle would not have put it forward. For, Castiglione has his protagonist reply to this argument with one that is similar to Gournay's argument about woman's creation:

> Just as one stone cannot, as far as its essence is concerned, be more perfectly stone than another stone, nor one piece of wood more perfectly wood than another piece, so one man cannot be more perfectly man than another; and so, as far as their formal substance is concerned, the male cannot be more perfect than the female, since both the one and the other are included under the species man, and they differ in their accidents and not their essence.[46]

The protagonist goes on to show that neither will various properties non-essential to being a human being work as a justification for the imperfection of women in relation to men. We have already seen that Castiglione holds that men's greater bodily strength cannot justify the general claim of men's superiority with respect to women.[47] And we have seen that this argument is not terribly far removed from Gournay's response to the "might makes right argument." As far as mental abilities go, the protagonist replies that "where a man's intellect can penetrate, so along with it can a woman's." This view, that woman is not by nature intellectually inferior to man, also bears comparison with Gournay's skeptical challenge to the "argument from nature."

Given the similarities between Gournay's first three main arguments, and Castiglione's reply to the "defective nature argument," one might be tempted to think that Gournay, like Castiglione, holds that this argument is not properly an Aristotelian one. One might think that this may partially explain why Gournay says of Aristotle that "he did not, in general – as far as I know – contradict the opinion that favors the ladies." But we need to remember Gournay's skeptical methodology: She would not claim to have knowledge about Aristotle's true view. Her point would be that for every reading of Aristotle as holding the natural inferiority of women, an equipollent argument can be adduced to show that he rejects this view.

Now we are in a position to see why Lewis is wrong to think both (1) that Gournay's reference to Aristotle is a lapse in her method, a case where Gournay is not being "a good reasoner"; and (2) that the appeals to any of the authorities have *any* "evidential import in the context of her argument for equality." Gournay offers us interpretations of Montaigne, Aristotle, St Basil, St Paul and others. She does not attempt to prove that these interpretations are correct; she does not even assent to the theoretical claims in the arguments. Nor need she. If her interpretations of the authorities give her interlocutors reason to doubt their original views, her skeptical arguments have done their job. But these are *skeptical* arguments challenging her opponents' views, not evidence for the positive thesis of equality.

We can also see why Rowan is wrong to think that Gournay should have abandoned her method of constructing unjustifiably selective interpretations of authoritative texts. As a skeptic, it is open to Gournay to make use of any and everything that might help her to produce equipollent arguments to match those of her interlocutors.

Following Gournay's challenge to the argument from woman's creation, her focus for the remainder of the treatise is what the Scriptures and faith reveal about the capacities and privileges that God has bestowed upon women. Here she does not merely rehearse isolated examples of extraordinary women, as was common in the *Querelle* tradition, she notes how throughout Scripture God made both men and women prophets, judges, teachers, leaders, and victors. But what about being a priest and administering the sacraments, or being the head of the family? Ultimately Gournay must provide equipollent readings of two Pauline texts that were commonplaces in Gournay's opponents' arsenal: Women must be silent in Church (1 Cor. 14:34–5); and the husband is the head of the wife (1 Cor. 11:3 and Eph. 5:23). It is in interpreting these passages, and in considering whether they assume the natural inferiority of woman, that Gournay is led to her final argument.

The Skeptical Challenge from God's Privileges against the Vanity of Man

> If we believed that the Scriptures command woman to submit to man, as unworthy to oppose him, see the absurdity that follows: woman would be worthy of having been made in the image of the Creator, worthy of enjoying the most holy Eucharist, the mysteries of the Redemption, Paradise and the vision of, indeed the union with, God, but not of the honors and privileges of man. Would this not be to declare man more precious and exalted than these things and consequently to commit the most grievous blasphemy?
>
> (Gournay, *The Equality of Men and Women*)

In this final argument, Gournay attempts to shed skeptical doubt on her opponents' view that women's subordinate place, in marriage and in the church, is due to her natural inferiority. The argument pits the opponents' readings of 1 Cor. 11:3, which claim that Scripture commands "woman to submit to man, as unworthy to oppose him," against the "examples, authorities, and reasons," which Gournay has chronicled, "by which the equality of God's favors and kindness toward the two . . . sexes, indeed their very unity, has been shown."[48] The argument takes the form of a *skeptical reductio* – that is an argument that displays a contradiction generated by the opponent's thesis, but that does not dogmatically infer from this that the negation of the thesis has been proved. Here is the argument:

1 Woman is not worthy of the status and privileges that God has bestowed upon man. (Thesis of the dogmatists)
2 Woman is worthy of the highest privileges that God bestows on anyone: she is made in His image, and is awarded the Eucharist, the Redemption, and the beatific vision. (A truth of faith, revealed in Scripture)
3 Therefore, the status and privileges that God has bestowed upon man are more exalted than the highest privileges that God bestows on anyone. (1 and 2)[49]
4 But it is not the case that the status and privileges that God has bestowed upon man are more exalted than the highest privileges that God bestows on anyone. (A truth of faith, revealed in Scripture)
5 Therefore, the status and privileges that God has bestowed upon man are more exalted than the highest privileges that God bestows on anyone, and it is not the case that the status and privileges that God has bestowed upon man are more exalted than the highest privileges that God bestows on anyone. (3 and 4)

Having reached this "absurdity," which follows validly from the thesis that woman is not worthy of the status and privileges that God has bestowed upon man, Gournay rests her case. Her dogmatic opponent – one who has theories about woman's nature independently of what is revealed in Scripture – must now either reject one or more of the other premises, or abandon the thesis. But the premises, (2) and (4), are articles of faith; they cannot be rejected. A dogmatist might conclude this *reductio* in the following way:

6 The above argument is valid.
7 Therefore, at least one of the premises must be false.
8 (2) and (4) are unassailable: they are articles of faith, and are revealed in Scripture.
9 Therefore, the thesis is false.
10 Therefore, woman is worthy of the status and privileges that God has bestowed upon man.

In true skeptical style, however, Gournay resists dogmatically drawing a conclusion. Instead, she raises a skeptical question: If one holds the thesis, "would this not be to declare man more precious and exalted than [God's honors and privileges] and consequently to commit the most grievous blasphemy?" Just as Montaigne used the interrogative form to avoid the appearance of a conclusion to his reasoning – a conclusion to which he would assent – so too, throughout

Gournay's treatise, until the very last sentence, the question remains the finale of each piece of skeptical reasoning. It returns the interlocutor's volley, showing that no dogmatic conclusion has been drawn by the skeptic herself.

Concluding Remarks

In this chapter, I have presented a new interpretation of Gournay's puzzling remarks about her method. I have argued that her method is rooted in Pyrrhonean skepticsm, albeit of the Renaissance stripe. And I have attempted to reconstruct her main arguments in accordance with a Pyrrhonean fideistic method.[50] One of the main claims in this chapter has been that the philosophical importance of the *Equality of Men and Women* lies in the fact that Gournay raises the level of discussion in a *Querelle* text to the point where the treatment of gender issues is recognizably philosophical. In fact, to my knowledge this is the first early modern philosophical text published by a woman.

To be sure, her Catholic fideism is philosophically problematic. Briefly, here is why. According to her Catholic fideism, it is not in virtue of reason that we assent to the articles of faith; rather on the basis of tradition and custom, we accept these articles of faith in the way that a pagan skeptic conforms to the appearances and customs of his country. But a genuine religious stance would seem to require assent to certain articles of faith, such as the existence of God and the fact that he has revealed truths to us.[51] The *Catholic Encyclopedia* makes the point in this way:

> We must first know with certitude that God exists, that He reveals such and such a proposition, and that His teaching is worthy of assent, all of which questions can and must be ultimately decided only by an act of intellectual assent based on objective evidence. Thus fideism not only denies intellectual knowledge, but logically ruins faith itself.[52]

But however problematic Renaissance fideism may be, it is Gournay's construction of equipollent arguments, for the purpose of skeptically challenging the dogmatism of her misogynist opponents, which makes *The Equality of Men and Women* a significant contribution to early modern philosophy – a contribution that warrants a place for Gournay in our histories of philosophy. Of course, the historical and philosophical work that has led to this conclusion has not been easy. Discovering Gournay's philosophical method, which allowed us to see the philosophical character of the text and the cogency of its reasoning, required a knowledge of the historical setting in which Gournay was situated, as well as a detailed understanding of the intellectual influences on her work. This is the sort of exacting work that historians of philosophy must always do to make the case for the significance of a forgotten figure's writings. Notice, however, that in the case of Gournay, as for many women philosophers of the past, there are additional features of her text that, until recently, have served to make it invisible as a work of *philosophy*, namely, genre and subject matter. It takes a highly nuanced reading of *The Equality of Men and Women* to be able to read past its position in the *Querelle* literature, and to see it as an example of Renaissance skepticism. Second, issues concerning gender have, since the time of Kant, been viewed as external to philosophy proper; they are of "anthropological" interest, matters of the social sciences that are beyond the purview of philosophy proper. But feminist historians of philosophy, with our acceptance of gender issues as constituting an important set of philosophical concerns, and with our openness to exploring different styles and genres of philosophy, are in an excellent position to excavate many of the women's long-forgotten texts, and to demonstrate the philosophical contributions that they make. The work will be hard, but the payoffs just may change the shape of our picture of western philosophy.[53]

Notes

1 Genevieve Lloyd, *The Man of Reason: Male and Female in Western Philosophy* (Minneapolis: University of Minnesota Press, 1984) and *Feminism and the History of Philosophy*, ed. G. Lloyd (New York/Oxford: Oxford University Press, 2002); Michèle Le Doeuff, *The Philosophical Imaginary*, tr. C. Gordon (Stanford, CA: Stanford University Press, 1989), *Hipparchia's Choice: An Essay Concerning Women, Philosophy, Etc.*, tr. T. Selous (Oxford/Cambridge, MA: Blackwell, 1991), and *The Sex of Knowing*, tr. K. Hammer and L. Code (New York/London: Routledge, 2003); Luce Irigaray, *Speculum of the Other Woman*, tr. G. Gill (Ithaca, NY: Cornell University Press, 1985), *This Sex which is not One*, tr. C. Porter (Ithaca, NY: Cornell University Press, 1985), *An Ethics of Sexual Difference*, tr. C. Burke and G. Gill (Ithaca, NY: Cornell University Press, 1993); Sister Prudence Allen, *The Concept of Woman: The Aristotelian Revolution, 750 BC–AD 1250*, rev. edn of 1985 original (Grands Rapids, MI: William B. Eerdmans Publishing Company, 1997), *The Concept of Woman: The Early Humanist Reformation, 1250–1500* (Grands Rapids, MI: William B. Eerdmans Publishing Company, 2002); Andrea Nye, *Feminist Theories and the Philosophies of Man* (New York/London: Routledge, 1988), *Philosophy and Feminism at the Border* (New York: Twayne Publishers, 1995); Nancy Tuana, *Woman and the History of Philosophy* (New York: Paragon Press, 1992), *The Less Noble Sex: Scientific, Religious and Philosophical Conceptions of Woman's Nature* (Bloomington: Indiana University Press, 1993); Elizabeth V. Spelman, *Inessential Woman: Problems of Exclusion in Feminist Thought* (Boston, MA: Beacon Press, 1988); Penelope Deutscher, *Yielding Gender: Feminism, Deconstruction, and the History of Philosophy* (New York/London: Routledge, 1997); Moira Gatens, *Feminism and Philosophy: Perspectives on Difference and Equality* (Bloomington/Indianapolis: Indiana University Press, 1991); and Karen Green, *The Woman of Reason: Feminism, Humanism and Political Thought* (New York: Continuum Publishing Company, 1995).
2 *Feminism and Ancient Philosophy*, ed. J. Ward (New York/London: Routledge, 1996); *Engendering Origins: Critical Feminist Readings in Plato and Aristotle*, ed. B. Bar On (Albany: SUNY Press, 1994).
3 See also *Modern Engendering: Critical Feminist Readings in Modern Western Philosophy*, ed. B. Bar On (Albany: SUNY Press, 1993).

4　Nancy Sherman, *The Fabric of Character: Aristotle's Theory of Virtue* (Oxford: Oxford University Press, 1989); Annette Baier, *A Progress of Sentiments: Reflexions on Hume's Treatise* (Cambridge: Cambridge University Press, 1991); Robin May Schott, *Cognition and Eros: A Critique of the Kantian Paradigm* (Boston, MA: Beacon Press, 1988); and Barbara Herman, *The Practice of Moral Judgment* (Cambridge, MA: Harvard University Press, 1993).

5　Carolyn Merchant, *The Death of Nature: Women, Ecology and the Scientific Revolution* (San Francisco: Harper and Row, 1980); and Evelyn Fox Keller, *Reflections on Gender and Science* (New Haven/London: Yale University Press, 1985); Londa Schiebinger, *The Mind Has No Sex? Women in the Origins of Modern Science* (Cambridge, MA/London: Harvard University Press, 1989).

6　Susan Moller Okin, *Women in Western Political Philosophy* (Princeton, NJ: Princeton University Press, 1979); and Carole Pateman, *The Sexual Contract* (Stanford, CA: Stanford University Press, 1988).

7　*The Sexism of Social and Political Theory*, eds. L. Clark and L. Lange (Toronto/Buffalo/London: University of Toronto Press, 1979); *Feminist Challenges: Social and Political Theory*, eds. C. Pateman and E. Gross (Boston, MA: Northeastern University Press, 1986); and *Women in Western Political Philosophy*, eds. E. Kennedy and S. Mendus (New York: St Martin's Press, 1987).

8　*A History of Women Philosophers*, ed. M.E. Waithe, 4 vols. (Dordrecht/Boston/London: Kluwer Academic Publishers, 1987–95). For references to additional women philosophers of the seventeenth and eighteenth centuries, see Eileen O'Neill, "Disappearing Ink: Early Modern Women Philosophers and Their Fate in History," in *Philosophy in a Feminist Voice: Critiques and Reconstructions*, ed. J. Kourany (Princeton, NJ: Princeton University Press, 1998).

9　See for example, *Hypatia: A Journal of Feminist Philosophy* 4 (1) (1989), Special Issue: The History of Women in Philosophy; *Hypatia's Daughters: Fifteen Hundred Years of Women Philosophers*, ed. L.L. McAlister (Bloomington: Indiana University Press, 1996); *Presenting Women Philosophers*, ed. C. Tougas and S. Ebenreck (Philadelphia, PA: Temple University Press, 2000); *A Princely Brave Woman: Essays on Margaret Cavendish, Duchess of Newcastle*, ed. S. Clucas (Aldershot/Burlington, VT: Ashgate, 2003); *Choosing the Better Part: Anna Maria van Schurman (1607–1678)*, ed. M. de Baar et al. (Dordrecht/Boston/London: Kluwer Academic Publishers, 1996); *Mary Astell: Gender, Reason, Faith*, ed. W. Kohlbrener and M. Michelson (Aldershot/Burlington, VT: Ashgate Press, forthcoming 2006).

10　*Women Philosophers of the Early Modern Period*, ed. M. Atherton (Indianapolis/Cambridge: Hackett Publishing Company, 1994); *Women Philosophers*, ed. M. Warnock (London: J.M. Dent and North Clarendon, VT: Charles E. Tuttle, 1996). See also *The Neglected Canon: Nine Women Philosophers: First to the Twentieth Century*, ed. T.B. Dykeman (Dordrecht/Boston/London: Kluwer Academic Publishers, 1999).

11　Jacqueline Broad, *Women Philosophers of the Seventeenth Century* (Cambridge: Cambridge University Press, 2002).

12　Erica Harth, *Cartesian Women: Versions and Subversions of Rational Discourse in the Old Regime* (Ithaca, NY/London: Cornell University Press, 1992).

13　Andrea Nye, *The Princess and the Philosopher: Letters of Elisabeth of the Palatine to René Descartes* (Lanham, MD: Rowman and Littlefield, 1999).

14　Susanna Åkerman, *Queen Christina of Sweden and Her Circle: The Transformation of a Seventeenth-Century Philosophical Libertine* (Leiden: E.J. Brill, 1991).

15 John J. Conley SJ, *The Suspicion of Virtue: Women Philosophers in Neoclassical France* (Ithaca, NY/London: Cornell University Press, 2002).

16 Connie Titone, *Gender Equality in the Philosophy of Education: Catharine Macaulay's Forgotten Contribution* (New York: Peter Lang, 2004).

17 Catherine Villanueva Gardner, *Women Philosophers: Genre and the Boundaries of Philosophy* (Boulder, CO/Oxford: Westview Press, 2003).

18 For a discussion of women's presence in early modern philosophy and subsequent disappearance from the histories of that period, see my "Disappearing Ink," and for an alternative view of the women's disappearance, see Jonathan Rée, "Women Philosophers and the Canon," *British Journal for the History of Philosophy* 10 (4) (2002): 641–52.

19 Patricia Springborg, "Introduction," to *Astell: Political Writings*, ed. Patricia Springborg (Cambridge/New York/Melbourne: Cambridge University Press, 1996).

20 Marie le Jars de Gournay (1565–1645) was the editor of the first complete edition of Montaigne's *Essais*, a writer of feminist, moral, and theological tracts, translator, literary and philological theorist, poet and novelist. An autodidact, she mastered Latin and translated Diogenes Laertius' *Life of Socrates* in her youth. At eighteen or nineteen she became an admirer of the early essays of Montaigne, secured a meeting with him in 1588, and became such an intimate friend that he referred to her as his "adopted daughter." This inspired her novel *Le Proumenoir de Monsieur de Montaigne* (1594). In 1594, Montaigne's widow sent her the final manuscript of his *Essais*; Gournay published an edition of it, together with a long "Préface" defending the work against all contemporary criticisms, in 1595. She defended the Jesuits against the charge that they were responsible for the assassination of King Henry IV in *Adieu de l'âme du roy de France . . . avec La Défence des Pères Jésuites* (1610), for which she was attacked in the *Anti-Gournay* (n.d.) and in *Remercîment des beurrières* (1610). She published classical translations in *Versions de quelques pièces de Virgile, Tacite et Saluste . . .* (1619) and a feminist tract *Égalité des hommes et des femmes* (1622), which were reprinted in her collected works: *L'Ombre de la Demoiselle de Gournay* (1626) and *Les Advis ou les presens de la Demoiselle de Gournay* (1634). She became well known for her defense of old terms in the French language, and the poetry of the Pléïade, against Malherbe and other Moderns. The 1641 edition of *Les Advis* contained her autobiographical sketch. During her last years, she participated in the salons of the Duchess de Longueville and the Comtesse de Soissons; her own salon included La Mothe le Vayer, Abbé de Marolles, Guillaume Colletet and was, arguably, the seed from which the French Academy grew. She numbered Anna Maria van Schurman, Justus Lipsius, Saint Francis de Sales, La Mothe le Vayer, Abbé de Marolles, Madame de Loges, Guez de Balzac, and Cardinal Richelieu among her correspondents.

21 See, for example, Ian MacLean, *Woman Triumphant: Feminism in French Literature 1610–1652* (Oxford: Clarendon Press, 1977), p. 25. For a view of the *Querelle* which views it as a more serious genre, see Joan Kelly, *Women, History and Theory: The Essays of Joan Kelly* (Chicago/London: The University of Chicago Press, 1984); and Margaret King and Albert Rabil, "The Other Voice in Early Modern Europe: Introduction to the Series," in Marie Le Jars de Gournay, *Apology for the Woman Writing and Other Works*, eds. R. Hillman and Colette Quesnel (Chicago/London: University of Chicago Press, 2002). On the *Querelle des femmes*, see also Lula McDowell Richardson, *The Forerunners of Feminism in French Literature of the Renaissance from Christine of Pisa to Marie de Gournay* in The Johns Hopkins Studies in Romance Literatures and Lan-

guages, vol. XII (Baltimore, MD: The Johns Hopkins Press, 1929); and Constance Jordan, *Renaissance Feminism: Literary Texts and Political Models* (Ithaca, NY: Cornell University Press, 1990).

22 Henricus Cornelius Agrippa, *Declamation on the Nobility and Preeminence of the Female Sex*, tr. A. Rabil, Jr. (Chicago/London: University of Chicago Press, 1996), p. 55.

23 Hélisenne de Crenne, *Les Epistres familières et invectives* (Paris, 1536); Louise Labé, *Euvres* (Lyon, 1555); Marie de Romieu, "Brief discours que l'excellence de la femme surpasse celle de l'homme," *Premieres oeuvres* (1581); Lucrezia Marinella, *La nobiltà, et l'eccellenza delle donne, co'diffetti, e mancamenti de gli huomini . . .* (Venice, 1600); Arcangela Tarabotti, *Che le donne siano della spezie degli uomini* (1651); Anna Maria van Schurman, *Amica dissertatio inter nobilissimam virginem Annam Mariam a Schurman et Andream Rivetum de ingenii muliebris ad scientias et meliores literas capacitate* (Paris, 1638).

24 All translations of Marie de Gournay's, *Égalité des hommes et des femmes* (1622) are my own. The copy text is the edition that appears in Mario Schiff's *La fille d'alliance de Montaigne, Marie de Gournay* (Paris: Librairie Honoré Champion, 1910).

25 Mary M. Rowan, "Seventeenth-Century French Feminism: Two Opposing Attitudes," *International Journal of Women's Studies* 3 (3) (1980): 273–91, p. 276.

26 Maya Bijvoet, "Marie de Gournay: Editor of Montaigne," in *Women Writers of the Seventeenth Century*, eds. K. Wilson and F. Warnke (Athens/London: The University of Georgia Press, 1989), p. 10.

27 Douglas Lewis, "Marie de Gournay and the Engendering of Equality," *Teaching Philosophy* 22 (1) (1999): 53–76, at p. 57.

28 Ibid., p. 64.

29 Ibid.

30 See, for example, the essays in *The Original Sceptics: A Controversy*, eds. M. Burnyeat and M. Frede (Indianapolis/Cambridge: Hackett, 1997).

31 For a reading of Montaigne in which the scope of his skepticism is wider, see Charles Larmore, "Scepticism," in *The Cambridge History of Seventeenth-Century Philosophy*, eds. D. Garber and M. Ayers (Cambridge: Cambridge University Press, 1998), vol. 2, pp. 1145–87. Since Montaigne is not the focus of the present chapter, and since I believe that the scope of Gournay's skepticism is closer to that which Burnyeat attributes to Montaigne, I do not discuss Larmore's reading here.

32 See Myles Burnyeat, "The Sceptic in His Place and Time," in *The Original Sceptics*, p. 92–126, for persuasive arguments highlighting the philosophical problems with this type of insulation.

33 Michel de Montaigne, *The Complete Essays of Montaigne*, tr. D. Frame (Stanford, CA: Stanford University Press, 1986), p. 326: "The knot that should bind our judgment and our will, that should clasp and join our soul to our creator, should be a knot taking its twists and its strength not from our considerations, our reasons and passions, but from a divine and supernatural clasp, having only one form, one face, and one aspect, which is the authority of God and his grace."

"Nor can man raise himself above himself and humanity; for he can see only with his own eyes, and seize only with his own grasp. He will rise, if God by exception lends him a hand; he will rise by abandoning his own means, and letting himself be raised and uplifted by purely celestial means. It is for our Christian faith, not for his Stoical virtue, to aspire to that divine and miraculous metamorphosis" (p. 457). See also Montaigne, pp. 321, 404, 415.

34 Montaigne, *Complete Essays*, pp. 374–5: "How many arts there are that profess to consist of conjecture more than of knowledge, that do not decide on the true and the false and merely follow what seems to be! There are, they say, both a true and a false, and there is in us the means to seek it, but not to test it by a touchstone. We are much better if we let ourselves be led without inquisitiveness in the way of the world. A soul guaranteed against prejudice is marvelously advanced towards tranquility. People who judge and check their judges never submit to them as they ought. How much more docile and easily led, both by the laws of religion and by political laws are the simple and incurious minds, than those minds that survey divine and human causes like pedagogues!"

"Equally acceptable and useful to me will be condemnation or approval, since I hold it as execrable if anything is found which was said by me, ignorantly or inadvertently, against the holy prescriptions of the Catholic, Apostolic, and Roman Church, in which I die and in which I was born. And therefore, always submitting to the authority of their censure, which has absolute power over me, I meddle rashly with every sort of subject, as I do here" (p. 229). See also pp. 386–7, 428.

For a groundbreaking work on the relation of fideism and skepticism, see Richard H. Popkin, *The History of Scepticism: From Savonarola to Bayle*, revised and expanded edition (Oxford/New York: Oxford University Press, 2003).

35 Gournay's argument appears to make use of some of Montaigne's views about the Italians. For example, in his *Essays* (1595), he notes that although unusual minds of the highest stature are rare and to be found equally in France as in Italy, there are more intellectuals in Italy than France, and there are more refined men in Italy, where "brutishness is incomparably rarer." And Montaigne notes that Italian custom typically imposes a "harsh" and "slavish" law on women, forbidding them any social interaction with men outside of their family. See Montaigne, *Complete Essays*, p. 673.

Gournay may also have been inspired by the following neglected passage from the *Essays* – a book which admittedly has many a harsh remark about women in it: "I say that males and females are cast in the same mold; except for education and custom, the difference is not great. Plato invites both without discrimination to the fellowship of all studies, exercises, functions, warlike and peaceful occupations, in his commonwealth. And the philosopher Antisthenes eliminated any distinction between their virtue and ours. It is much easier to accuse one sex than to excuse the other. It is the old saying: The pot calls the kettle black" (p. 685).

36 Christine de Pisan, *The Book of the City of Ladies*, I.27.1, p. 63.

37 Baldesar Castiglione, *The Book of the Courtier*, tr. G. Bull (London/New York: Penguin, 1976), p. 218.

38 Notice how my reading differs from that of Lewis. He reads this as Gournay's dogmatic theory that explains women's inferior intellectual performance. If Lewis is correct, it has to be conceded that there is not much of a theory here. On my reading, Gournay has raised a powerful skeptical challenge.

39 Castiglione, *The Book of the Courtier*, p. 218.

40 Augustine, *De Libero arbitrio voluntatis/St Augustine on Free Will*, tr. C.M. Sparrow (Charlottesville: The University of Virginia Press , 1947), p. 14.

41 On this point I am indebted to Maryanne Cline Horowitz, "The Image of God in Man – Is Woman Included?" *Harvard Theological Review* 72 (3–4) (1979): 175–206. See also Ian Maclean, *Woman Triumphant* and his *The Renaissance Notion of Woman: A Study in the Fortunes of Scholasticism and Medical Science in European Intellectual Life* (Cambridge/New York/Melbourne: Cambridge University Press, 1980).

42 Among the various "arguments" in the anonymous treatise that attempt to demonstrate that women are not human – that they do not participate in the image or form of man – is this: "Let whoever so desires peruse the whole Bible: Is it written anywhere, 'Let us make her in our image,' or perchance, that she has been made in the image of God? The divine Paul says expressly, "Man [Vir] is the image and glory of God, woman is the glory of man [viri]' [1 Cor. 11:7] You see that the Apostle views women as lacking the image of God, and here this title is denied to her. Let us beware, therefore, of afflicting God with insult, and deciding that she, whom he has not wanted to dignify with his image, is a human being" (*"Women Are not Human": An Anonymous Treatise and Responses*, ed. and tr. T. Kenney (New York: Crossroad, 1998), p. 25).

43 Simon Gedik, *Defensio sexus muliebris* [Defense of the Female Sex] (1595); J.U. Wolff, *Discursus: de foeminarum in jure civili et canonico privilegiis, immunitatibus et praeeeminentia* [Discourse: on the Privileges, Immunities and Preeminence of Women in Civil and Canon Law] (1615); and Arcangela Tarabotti, *Che le donne siano della spezie degli uomini* [That Women Are of the Human Species][(1651).

44 Castiglione, *The Book of the Courtier*, p. 217.

45 Ibid.

46 Ibid., p. 218.

47 Ibid.

48 Cf. this argument with the concluding discussion in Agrippa, pp. 95–6.

49 This follows from (1) and (2) and the analytical principle that "if x is worthy of y, but not worthy of z, then z is more exalted than y."

50 Someone might raise the following objection to my attribution of this method to her: In this text and others, Gournay *does* assent to certain propositions. For example, in her nature vs. nurture argument she asserts that "women surely achieve a high degree of excellence less often than men do." My reply here is that this belief is a non-theoretical, one of ordinary life; as such it is insulated from her skepticism.

    A more difficult challenge may be raised about the Preface to her 1595 edition of Montaigne's *Essais*. Here she seems to assent to a number of evaluative claims about the merits of Montaigne's text, saying such things as that the book is "the judicial throne of reason," "the resurrection of truth," and "perfection in itself and the means of perfecting others" (*Preface to the* Essays *of Michel de Montaigne by his Adoptive Daughter, Marie le Jars de Gournay*, trs. R. Hillman and C. Quesnel (Tempe, AZ: Medieval and Renaissance Texts and Studies, vol. 193, 1998), p. 85) All of Gournay's remarks in this Preface are in dialectical response to published criticisms of the first published set of Montaigne essays. Still, it does not seem correct to think that Gournay is merely attempting to produce reasons on behalf of the book's merit that are equipollent to those of the detractors. But viewed in context, it also does not seem that her acclaim for the book is a dogmatic judgment about dogmatic views that Montaigne holds. She is merely observing the therapeutic value of the equipollent arguments that Montaigne himself provides: "He, on the contrary, has as his design the fencing that sharpens judgment, and perhaps intellect, the perpetual scourge of common errors. The others teach wisdom; he un-teaches foolishness . . . And whoever seeks to know what perfection means will see what a service he often does them by anatomizing them" (*Preface*, p. 83; p. 85)

    That this is a fideistic skeptical text is clear from her claims: "Who, moreover, could tolerate those heaven-climbing Titans that think to arrive at God by their means and circumscribe His works by the limits of their reason" (*Preface*, p. 55; p. 57); and her statement that "Judgment alone puts us in true possession of God; this is called adoring Him, and not knowing Him" (*Preface*, p. 31; 33). Finally, the Catholic slant on her fideism is evident when she says of Montaigne that "none was ever a greater enemy to all that impaired respect for the true one [religion], and the touchstone of that religion was, both for him, as the *Essays* declare, and for me, his creature, the holy law of the fathers" (*Preface*, p. 55).

51 On this issue, see Terence Penelhum, *God and Skepticism: A Study in Skepticism and Fideism* (Dordrecht/Boston/Lancaster: D. Reidel, 1983).

52 As cited in Craig Brush, *Montaigne and Bayle: Variations on the Theme of Skepticism* (The Hague: Martinus Nijhoff, 1966), p. 18.

53 I wish to thank the audiences at the conference on "Early Modern Women Philosophers" at the University of Florida-Gainesville, and at the Second Biennial Margaret Dauler Wilson Conference at Grafton, Vermont, as well as the students in my 2003 course on "Early Modern Women Philosophers" at UMass for helpful comments. Special thanks go to Dan Kaufman, Lisa Shapiro, Alice Sowaal, Susan Peppers-Bates, Tad Schmaltz, Kirk Ludwig, Marge Dunehew, Gary Ostertag, Andy Platt, Creighton Rosental, Jennifer Church, Don Rutherford, Martha Bolton and Stephen Menn. I especially wish to thank Eva Kittay and Linda Alcoff for their encouragement and patience.

This chapter is dedicated to the memory of Richard Popkin whose seminal work in the history of modern skepticism, and whose knowledge of early modern women philosophers have informed and inspired this chapter.

Chapter 2

Feminism and the History of Philosophy[1]

Robin May Schott

Introduction

First among the burgeoning new work of feminist philosophy in the early 1970s were the feminist rereading(s) of the history of philosophy. After all, philosophers who made up the core canon in western philosophy were without exception men, most of whom had made reprehensible comments about women. One could open a text of Plato, Aristotle, Rousseau, or Kant and find one's feminist suspicions confirmed: Philosophers *had* been sexist. And should one point out this pattern to fellow students or teachers, their attitudes merely reinstated those of this tradition. For their response, still typical today in Denmark, was: "Oh there she goes again." This response was meant to point out what they took to be obvious, that the feminist philosopher or student in question simply did not understand that what Aristotle or Kant wrote about women is wholly irrelevant to their philosophical theories. It may be unfortunate that Kant had written, "I hardly believe that the fair sex is capable of principles," but surely one should ignore this sentiment in dealing with his moral theory. If anything, this example of Kant's historical prejudice buttressed one's colleagues own confident belief in progress, since none of them would be caught dead writing that "a woman who had a head full of Greek . . . or carries on fundamental controversies about mechanics . . . might as well even have a beard, for perhaps that would express more obviously the mien of profundity for which she strives."[2] (Though these same colleagues may have their own views about who counted as a real woman.)

So the early attempts to trace the history of what philosophers had written about women located itself on a negative affective range. One faced what the French philosopher Michèle Le Doeuff has termed the paradoxes of sexism: "It has all been over since about the day before yesterday, and yet I experience it just this instant."[3] Hence, feminist philosophers sought to use their anger productively in creating new approaches to the history of philosophy.

Since the publication of the first source books, like Mary Mahowald's *Philoso-phy of Woman* (1978),[4] the relation between feminism and history of philosophy has become more nuanced and sophisticated, though no less difficult. How can the terms "feminist" and "history of philosophy" sit comfortably together in one phrase? On the one hand, one meets skeptics from the ranks of philosophers. First of all, many philosophers expect to hear a compelling justification for why they should be concerned about the *history* of philosophy at all, rather than address contemporary problems in philosophy. Second, those historians of philosophy who valiantly defend their efforts will ask: "What does gender have to do with it?" What, for example, do Aristotle's views of women have to do with philosophy? On the other hand, one meets skeptics among other feminists who voice a sense of dis-proportion of the effort involved given the desired outcome.[5] How can women's access to, and representation in, philosophy be vital for ongoing emancipatory struggles?

Here I will try to show some of the overlapping interests of both critics and defenders of feminist work in the history of philosophy. Instead of presupposing that work in history of philosophy and work in feminism are naturally at odds with each other, and arguing for a post-war pact of reconciliation, I will try to show that feminism helps philosophy do its job better. Further, I will argue that feminist work in the history of philosophy is an important contribution to *contemporary* philosophical work. As Michèle Le Doeuff writes in *Hipparchia's Choice*:

"[T]hinking philosophically" and "being a feminist" appear as one and the same atti-tude: a desire to judge by and for oneself . . . If philosophy particularly consists in questioning what happens in towns, houses and people's daily lives (and, according to Cicero, such is philosophy's task as seen by Socrates), then the issue of women's lives is necessarily on the agenda. But has it really been so, as an issue, in the twenty-five centuries of philosophy that we can observe? Too little or not in the right way, the feminist would say: so here we have an enquiry and a process to be taken further.

For the project of philosophy and that of feminist thinking have a fundamental structure in common, an art of fighting fire with fire and looks with looks, of objec-tifying and analyzing surrounding thought, of regarding beliefs as objects that must be scrutinized, when the supposedly normal attitude is to submit to what social life erects as doctrine. Nothing goes without saying, including what people think about the roles which have come down to men and women.[6]

And yet, though the most lively philosophical attitude is in harmony with fem-inism, uniting feminist and philosophical identities in one person still produces a kind of contradiction. And that is because being a philosopher has not been defined strictly in terms of rigorous intellectual inquiry and self-reflection. Instead, being a philosopher has typically carried with it certain aspects of what Le Doeuff calls an *imaginary*. The imaginary dimension of philosophy does not mean that philosophy is unreal. The term "imaginary" brings into focus the theatrical staging of the philosopher's body: the seriousness of the face, a demeanor that focuses on the austerity of thought as opposed to the frivolity of personal grooming. This comportment may help lead a young man with the conviction of the superiority of his own thought onto a path by which he becomes the sage whom the next generation must simultaneously emulate and surpass.[7] Already one can detect the difficulties for women philosophers, for nowhere in our cultural heritage have we learned that philosophers may be young, attractive women wearing shirts that expose their navels, are women with full pregnant bellies, or are mothers who also run after toddlers.

The imaginary focuses on certain assumptions about how to write philosophy as well, which separate those who write "commentary" from those who create something "original." In commenting on the different kinds of philosophical writing that one can distinguish in French examination systems, typically linked to the sexes of the candidates, Le Doeuff notes:

> a paper can be identified as masculine by its authoritative tone, by the way interpretation dominates over receptivity to the text, resulting in a decisive and profound reading or in fantastic misinterpretation. Women, on the other hand, are all receptivity, and their papers are characterized by a kind of polite respect for the fragmentation of the other's discourse (this is called 'acuteness in detailed commentary but lack of overview') . . . Men treat the text familiarly and knock it about happily; women treat it with a politeness.[8]

And although the latter type of writing may have a number of virtues associated with it, e.g., a nuanced attention to detail or an awareness of gaps in thinking, or it may display a peculiar displacing relation to the text, these types of commentaries are not considered the most authoritative. Hence, women philosophers in France are unlikely to be viewed as the most reliable commentators on a historical text, and their work is rarely used in mainstream courses in history of philosophy.[9] Thus, texts which display a non-authoritative style of writing do not become viewed as original philosophical interventions.

A certain style of writing that one can call masculinist, as opposed to male (so as not to identify with it men who refuse to see themselves in this type of imaginary)[10] is one aspect of the philosophical imaginary, as is the assumption that philosophical thinking issues in a complete philosophical system. This philosophical ideal of systematic completeness positions women outside of this system. For example, in Aristotle's view, woman is characterized by a certain lack of qualities. As Le Doeuff writes, "the fact that there is someone (women) incapable of philosophizing is comforting because it shows that philosophy is capable of something." One of the disturbances of thought created by feminism, which takes up the Socratic injunction to examine one's thoughts up to and beyond the point of discomfort, is to challenge the view that philosophy should even strive for completeness. Instead, as feminists have stressed, the philosophical task must be to retain the notion of the unknown and unthought.[11] Far from refusing the questions raised by feminists to the history of philosophy, it is imperative to include questions that historically have been officially excluded from philosophy in the process of pushing us to the borders of thought.

Canonical Figures and Feminist Questions:
Ancient and Medieval Philosophers

There have been many strategies developed to examine the masculinism of the history of philosophy: the investigation of the philosophical imaginary, and of how images used in argumentation have the function of distracting attention from an argument's gaps or weaknesses; the examination of metaphors used to symbolize the masculine and feminine in philosophy; the focus on how culturally coded qualities of masculinity become identified with shifts in philosophical discourse.[12] All of these strategies, however, thematize the question of how feminists relate to the western philosophical canon. In one sense, feminist philosophers are using the history of philosophy as other philosophical movements have done, to provide a justification for their contemporary concerns.[13] However, feminist readings are distinguished from non-feminist readings by an interest in and sensitivity to questions about sexual difference and gender. By way of contrast, consider the following remark by noted American philosopher Richard Rorty: "Each historian of philosophy is working for an '*us*' which consists, primarily, of those who see the contemporary philosophical scene as *he* does. So each will treat in a '*witchcraft*' manner what another will treat as the antecedents of something real and important in contemporary philosophy."[14] As illustrated by Rorty, the philosophical "us" which reads the history of a philosophy is a "he" that uses gendered terms (e.g., "witchcraft") to describe what "he" considers to be bad philosophy. For a feminist historian of philosophy, the problem is how "she" can create a philosophical "us" that includes both women and men, instead of taking "he-ness" as a natural philosophical attribute.

There are a number of ways by which feminists relate to the western philosophical canon: First, they may relate negatively to this canon by pointing to the misogyny of philosophers' views of women; the gendered interpretations of theoretical concepts, like matter and form in Aristotle; or the ways in which overarching philosophical concepts of reason and objectivity have been gendered as male, or have arisen out of a world-view that is gendered male. By virtue of this critical relation to the western philosophical canon, feminist philosophers also point out concepts that should be resisted in contemporary theory, and thus the canon functions as a negative resource as well.[15] For example, Elizabeth Spelman's book *Inessential Woman* takes as its starting point a critical assessment of the concept of essence in Platonic philosophy, and then uses this vantage point to assess critically how contemporary feminist theorists use the concept "women."[16]

Second, feminist historians of philosophy may relate to the western philosophical canon by providing an alternative selection of figures or texts that should be viewed as canonical. This strategy includes the attempt to record the lost voices of women philosophers, as in Mary Ellen Waithe's *A History of Women Philosophers* and the recent series Re-Reading the Canon which upgrades Mary Wollestonecraft, Hannah Arendt, and Simone de Beauvoir as canonical. Note, however, that the *Encyclopedia of Philosophy* which contains articles on over 900 philosophers does not have an entry for any of them.[17] By creating an alternative canon, feminist historians of philosophers are also looking for antecedents to issues discussed by contemporary feminist philosophers. This strategy also includes giving renewed attention to male figures in the history of philosophy who often are viewed as marginal (e.g., Anaximander, Heraclitus, Democritus, and Gorgias).[18] Creating an alternative canon may also include developing reading strategies that focus on non-orthodox texts or moments by those authors who are firmly established in the canon. The French philosopher Barbara Cassin writes that canonical texts contain "heterodoxical moments, when they are obliged to confront the 'others': witness the extreme difficulty of Book Gamma of Aristotle's *Metaphysics* or Plato's *Sophist*." Cassin's reading of canonical texts focuses on "the very singularity of the works that are created, torn between denials and inventions."[19]

Third, feminists may turn to the history of philosophy for positive resources to address contemporary issues that feminist philosophers confront. For example, Martha Nussbaum turns to Aristotle for an understanding of the role of emotion, relationships, and context in ethical life; Moira Gatens and Genevieve Lloyd turn to Spinoza's understanding of the body as "in relation" for a reconceptualization of the imaginary and of the possibility of social inclusion; Annette Baier finds inspiration in David Hume's reflections on moral sentiment and actual moral practices, and Charlene Seigfried argues for the value of pragmatism for contemporary feminism.[20] Other feminists focus on John Stuart Mill's and Friedrich Engels' reflections on the rights and liberties of women – who they argued deserve the same rights and liberties as men – and thus view their works as supportive of contemporary feminist principles.[21]

Before I turn to questions of methodology, I will illustrate the original impetus for feminist work in this field found in the statements made by philosophers about women and femininity.[22] There are highly divergent ways in which feminist philosophers have interpreted texts by figures in the history of philosophy such as Plato, Aristotle, and Kant, and I will give some examples of these differences.[23]

The statements made by philosophers about women and concepts frequently associated with women such as the body and emotion today are embroiled in controversy – often a controversy over feminism's core values and theoretical commitments. For example, some feminist philosophers consider Plato's *The Republic* to be a compelling declaration about the equality of men and women in the guardian class. Yet other feminists call attention to the passages in the *Timaeus* where Plato describes the creation of women as follows: "Of the men who came into the world, those who were cowards or led unrighteous lives may with reason be supposed to have changed into the nature of women in the second generation . . . Thus were created women and the female sex in general" (*Timaeus* 90e–91e).[24] In *The Republic*, one can find evidence for both generous and critical interpretations of Plato's views on women. For example, in Book V he explicitly rejects the view that sexual differences influence men's and women's natural capacities to rule. He writes:

If it appears that the male and the female sex have distinct qualifications for any arts or pursuits, we shall affirm that they ought to be assigned respectively to each. But if it appears that they differ only in just this respect that the female bears and the male begets, we shall say that no proof has yet been produced that the woman differs from the man for our purposes, but we shall continue to think that our guardians and their wives ought to follow the same pursuits.

(*The Republic*, 454d–e)

And yet he immediately qualifies this claim, "women naturally share in all pursuits and men in all – yet, for all, the woman is weaker than the man" (*Republic*, 455d–e). Moreover, in Book IV, he introduces women in the class of individuals in whom the worse part rules the better. He contrasts "the mob of motley appetites and pleasures and pains one would find chiefly in children and women and slaves and in the base rabble of those who are free men in name" with "the simple and moderate appetites which with the aid of reason and right opinion are guided by consideration" (*Republic* 431c). Elsewhere, he confines the lamentations of grief to women and inferior men and exhorts young men seeking to become "brave, sober, pious, free" (*Republic* 395c) to avoid imitating women. So the controversy about the feminist implications of Plato's texts to a considerable extent revolves about how to situate the egalitarianism of Book V of *The Republic* in relation to Plato's inegalitarianism, which posits that different natures are rooted in different kinds of souls.[25]

Feminist scholars also disagree about how to understand the most important female figure in the dialogues, namely the priestess Diotima in the *Symposium*, whom Socrates calls his teacher about love. How did Diotima learn about love's true nature and gain philosophical wisdom? Luce Irigaray cautions against taking literally this description of Diotima in the dialogue. Although Socrates cites Diotima's teaching, Irigaray reminds us: "She does not take part in these exchanges or in this meal among men. She is not there. She herself does not speak . . . And Diotima is not the only example of a woman whose wisdom, especially about love, is reported in her absence by a man."[26] Irigaray's ironic comment about Diotima's absence becomes a starting point for an alternative reading of Diotima's views about love that includes the fecundity of both body and soul.

In reading Aristotle, feminists have debated the relation between his views about human biology and his metaphysical and political concepts. For example, in *The Generation of Animals* Aristotle characterizes the male and female principles by the contrasts between form and matter, active and passive (716b11).[27] Although both the female, material principle and the male, formative principle are necessary for reproduction, the female remains inferior to the male. Aristotle writes, "the female, in fact, is female on account of inability of a sort" (728a18). And Aristotle sees these principles not only in physical existence, but in the "mental characteristics of the two sexes" (*History of Animals* 608a21–2). In the *Politics* Aristotle also writes, "It is clear that the rule of the soul over the body and of the mind and the rational element over the passionate is natural and expedient; whereas the equality of the two is always hurtful. The same holds good of animals in relation to men . . .

Again, the male is by nature superior, and the female inferior, and the one rules and the other is ruled" (*Politics* 1254b5–15). Commentators who disagree on the value of Aristotle's philosophy for contemporary feminist debates agree that he is sexist. Cynthia Freeland writes,

> Aristotle says that the courage of a man lies in commanding, a woman's lies in obeying; that "matter yearns for form," as the female for the male and the ugly for the beautiful; that women have fewer teeth than men; that a female is an incomplete male or "as it were, a deformity": which contributes only matter and not form to the generation of offspring; that in general "a woman is perhaps an inferior being"; that female characters in tragedy will be inappropriate if they are too brave or too clever.[28]

Given these views, the question now becomes: should Aristotle's sexist comments give rise to a gendered interpretation of his metaphysical views?

A gendered interpretation implies that Aristotle's metaphysical concepts are connected either explicitly or implicitly with his views on gender and sexual difference. The argument for a gendered interpretation takes the following form: The hierarchical relation between form and matter provides a conceptual framework that informs most of Aristotle's philosophy, from biology to metaphysics and politics. If one argues that form and matter are intrinsically associated with masculinity and femininity, then Aristotle's work is fundamentally "masculinist."[29] Hence, one cannot merely remove Aristotle's theory of sex difference from the rest of his philosophy, because it expresses social values that become the basis for a metaphysics that is politicized and is used to justify the subordination of all women as well as of some men (slaves).[30] Alternatively, those who reject a gendered interpretation argue that the gender associations of matter and form are extrinsic to Aristotle's theory. Although Aristotle's metaphysical framework captures a reality that is already value-laden, the fact that maleness became associated with form and femaleness with matter was incidental to his metaphysics as such. This reformist interpretation of Aristotle suggests that gender associations can be removed without undermining his metaphysical theory. For the reformist interpretation, Aristotle's theory highlights the relation between normative values and description and thus his theory of substance provides a positive resource for the present.[31]

Feminist philosophers have also highlighted what key thinkers in the Christian tradition have written about women and the feminine. St Augustine's texts express his views that women are more closely linked to the corrupt body than men, making their subordination both natural and commendable. He writes, "There is nothing I am more determined to avoid than relations with a woman. I feel that there is nothing which so degrades the high intelligence of a man than the embraces of a woman and the contact with her body, without which it is impossible to possess a wife."[32] And in the *Confessions* he writes,

> And just as in man's soul there are two forces, one which is dominant because it deliberates and one which obeys because it is subject to such guidance, in the same way, in the physical sense, woman has been made for man. In her mind and her rational

intelligence she has a nature the equal of man's, but in sex she is physically subject to him in the same way as our natural impulses need to be subjected to the reasoning power of the mind, in order that the actions to which they lead may be inspired by the principles of good conduct.

(13.32.344)

In Augustine's view, the subjugation of woman to man incarnates the spiritual hierarchy that man must strive to achieve within his own soul. In insisting on both women's rational equality and physical subordination, Augustine suggests that women experience a split between their rational soul and their embodied existence that men do not experience.[33] Hence, Genevieve Lloyd has argued that "despite this conscious upgrading of female nature, his own interpretations still put women in an ambivalent position with respect to Reason."[34]

Augustine's dual conception of women's spiritual and physical being leads him to attribute conflicting qualities to women's nature. He writes, "A good Christian is found in one and the same woman to love the creature of God whom he desires to be transformed and renewed, but to hate in her the corruptible and moral conjugal connection, sexual intercourse and all that pertains to her as wife."[35] Although women were created for the purpose of aiding in generation, Augustine argues that after resurrection, this function will be transcended. Women's bodies will retain their "nature," not their "vice"; they shall be "superior to carnal intercourse and child-bearing."[36] Thus, the resurrection of women's true nature negates the function for which they were created in earthly existence.

Thus, Augustine is inconsistent with regard to the question of women's equality. He maintained women's *equality* in the "City of God," but stressed their social and political *inequality*. As Penelope Deutscher argues in *Yielding Gender*, the issue for feminist theorists is what methodologies can be used to interpret such inconsistencies in the history of philosophy.[37] Should the ambivalence in these texts be pardoned in light of the relative progress Augustine's views represents over those of the other Church Fathers? Are there alternative strategies to interpret the ambivalence in these texts? I will return to these questions of methodology below.

Thomas Aquinas problematizes the very creation of women in *Summa Theologica* (*ST*). He poses the question of "whether woman should have been made in the first production of things."[38] Aquinas suggests that woman's existence is problematic because she is naturally subjugated to man, she is the occasion for sin, and as Aristotle says, she is a "misbegotten male." If God's creation is in all respects good, it is puzzling to Aquinas how such an imperfect being as woman could have been made in this original act of production. Thus, Aquinas explains women's role in the following terms: "It was necessary for a woman to be made, as the Scripture says, as *a helper* to man; not, indeed, as a helpmate in other works, as some say, since man can be more efficiently helped by another man in other works; but as a helper in the work of generation" (*ST* 1.92.1). As to the question of why sexual differentiation is at all necessary for human biology, Aquinas' answer is that sexual differentiation allows for a separation across the sexes between the active and passive powers in generation, which makes possible man's pursuance of the noble, "vital operation" of intellection. Aquinas reinforces this identification of male with the operations of reason when he claims that man serves as the "principle" of human existence. He writes, "As God is the principle of the whole universe, so the first man, in likeness to God, was the principle of the whole human race" (*ST* 1.92.2) If man is the principle of the human race, then he must contain all the perfections of human existence. Since reason is the noblest function of human existence, intellectual operations must be contained in this first principle of the human race.

Because of women's inclination to be led by passion, marriage cannot be a relationship between equals, but is one of "proportional" equality (*Suppl.* 64.5).[39] Aquinas compares this proportional equality between husband and wife to the complementary relation between active and passive elements. And he argues that woman's subjection to man existed even before the Fall: "woman is naturally subject to man, because in man the discretion of reason predominates" (*ST* 1.92.1).

Thus, Aquinas presents an ambiguous picture of women's relation to reason. On the one hand, he attributes to her an intellectual soul which is the image of God, and is itself without sexual differentiation: "The image of God belongs to both sexes, since it is in the mind, wherein there is no distinction of sexes" (*ST* 1.93.6). On the other hand, Aquinas persists in claiming that in a secondary sense, the image of God is found only in man and not in woman: "For man is the beginning and end of woman; as God is the beginning and end of every creature" (*ST* 1.93.4). For feminist philosophers, the question is not whether Aquinas' writings express sexist sentiments. More significantly, the question is whether his ideals of reason themselves carry a gendered meaning. As Genevieve Lloyd has argued, although woman does not symbolize for Aquinas an inferior form of rationality, because woman's meaning is bound up with reproduction, she is "symbolically located outside the actual manifestations of Reason within human life." Hence, more is at stake in Aquinas' texts than a "succession of surface misogynist attitudes within philosophical thought. It is not a question simply of the applicability to women of neutrally specified ideas of rationality, but rather of the genderization of the ideals themselves."[40]

Although one could continue discussing the philosophical implications of texts in the western philosophical canon that explicitly address women's nature, it is not my project to provide a complete resource to the reader. I merely have pointed to some of the examples which have been a reference point for feminist historians of philosophy. Hence, I will include only one more philosopher in this section, Immanuel Kant, who has been a focal point for my own work in feminist history of philosophy.

Canonical Figures and Feminist Questions: Kant

Kant's comments on women are hardly a positive testimony to the progressive character of the Enlightenment project. Kant considers women's character, in contrast to men's, to be wholly defined by natural needs. He writes, "Nature was concerned about the preservation of the embryo and implanted fear into the woman's character, a fear of physical injury and a timidity towards similar dangers. On the basis of this weakness, the woman legitimately asks for masculine protection."[41] Because of their natural fear and timidity, women are viewed as unsuited for scholarly work. Kant mockingly describes the scholarly women who "use their books somewhat like a watch, that is, they wear the watch so it can be noticed that they have one, although it is usually broken or does not show the correct time."[42] And in his view, women's philosophy is "not to reason, but to sense."[43] No wonder that under these conditions the woman "makes no secret in wishing that she might rather be a man, so that she could give larger and freer latitude to her inclinations; no man, however, would want to be a woman.[44] Although one might be tempted to dismiss Kant's misogynist views as merely a reflection of an earlier epoch, Kant himself was exposed to more progressive views. The lawyer Theodor von Hippel, mayor of Königsberg and friend of Kant, was a spokesperson for equal human and civil rights for women.

Because of Kant's misogyny and his apparent disdain for the body, Kant is the modern philosopher that feminists find most objectionable.[45] However, many feminists seek to redefine the ground on which a sympathetic dialogue with Kant can be found.[46] These competing views are generated about Kant's categorical imperative, which he at one point formulated as "I should never act in such a way that I could not also will my maxim should be a universal law."[47] Kant's moral philosophy demands respect for persons as rational beings, warns against treating persons as means to an end, and argues against any role for emotion in ethical judgment except the feeling of respect for the moral law. Some feminist philosophers have argued that Kant's formalist conception of the moral law is based on a false dichotomy between reason and nature, and cannot be adequate to understanding the complexities of human life.[48] Other feminist philosophers argue that Kant's formal rule of morality is both universalist and radically individualizing, and that Kant's ethics can be an important tool in identifying the wrongs to which women are subjected because of their gender, or that it can be a resource in developing a duty to care.[49]

Kant's aesthetic reflections in the *Critique of Judgment* have been central for contemporary resurgence of interest in Kant. In this text, Kant moves away from the mechanistic conception of nature that is dominant in the *Critique of Pure Reason*, and emphasizes the harmonious interplay of the imagination and understanding, which gives rise to the experience of objects *as if* they were designed for our own purposes. In a sympathetic feminist account, one philosopher argues that Kant's notion of common sense – *sensus communis* – opens up the possibility not just of thinking with others, but of feeling with others, and thus creates a space for imagination and feeling that revises Kant's earlier account of moral subjectivity.[50] In a critical feminist account, another philosopher argues that Kant's theory about the beautiful and the sublime continues the long list of dualisms in western culture, including the dualisms between form/matter, mind/body, reason/emotion, transcendence/immanence, all of which have a gendered meaning in western civilization.[51] Similarly, there are competing interpretations by feminist philosophers of Kant's rationalism. For example, in my book *Cognition and Eros; A Critique of the Kantian Paradigm*, I focused on reason's role in scientific knowledge, and on the cognitive relation between the knower and the object of knowledge.[52] In Kant's formalistic conception of knowledge, he treats observation as paradigmatic for knowing, and thus excludes awareness of our own sensory involvement with the object of knowledge. In excluding feeling from knowledge, even from knowledge of oneself, Kant develops a cognitive corollary to his earlier views that compare emotions and passions to "an illness of mind because both emotion and passion, exclude the sovereignty of reason."[53] Moreover, the abstract nature of the "I think" which accompanies all knowledge indicates that the subject does not develop or change through the process of knowing. And the role of a priori concepts of the understanding, which are prior to and independent of experience, leads to a conception of knowledge that is impervious to any historical changes in relations between subjects and objects of knowledge. Hence, I argue that Kant's philosophy illustrates an ascetic posture that is based on a distancing from and denigration of feeling, sensuality, and the feminine.

Other feminist philosophers offer a more positive reading of the formal features of Kant's epistemology. Adrian Piper focuses on the resources available in Kant's conception of the self for knowing other persons.[54] Piper takes up the question of xenophobia, which she defines as "a fear of individuals who violate one's empirical conception of persons and so one's self-conception."[55] She asks, what is it that prevents one from recognizing a particular third-person other as a person? And can one correct for this exclusion of a particular empirical other from personhood? Piper argues that Kant's theory of the self is a positive resource because it provides for the possibility of correcting against xenophobia. The main points of her argument are as follows: Even though an individual might have an empirically limited conception of persons (e.g., they may not have wide acquaintance with blacks), reason always works to enlarge our understanding by searching for further data by which to explain our experiences. Thus, the rational subject welcomes new experiences as cognitive challenges. Piper concludes that Kant's conception of the rational self not only has the resources for correcting for xenophobia in the self's relation to the other, but this conception of the self can even be characterized by a kind of xenophilia, "a positive valuation of human difference as intrinsically interesting . . . and a disvaluation of conformity to one's honorific stereotypes as intrinsically uninteresting."[56]

Although feminist rereadings of the history of western philosophy were motivated initially by the desire to analyze critically philosophical misogyny, these interpretations have had much more far-reaching results. They have led to a rethinking of themes within ethics, aesthetics, epistemology, and metaphysics. Though there is no one feminist way of reading a particular philosopher, there are certain common threads in these interpretations. Feminist philosophers raise questions about embodiment, emotion, imagination, community, and power relations.

Feminist interpretations are guided by an ethical interest as well, as they explore the ways in which philosophical theories either sustain a logic of domination or provide resources to resist such a logic.

Methodological Reflections

Although feminist work in the history of philosophy began with what one might now consider to be a banal recitation of misogynist comments on women, it has developed into a field that is reflective about methodology in a way that contributes to making the field of history of philosophy profoundly philosophical.[57] Methodology refers to a systematic procedure for approaching something, gaining knowledge, or teaching. Earlier feminist work in the history of philosophy proceeded by asking the question, "Is Plato or Aristotle or Kant sexist?" Later work has broadened the range of questions to pursue and has become self-reflective about its relation to other strategies of reading texts. Feminist historians of philosophy now analyze the range of affective, conceptual, and institutional issues that mediate both women's and men's relation to the history of philosophy. Affective issues may include questions such as: Does the reader relate to the text through anger or through pleasure? How does the position and content of imagery in an argument produce the effect of conviction? Conceptual issues include questions about knowledge, ethics, politics, or aesthetics, as well as reflections on strategies of textual interpretation. Institutional issues include questions about how certain forms of commentary are viewed as authoritative and as legitimate topics for professional research, and how other kinds of commentary are viewed as nonauthoritative and illegitimate.[58]

In the beginning of this chapter I referred to three classifications for feminist work in the history of philosophy: (1) A *negative* relation to the canon includes approaches that focus on the misogyny of a philosopher, on gendered interpretations of specific concepts, and on gendered interpretations of overarching themes in the history of philosophy. (2) An *alternative* canon consists in revisons about which writers and texts should be included in the canon of the history of philosophy. (3) A *positive* relation to the philosophical canon emphasizes how feminists inherit resources from this tradition that are productive for contemporary feminist concerns. Although this classification is useful, it does hold the danger of oversimplification. What about interpretations that express more than one of these ways of relating to the canon, or none of them? For example, the strategies of reading history of philosophy inspired by deconstruction do not fit neatly into this classification. Deconstructive strategies of reading focus on the effects of the unstable or contradictory character of concepts in texts. Penelope Deutscher, in *Yielding Gender*, uses this approach in a specifically feminist spirit to analyze how the unstable or contradictory character of the concepts of reason, male, female, and human have the effect of sustaining a phallocentric argument in a text. In this sense, deconstructive feminism has a negative or critical relation to canonical texts. But deconstructive feminism also has a more general project of analyzing the tensions and ambivalences that saturate philosophical writing, despite textual claims for rational consistency and completeness. Thus, for deconstructionist feminism, the interesting question is not just, "Do feminists relate to the history of philosophy negatively or positively?" Rather, they ask: "What are the reading strategies developed by feminist philosophers?" and "How do these strategies complicate or deepen interpretations of texts in the history of philosophy?"

Feminist philosophers have chosen various strategies for interpreting how the terms masculinity and femininity are used in an ambiguous or contradictory fashion in philosophical texts. One strategy is to argue that *despite* the uneven statements of thinkers like St Augustine or Jean-Jacques Rousseau, the masculine connotations of reason prevails. For example, in *The Man of Reason* Genevieve Lloyd argues that *despite* the complexity of Rousseau's view of the relation between nature and reason, he excludes women from a concept of reason which is associated as masculine. A second strategy is to argue that the complexity and contradiction within a thinker like Rousseau *mitigates* or *diminishes* the misogyny of the text. Deutscher draws from deconstruction a third strategy for reading contradictions. She criticizes both these two approaches for having the effect of making the text more consistent or stable than it actually is. She writes, "Feminist philosophy also needs to focus on contradictory textual tendencies, rather than looking between or beyond them to the 'real meaning' of a confused philosophical argument, or looking behind them, as when critics think such tendencies are trivial, or attempt to explain or account for them."[59] Therefore, she asks: what are the effects of contradictions and ambiguities in a text? Her thesis is that the contradictions in the concept of reason have the effect of sustaining the phallocentric alignment of reason and humanity with masculinity. Not only do these thinkers give contradictory accounts of women, but they also give contradictory accounts of men. And the alignment of masculinity with reason is actually an effect of the contradictory account of woman as *both* rational and irrational.

Three prominent French feminist philosophers have focused on the problem of textual instability: Michèle Le Doeuff, Sarah Kofman, and Luce Irigaray. All three of these philosophers have focused on how women and femininity have been represented as other in the history of philosophy, and how this representation is linked to textual contradictions and ambiguities. Michèle Le Doeuff, as noted earlier, works with the imagery in philosophical arguments. She describes her work as follows, "My work is about the stock of images you can find in philosophical works, whatever they refer to: insects, clocks, women, or islands. I try to show what part they play in the philosophical enterprise."[60] Le Doeuff analyzes how textual elements that appear as strictly marginal in a philosophical work have the effect of concealing or substituting for problems in the argument. She writes, "The perspective I am adopting here . . . involves reflecting on strands of the imaginary operating in places where in principle, they are supposed not to belong and yet where, without them, nothing would have been accomplished."[61] Thus, Le Doeuff analyzes the rhetoric in a philosophical text by looking at points of weakness and contradictions in an argument.

Sarah Kofman's readings of Nietzsche, Freud, Comte, Kant, and Rousseau draws on a methodology which she considers to be both deconstructive and psychoanalytical. She focuses on the distinction between what texts purport to do and what they really do. For example, she interprets Rousseau's use of the term "respect" for women as a symptom of a complex structure of ambivalence towards women. And she looks at how Rousseau's contradictions about women are functional for his text. But at the same time, she offers a causal explanation for these contradictions, e.g., by looking at the author's unconscious intent. In this respect, Kofman's emphasis is on what motivates the contradictory logic in a philosopher rather than on what this logic enables in the text.

Of these three French philosophers, Luce Irigaray most systematically explores the logic of instability. For Irigaray, the representations of masculine and feminine are themselves generated by a paradoxical structure. Her hypothesis is that "woman" has always been defined as the necessary complement to, or negative image of, masculinity in philosophy. Women have been represented only in terms that are relational to a masculine reference. Therefore, Irigaray's project is to analyze how a text does *not* represent women. She argues that philosophy has the power to "reduce all others to the economy of the Same" and "eradicate the difference between the sexes."[62] And thus Irigaray's thesis is that the concept of femininity is a possibility that is both outside and inside the borders of philosophy. The concept of femininity is outside the history of philosophy, since the representation of women has been excluded from philosophy. But the concept of femininity is not entirely outside, since philosophy gestures towards it as an excluded possibility. Hence, the concept of femininity has a paradoxical inside/outside structure. Irigaray's strategy for reading texts in the history of philosophy shows how the contradictions implicit in these terms have the effect of sustaining the phallocentric premises of the text.

These three authors use the analysis of textual instability to point to negative features in the philosophical canon, i.e., they show how contradictions sustain phallocentrism. In this sense they exemplify a "disinvestment approach" – i.e., they do not take ownership of this philosophical tradition, as philosophers who invoke the inheritance model do, since they see in this tradition the perpetuation of relations of domination. Nor do they abandon philosophy. Since the philosophical tradition cannot be a straightforward resource, they use unorthodox techniques of reading to return uneasily to the house of philosophy.[63] But Michèle Le Doeuff also has contributed significantly to building an "alternative" to the canonical texts, e.g, through her substantial work on Simone de Beauvoir. And Luce Irigaray is also deeply inspired by the work of Emmanuel Lévinas, as is evident in her book *An Ethics of Sexual Difference*, and thus she uses the history of philosophy for its positive resource as well. Therefore, instead of highlighting negative, positive, or alternative relations to the canon, their work illustrates how methodological innovation in interpreting texts can cut across these categorizations.

If conceptual contradictions point to contradictions in social relations, then an analysis of philosophical writing becomes a tool for social critique.[64] But deconstruction explicitly rejects a reference to the extra-textual terrain. Derrida writes, "Reading . . . cannot legitimately transgress toward something other than it, toward a referent (a reality that is metaphysical, historical, psychobiographical, etc.)"[65] Can ethical or political intervention occur strictly by pointing to the textual level? Arguably, Irigaray's readings in the history of philosophy give one example of how textual intervention can have ethical effects. She uses irony, humor, mimicry, and parody to subvert the prevalent readings of Plato, Descartes, and other philosophers and to explore the fecundity of sexual difference.[66] Feminist deconstruction also needs to clarify the scope of its strategy. Can feminist deconstruction be applied to all texts within the history of philosophy, even texts that do not address explicitly questions of women and femininity? Or is it focused exclusively on contradictions surrounding gender? If the latter, it could be argued that feminist deconstruction limits feminist readings in the history of philosophy to a narrow domain.

Concluding Remarks

In the preceding section, I have focused on the methodological innovations engendered by a deconstructionist approach to texts. But feminist historians of philosophy also address the standard methodological issues of the field, and debate the following questions: Is the task of the (feminist) historian of philosophy to be primarily a *historian*, i.e., to tell it like it was and study the history of philosophy on its own terms? Or is the task of the (feminist) historian of philosophy to use the resources of the history of philosophy to address the *philosophical* issues.[67] The limit of the *historical* approach to texts is that it presumes it is possible to be a neutral historian with no specific interest in a text. Feminist historians of philosophy are often critical of this reading practice because it rejects using one's specific interest in the present, e.g., an interest in gender as an interpretative tool. Moreover, the claim for neutrality in history of philosophy often accompanies practices of selective focus, and thus raises serious doubts about this ideal of neutrality. The *philosophical* approach to texts uses the history of philosophy as inspiration for seeking truths or at least as solutions to current problems or puzzles. Among feminist historians of philosophy, this approach characterizes feminists who view the history of philosophy as an inheritance which can be mined for contemporary feminist concerns. Yet this approach also makes a number of problematic assumptions: that the history of philosophy is primarily a positive resource rather than a negative inheritance; that history is sufficiently continuous so that past truths can address present problems; and that philosophy's goal is to further progress towards truth. Cynthia Freeland suggests a third approach, invoking a pragmatist vision of history of philosophy as an ongoing project of explaining puzzles, rather than as a quest for true views or arguments.[68] This approach recognizes that the resources of the past are always a mixed bag, and that they cannot provide justifications for present views; but these past resources are potentially stimulating for reflection on the present. Feminist pragmatism in reading the history of philosophy incorporates analyses of the context of historical texts, of the values or interests that guide (feminist) research in the present, and is critical of claims for progress in truth without giving up claims for epistemic superiority.

How then do feminist debates contribute to methodological reflections on the history of western philosophy? For one thing, these debates show that approaches to history of philosophy that *exclude* feminist questions are themselves ideological, both because they are epistemologically flawed and because they contribute to the justification of social relations of dominance. Feminist philosophers do not claim that all work in the history of philosophy should be guided by questions of gender and sexuality. But they protest against the view that philosophy can interrogate all of the fundamental issues of human life except the fact that humans are both male and female, and how these differences have been sedimented in social, cultural, and intellectual history.

One can detect a shift amongst feminist commentators from an early negative interest in the philosophical canon to a more recent positive interest. In an interview published in 2000 Genevieve Lloyd commented,

> The positive and negative approaches can both be seen as reflecting a feminist perspective on the history of philosophy, but they're very different in spirit. I'm now much more interested in the positive appropriations – in looking *to* sources in the philosophical tradition for ways of reconceptualizing issues that are under current debate, and for ways of opening up our imaginations to alternative ways of thinking, than I am in the more negative criticisms of past philosophers.[69]

Penelope Deutscher speculates that this turn to a more positive relation to the history of western philosophy should be explained not just in intellectual terms, but in affective terms as well. Women philosophers are interested in the practice of philosophy, and ask: What does philosophy enable us to be? What affective range does it allow us to occupy? How can one find surprise, pleasure, and humor in the text? In discussing the work of contemporary French women philosophers, Deutscher articulates the questions they implicitly pose to philosophy:

> Not just, what can we know, but what range of emotions, stances, and actions does it allow us to occupy? Does it expand our subjective possibilities as negative critics, or as lovers of the new, for example the new that we find amongst the letter of the old? Could feminism engage in a therapeutic assessment of its relationship to the history of philosophy?[70]

There is no consensus on methodology by feminists who work in the history of philosophy. They work with methodologies that draw on inheritance models, ideology-critique, deconstructionism, psychoanalysis, and pragmatist views; nor should this be understood as an exhaustive account of feminist methodologies. But the multiplicity of approaches does not mean "anything goes." Feminist philosophers are good scholars who contribute subtle, nuanced, and innovative readings. Feminist philosophers generally acknowledge that they are participating in a collaborative project, and that no one individual interpretation or approach can be final and complete. This spirit of collaboration implies that feminist scholars do not merely tolerate other methods, since the notion of toleration retains the presumption that one's own methodology is the yardstick by which all others should be measured. Rather, feminist debates issue in a perspectivism that acknowledges that differing approaches to history are productive in very different ways. But amidst this diversity, feminist historians of philosophy are animated by the spirit of living the present critically. As the French philosopher Françoise Dastur says in her reading of Heidegger's Rectorat address of 1933, "To be in one's time . . . is to resist one's time, to be in one's time in a critical fashion, out of phase."[71] And since one cannot be utopian about the present, it is in the spirit of living the present critically that feminist readers open up places for innovative readings, dissenting views, and maverick approaches.

Notes

1 This chapter was first published in Robin May Schott, *Discovering Feminist Philosophy* (Lanham, MD: Rowman and Littlefield, 2003), pp. 25–52 and is reprinted here by permission of the publishers.

2 Immanuel Kant, *Observations on the Feeling of the Beautiful and Sublime*, tr. John T. Goldthwait (Berkeley: University of California Press, 1960), pp. 132–3, p. 78.

3 Michèle Le Doeuff, *Hipparchia's Choice; An Essay Concerning Women, Philosophy, Etc*, tr. Trista Selous (Oxford and Cambridge, MA: Blackwell, 1991), p. 6.

4 Mary Mahowald, ed., *The Philosophy of Woman; Classical to Current Concepts* (Indianapolis, IN: Hackett Publishing, 1978).

5 Le Doeuff, p. 5.

6 Ibid., p. 29.

7 Ibid., pp. 31, 156.

8 Le Doeuff, "Women and Philosophy," in *French Feminist Thought*, ed. Toril Moi (Oxford: Basil Blackwell, 1987), pp. 204–5.

9 Penelope Deutscher, "A Matter of Affect, Passion and Heart: Our Taste for New Narratives of the History of Philosophy," introduction to *Hypatia: A Journal of Feminist Philosophy* 15 (4) (Fall 2000), Special Issue: Contemporary French Women Philophers, ed. Penelope Deutscher: 1–17.

10 Le Doeuff, *Hipparchia's Choice*, p. 139.

11 Le Doeuff, "Women and Philosophy," pp. 193, 209.

12 See for example Michèle Le Doeuff, *The Philosophical Imaginary*, tr. Colin Gordon (London: Athlone Press, 1989); Genevieve Lloyd, *The Man of Reason; "Male" and "Female" in Western Philosophy* (Minneapolis: University of Minnesota Press, 1984); Susan R. Bordo, *The Flight to Objectivity; Essays on Cartesianism and Culture* (Albany:

SUNY Press, 1987), and Susan Bordo, ed., *Feminist Interpretations of René Descartes* (University Park: Pennsylvania State University Press, 1999): See also Eva Feder Kittay's essay, "Womb Envy as an Explanatory Concept," in *Mothering, Essays in Feminist Theory*, ed. Joyce Trebilcot (Totowa, NJ: Rowman and Allanheld, 1984), pp. 94–128.

13 See Charlotte Witt, "How Feminism is Re-writing the Philosophical Canon," The Alfred P. Stiernotte Memorial Lecture in Philosophy at Quinnipac College, October 2, 1996, reprinted on SWIP-Web, p. 11. http.//www.uh.edu/cfreelan/SWIP

14 *Philosophy in History*, eds. Richard Rorty, J.B. Schneewind, and Quentin Skinner (Cambridge: Cambridge University Press, 1984), p. 7, cited in Witt, p. 1; my italics.

15 Witt, "How Feminism is Re-writing the Philosophical Canon,"p. 3. See also Cynthia Freeland's "Feminism, Ideology, and Interpretation in Ancient Philosophy," *Apeiron*, 33 (4) December 2000, pp. 365–406.

16 Elizabeth V. Spelman, *Inessential Woman: Problems of Exclusion in Feminist Thought* (Boston, MA: Beacon Press, 1988).

17 Witt, "How Feminism is Re-writing the Philosophical Canon,"p. 7. See Mary Ellen Waithe, *A History of Women Philosophers* (Boston, MA: Kluwer Academic Publishers, 1989) and Nancy Tuana, General editor, Re-Reading the Canon series (University Park: The Pennsylvania State University Press, 1994–).

18 Deutscher, "A Matter of Affect," p. 5.

19 Quoted in ibid., p. 6.

20 Witt, "How Feminism is Re-writing the Philosophical Canon," p. 9. Martha Nussbaum, *Love's Knowledge; Essays on Philosophy and Literature* (Oxford: Oxford University Press, 1990); Susan James interviews Genevieve Lloyd and Moira Gatens, "The Power of Spinoza: Feminist Conjunctions," in *Hypatia: A Journal of Feminist Philosophy*15 (2) Spring 2000, Special Issue, Going Australian: Reconfiguring Feminism and Philosophy, eds. Christine Battersby, Catherine Constable, Rachel Jones, and Judy Purdom, pp. 40–58; Annette Baier, *Postures of the Mind; Essays on Mind and Morals* (Minneapolis: University of Minnesota Press, 1985); Charlene Haddock Seigfried, *Pragmatism and Feminism* (Chicago: University of Chicago Press, 1996). I will discuss the turn towards a positive orientation to the history of philosophy at the end of this chapter.

21 See Mahowald, *The Philosophy of Woman*.

22 There are significant resources for this discussion. I have already mentioned Genevieve Lloyd's *The Man of Reason* and the series Re-Reading the Canon. I can also recommend the following texts: Vigdis Songe-Møller, *Den græske drømmen om kvinnens overflødighet. Essays om myter og filosofi i antikkens Hellas* (Oslo: Cappelon Akademisk Forlag, 1999: English translation: *Philosophy without Women*, London: Continuum, forthcoming); Mary Wollestonecraft, *A Vindication of the Rights of Woman* (Buffalo: Prometheus Books, 1989) for her comments on Rousseau; Penelope Deutscher, *Yielding Gender; Feminism, Deconstruction and the History of Philosophy* (London and New York: Routledge, 1997) with sections on St Augustine and Rousseau; Christine Battersby's *The Phenomenal Women; Feminist Metaphysics and the Patterns of Identity* (Cambridge: Polity Press, 1998), with sections on Kant, Hegel, Kierkegaard, and Adorno; Nancy Tuana's *The Less Noble Sex: Scientific, Religious and Philosophical Conceptions of Women's Nature* (Bloomington: Indiana University Press, 1993), as well as Irigaray's provocative interpretations in *Speculum of the Other Woman*, tr. Gillian C. Gill (Ithaca, NY: Cornell University Press, 1985) and *An Ethics of Sexual Difference*, tr. Carolyn Burke and Gillian C. Gill (London: Athlone Press, 1993).

23 In the following discussion, I will draw on my own work in *Cognition and Eros; A Critique of the Kantian Paradigm* (Boston, MA: Beacon Press, 1983), especially chapters 1, 3, 4, and 8.

24 Plato, *The Collected Dialogues of Plato including the Letters*, eds. Edith Hamilton and Huntington Cairns (Princeton, NJ: Princeton University Press, 1961).

25 Spelman, *Inessential Woman*, pp. 25–6.

26 Irigaray, *An Ethics of Sexual Difference*, p. 20. For an alternative interpretation of Diotima's role, see for example Andrea Nye in "Irigaray and Diotima at Plato's Symposium," in Nancy Tuana, ed. *Feminist Interpretations of Plato* (University Park: Pennsylvania State University Press). See also Martha Nussbaum's reading of the dialogue, which emphasizes the importance of Alcibiades' speech in "The Speech of Alcibiades: A Reading of Plato's *Symposium*," *Philosophy and Literature* 3 (Fall 1979): 131–72.

27 Aristotle, *The Generation of Animals*, tr. A.L. Peck, Loeb Classical Library (Cambridge, MA: Harvard University Press, 1942). The citations to other texts refer to *The Basic Works of Aristotle*, ed. Richard McKeon (New York: Random House, 1941).

28 Cynthia Freeland, "Nourishing Speculation: A Feminist Reading of Aristotelian Science," in *Engendering Origins: Critical Feminist Readings in Plato and Aristotle*, ed. Bat-Ami Bar On (Albany: SUNY Press, 1994), pp. 145–6.

29 For this discussion, see Witt, "How Feminism is Re-writing the Philosophical Canon," pp. 4–5.

30 See Elizabeth V. Spelman, "Aristotle and the Politicization of the Soul," in *Discovering Reality; Feminist Perspectives on Epistemology, Metaphysics, Methodology, and Philosophy of Science*, eds. Sandra Harding and Merrill B. Hintikka (Dordrecht/Boston/Lancaster: D. Reidel, 1983), pp. 17–30.

31 Witt, "How Feminism is Re-writing the Philosophical Canon," p. 5.

32 *Soliloquia* I.10.17, quoted in Kari Elisabeth Børresen, *Subordination and Equivalence: The Nature and Role of Woman in Augustine and Thomas Aquinas*, tr. Charles H. Talbot (Washington, DC: University Press of America, 1981), p. 7.

33 Ibid., p. 27.

34 Lloyd, *The Man of Reason*, p. 29.

35 Quoted in Rosemary Radford Ruether, "Misogynism and Virginal Feminism in the Fathers of the Church," in *Religion and Sexism*, ed. Rosemary Radford Ruether (New York: Simon and Schuster, 1974), p. 161.

36 St Augustine, *The City of God*, tr. Marcus Dods (New York: Random House, 1950), 22.17.839.

37 Deutscher, *Yielding Gender*, p. 145.

38 Thomas Aquinas, *Summa Theologica*, tr. the Fathers of the English Dominican Province (New York: Benzinger Bros., 1947), vol. 1, part 1, question 92.

39 Ibid. vol. 3.

40 Lloyd, *The Man of Reason*, pp. 36–7.

41 Kant, *Anthropology from a Pragmatic Point of View*, p. 219.

42 Ibid., p. 221.

43 Ibid., pp. 132–3.

44 Ibid., p. 222.

45 Barbara Herman, "Could It Be Worth Thinking about Kant on Sex and Marriage?" in *A Mind of Her Own*, eds. Louise Antony and Charlotte Witt (Boulder, CO: Westview Press, 1993), p. 50.

46 For examples of some of these competing views, see my article,"Kant," in *A Companion*

to *Feminist Philosophy*, ed. Alison M. Jaggar and Iris Marion Young (Oxford: Black-well, 1998) and my anthology *Feminist Interpretations of Immanuel Kant* (University Park: Pennsylvania State University Press, 1997). For a Kantian-inspired approach to feminist philosophy, see also Herta Nagl-Docekal, *Feministische Philosophie; Ergebnisse, Probleme, Perspektiven* (Frankfurt am Main: Fischer Taschenbuch Verlag, 2000).

47 Kant, *Foundations of the Metaphysics of Morals*, tr. Lewis White Beck (New York: Mac-millan, 1963), p. 18.

48 Sally Sedgwick, "Can Kant's Ethics Survive the Feminist Critique?" in Schott, *Feminist Interpretations of Immanuel Kant*.

49 Herta Nagl-Docekal, "Feminist Ethics: How It Could Benefit from Kant's Moral Phil-osophy," in Schott, *Feminist Interpretations of Immanuel Kant*; Sarah Clark Miller, "A Kantian Ethic of Care?" in *Feminist Interventions in Ethics and Politics*, eds. Barbara Andrew, Jean Keller, and Lisa Schwartzman (Lanham, MD: Rowman and Littlefield, 2005), pp. 111–27.

50 Jane Kneller, "The Aesthetic Dimension of Kantian Autonomy," in Schott, *Feminist Interpretations of Immanuel Kant*. See also Marcia Moen's analysis of intersubjectiv-ity in the *Critique of Judgment* in "Feminist Themes in Unlikely Places: Re-Reading Kant's *Critique of Judgment*" in the same volume.

51 Cornelia Klinger, "The Concepts of the Sublime and the Beautiful in Kant and Lyotard," in Schott, *Feminist Interpretations of Immanuel Kant*. Another critical view is offered by Kim Hall, "*Sensus Communis* and Violence: A Feminist Reading of Kant's *Critique of Judgment*" in the same volume. See also Bonnie Mann, *Women's Liberation and the Sublime* (Oxford: Oxford University Press, 2006) for her interpretation of the Kantian sublime as providing a narrative of the unity of the subject that is reconstituted through projecting physical helplessness onto abject others, such as women and non-European "savages."

52 Today I would no longer argue that Kant's analysis of reason's role in scientific know-ledge is paradigmatic for all of the tasks of reason. Instead, I am persuaded by Susan Neiman's interpretation of Kant, in *The Unity of Reason* (Oxford: Oxford University Press, 1994) which focuses on Kant's analysis of reason beyond the limits of the cogni-tive. From this point of view, rationality for Kant is not centrally concerned with the cognitive, but with the unity of theoretical and practical reason and the primacy of practical reason within this unity.

53 Kant, *Anthropology*, p. 155, para. 73.

54 Adrian M.S. Piper, "Xenophobia and Kantian Rationalism," in Schott, *Feminist Inter-pretations of Immanuel Kant*, pp. 21–73.

55 Ibid., p. 48.

56 Ibid., p. 66.

57 Freeland, "Feminism and Ideology in Ancient Philosophy," *Apeiron: A Journal for Ancient Philosophy and Science*, 33 (4) December 2000, p. 370.

58 See Deutscher, "A Matter of Affect," as well as "'Imperfect Discretion': Interventions into the History of Philosophy by Twentieth-Century French Women Philosophers," in *Hypatia: A Journal of Feminist Philosophy*, 15 (2), Spring 2000, Special Issue, Going Australian: Reconfiguring Feminism and Philosophy, eds. Christine Battersby, Cather-ine Constable, Rachel Jones, and Judy Purdom, pp. 160–80. Deutscher argues that the distinction between commentary and originality is a feminist issue, since it fails to iden-tify as original the philosophy that women have written in letters, treatises on education and theology, and commentary on the history of philosophy. For Deutscher the ques-

tion is "what practices preclude women from being identified as original and innovative philosophers?" (p. 165)

59 Deutscher, "A Matter of Affect," pp. 7–8.

60 Cited in Deutscher, *Yielding Gender*, pp. 60–1.

61 Cited in ibid., p. 60. Deutscher notes, however, that there is a second strain in Le Doeuff's analysis, which leans towards a causal or motivational approach, e. g., in an effort to explain why certain contradictions and imagery emerge as central.

62 Cited in ibid., p. 77.

63 Freeland, *Feminism and Ideology*, p. 385.

64 For example, Lucien Goldmann's *The Hidden God: A Study of Tragic Vision in the Pensées of Pascal and the Tragedies of Racine*, tr. Philip Thody (London: Routledge and Kegan Paul, 1964). I raise these issues in my review of Deutscher's book in *Hypatia: A Journal of Feminist Philosophy*, 14 (3) Summer 1999, pp. 157–62.

65 Jacques Derrida, *Of Grammatology*, tr. Gayatri Chakravorty Spivak (Baltimore, MD and London: Johns Hopkins University Press, 1976), pp. 159, 158, cited in Deutscher, *Yielding Gender*, pp. 86–7.

66 Irigaray, *An Ethics of Sexual Difference*, p. 5. Note that Irigaray's more recent work explicitly seeks to live up to the injunction for ethical and political intervention, through her discussion of civil codes and her argument for sexed civil rights. (See *Le Temps de la différence: pour une révolution pacifique* (1989) and *Je, tu, nous* (1990).)

67 Cynthia Freeland's article discusses these two approaches laid out in Michael Frede's paper, "The History of Philosophy as a Discipline" (1988). He names the first approach as exegetical history of philosophy and the second approach as doxography (Freeland, *Feminism and Ideology*, p. 371ff.)

68 Ibid., p. 403.

69 Susan James interviews Genevieve Lloyd and Moira Gatens, p. 45.

70 Deutscher, "A Matter of Affect," p. 15.

71 Ibid., p. 10.

Chapter 3

Pragmatism

Shannon Sullivan

Pragmatism and Experience

Because "pragmatic" often is used colloquially to mean realistic or levelheaded, a word about the philosophical meaning of the term is in order before turning to the intersections of pragmatism and feminism. The roots of American philosophy, of which pragmatism arguably is the best-known branch, often are located in the transcendentalism of Emerson and Thoreau. The so-called classical period of American philosophy was later developed in the United States from the late nineteenth to the middle of the twentieth century by figures such as Jane Addams, W.E.B. Du Bois, John Dewey, Charlotte Perkins Gilman, William James, Alain Locke, George Herbert Mead, Charles Sanders Peirce, Josiah Royce, George Santayana, and Alfred North Whitehead. I say "so-called" since the issue of who is included in the American philosophical canon has been contentious. Often it is restricted to the Anglo-American men on the list – Peirce, Dewey, James, Mead, Whitehead, and Royce – with a particular focus on the first three as the "holy triumvirate" of American pragmatism. In the past decade or so, however, the canon has expanded to include the distinctive contributions to American philosophy of white women and African-American men, especially Addams, Du Bois, Gilman, and Locke.

Waning in popularity after the Second World War, American pragmatist philosophy experienced a revival in the 1970s, often credited to the neo-pragmatist work of Richard Rorty (see especially Rorty 1979) that continues today. In its published form, contemporary pragmatist feminism was born in the 1980s with Charlene Haddock Seigfried's criticism of Simone de Beauvoir from the perspective of Jamesian "Pragmatic radical empiricism" (Seigfried 1985). The young field fully secured a place on the philosophical map in the mid-1990s when Seigfried edited a special issue of *Hypatia* on pragmatism and feminism (1993) and published her monograph *Pragmatism and Feminism: Reweaving the Social Fabric* (1996). *Pragmatism and Feminism* broke new ground by reclaiming as pragmatist feminists women such as Elsie Ridley Clapp and Lucy Sprague Mitchell, who were educational innovators in the early 1900s, and the better-known Addams and Gilman, and exploring some of the benefits and tensions produced by bringing contemporary feminist theory together with American philosophy, particularly on the topics of science, experience, and ethics (Sullivan 2001a: 70). Since the publication of Seigfried's book, a wide array of essays on or from the perspective of pragmatist feminism have appeared, and four book-length explorations of pragmatist feminism have urged feminist science studies to avoid entrapment in artificial epistemological problems (Clough 2003), developed a process model of utopia that envisions a dynamic future formed by critical intelligence (McKenna 2001), connected pragmatist feminism to Continental philosophy on the topic of the body (Sullivan 2001b), and argued for an intellectual continuum that begins with William James and ends with postmodern feminist Judith Butler (Livingston 2001).

Pragmatism is especially useful for feminism because far from being an anti-theoretical position that simplistically champions matter-of-fact practicality, pragmatist philosophy stresses the dynamic relationship between theory and practice and especially the value of each for transforming the other. It seeks to undermine other dichotomies as well, including those between body and mind, subject and object, ends and means, and nature and culture, because such sharp divisions eradicate the fluid continuities of lived experience. Viewing knowledge as a tool for enriching experience, pragmatism rejects the quest for absolute certainty. Fallibilist, pluralistic, experimental, and naturalistic, it takes a meliorist attitude that human action sometimes can improve the world (Sullivan 2002).

Pragmatism's emphasis on experience, developed in the wake of Darwin's evolutionary theory, perhaps best distinguishes it from other philosophical fields. Pragmatism demands that philosophy grow out of and test its merits in the "soil" of lived experience. This is not to abjure abstraction, but rather to insist that philosophy deal with the genuine problems of living organisms, not the artificial problems of an academic discipline. It is important to realize, however, that pragmatists understand the concept of experience as "double-barrelled," in James' words (James quoted in Dewey 1988b: 18). Experience refers not only to the so-called "subjective" experience of a living being, but also to the "objective" world that is experienced by it. Biology and evolutionary theory teach that plants and non-human animals cannot live apart from the environments that feed and sustain them. Pragmatist philosophy incorporates this lesson by insisting that all of experience, including human experience, needs to be understood as a co-constitutive transaction between organism and environment. Functional distinctions can be made between the two, but for pragmatism, no substantive opposition between them exists (Sullivan 2002).

What if, however, the double-barrelled experience of human beings is shot through with hierarchy, oppression, and privilege? While Dewey once noted that the introduction of women into academic philosophy had the potential to radically transform it (Dewey 1988a: 45), most classical American philosophers neglected the impact of gender and sexism, and race and racism, on lived experience. On the one hand, this neglect is ironic and yet, on the other, it can be seen as a fitting illustration of classical pragmatism's own claims. Given pragmatism's insistence that all experience is shaped by a selective interest that picks out some features of the world while overlooking others, white male pragmatists can be viewed as theoretically equipped but often practically unable to recognize the ways that gender, race, and other salient features of human experience shaped the transactions of organism and environment.

In this respect, pragmatist feminism perhaps lives up to pragmatism's emphasis on the dynamic relationship between theory and practice better than does traditional pragmatism itself. The situation of oppressed groups, such as women, cannot be adequately accounted for merely with a pragmatist critique of the hierarchy of theory over practice (Seigfried 1996: 150). By bringing feminist insights to pragmatism, pragmatist feminism helps develop the radical potential of American philosophy that was not always fully recognized by its founders. From the pragmatist side of their heritage, pragmatist feminists gain rich metaphysical, epistemological, and other resources to support their emphasis upon experience, their appreciation of context and environment, their pursuit of plurality and community, their connections between theory and practice, and their rejection of a neutral, "God's eye" point of view. From feminism they gain focus on the relevance of gender, race, and sexuality to people's environments, communities, practices, and other areas of lived experience. In particular, feminist theory helps pragmatism realize that its emphasis upon democratic inclusiveness itself is the product of a situated, historical perspective and thus that, like all perspectives, it too (as does pragmatist feminism) has hidden assumptions and potentially exclusive effects that are difficult for it to recognize without the assistance of other perspectives (Sullivan 2001a: 70–1).

Classical Intersections of Pragmatism and Feminism

Of all the women who made distinctive contributions to the formation of classical American philosophy, Jane Addams arguably is the most important. Founder of Chicago's Hull House settlement with Ellen Gates Starr in 1889 and winner of the Nobel Peace Prize for a life-time of pacifist work in 1931, Addams was responsible for the pragmatist conception of democracy not just as a political system, but as a way of life, which became a centerpiece of Dewey's philosophy (Seigfried 2002, xi). For Addams and Dewey, the inclusion of diverse groups in election and voting procedures is not sufficient to create a democratic community. Democracy depends on an expansive consideration and appreciation of the experiences of diverse people in their everyday transactions with one another.

Demonstrating how pragmatist theory grows out of concrete practice, Addams developed her ideas about democracy and community from her experience working with Irish, Italian, Greek, Polish, Jewish, and other European immigrants to the United States. Established in the midst of these ghettoized communities, Hull House demonstrated that ethics is a social enterprise that involves "mixing on the thronged and common road where all must turn out for one another, and at least see the size of one another's burdens" (Addams 2002, 7).

Addams firmly believed that different classes and races of people were dependent upon each other. The problem in Chicago and much of the United States, however, was that their reciprocal dependence and need often was denied or misunderstood. The goal of Hull House thus was to increase reciprocity between new immigrants and Chicago's white middle-class, as well as between the different immigrant groups themselves (Addams 1893: 1–2). Ending the isolation and segregation of these various groups would help them to expand their sense of ethical obligation and enrich their lives with social aims that take them beyond the narrow interests of their own class or ethnic group.

An important feature of Addams' social ethics is that it not only values the experiences and perspectives of diverse peoples, but also obliges people to pay attention to how they choose their experiences. This obligation is not an implicit claim that a person can control every aspect of her life; certainly there are experiences that one is thrust into without any choice. Choice nevertheless can sometimes be exercised. Here we can see Addams' development of the pragmatist claim that selective interest shapes all of human experience. Human beings can selectively open up or close off their selves from other people and situations. Addams thus considers the claim that a person can never choose her experiences to be a dishonest attempt to maintain a narrow way of life that disregards the perspectives of others. As she argues, "if we grow contemptuous of our fellows, and consciously limit our intercourse to certain people whom we have previously decided to respect, we not only tremendously circumscribe our range of life, but limit the scope of our ethics" (Addams 2002: 8).

Addams is at her best when she relates theory with practice by showing the perplexities that thoughtful upper-class charity workers encounter when they attempt to help the working-class poor. The charity worker arrives with bourgeois ideals that associate financial success with hard work and poverty with idleness but soon is puzzled by the applicability of those ideals when she sees how hard the impoverished washerwomen that she visits work. This perplexity is the sign of the charity worker's broadening ethical sensibilities for it demonstrates her growing awareness that the lived experiences and moral standards of both the upper and working classes must be taken into consideration when determining what is best in any particular situation. It also is a sign of her growing awareness of the reciprocity of the two classes and the hypocrisy of the upper class that wants to ignore it. Stepping into the home of a washerwoman that is strewn with dirty laundry taken in for pay, the delicately dressed and impeccably clean charity worker begins to realize that her cleanliness and social standing are dependent upon washerwomen who better exemplify the ideal of hard work than do most charity workers (Addams 2002: 12–13).

Addams' work becomes problematic, however, when it turns to the issue of what the different classes have to offer in their reciprocal relationship with each other. Like many others at the end of the nineteenth and beginning of the twentieth century, Addams implicitly posited a racial hierarchy that opposed (allegedly) civilized and sophisticated white people to (allegedly) primitive and savage non-white people, including the Irish, Italian, Greek, Polish, and Jewish neighbors of Hull House, who did not count as white at the turn of the century. Addams thought that "primitive" people possessed a wild, life-giving energy that civilization had tamed out of white people. They thus can provide the white upper class "something of that revivifying and upspringing of culture from our contact with groups who come to us from foreign countries, and that we can get it in no other way" (Addams 1930: 410). In turn, the white upper class can provide "as much as possible of social energy and the accumulations of civilization to those portions of the [human] race which have little" (Addams 1893: 2). Addams' valuable emphasis upon reciprocity thus includes a racial hierarchy that tends to undercut the democratic thrust of her work. While non-white people are included in Addams' ideal of community, their inclusion as primitives in need of civilization perpetuates racist stereotypes and values the lives of non-white people from the narrow interests of the white upper class only.

A similar racial hierarchy can be found in the work of another foremother of American philosophy, Charlotte Perkins Gilman. Gilman perhaps is best known for her semi-autobiographical short story *The Yellow Wallpaper* (1973), in which a young woman goes mad after being confined to inactivity in her house as part of a "rest cure" for her allegedly weak nerves. Gilman made her most significant contributions to pragmatist feminism, however, in her writings on economics and the home. An "architectural feminist," as she has been called (Allen 1988), Gilman believed that women's emancipation depended on a radical restructuring of both the physical space of the home and women's economic place in it. Her focus on the lived environment and use of evolutionary theory to argue for social change utilized pragmatist ideas for distinctively feminist ends. Because Gilman combined them with a teleological progressivism and pernicious racial hierarchies, however, they also entangled classical pragmatist feminism in racism and white supremacy.

Gilman did not think of herself as a feminist; she preferred to be known as a sociologist. This is because Gilman thought that most feminists of her day were myopically focused on women's suffrage while economic freedom also was needed for women's full emancipation. Like Dewey and Addams, Gilman held that politics alone – at least, when narrowly conceived – could not solve society's problems. Larger environmental conditions, such as economic relationships and their effect on lived spatiality, must be altered. This change would be to the benefit not just of women, moreover, but of all of humanity. According to Gilman, women's economic dependence on men was having a deleterious effect on the entire human race. It prevented women from helping to uplift humanity through their contributions to wider society. Trapped in the home with all its domestic burdens, women have become a drag on rather than a stimulus to the evolutionary advancement of the human race.

It was not always this way, however. Gilman explains that women's economic dependence on men and their excessive development of feminine characteristics has had an important role to play in the development of humanity. Anticipating contemporary care ethics, Gilman claims that in an earlier stage of the human race, women's caring, maternal energy made them superior to men, who tended to be blindly competitive and individualistic. For men to catch up with women on the evolutionary scale, women had to temporarily subsume themselves to men. Overdeveloping their beauty, frailty, and other stereotypically feminine attributes, women attracted men to them. Wishing to retain these dependent creatures, men learned to work to support women rather than just themselves. Thus a union was formed in which women's subordination helped transform men into more caring, "maternal" people.

Gilman argues that once the role of women's subordination in the development of the human race is properly understood, women should not resent their temporary social inferiority to men. Women have made sacrifices, to be sure, but their "subjugat[ion] to the male during the earlier period of development [was] for such enormous racial gain, such beautiful and noble uses, that the sacrifice should never be mentioned nor thought of by a womanhood that knows its power" (Gilman 1966: 135). Without her sacrifice, men would have remained evolutionarily backward, causing both men's and women's further development to stagnate (1966: 132).

Now that men have been transformed, however, the excessive development of women's sex characteristics is no longer needed. Even stronger, Gilman's concern is that women's excessively developed sex characteristics, including their economic dependence on men, now are retarding the further civilization of humanity. The race wants to move on – so evolution will have it on Gilman's teleological view – but women are simultaneously being held back and holding back the race through their confinement to the home. For Gilman, "[s]ocial development is an organic development," which means that a people becomes more and more civilized when its various members specialize their work and thus become increasingly interconnected and dependent upon one another for their human needs (Gilman 1966: 73). Mixing a pragmatic emphasis on human sociality and interdependence with a progressivist insistence on the necessary development of humanity, Gilman argues that women need productive and meaningful lives outside their own homes. As Gilman claims, "to serve each other more and more widely; to live only by such service; to develope [sic] special functions, so that we depend for our living on society's return for services that can be of no direct use to ourselves, – this is civilization, our human glory and race-distinction" (1966: 74). To force women to be a jack-of-all-domestic-trades – cooking, cleaning, raising children, and managing a household – is to deny both them and society the opportunity for professional, specialized labor.

Gilman thus pragmatically and creatively calls for environmental change, namely the physical reorganization of homes in which adjacent, kitchenless houses share an "eating-house" that can be reached by covered walkways (Gilman 1966: 243). Not only would removing kitchens from individual homes produce more healthful food prepared by nutritionally savvy cooks, but it also would eliminate one of the primary sources of household grease and dirt. What housekeeping and cleaning remained, moreover, should also be performed by trained professionals who specialize in care of linens, ironware, plumbing, and so on. Likewise, nurseries outside the home offering expert childcare should be readily available for women with children. By allowing women to specialize in paid labor of their choice outside their particular home, these physical and social changes to domestic life would simultaneously improve the quality of everyone's lives by better providing for their basic needs and free women from their crippling confinement to the home and economic dependence upon men.

The power and ingenuity of many of Gilman's ideas should not be underestimated. She was one of the first to concretely explore pragmatist claims concerning the relationship of the physical environment to social causes such as women's liberation, and affordable childcare continues to be an important feminist issue over one hundred years after Gilman called for it. Yet neither should the racist undertones of her teleological interpretation of evolutionary theory be overlooked. Gilman often equivocates when using the term "the race." She speaks of uplifting the human race, as if all human beings are or can be involved in this process. It is only the white race, however, that is civilized enough to progress beyond women's subordination. Other, "primitive" races have not even advanced to the point of extreme sex differentiation upon which women's subordination and subsequent emancipation depends (Gilman 1966: 29, 65, 72). It is in the life of the "Anglo-Saxon," who is "the most powerful expression of the latest current of fresh racial life from the north," that social evolution can be found (1966: 147).

To hold (white) women back by maintaining their economic dependence on men thus is to create a situation of "moral miscegenation" between (white) men and women (Gilman 1966: 339). Comparing young women vying for men at a summer resort with "savages in a too closely hunted forest," Gilman depicts (white) women as resembling the allegedly lower races because they rely upon individual efforts to secure their livelihood (1966: 109). To pair such "lower" creatures with (white) men who are more civilized is to produce a weak, hybrid humanity rather than to further the human (white) race. Gilman could not be clearer about the deleterious effects of the incongruity of such "cross-bred products" (1966: 331):

> Marry a civilized man to a primitive savage, and their child will have a dual nature. Marry an Anglo-Saxon to an African or Oriental, and their child has a dual nature. Marry any man of a highly developed nation, full of the specialized activities of his race and their accompanying moral qualities, to the carefully preserved, rudimentary female creature he has so religiously maintained by his side, and you have as result what we all know so well, – the human soul in its pitiful, well-meaning efforts, its cross-eyed purblind errors, its baby fits of passion, and its beautiful and ceaseless upward impulse through all this wavering.
>
> (Gilman 1966: 332)

Gilman's pragmatist feminist argument for (white) women's liberation from the home thus is marred by its exclusive focus on white middle- and upper-class women and its dependence upon racist assumptions about non-white people's "savagery." While an implicit and unintentional racism can be found in the work of many classical pragmatists, Gilman's particular use of evolutionary theory and concern for environmental transformation explicitly assume that white people are morally and developmentally superior to non-white people.

Contemporary Intersections of Pragmatism and Feminism

While contemporary pragmatist feminism addresses a variety of issues and themes, some of the most prominent concern the related topics of epistemology and science, including evolutionary theory. Drawing on John Dewey and feminists such as Evelyn Fox Keller and Sandra Harding, Lisa Heldke has developed a "Coresponsible Option" in epistemology that avoids the pitfalls of both absolutism and relativism (Heldke 1987: 1988). Absolutism holds that there are acontextual grounds for knowledge, found, for example, in the "facts" of a real world independent of human knowers. Relativism, on the other hand, claims that there are no grounds for knowledge at all and thus no way to adjudicate different claims about morality or truth. Rejecting both absolutism and relativism, the coresponsible option locates the grounds for knowledge in communal processes of inquiry. These epistemological grounds are historical and contextual (unlike absolutism), but not arbitrary (unlike relativism). Or, better put: precisely because they are historical, contextual, and thus provisional, they are not arbitrary for they are formed in response to and must answer the needs of participants in inquiry. The coresponsible option thus attempts to both satisfy the demand for epistemological standards by which to judge right and wrong and relate those standards to everyday practices of knowing rather than knowledge for knowledge's sake alone.

As the term "coresponsible" suggests, knowledge involves responsibility. According to Heldke, a communal process of inquiry is "an activity that takes place between two 'things' that have *responsibilities* to each other, obligations to treat each other with respect and care" (Heldke 1987: 129; emphasis in original). Absolutism is wrong that a fixed, static world stands apart from human beings, waiting to be known but untouched by their knowing of it. Like the plant that alters the world as it takes in sun, water, and nutrients from the soil, human beings modify the world through their epistemological and other transactions with it. Understanding a condescending remark made by a man to his female colleague as evidence of sexism and male privilege, for example, produces a very different world than understanding it as a reflection of women's innate inferiority. This does not mean that "anything goes" or that human beings can fashion the world totally at their will. It does mean, however, that knowers should take responsibility for how and what they know. "Whether we acknowledge it or not, we enter into relationships when we engage in inquiry," relationships with other knowers and with the "objects" that we come to know (Heldke 1988: 17). Whether the world is seen as a mere tool for human use or as a partner in inquiry deserving of respect depends in large part on the responsibility we take in our relationships with it.

Heldke's coresponsible option in epistemology is closely connected to her redefinition of objectivity as responsibility. If the world is not a ready-made given that presents itself to us, then objectivity cannot be attained by providing a "neutral" description of the world, allegedly free from all subjective or individual perspective. Instead, Heldke argues, objectivity is found in acknowledging, fulfilling, and then expanding responsibility in the process of communal inquiry. Objectivity is found in increasing degrees as one first merely recognizes and accepts that relationships with other knowers and the world are central to the process of knowing. The next step is to fulfill one's responsibilities in those relationships. This does not mean that every demand made by others must be met on its own terms, but one cannot merely dismiss another's needs without being accountable for that dismissal. Finally, objectivity is at its maximum when one expands the network of responsibilities one is involved in. Here Heldke's coresponsible option complements well the classical pragmatist insistence that objectivity does not concern a "God's eye" viewpoint on the world. Given that the purpose of knowledge is to increase human flourishing, objectivity is attained when the greatest number possible of human needs and desires are fulfilled in any given situation. Pragmatist objectivity, in other words, is pervaded by selective interest; increasing the number of biases under consideration is the way to attain greater objectivity. This expansive aspect of objectivity relates to Jane Addams' demand that we augment our ethical sensibilities by enlarging the range of experiences to which we are exposed. Seeking out additional people and situations to be responsible to and for, we become both more objective and more ethical as we increase our moral obligations (Heldke and Kellert 1995: 367–9; see also Seigfried 1996: 152–3, 178).

Donna Haraway also engages questions of objectivity and responsibility in her examination of the roles that gender and race play in western scientific culture. Haraway's work is easily recognized as feminist, but its pragmatist dimensions often are overlooked. As Haraway (1997: 297 n.21) explains, the process philosophy of Alfred North Whitehead has been important to her thinking since at least her days as a graduate student. Much of Haraway's work thus can be read as a pragmatist feminist response to the practices and obsessions of western science and technology.

Whitehead's influence, and thus Haraway's distinctively pragmatist feminism, is most apparent in her recent critique of the fetishism of technoscience. Fetishism occurs when one mistakes "a fixed thing for the doings of power-differentiated lively beings" (Haraway 1997: 135). In Whitehead's terms, technoscience is guilty of the fallacy of misplaced concreteness. This error occurs when abstract logical constructions – such as the notion of a thing's primary qualities or of its simple location in space-time – are (mis)taken for the concreteness of processual, actual entities. Contemporary western scientific practices tend to treat the objects of their inquiry as static and given, congealing and obscuring social relations such that they can be taken as decontextualized things-in-themselves. In Heldke's terms, science's fetishism thus prevents it from being objective since it does not acknowledge – much less fulfill or expand – its responsibilities in the context of inquiry.

Along with genes, fetuses, and OncoMouse™, Haraway demonstrates how technoscientific fetishism occurs in the case of the computer chip, an incredibly valuable and necessary component of late capitalist, technological society. Locating the chip's value in pieces of metal and plastic and electronic codes, however, we lose sight of the historical and labor processes that produce and sustain the computer's existence. A product of World War II, the computer was developed to help calculate artillery trajectories so that bombs would be more effective (read: destroy more property and kill more people). Today, computer chips and mother boards often are produced by Asian women in the US and various third-world countries, who are seen as especially appropriate for such jobs because of their "Oriental" nimble finger work and attentiveness to small details (Haraway 1991: 154, 177). When we fetishize the chip, we are incapable of seeing this "final appropriation of women's bodies in a masculinist orgy of war" (1991: 154). That is to say, we render ourselves incapable of understanding how the materials, processes, and concerns of a highly militarized, technoscientific culture shape the world and our very selves. And without this understanding, we cannot be objective about – coresponsible for – computer chips because we are unable to be responsible to the exploited women who produce them and for the network of complex relationships that bind us to them. While the elimination of technoscientific fetishism does not automatically produce responsibility, it is a necessary step toward becoming fully coresponsible to others and for one's own knowledge and practices (Sullivan 2002).

Finally, another feminist concerned with science who recently has highlighted the pragmatist influences on her work is Elizabeth Grosz. Grosz's explorations of architecture appeal to "pragmatic models" to rethink space as dynamic and creative, rather than static and fixed (Grosz 2001: 120). With the term "pragmatic," Grosz includes thinkers in both American and Continental philosophy who operate with a "self-consciously evolutionary orientation" (2001: 169). This "philosophical pragmatism meanders from Darwin, through Nietzsche, to the work of Charles Sanders Peirce, William James, Henri Bergson, and eventually through various lines of descent, into the diverging positions of Richard Rorty, on the one hand, and Gilles Deleuze on the other" (2001: 169).

Grosz appeals to evolutionary theory for very different purposes than does Charlotte Perkins Gilman. While Gilman interprets it teleologically to shore up racist oppositions between backward "savages" and an advanced "civilization," Grosz finds in evolutionary thought the means for undercutting the necessity of sharp binaries and rigid dualisms, which often support male privilege and white supremacy. Positioning herself within the lineage of Darwin, Peirce, James, and others, Grosz affirms "pragmatist philosophers who put the questions of action, practice, and movement at the center of ontology" (Grosz 2001: 169). The result, she hopes, [will be a rethinking of material life as becoming rather than static being, which might produce positive changes in the lived experience of spatiality.] Realizing that physical structures such as buildings are capable of change – they are not "set in stone" even when they literally are built of stone – opens up the possibility of restructuring them to better meet the physical, psychological, emotional, and other needs they serve. Like Gilman, Grosz can be seen as an architectural feminist who takes seriously the power of environmental space to further feminist aims, but unlike Gilman, Grosz strives to include more than white women in her evolutionary project of emancipation.

Grosz values Darwin because he helps her to "understand the [inorganic] *thing as question*, as provocation" for organic life (Grosz 2001: 169; emphasis in original). This would be to take becoming and an evolutionary openness to the future seriously for it would dare to think of the so-called inanimate, static thing as continuous with animate, dynamic, organic – including human – life. [Doing so would operate with the distinction between animate and inanimate in order to show their co-constitutive transactions.] It would acknowledge that the animate and the inanimate exist as poles on a continuum, where differences shade into one another rather than stand starkly apart. It would, in other words, end the fetishization of the thing that prevents us from being responsible to the network of relationships that produce it (Sullivan 2002).

While Grosz never references Whitehead's process philosophy, her work demonstrates that many philosophers' and architects' treatment of things is guilty of the fallacy of misplaced concreteness. For Grosz, the process of a thing's becoming, not its static location in space-time, is its concrete reality. Emphasizing becoming and questioning conventional boundaries between thing and non-thing, Grosz's goal is not, however, to completely collapse all distinctions between binary categories. [It rather is to complicate their relationships so that new possibilities might open up.] This complication might be seen as a Heldkean expansion of objectivity for it increases the number of connections with things for and to which we should be responsible. But neither is the purpose of Grosz's work to urge the attempt to live in a world of total flux – as if such a thing were possible. Following James, Grosz instead insists that the "teeming flux of the real" must be rendered into discrete objects and that human beings are not able to choose not to do so (Grosz 2001: 179). What she adds, however, is that philosophy and architecture need to objectively – that is, responsibly – acknowledge that categories for slicing up the world do not fully capture it in all its complex multiplicity and that a residue remains. This residual excess is not in rigid opposition to objects and categories; rather it and the world of flux are continuous with the world of discrete objects, moving back and forth in dialogue with them. While discretion is unavoidable, there is no ahistorical necessity to the particular forms that it takes. We could cut up the world differently in the future, drawing on aspects of the world's multiplicity that were previously minimized or neglected. Flux is the material, so to speak, out of which discrete objects are formed, which means that no sharp line exists between flux and discretion. For Grosz, to think the relationship between flux and object as fluid is to think it in its complex, dynamic concreteness rather than fetishize it as a simple, static abstraction (Sullivan 2002).

Conclusion

There is much more to pragmatist feminism than this short essay can reveal. Contemporary pragmatist feminists are continuing the work of both reclaiming "lost" foremothers (see, e.g., McDonald 2003) and relating the American philosophical tradition to feminist issues and concerns (see, e.g., Keith 2001). As Addams' and Gilman's ambiguous legacy demonstrates, however, that work must include careful examination of the intersections of gender with race, ethnicity, nationality, class, sexuality, and other salient axes of lived experience. W.E.B. Du Bois' discussion of the situation of black women provides an admirable model for such analyses. Like Gilman, Du Bois thought that women's emancipation depended on structural transformations that would free women from their limited roles of caregiver and homemaker. Rather than exclusively focus on white women, however, Du Bois argues that since black women are central to the homes of both black and white families, their struggle will be vital to the emancipation of all women (Du Bois 1999: 95–108).

More recently, Cornel West's "prophetic pragmatism" has shown the value of American philosophy for anti-racist struggle. Combining Emersonian, Deweyan, and Du Boisian pragmatism with socialism and Christianity, West's work promotes a culture of creative democracy in which all humans can participate. Focusing on the plight of the wretched of the earth, prophetic pragmatism is simultaneously utopic and tragic. It energetically confronts racism and other evils in the world yet without the expectation that all evil can necessarily be eliminated. Cognizant of the vast and multifaceted operations of power, it nonetheless refuses to conceptualize the world exclusively in terms of impersonal forces and instead appeals to human agency to transform human societies, histories, and practices. Calling for cultural criticism and political engagement, prophetic pragmatism thus insists that philosophy put itself in the service of human flourishing (West 1989: 211–39).

Du Bois and West thus suggest how the concerns of pragmatist feminism can reach beyond white, middle- and upper-class women (as do Heldke 1998 and Pappas 2001). As is true for feminism more broadly, pragmatist feminism cannot be effective if it focuses on gender to the exclusion of race, class, and other significant aspects of lived experience. Expanding their focus, pragmatism and feminism can continue to invigorate each other, sharing the belief that philosophy should concern itself with improving the lives of all men and women rather than solving artificial problems created by academic philosophers.

References

Addams, Jane (1893) "The Subjective Necessity for Social Settlements," in *Philanthropy and Social Progress*, eds. Jane Addams, Robert A. Woods, J.O.S. Huntington, Franklin H. Giddings, and Bernard Bosanquet, New York: Thomas Y. Crowell.

—— (1930) *The Second Twenty Years at Hull-House*, New York: Macmillan.

—— (2002) *Democracy and Social Ethics*, Chicago: University of Illinois Press.

Allen, Polly Wynn (1988) *Building Domestic Liberty: Charlotte Perkins Gilman's Architectural Feminism*, Amherst: University of Massachusetts Press.

Clough, Sharyn (2003) *Beyond Epistemology: A Pragmatist Approach to Feminist Science Studies*, Lanham, MD: Rowman and Littlefield.

Dewey, John (1988a) "Philosophy and Democracy," in vol. 11 of *The Middle Works, 1899–1924*, ed. Jo Ann Boydston, Carbondale: Southern Illinois University Press.

—— (1988b) *Experience and Nature*, vol. 1 of *The Later Works, 1925–1953*, ed. Jo Ann Boydston, Carbondale: Southern Illinois University Press.

Du Bois, W.E.B. (1999) *Darkwater: Voices from within the Veil*, New York: Harcourt, Brace, and Company.

Gilman, Charlotte Perkins (1966) *Women and Economics: A Study of the Economic Relation between Men and Women as a Factor in Social Condition*, New York: Harper and Row.

—— (1973) *The Yellow Wallpaper*, Old Westbury, NY: The Feminist Press.

Grosz, Elizabeth (2001) *Architecture from the Outside: Essays on Virtual and Real Space*, Foreword by Peter Eisenman, Cambridge, MA: The MIT Press.

Haraway, Donna J. (1991) *Simians, Cyborgs and Women: The Reinvention of Nature*, New York: Routledge.

—— (1997) *Modest_Witness@Second_Millennium.FemaleMan©_Meets_OncoMouse™: Feminism and Technoscience*, New York: Routledge.

Heldke, Lisa (1987) "John Dewey and Evelyn Fox Keller: A Shared Epistemological Tradition," *Hypatia: A Journal of Feminist Philosophy* 2 (3): 129–40.

—— (1988) "Recipes for Theory Making," *Hypatia: A Journal of Feminist Philosophy* 3 (2): 15–29.

—— (1998) "On Being a Responsible Traitor: A Primer," in *Daring to Be Good: Essays in Feminist Ethico-Politics*, eds. Bat-Ami Bar On and Ann Ferguson, New York: Routledge.

Heldke, Lisa M. and Kellert, Stephen H. (1995) "Objectivity as Responsibility," *Metaphilosophy* 26 (4): 360–78.

Keith, Heather (2001) "Pornography Contextualized: A Test Case for a Feminist-Pragmatist Ethics" *Journal of Speculative Philosophy* 15 (2): 122–36.

Livingston, James (2001) *Pragmatism, Feminism, and Democracy: Rethinking the Politics of American History*, New York: Routledge.

McDonald, Dana Noelle (2003) "Achieving Unity through Uniqueness: Mary Whiton Calkins' Proof of Immortality," *Transactions of the C.S. Peirce Society* 39 (1): 113–25.

McKenna, Erin (2001) *The Task of Utopia: Pragmatist and Feminist Perspectives*, Lanham, MD: Rowman and Littlefield.

Pappas, Gregory Fernando (2001) "Dewey and Latina Lesbians on the Quest for Purity," *Journal of Speculative Philosophy* 15 (2): 152–61.

Rorty, Richard (1979) *Philosophy and the Mirror of Nature*, Princeton, NJ: Princeton University Press.

Seigfreid, Charlene Haddock (1985) "*Second Sex*: Second Thoughts," *Hypatia: Women's Studies International Forum* 8 (3): 219–29.
—— (1996) *Pragmatism and Feminism: Reweaving the Social Fabric*, Chicago: University of Chicago Press.
—— ed. (1993) *Hypatia: A Journal of Feminist Philosophy* 8 (2), Special Issue: Feminism and Pragmatism.
—— (2002) "Introduction" to Jane Addams, *Democracy and Social Ethics*, Chicago: University of Illinois Press.
Sullivan, Shannon (2001a) "Guest Editor's Introduction," *Journal of Speculative Philosophy* 15 (2): 69–73.
—— (2001b) *Living Across and Through Skins: Transactional Bodies, Pragmatism, and Feminism*, Bloomington: Indiana University Press.
—— (2002) "Feminist Approaches to Intersection of Pragmatism and Continental Philosophy," in *The Stanford Encyclopedia of Philosophy* (Winter 2002 edn), ed. Edward N. Zalta, <http://plato.stanford.edu/archives/win2002/entries/femapproach-prag-cont/>.
West, Cornel (1989) *The American Evasion of Philosophy: A Genealogy of Pragmatism*, Madison: University of Wisconsin Press.

Suggested Further Reading

Bederman, Gail (1995) *Manliness and Civilization: A Cultural History of Gender and Race in the United States, 1880–1917*, Chicago: The University of Chicago Press.
Clark, Ann (1993) "The Quest for Certainty in Feminist Thought," *Hypatia: A Journal of Feminist Philosophy* 8 (3): 84–93.
Fraser, Nancy (1990a) "Solidarity or Singularity? Richard Rorty between Romanticism and Technocracy," in *Reading Rorty*, ed. Alan Malachowski, Cambridge, MA: Basil Blackwell.
—— (1990b) "From Irony to Prophecy to Politics: A Response to Richard Rorty," *Michigan Quarterly Review* 30 (2): 259–66.
Gatens-Robinson, Eugenie (1991) "Dewey and the Feminist Successor Science Project," *Transactions of the C.S. Peirce Society* 27 (4): 417–33.
Green, Judith M. (1999) *Deep Democracy: Community, Diversity, and Transformation*, Lanham, MD: Rowman and Littlefield.
Heldke, Lisa (2001) "How to Be Really Responsible," in *Engendering Rationalities*, eds. Nancy Tuana and Sandra Morgen, Albany, NY: SUNY Press.
Kruse, Felicia (1991) "Luce Irigaray's *Parler Femme* and American Metaphysics," *Transactions of the C.S. Peirce Society* 27 (4): 451–64.
Lawson, Bill E. and Koch, Donald F., eds. (forthcoming) *Pragmatism and the Problem of Race*, Bloomington: Indiana University Press.
McKenna, Erin (2003) "Pragmatism and Feminism: Engaged Philosophy," *American Journal of Theology and Philosophy*, 24 (1): 3–21.
Miller, Marjorie C. (1992) "Feminism and Pragmatism: On the Arrival of a 'Ministry of Disturbance, A Regulated Source of Annoyance: A Destroyer of Routine; An Underminer of Complacency,'" *Monist* 75 (4): 445–57.
—— (1994) "Essence and Identity: Santayana and the Category 'Women,'" *Transactions of the C.S. Peirce Society* 30 (1): 33–50.

Moen, Marcia (1991) "Peirce's Pragmatism as a Resource for Feminism," *Transactions of the C.S. Peirce Society* 27 (4): 435–50.

Rorty, Richard (1991) "Feminism and Pragmatism," *Radical Philosophy* 59: 3–14.

—— (1993) "Feminism, Ideology, and Deconstruction: A Pragmatist View," *Hypatia: A Journal of Feminist Philosophy* 8 (2): 96–103.

Seigfried, Charlene Haddock (1999) "Socializing Democracy: Jane Addams and John Dewey," *Philosophy of the Social Sciences* 29 (2): 207–30.

Sullivan, Shannon, ed. (2001) *Journal of Speculative Philosophy* 15 (2), Special Issue: Pragmatism and Feminism.

—— (2003) "Reciprocal Relations between Races: Jane Addams's Ambiguous Legacy," *Transactions of the C.S. Peirce Society* 39 (1): 43–60.

Part II
Ethical Inquiries

Chapter 4

Ethics and Feminism

Marilyn Friedman and Angela Bolte

Human morality and the philosophical specialty of ethics have long been vital subjects of feminist thought. In the "Second Wave" of feminism that became prominent in the 1960s, much of the earliest work in feminist ethics took the form of "applied ethics." Those early writings often applied pre-existing moral and political theories to specific social issues of special concern to women, such as abortion, sex discrimination in the workplace, gender roles, and violence against women. Feminist ethics soon expanded into more abstract ethical issues of character, value, responsibility, and perspective. This shift in attention was accompanied by the development of autonomous feminist moral theories, such as care ethics. Feminists also began to scrutinize the dominant ethical theories and methods of the discipline of philosophy to uncover biases that had resulted from centuries of male domination of academic and professional philosophy.

In this essay, we summarize important feminist ethical developments regarding the following areas: (1) care ethics, (2) applied ethics, (3) the ideal of autonomy, and (4) discourse ethics. We conclude by summarizing some widespread contemporary feminist methodological strategies in ethics.

Care Ethics

Moral psychologist Carol Gilligan's *In a Different Voice*, published in 1982, set the stage for major advances in feminist ethical theorizing.[1] Gilligan's writings suggested that there were substantial differences between the moral perspectives she found among women and those that were typical of men. Women's moral concerns were more likely than those of men to focus on caring for particular others, not hurting them, responding empathically to them, and maintaining relationships with them. Men's moral concerns were more likely than those of women to focus on abstract matters of justice and rights in relation to other persons considered impartially. In their methods of moral reasoning, women were more likely than men to avoid deriving conclusions from abstract principles and instead to consider particular persons in their situational contexts. By contrast, male moral reasoning was more likely than that of women's reasoning to rely on derivations from abstract moral principles.

Gilligan's work stimulated developments in feminist ethics that appear to constitute a new theoretical paradigm.[2] This approach tends to avoid abstract moral rules and principles, trying instead to derive its moral judgments from the contextual detail of situations grasped as specific and unique. The predominant substantive concerns for this perspective are care and responsibility, particularly as these arise in the context of interpersonal relationships. Moral judgments, for care reasoners, are tied to feelings of empathy and compassion. The major moral imperatives for this approach center around caring, not hurting others, and avoiding selfishness. And the motivating vision of this ethic is that "everyone will be responded to and included, that no one will be left alone or hurt."[3]

The theoretical perspectives feminists had advanced prior to this time generally involved adaptations of pre-existing frameworks of thought that had not been specifically feminist in origin. Thus, early feminist normative writings were often anthologized under headings such as "liberal feminism," "socialist feminism," and "Marxist feminism."[4] This format persists today with the addition of a few new categories such as "postmodern feminism."[5] In contrast to these feminist adaptations, care ethics is largely a homegrown product of feminist thought and practice.[6]

To be sure, care ethics has had its share of feminist critics. Early critics questioned Gilligan's apparent association of the care perspective with women and the justice perspective with men. Critics also charged that while care ethics might constitute a *feminine* ethic, it was not necessarily a *feminist* ethic. The concern with caring for others is emblematic of women's traditional role as wife, mother, and family nurturer. Claudia Card explores various moral limitations attached to this role. It has historically been subordinated to the role of male head of household, compromised by a normative ideal of extensive self-sacrifice, and made socially vulnerable to domestic violence. In addition, the domestic caregiving role is not equipped to deal adequately with strangers. The enforcement of rights and justice, supposedly disregarded by care reasoners, may actually offset some of the role's limitations.[7] Critics have also charged that early versions of care ethics were biased toward white women and ignored differences among women due to race and class.[8]

These criticisms are not decisive, however. Care ethics can be revised to take account of them. For one thing, care ethics need not exclude considerations of rights and justice. Indeed, Gilligan sometimes suggests that the most advanced form of moral reasoning will combine both sets of concepts. Care ethics should also be able to accommodate differences in caring attitudes and practices that derive from differences in race, class, sexual identity, ableness, and so on. Finally, even if care ethics is not significantly correlated with female gender, the continuing feminist interest in the concepts of caring and care work suggests that these concepts are fruitful for feminist thought beyond the question of their gendered origin.

Care ethics is significant for mainstream philosophical ethics in a number of ways. First, in focusing on caring attitudes and relationships, care ethics directs moral attention to aspects of human life that have undeniable human value but which had been neglected by centuries of moral thought written by men, that is, by persons who rarely engaged in the work of taking care of and nurturing others. Second, as suggested earlier, care ethics seems to be much more than merely a negative critique of existing moral viewpoints and more than simply a feminist perspective derived by adding gender considerations to a pre-existing theory such as Marxism. Care ethics seems to constitute a substantive ethic in its own right.[9]

Third, as a moral theory in its own right, care ethics seems to be distinct from the three paradigms of contemporary moral philosophy: utilitarianism, Kantian ethics, and virtue theory. To be sure, some theorists, such as Margaret McLaren, defend an alliance between care ethics and virtue theory. McLaren argues care ethics suffers from certain theoretical flaws, among them that it reinforces stereotypic feminine traits that happen to be products of oppressive conditions and that it ignores broad political concerns such as justice. Virtue theory, in McLaren's estimation, avoids these problems by emphasizing stereotypic feminine traits and encompassing the political realm in its theoretical scope.[10] Other feminists, such as Virginia Held, however, regard the connection between the two theories as weak.[11] Held argues that care ethics, unlike virtue ethics, is distinctive in emphasizing the relational and dependent nature of persons, the nonvoluntary nature of many crucial caring relationships, and the inequalities of power that characterize those and most other interpersonal relationships.

Fourth, care ethics is important because its focus on close personal relationships has helped to move those sorts of relationships to philosophical center stage, where they now challenge the theoretical adequacy of longstanding ethical norms of impartiality and universality.

Care ethics has led to conceptual innovations across a wide range of topics. Sara Ruddick, for example, drew upon the caring attitudes of mothering to develop a peace ethic with international implications. She investigated how mothering practice gives rise to modes of thought infused with the normative demands of protection, nurturance, and development. In Ruddick's view, these norms can provide, in turn, a foundation for a nonviolent approach to resolving problems that range from the interpersonal and intimate level to the international and global level.[12]

Joan Tronto articulated the more general political significance of care ethics. She observes that despite the crucial importance of care work in social life, this work is politically devalued. Devaluing care work is one way in which privileged members of a society, who typically do not engage in care work themselves, maintain their privileged status. The people who do care work for pay are typically women, and even more often, they are people of color and of low socio-economic status (and usually female as well). These are the people whose social standing and political power is most diminished when care work is devalued.[13] Tronto and other feminists working on this issue, such as Virginia Held,[14] argue that care work should be recognized as crucial to the survival of any society and incorporated into accounts of both justice and ideals of citizenship.[15]

Eva Kittay further develops care ethics by exploring the dependency which is found in most, if not all, caring relationships. Dependency is universal among human beings, who each experience it for at least some period of time in their lives. Kittay proposes that theories of justice be altered to take account of human dependency. In particular, conceptions of social goods and social cooperation need to be modified in existing political theories if those theories are to take account of what is required for the adequate care of dependents. Kittay proposes that the capacity to care should be considered a distinct moral power and that the social position of a dependency worker should be used as a paradigm standpoint for assessing issues of fairness and the justice of social distributions.[16]

In addition to the issues mentioned above, care ethics has contributed to contemporary feminist thought on topics such as social welfare programs, disability policies, health care practices, and international relations.[17]

Applied Ethics

The distinction between theoretical and applied ethics is not always easy to draw, as suggested by the previous discussion of how care ethics applies to specific domains of female experience. For the sake of this discussion, however, we shall consider applied ethics to be an area of ethical study that has the aim of determining what to do regarding specific types of morally controversial situations, rather than of solving more abstract problems of moral theory. Feminists are especially interested in moral controversies in which gender figures prominently, an interest that encompasses attention to matters such as race, class, and sexual identity as well. What gives a distinctively feminist cast to the consideration of moral situations is a concern for the perspectives of the various women who are significantly involved in them or a concern for female images or stereotypes that are involved. Reproduction, marriage and family life, the workplace, and the environment present a great variety of situations that have engrossed feminist attention for some time now and we survey some of those topics here. It is noteworthy that another line is often blurred in these studies: that between distinct disciplinary boundaries. When seeking to understand the varied domains of female experience, feminist philosophers engage intensely with the work of non-philosophers, such as feminist legal theorists, in mutually enriching exchanges.

Reproduction

Feminists generally favor broad rights of legalized abortion. The feminist defense of this stance typically differs from that of non-feminists who hold the same position. Non-feminist approaches to the topic of abortion may try to decide this issue simply by determining the status of the fetus: does it have an inviolable right to life or does it not? Feminist approaches to the topic of abortion focus on the perspectives, experiences, and situations of pregnant women and girls.[18] On a feminist approach such as that of Susan Sherwin, the morality of abortion is decided by giving due attention to what pregnancy means in the life of the pregnant woman or girl, whether she had control over the circumstances by which she came to be pregnant, how pregnancy might affect her health, and the care-taking responsibilities and economic circumstances that face her. Feminist theorists, such as Catharine A. MacKinnon, also challenge the social and political control that men have historically exercised over women's reproductive lives and choices.[19]

Marriage and family life

Feminists have criticized traditional forms of male-dominant, heterosexual marriage and family life, arguing, for example, that the manifestations of male dominance within marriage and family, such as gender inequality, domestic violence, and marital rape, should be abolished. According to Susan Moller Okin, these conditions have persisted because normative gender roles have confined women to domestic life and women lacked the resources and opportunities to "exit" from unsatisfying or unjust family situations. Women's lack of resources derived from women's excess share of unpaid family labor and from the lack of opportunities to acquire adequate income outside the home.[20]

Although feminists have criticized the traditional forms of marriage and family, they have also recognized that marriage and family life are organized socially to provide some genuine benefits for those who are recognized as legitimate participants in these institutions, benefits such as inheritance rights and access to health care coverage. The problems with these social arrangements, argues Iris Young, is that they are available in a discriminatory and unjust manner.[21] Young calls for the same marital privileges to be extended to partners in any comparable long-term sexual or affectionate relationship.

Angela Bolte has argued specifically for legal recognition of same-sex marriage.[22] Bolte criticizes arguments against same-sex marriage that invoke tradition. She also argues that legalizing same-sex marriages will increase the protection of children. At the same time, Bolte argues against Claudia Card's view that gays and lesbians should reject marriage.[23] Rather than allowing the state into their relationships, Card argues that gays and lesbians should adopt contractual relationships. However, the problems Card identifies within same-sex marriage, Bolte argues, will not be avoided through private contracts nor will these private contracts allow access to needed rights granted exclusively by the government. Bolte thus argues that same-sex marriage should be recognized by the state and that the gay and lesbian rights movement should demand this recognition.

Violence against women

This theme encompasses a number of distinct issues, of which we will mention two: rape and sexual violence, and domestic violence. These issues, of course, overlap. Susan Brownmiller gave high visibility to the problem of rape with the publication of her 1975 book, *Against Our Will: Men, Women, and Rape*.[24] Until feminists began to investigate this topic, both law and culture treated rape in a shameful manner. Rape law tended both to allow perpetrators to go free (with the racist exception of black men accused of raping white women) and to punish rape victims in court, for example, by permitting cross-examination regarding her sexual history. At a cultural level, rape victims were frequently held responsible for provoking their attackers, women's resistance to sexual overtures were often disregarded, and rape jokes abounded. Feminists argued that, apart from any violence that might be involved, rape perpetrated a profound violation of the victim's personhood. Feminists also successfully called for greater protection for female rape victims and for legal improvements in the manner in which rape was prosecuted as a crime.

An analogous situation obtained regarding domestic violence. In many societies, husbands have been given leeway to beat up their wives and domestic violence has not been seriously prosecuted by the legal system. Feminists defended an ideal of gender equality in family life that called for an end to domestic assault and battery by men against women. They also founded battered women's shelters to provide safe refuge for domestic violence victims and called for legal improvements in the manner in which domestic violence was prosecuted as a crime.[25]

Workplace

Feminists have generally supported pay equity for women, affirmative action, rights against sexual harassment in the workplace, and worker safety. Significant feminist discussion has focused on the question of how best to define equality of opportunity, with some theorists arguing that it requires treating women and men in the same way while other theorists argue that it requires treating women and men differently so as to take account of differences among them such as women's capacity for childbearing. Linda Krieger, for example, defends what Elizabeth Wolgast would call a "special right" to pregnancy leave but suggests that this "special" right for women is necessary in order for women to achieve genuinely equal rights with men.[26] Other feminists defend policies of treating women and men in the same way but basing this treatment on the typical needs and interests of women rather than men, thus achieving gender equality in a different manner. Thus, Marjorie Weinzweig calls for an androgynous workplace where each person has access to greater flexibility in her or his work schedules, flexibility that includes access to parental leave for childrearing.[27]

Ever since the publication of Catharine MacKinnon's groundbreaking book on the subject of sexual harassment, feminists have denounced this form of exploitation and harassment of women in the workplace (and elsewhere).[28] However, despite an extensive effort by many to eliminate sexual harassment from the workplace, it continues to occur there. S. Gayle Baugh explains this persistence in terms of "a pervasive tendency to blame the victim for her own plight by discounting her definitions of sexual harassment or searching for causes of harassment in her own behavior."[29] Jean Cohen, who worries about employers over-regulating the private behavior and speech of their employees,[30] nevertheless fears that employers will tend to suppress genuine sexual harassment charges. Cohen argues that an increase in employment "at will" allows employers easily to ignore sexual harassment charges or to terminate those who bring charges.[31] In the end, employers may apply sexual harassment policies inconsistently by aggressively pursuing accusations made against low-level or disliked employees and protecting high-level or favored employees when similar accusations are leveled against them.

Feminists have strongly supported affirmative action in employment and education. Uma Narayan and Luke Charles Harris, for example, argue that the historical exclusion of women and people of color from both white-collar positions of power and skilled blue-collar professions makes affirmative action policies crucial for transforming the status quo.[32] They argue that affirmative action policies have stimulated critical discussions of the idea of merit and, in post-secondary educational institutions, have promoted revisions of the curriculum toward greater diversity. Partly because of affirmative action, historically excluded groups of persons have been part of the debates surrounding these matters.

Some feminists, however, have raised concerns about affirmative action policies. Iris Young argues that such policies have too limited a focus. They emphasize matters of distributive justice and the distribution of privileged positions across racial and gender lines. Young argues that this focus "fails to bring into question issues of institutional organization and decision-making power" and, as such, is too limited in scope.[33] Other feminists worry that general antidiscrimination policies, including affirmative action policies, fail to help adequately those who fall into multiple traditionally stigmatized groups. As Kimberlé Crenshaw points out, sex and race discrimination are traditionally conceptualized in terms of a single axis of discriminatory treatment.[34] Victims of sex discrimination, for example, are typically thought of as if they were white, heterosexual, middle-class women rather than, say, black, lesbian, lower-class women. This conventional view of discrimination, upon which most affirmative action policies are based, fails to be, in Crenshaw's terms, *intersectional*; that is, it fails to recognize that multiple axes of discrimination may combine in many cases.

Increasingly important employment issues for feminists have to do with domestic labor, and especially those workers who provide traditional feminine care work. Such labor typically is poorly compensated and the potential for exploitation is great, particularly for care workers who also reside in the home as full-time nannies or housekeepers. Additionally, the typical domestic worker is female and either

African-American, Latina, or foreign born (and possibly illegal and "undocu-mented"), facts which make such workers vulnerable to multiple and overlapping forms of oppression. Yet feminists disagree about the best means for overcoming these problems.

Joan Tronto, for example, points out that the hiring of domestic workers such as nannies, which allows upper-middle-class families to reap the benefits of feminism while lessening their family burdens, depends on the domestic worker functioning in many ways as a traditional housewife.[35] Concerned about the potential for exploi-tation posed by this similarity, Tronto argues for humane working conditions for domestic workers, a move away from individualized childcare, and a rethinking of responsibilities that will lead to profound change regarding the raising of children.

Gabrielle Meagher, by contrast, argues that ending domestic labor would have a negative impact on those who rely on it for their own employment. She calls instead for a "formalization" of domestic labor.[36] By "formalization" Meagher means the creation of what she terms "contracts *for* service," rather than "contracts *of* service," involving good pay for domestic workers as well as well-defined, mutu-ally agreeable boundaries for both the job and the relationship to the employer.[37] Such formalization, Meagher suggests, will be best accomplished through the use of worker cooperatives or well-regulated agencies or companies. Meagher believes that formalization ultimately will enable workers to have more control over their work by ending the potentially harmful familiarity that often exists between employer and employee in domestic situations.

Environment

Feminist approaches to environmental ethics began to appear in the early 1970s and this area blossomed in the late 1980s.[38] Ecological feminism, or ecofeminism, as these theories came to be known, has expanded to take account of animal rights and the plight of animals in the agricultural industry as well as issues of postcolo-nialism. In large part, ecofeminism rests on a critique of value dualisms.[39] Value dualisms are comprised of disjunctive pairs of traits or entities that are conceptual-ized as being mutually exclusive, oppositional, and ranked in such a way that one member of the pair is more highly valued than the other, for example, reason over emotion, masculine over feminine, and culture over nature. These value dualisms are culturally correlated with forms of domination so as to rationalize those forms, for example, the domination of emotional women by rational men and the domi-nation of feminine nature by masculine culture.

Karen J. Warren considers the domination of women by men and the domi-nation of nature by humans to be both dependent on what she terms the *logic of domination*.[40] According to this logic, some groups of persons are superior to other beings in ways that embody significant value dualisms, and superior groups are considered entitled to oppress their respective inferiors. Standard arguments for patriarchy link women to nature and use the logic of domination to advocate the oppression of both by men. Thus, any movement to liberate one must also strive to liberate the other in order to be successful.

Other ecofeminists have focused on exposing the abhorrent conditions endured by processing plant workers within the agricultural industry, a majority of whom are women of color.[41] Linking these conditions to the oppression of both nature and women, some ecofeminists argue that vegetarianism must become a central aspect of ecofeminism.[42] Other ecofeminists focus on the problems of western-style development in so-called underdeveloped countries.[43] Vandana Shiva thus argues that such development actually destroys the sustainable systems already in place thereby creating real poverty where there was only perceived poverty before, an outcome from which women suffer especially badly.

Autonomy

Concerns about sex role norms and stereotypes prompted early feminist attention to matters of character, virtue, responsibility, and identity. The character ideal of autonomy lies at the juncture of these issues. Feminists in the 1970s and 1980s esteemed autonomy for its liberatory potential for women.[44] In the 1980s and 1990s, however, feminists challenged the ideal of autonomy on several grounds.[45] For one thing, autonomy had been historically inaccessible to subordinated and oppressed social groups, such as women, whose labors were often precisely what freed middle- and upper-class white males to live autonomous lives. Feminists were also concerned that, because of the historical association of autonomy with men, conceptions of autonomy had become biased toward traditional norms of masculinity. The masculine norm most frequently cited in these feminist critiques was that of individualism.

Feminist philosophers who continued to defend the ideal of autonomy reconceptualized it so as to address these concerns. The conception of autonomy that most feminists defend now is a relational version of autonomy that focuses on the social context in which autonomy emerges and on the social nature of the self who realizes autonomy. Feminist accounts of autonomy thus treat social relationships as necessary for the achievement of autonomy.[46] This approach to autonomy is an outgrowth of care ethics and its relational conception of the self.

Emphasis on the social nature of autonomy shows that this character ideal is not antithetical to women or their experience. Marilyn Friedman argues further that autonomy has the potential to be particularly valuable for women who are seeking to end oppressive gender practices.[47] Personal autonomy enables individuals to reflect critically on the norms and conventions according to which they are expected to live. A culture that idealizes and fosters autonomy makes it easier for some individuals to resist or challenge existing practices. In addition, the political legitimacy of a political system may depend on whether or not the members of that system autonomously accept it.[48] A diverse public does not consent to its political system as one homogeneous whole. It is particularly important for a political system to be acceptable to all the significant groups living under it, especially those that have been historically disenfranchised, marginalized, or oppressed. Women's autonomous acceptance of their political system, according to Friedman, is thus a distinct criterion of political legitimacy as are acceptances by members of other oppressed or subordinated groups, most of which overlap with that of women.

One issue regarding autonomy that has generated debate among feminists is whether being autonomous requires someone to make choices that accord with the ideal of autonomy itself, or, at the very least, that do not violate it. If a woman chooses to live a life that subordinates her to men or to male-dominated institutions, is she choosing autonomously or not? There are "content-neutral," or "procedural," conceptions of autonomy which place no restrictions on the content of what someone chooses and count someone as autonomous merely if she has reflected on her choices in the right way, for example, with adequate information and an absence of undue pressure or coercion by others.[49]

A content-neutral account of autonomy, however, does not take sufficient account of female socialization, which often instills in women values and dispositions of character that lead even a reflective woman to behave in ways that preserve her subordination to men.[50] Such choices may meet the requirements of a content-neutral conception of autonomy yet still seem to be non-autonomous. The alternative to a content-neutral approach is to conceptualize autonomy as requiring the choice of a non-subordinated life. This approach, however, has problems of its own. For one thing, it ignores the differences among women and the fact that subordinated lives may nevertheless allow women to experience values that are important to them. Autonomy is not the only important value or character ideal. As well, no one escapes the influence of socialization. Choices of non-subordination may simply be the result of different sorts of socialization than oppressive choices. Finally, value-laden, or "substantive," conceptions of autonomy may disregard the forms of agency women do manage to exercise under subordinating conditions.

To avoid the difficulties of both the value-neutral and the value-laden accounts of autonomy, Diana Tietjens Meyers recommends an account of autonomy that she calls a "feminist voice theory." This account relies on the idea that "silencing disables agency."[51] According to the feminist voice theory, women must be able to express their concerns and values in their own voices; they must not be culturally silenced. Meyers recognizes that this requirement alone is not sufficient to ensure autonomy, however, because "voices," too, may be manipulated and oppressively socialized. Feminist voice accounts of autonomy must include some means of differentiating the more authentic voices from those that are less so. In Meyers' view, autonomous persons must have a developed set of "agentic skills" upon which they can draw in the living of their daily lives. These skills, in her view, differentiate the more from the less autonomous voices. Agentic skills include introspection, communication, imagination, analytic and reasoning ability, self-nurturance, and the ability to work in concert with others to resist oppressive social practices.[52] On Meyers' view, then, persons are autonomous if they have a significant repertoire of agentic skills on which they draw to express their values and concerns in their own voices.

Communicative Ethics

Jürgen Habermas' work on communicative or discourse ethics,[53] while not focusing on issues of gender, has been a valuable resource for some feminists in their search for an alternative to more traditional theories of ethics.[54] Johanna Meehan argues that Habermas' work can offer to feminists a framework for understanding the structures of modern life, a radical reconceptualization of the subject and the intersubjective nature of self-identity, and an account of what is pragmatically presupposed by discursive validity. Habermas' emphasis on the socially mediated nature of the subject and its constitution through social relationships is particularly useful for feminism. Identities are formed when subjects can distance themselves from their own social roles and grasp the social norms that structure and constitute roles. Subjects thereby take up the standpoint of the "generalized other," a perspective from which they can question conventional norms, beliefs, and values.[55] To be adequate for feminist theory, however, these notions have to be corrected by considerations of gender. According to Jodi Dean, gender disrupts the ability of people to take up the social roles of others and under social conditions of male domination, masculinity afflicts the supposedly neutral standpoint of the generalized other.[56] A feminist appropriation of Habermas' social conception of the subject would modify his account with specific attention to gender norms, roles, and identities.

Seyla Benhabib defends the "universalism" of Habermas' discourse ethics which is intended to correct the defects of Kantian universalizability. Benhabib considers a key insight of discourse ethics to be its insistence that the legitimacy of social institutions depends on the free consent of individuals who are engaged together in certain communicative practices regarding their common interests.[57] The search for ethical legitimacy is thus portrayed as a communal endeavor rather than the solitary quest of an individual moral reasoner.

This Habermasian communal dialogue around moral issues is governed by certain ideal requirements. First, the participants must admit into the moral conversation all those who are capable of speech and action; this is the requirement of "universal moral respect." Second, within such conversations, all participants have the right to utilize all methods of argumentative discourse such as introducing new topics or examining presuppositions; this is the requirement of "egalitarian reciprocity." These two rules reflect the ideal of fair debate, in which every participant's standpoint is respected as worthy of equal consideration.[58] The only moral norms that can claim social validity are those that are or could be approved by all participants in a practical discourse governed by the rules of universal moral respect and egalitarian reciprocity.[59] Benhabib objects, however, that Habermas narrows the domain of the moral, as governed by the above constraints, to matters of justice, thereby excluding matters of care and personal relationships. The latter are relegated to questions of the good life. Benhabib argues by contrast that universalism covers all moral matters, not simply those of justice.[60] Benhabib thus corrects the Habermasian system by incorporating into it moral issues that have been associated with women's moral reasoning (see the section on care ethics above).

Alison Jaggar advocates a global feminist discourse and argues that "dialogue with those who share many of our values and commitments is . . . practically indispensable for making social change within democratic contexts."[61] Jaggar, however, adds to Habermasian theory a consideration of power relationships that affect all aspects of discourse, including who speaks and who listens. This power differential, she emphasizes, is even more pronounced in cross-cultural dialogues, especially those involving the inequalities between westerners and nonwesterners. Jaggar calls generally for feminists to engage in inclusive moral discourse. She does allow for certain exceptions, however.[62] For example, Jaggar considers it reasonable for certain subordinated communities to engage in internal debate that excludes members of the dominant community. Such exclusions may allow for more vigorous discourse than would be possible otherwise.

The importance of discourse as a method of moral reasoning is emphasized even by feminist moral philosophers who do not otherwise discuss Habermasian texts. Thus, Margaret Walker presents a feminist discourse model of moral thought in her concept of an *expressive-collaborative* approach to moral understanding. Walker contrasts her model to the dominant model of moral reasoning in mainstream ethics, which she calls the "theoretical juridical model." According to theoretical-juridical models of moral reasoning, morality consists of a compact set of moral rules or procedures that any person can use in isolated inquiry to determine how to behave in particular situations.[63] Walker's expressive-collaborative model, by contrast, "pictures morality as a socially embodied medium of understanding and adjustment in which people account to each other for the identities, relationships, and values that define their responsibilities."[64] In Walker's view, communities support moral understanding with shared vocabularies, exemplars, and formats for deliberation and argument. These communal resources are not fixed but remain open for debate and further elaboration. They provide people with the shared means to negotiate and assign responsibilities and to hold each other accountable in an "ongoing process of self-expression and mutual influence."[65] Ideally, groups that have been historically excluded from moral debate should be allowed to add their voices to this ongoing process of shared moral understanding.

Feminist Ethical Strategies

James Sterba portrays the feminist challenge to traditional moral philosophy as consisting largely in the criticism that traditional ethical concepts and theories have been applied badly when applied to specific women's issues or gender issues.[66]

Exposing such faulty applications is certainly part of the feminist challenge to ethics. For example, feminists have shown how the public/private distinction has shielded family life from public moral scrutiny and obscured its political nature, in particular, its injustices and abuses.[67] However, feminism does more than simply criticize the traditional application of moral concepts. It also raises fundamental challenges to the very concepts, theories, and methods of traditional ethics. Feminists have tried to show that traditional ethical concepts, theories, and methods are male-biased *as such*, and not simply that they have been misapplied in practice. These challenges strike moral philosophy at its most foundational level.

Four feminist criticisms of the foundations of moral philosophy are particularly noteworthy. We recommend viewing these challenges as critical *strategies* rather than as substantive conclusions. They are strategies for evaluating work in traditional ethics on the basis of general suspicions about where male-bias might be hidden in moral thought. The four feminist challenges we discuss below pertain to: (1) individualism; (2) universalism and difference; (3) rationalism; and (4) the social locations and standpoints of academic ethics and of professional moral philosophers. These critical strategies overlap somewhat and they do not exhaust feminist concerns about traditional ethics. Furthermore, none of these strategies is accepted by all feminists.

Individualism

First, many feminists are suspicious of excessive individualism. They often view it as exemplifying a narrow liberal bias.[68] Apart from that, many feminists view individualism as exemplifying a (contingently) masculine bias toward certain styles of social and political interaction. In recent centuries, individualism has been bolstered by the rewards achieved by competitive, self-interested agents in the capitalist marketplace, a realm that males have long dominated. Individualism has also been enshrined at the foundation of the liberal state in the form of individual rights and contraction defenses of the liberal state, itself a domain of exclusionary male citizenship until the twentieth century.[69] Thus, the association of individualism with masculinity, while not a matter of biological or metaphysical essence, is a key historical gender formation that feminists believe has influenced white, western male perspectives for at least several centuries now. By contrast, women's perspectives seem to be more influenced by close interpersonal connections and the responsiveness and responsibilities that arise within them. Accordingly, feminists tend to champion *social or interpersonal* accounts of any ethical concept or phenomenon under investigation and to be suspicious of individualistic concepts and theories.[70]

This suspicion about individualism has led feminists, for example, to repudiate "monological" methods or models of moral reasoning and justification in favor of "dialogical," or communicative methods or models. As noted in the previous section, this theoretical strategy gains impetus from the critical theory of Jürgen

Habermas.[71] Feminists tend to reject any method of moral reasoning that lacks an explicit call for interpersonal dialogue or communication as part of the process of moral understanding or justification.[72]

Universality and difference

A second feminist critical strategy is to challenge the legitimacy of universal claims. At least since the 1980s, feminists have paid a great deal of attention to human differences, not only *between* genders, but also *within* genders, especially differences among women due to race, class, sexuality, ableness, and other social saliencies. Universal claims disregard human differences; yet in many moral situations, particularly those involving oppression, those differences are crucial to understanding the moral significance of what is happening and what ought to happen.[73]

Difference has loomed so large for feminists of late that some doubt whether anyone can understand viewpoints arising from backgrounds and experiences very different from her own, especially when these differences reflect systems of social hierarchy and oppression. Feminists therefore often doubt the usefulness of any ethical theory or method that requires people to project themselves imaginatively into the situation of others. Lynne Arnault, for example, has criticized R.M. Hare's universal prescriptivism on this point.[74] A monological method of moral reasoning, in which one tries to understand the situations of different others by one's own imaginative projection into their social locations, is no substitute for moral understanding through actual dialogue with others.[75]

Rationalism

Feminists tend to question moral theories that give overriding authority to rationality in the search for moral understanding.[76] Feminist concern about this theoretical elevation of rationality springs from several sources. One is the long-standing traditional dichotomy between reason and emotion, and the familiar association of reason with men and emotion with women. Feminists worry that this dichotomous association continues to exercise a covert influence over contemporary ethical thinking by implicitly enshrining the rational perspective (covertly stereotyped as male or masculine) into a position of moral authority over a devalued emotional perspective (covertly stereotyped as female or feminine). Another concern about reason-based moral theories is that they may obscure a variety of other capacities that full moral competence requires, for example, perceptiveness, emotionality, imagination, and sociability.

Professionalism

Finally, feminists are concerned about the social location both of moral philosophy as an academic discipline and of moral philosophers themselves as people able to practice this discipline from positions of social privilege.[77] Professional philosophers together exhibit only some of the varied socio-economic locations in a society. In the United States today, the vast majority of professional philosophers are white, male, middle-class and (given the absence of evidence to the contrary) presumptively heterosexual. They do not mirror the entire socio-economic composition of society at large. For example, the number of professional philosophers in the United States who are African-American, male *or* female, is under 2 percent.[78] Such a limited range of backgrounds hampers the ability of professional philosophers to represent the full gamut of human intuitions, experiences, and concerns in their ethical theorizing.[79] Feminists are particularly sensitive to the way in which the social locations of professional philosophers thus affect the moral philosophies and preoccupations that emerge – or do not emerge – from professional ethical theorizing.

Notes

1 Carol Gilligan, *In a Different Voice: Psychological Theory and Women's Development* (Cambridge, MA: Harvard University Press, 1982). Similar ideas were also presented at about the same time by Nel Noddings, *Caring: A Feminine Approach to Ethics* (Berkeley: University of California Press, 1984), but it is Gilligan's work that has had the widest impact on feminist ethics.

2 See, for example, Eva F. Kittay and Diana T. Meyers, eds., *Women and Moral Theory* (Totowa, NJ: Rowman and Littlefield, 1987); Mary Jeanne Larrabee, ed., *An Ethic of Care: Feminist and Interdisciplinary Perspectives* (New York: Routledge, 1993); and Virginia Held, ed., *Justice and Care: Essential Readings in Feminist Ethics* (Boulder, CO: Westview Press, 1995). More recent publications are cited in subsequent notes.

3 Gilligan, *In a Different Voice*, pp. 19, 63, 69, 90, 100. This paragraph is drawn largely from Marilyn Friedman, *What Are Friends For? Feminist Perspectives on Personal Relationships and Moral Theory* (Ithaca, NY: Cornell University Press, 1993), p. 92.

4 See, for example, Alison M. Jaggar and Paula Rothenberg Struhl, eds., *Feminist Frameworks: Alternative Theoretical Accounts of the Relations between Women and Men* (New York: McGraw-Hill, 1978).

5 See, for example, Janet A. Kourany, James P. Sterba, and Rosemarie Tong, eds., *Feminist Philosophies*, 2nd edn (Upper Saddle River, NJ: Prentice Hall, 1999).

6 In addition to care ethics, there have been other perspectives that seem home-grown to feminism. In the Jaggar and Struhl anthology cited in note 4, one of the feminist perspectives represented in the book is "radical feminism." This viewpoint was defined by the conviction that gender subordination was the original and most basic form of subordination. However, that conviction gave way in the 1980s to the argument that differences among women, such as those of race, marked out forms of subordination

and oppression that were at least as fundamental as that of gender. Thus, radical feminism in its original sense has given way to "multicultural feminism." However, in light of the independent sources of concern for multiculturalism, this is yet another feminist "ism" that is largely not "indigenous" to feminist thought or the experiences of (any group of) women.

7 Claudia Card, *The Unnatural Lottery: Character and Moral Luck* (Philadelphia, PA: Temple University Press, 1996), chapter 2; see also Friedman, *What are Friends For?* Part II.

8 See, for example, Michele Moody-Adams, "Gender and the Complexity of Moral Voices," in *Feminist Ethics*, ed. Claudia Card (Lawrence: University Press of Kansas, 1991).

9 Joan Tronto, "Care as the Work of Citizens: A Modest Proposal," in *Women and Citizenship*, ed. Marilyn Friedman (New York: Oxford University Press, 2005), pp. 131–47.

10 Margaret McLaren, "Feminist Ethics: Care as a Virtue," in *Feminists Doing Ethics*, eds. Peggy DesAutels and Joanne Waugh (Lanham, MD: Rowman and Littlefield, 2001), pp. 101–17.

11 Virginia Held, "Care and Justice in the Global Context," *Associations: Journal for Legal and Social Theory*, 7 (1) 2003, p. 160.

12 Sara Ruddick, *Maternal Thinking: Toward a Politics of Peace* (New York: Ballantine Books, 1989).

13 Joan Tronto, *Moral Boundaries: A Political Argument for an Ethic of Care* (New York: Routledge, 1993).

14 Virginia Held, *Feminist Morality: Transforming Culture, Society, and Politics* (Chicago: University of Chicago Press, 1993).

15 See, for example, Selma Sevenhuijsen, *Citizenship and the Ethics of Care: Feminist Considerations on Justice, Morality, and Politics*, tr. Liz Savage (New York: Routledge, 1998; original publication 1996).

16 Eva Feder Kittay, *Love's Labor: Essays on Women, Equality, and Dependency* (New York: Routledge, 1999).

17 These issues are variously addressed by the papers collected in Eva Feder Kittay and Ellen K. Feder, eds., *The Subject of Care: Feminist Perspectives on Dependency* (Lanham, MD: Rowman and Littlefield, 2002); Nancy J. Hirschmann and Ulrike Liebert, eds., *Women and Welfare: Theory and Practice in the United States and Europe* (New Brunswick, NJ: Rutgers University Press, 2001); and by Fiona Robertson, *Globalizing Care: Ethics, Feminist Theory, and International Relations* (Boulder, CO: Westview Press, 1999).

18 Susan Sherwin, "Abortion through a Feminist Ethics Lens," *Dialogue* 30 (1991), pp. 327–42.

19 Catharine A. MacKinnon, *Feminism Unmodified: Discourses on Life and Law* (Cambridge, MA: Harvard University Press, 1987), pp. 93–102.

20 Susan Moller Okin, *Justice, Gender, and the Family* (New York: Basic Books, 1989), esp. chapter 7. See also: Barrie Thorne with Marilyn Yalom, eds., *Rethinking the Family: Some Feminist Questions* (New York: Longman, 1982); and Hilde Lindemann Nelson, ed., *Feminism and Families* (New York: Routledge, 1997).

21 Iris Young, "Reflections on Families in the Age of Murphy Brown: On Gender, Justice, and Sexuality," in *Intersecting Voices: Dilemmas of Gender, Political Philosophy, and Policy* (Princeton, NJ: Princeton University Press, 1997), pp. 95–113.

22 Angela Bolte, "Do Wedding Dresses Come in Lavender? The Prospects and Implications of Same-Sex Marriage," *Social Theory and Practice* 24 (1998), pp. 111–31.

23 It should be noted that Card considers it wrong for the state to ban same-sex marriage; her view is about what lesbians and gays should themselves choose to do. Cf., Claudia Card, "Against Marriage and Motherhood" *Hypatia: A Journal of Feminist Philosophy* 11 (1996), pp. 1–23.

24 Susan Brownmiller, *Against Our Will: Men, Women, and Rape* (New York: Simon and Schuster, 1975). See also MacKinnon, *Feminism Unmodified*, and Susan Brison, "Surviving Sexual Violence," *Journal of Social Philosophy* 24 (Spring 1993), pp. 5–22.

25 See Marilyn Friedman, *Autonomy, Gender, Politics* (New York: Oxford University Press, 2003), chapter 7.

26 Linda J. Krieger, "Through a Glass Darkly: Paradigms of Equality and the Search for a Woman's Jurisprudence," *Hypatia: A Journal of Feminist Philosophy* 2 (1987), pp. 45–61, p. 57.

27 Marjorie Weinzweig, "Pregnancy Leave, Comparable Worth, and Concepts of Equality," *Hypatia: A Journal of Feminist Philosophy* 2 (1987), pp. 71–101.

28 Catharine MacKinnon, *Sexual Harassment of Working Women: A Case of Discrimination* (New Haven, CT: Yale University Press, 1979).

29 S. Gayle Baugh, "On the Persistence of Sexual Harassment in the Workplace," *Journal of Business Ethics* 16 (1997), pp. 899–908, p. 903.

30 Jean L. Cohen, "Personal Autonomy and the Law: Sexual Harassment and the Dilemma of Regulating 'Intimacy'," *Constellations* 6 (1999), pp. 443–72, p. 463.

31 Ibid., p. 464. Employment "at will" allows an employer to terminate or discipline an employee without cause at any time.

32 Luke Charles Harris and Uma Narayan, "Affirmative Action and the Myth of Preferential Treatment: A Transformative Critique of the Terms of the Affirmative Action Debate," *Harvard Blackletter Journal* 11 (1994): 1–35.

33 Iris Marion Young, *Justice and the Politics of Difference* (Princeton, NJ: Princeton University Press, 1990), p. 193.

34 Kimberlé W. Crenshaw, "Demarginalizing the Intersection of Race and Sex," *University of Chicago Legal Forum* (1989), pp. 139–67.

35 Joan Tronto, "The 'Nanny' Question in Feminism," *Hypatia: A Journal of Feminist Philosophy* 17 (2002), pp. 34–51, p. 37.

36 Gabrielle Meagher, "Is it Wrong to Pay for Housework?" *Hypatia: A Journal of Feminist Philosophy* 17 (2002), pp. 52–66, pp. 60–3.

37 Ibid., p. 60.

38 See Judith Plant, *Healing the Wounds: The Promise of Ecofeminism* (Philadelphia, PA: New Society Publishers, 1989). See also Irene Diamond and Gloria Feman Orenstein, eds., *Reweaving the World: The Emergence of Ecofeminism* (San Francisco: Sierra Club Books, 1989).

39 Val Plumwood, *Feminism and the Mastery of Nature* (London: Routledge, 1993).

40 Karen J. Warren, "The Power and Promise of Ecological Feminism," *Environmental Ethics* 12 (1990), pp. 25–146.

41 See Carol J. Adams, *The Sexual Politics of Meat: A Feminist-Vegetarian Critical Theory* (New York: Continuum, 1990). See also Chris J. Cuomo, *Feminism and Ecological Communities: An Ethic of Flourishing* (London: Routledge, 1998).

42 See Carol J. Adams, "Ecofeminism and the Eating of Animals," *Hypatia: A Journal of Feminist Philosophy* 6 (1991), pp. 125–45; Deane W. Curtin and Lisa W. Heldke, eds.,

Cooking, Eating, Thinking: Transformative Philosophies of Food (Bloomington: Indiana University Press, 1992); Greta Gaard, ed., *Ecofeminism: Women, Animals, and Nature* (Philadelphia, PA: Temple University Press, 1993).

43 Vandana Shiva, *Staying Alive: Women, Ecology, and Development* (London: Zed Books, 1989).

44 See Sharon Bishop Hill, "Self-determination and Autonomy," in Richard Wasserstrom, ed., *Today's Moral Problems* (New York: Macmillan, 1975). See also Jean Grimshaw, "Autonomy and Identity in Feminist Thinking," in Morwenna Griffiths and Margaret Whitford, eds., *Feminist Perspectives in Philosophy* (Bloomington: Indiana University Press, 1988).

45 See Evelyn Fox Keller, *Reflections on Gender and Science* (New Haven, CT: Yale University Press, 1985); Sarah Hoagland, *Lesbian Ethics: Toward New Value* (Palo Alto, CA: Institute for Lesbian Studies, 1988); Jennifer Nedelsky, "Reconceiving Autonomy: Sources, Thoughts and Possibilities," *Yale Journal of Law and Feminism* 1 (1989), pp. 7–36; Lorraine Code, "Second Persons," in *What Can She Know? Feminist Theory and Construction of Knowledge* (Ithaca, NY: Cornell University Press, 1991); Seyla Benhabib, *Situating the Self: Gender, Community, and Postmodernism in Contemporary Ethics* (Oxford: Polity Press, 1992).

46 See Diana Tietjens Meyers, *Self, Society, and Personal Choice* (New York: Columbia University Press, 1989); Lynne Arnault, "The Radical Future of a Classic Moral Theory," in Alison Jaggar and Susan Bordo, eds., *Gender/Body/Knowledge: Feminist Reconstructions of Being and Knowing* (New Brunswick, NJ: Rutgers University Press, 1989); Code, *What Can She Know?*; Trudy Govier," Self-Trust, Autonomy, and Self-Esteem," *Hypatia: A Journal of Feminist Philosophy* 8 (1993), pp. 99–120; Johanna Meehan, "Autonomy, Recognition and Respect: Habermas, Benjamin and Honneth," *Constellations* 1 (1994), pp. 270–85; Patricia Huntington, "Toward a Dialectical Concept of Autonomy," *Philosophy and Social Criticism* 21 (1995), pp. 37–55; and Catriona Mackenzie and Natalie Stoljar, eds., *Relational Autonomy: Feminist Perspectives on Autonomy, Agency, and the Social Self* (New York: Oxford University Press, 2000).

47 Friedman, *Autonomy, Gender, Politics*, p. 78.

48 Ibid.

49 See, for example, John Christman, "Feminism and Autonomy," in *Nagging Questions: Feminist Ethics and Everyday Life*, ed. Dana Bushnell (Lanham, MD: Rowman and Littlefield, 1995), pp. 17–39.

50 See, for example, Paul Benson, "Autonomy and Oppressive Socialization," *Social Theory and Practice*, 17 (1991), pp. 385–408; and Marina Oshana, "Personal Autonomy and Society," *Journal of Social Philosophy*, 29 (Spring 1998), pp. 81–102.

51 Diana Tietjens Meyers, *Gender in the Mirror: Cultural Imagery and Women's Agency* (New York: Oxford University Press, 2002), p. 17.

52 Ibid., chapter 1.

53 See, for example, Jürgen Habermas, *The Theory of Communicative Action*, vol. I (Boston, MA: Beacon Press, 1985); and Jürgen Habermas, *Moral Consciousness and Communicative Action*, trs. Christian Lenhardt and Shierry Weber Nicholsen (Cambridge, MA: MIT Press, 1990).

54 See, for example, Nancy Fraser, *Unruly Practices: Power, Discourse and Gender in Contemporary Social Theory* (Minneapolis: University of Minnesota Press, 1989); Jean L. Cohen, "The Historicist Critique," in Jean L. Cohen and Andres Arato, eds., *Society*

and Political Theory (Cambridge, MA: MIT Press, 1992); Joan Landes, "The Public and Private Sphere: A Feminist Reconsideration," in Johanna Meehan, ed., *Feminists Read Habermas: Gendering the Subject of Discourse* (New York: Routledge, 1995); Georgia Warnke, "Feminism and Democratic Deliberation," *Philosophy and Social Criticism* 26 (2000), pp. 61–74.

55 Meehan, *Feminists Read Habermas*, pp. 1–6.

56 Jodi Dean, "Discourse in Different Voices," in Meehan, *Feminists Read Habermas*, pp. 215–17.

57 Benhabib, *Situating the Self*, p. 24.

58 Ibid., p. 29.

59 Ibid., p. 37.

60 Ibid., pp. 185–7.

61 Alison M. Jaggar, "Globalizing Feminist Ethics," *Hypatia: A Journal of Feminist Philosophy* 13 (1998), pp. 7–31, 17.

62 Ibid. p. 20.

63 Margaret Urban Walker, *Moral Understandings: A Feminist Study in Ethics* (New York: Routledge, 1998), pp. 52–3.

64 Ibid., p. 61.

65 Ibid., p. 62.

66 See, for example, James Sterba, *Three Challenges to Ethics: Environmentalism, Feminism, and Multiculturalism* (New York: Oxford University Press, 2001).

67 See, for example, Susan Moller Okin, *Justice, Gender, and the Family* (New York: Basic Books, 1989); Nelson, *Feminism and Families*.

68 Alison Jaggar, "Feminism in Ethics: Moral Justification," in Miranda Fricker and Jennifer Hornsby, eds., *The Cambridge Companion to Feminism in Philosophy* (Cambridge: Cambridge University Press, 2000), pp. 225–44.

69 For several centuries, liberal citizenship was of course exclusionary also along lines of race and class. And liberal citizenship was certainly not the first form of citizenship to exclude various groups from its domain. However, the liberal association of individualism, exclusivity, and masculinity was historically entrenched enough to influence ideological developments for several centuries.

70 Writings that show how individualist normative theories, such as contractarianism, are detrimental to women include the following: Alison M. Jaggar, *Feminist Politics and Human Nature* (Totowa, NJ: Rowman and Allenheld, 1983); Annette Baier, *Postures of the Mind: Essays on Mind and Morals* (Minneapolis: University of Minnesota Press, 1985), esp. chapter 5, "Cartesian Persons"; Carole Pateman, *The Sexual Contract* (Stanford, CA: Stanford University Press, 1988); Benhabib, *Situating the Self*; Held, *Feminist Morality*; and Kittay, *Love's Labor*. A feminist defense of social contract theory can be found in Jean Hampton, "Feminist Contractarianism," in *Feminist Theory: A Philosophical Anthology*, eds. Ann E. Cudd and Robin O. Andreasen (Malden, MA: Blackwell, 2005), pp. 280–301.

71 Habermas, *The Theory of Communicative Action*, I.

72 Young, *Justice and the Politics of Difference*, and Benhabib, *Situating the Self*.

73 For a feminist defense of universalism in ethics, see Martha C. Nussbaum, *Sex and Social Justice* (Oxford: Oxford University Press, 1999).

74 Arnault, "The Radical Future of a Classic Moral Theory."

75 See, for example, Young, *Justice and the Politics of Difference*, Jaggar, *Feminism in Ethics*, and Benhabib, *Situating the Self*.

76 See, for example, Genevieve Lloyd, *The Man of Reason: "Male" and "Female" in Western Philosophy* (Minneapolis: University of Minnesota Press, 1984); Alison M. Jaggar, "Love and Knowledge: Emotion in Feminist Epistemology," in Jaggar and Bordo, *Gender/Body/Knowledge*, pp. 145–71; and Martha C. Nussbaum, *Love's Knowledge: Essays on Philosophy and Literature* (New York: Oxford University Press, 1990).

77 See, for example, Walker, *Moral Understandings*.

78 In 1991–2, a one-time survey of the membership of the American Philosophical Association asked respondents to indicate their racial identity. Of the 6,790 members surveyed, 2,831, or 42 percent, responded. At that time, the number of Blacks who were members of the APA was 37, or 1.7 percent of the membership. See *Proceedings and Addresses of the American Philosophical Association* 65 (7) (June 1992), pp. 41–2.

79 J.M. Doris and S.P. Stich have drawn on empirical studies in moral psychology to show that the guiding "intuitions" on which many moral philosophers rest their theorizing do not represent the intuitions of people in general; see their "As a Matter of Fact: Empirical Perspectives on Ethics," in *The Oxford Handbook of Contemporary Analytic Philosophy*, eds. F. Jackson and M. Smith (Oxford: Oxford University Press, forthcoming).

Further Reading

Alcoff, Linda and Elizabeth Potter, eds. (1993) *Feminist Epistemologies*, New York: Routledge.

Allen, Amy (2000) "Reconstruction or Deconstruction? A Reply to Johanna Meehan," *Philosophy and Social Criticism* 26 (3): 53–60.

Babbitt, Susan (1993) "Feminism and Objective Interests: The Role of Transformation Experiences in Rational Deliberation," in *Feminist Epistemologies*, eds. Linda Alcoff and Elizabeth Potter, New York: Routledge.

Baber, H.E. (1990) "Two Models of Preferential Treatment for Working Mothers," *Public Affairs Quarterly* 4 (October): 323–34.

Benhabib, Seyla (1989–90) "In The Shadow of Aristotle and Hegel: Communicative Ethics and Current Controversies in Practical Philosophy," *The Philosophical Forum* 21 (1–2): 1–31.

Bergman, Barbara R. (1986) *The Economic Emergence of Women*, New York: Basic Books.

Bushnell, Dana, ed. (1995) *Nagging Questions: Feminist Ethics and Everyday Life*, Lanham, MD: Rowman and Littlefield.

Claudia Card ed. (1991) *Feminist Ethics*, Lawrence: University Press of Kansas.

Chambers, Simone (2000) "The Cultural Foundations of Public Policy," *Philosophy and Social Criticism* 26 (3): 75–81.

Cohen, Jean L. and Arato, Andres, eds. (1992) *Society and Political Theory*, Cambridge, MA: MIT Press.

Couture, Tony (1995) "Feminist Criticisms of Habermas's Ethics and Politics," *Dialogue* 34: 259–79.

Fleming, Marie (1993) "Women and the 'Public Use of Reason'," *Social Theory and Practice* 19 (1): 27–51.

Fricker, Miranda and Hornsby, Jennifer (2000) *The Cambridge Companion to Feminism in Philosophy*, Cambridge: Cambridge University Press.

Gibson, Mary (1983) *Worker's Rights*, Totowa, NJ: Rowman and Allanheld.

Gould, Carol C., ed. (1984) *Beyond Domination*, Totowa, NJ: Rowman and Allanheld.

Griffiths, Morwenna and Whitford, Margaret, eds. (1989) *Feminist Perspectives in Philosophy*, Bloomington: Indiana University Press.

Heilman, Madeline E. (1997) "Sex Discrimination and the Affirmative Action Remedy: The Role of Sex Stereotypes," *Journal of Business Ethics* 16: 877–89.

Hepburn, Elizabeth R. (1997) "The Situated but Directionless Self: The Postmetaphysical World of Benhabib's Discourse Ethics," *Journal of Applied Philosophy* 14 (1): 59–68.

Moulton, Janice (1984) "Women's Work and Sex Roles," in *Beyond Domination*, ed. Carol C. Gould, Totowa, NJ: Rowman and Allanheld.

Rhode, Deborah (1988) "Occupational Inequality," *Duke Law Journal* December: 1207–41.

Wasserstrom, Richard A. (1985) *Today's Moral Problems*, 3rd edn, New York: Macmillan.

Weiss, Penny A. and Friedman, Marilyn (1995) *Feminism and Community*, Philadelphia, PA: Temple University Press.

Williams, Christine L. (2002) "Sexual Harassment and Sadomasochism," *Hypatia: A Journal of Feminist Philosophy* 17 (2): 99–117.

Wolgast, Elizabeth (1987) "Wrong Rights," *Hypatia: A Journal of Feminist Philosophy* 2 (1): 25–43.

Young, Iris M. (1997a) *Intersecting Voices: Dilemmas of Gender, Political Philosophy, and Policy*, Princeton, NJ: Princeton University Press.

Chapter 5

Moral Psychology

Margaret Urban Walker

Moral psychology is a loosely defined area within philosophy. It encompasses the roles of knowledge, perception, judgment, emotion, and action in our lives as moral agents. It seeks to understand how we can function as moral beings, as well as our capacities and vulnerabilities in doing so. Moral psychology studies our abilities to perceive situations in moral terms and our capacities to transform those perceptions into judgment and action. It also explores why we fail, as we often do, to do any of these things, or some of them: we may come to situations prepared with moral convictions and yet fail to notice that they apply; or notice that they apply but fail to act on them. Moral psychology tries to understand the "how" of ethics, what makes us able and unable to do and be what we should, and what makes it possible and fair for us to judge ourselves and each other for what we do. This opens up a wide territory for investigation. There is no single defining question of moral psychology. It takes in clusters of questions that address different faculties, capacities, motivations, and feelings that account for our specifically human moral agency. Our "equipment" for morality must explain our abilities to engage in complex practices of reasoning, self-control, and mutual accountability in response to understandings about value and responsibility. Anything that helps explain this is subject matter for moral psychology.

In the empirical science of psychology, there are highly developed literatures on moral development, on socially sanctioned harm doing, and on the situational constraints that explain and predict human action, often with surprising results. In philosophy, there is some ambiguity concerning the sense in which moral psychology is "moral," as well as the sense in which it is "psychology." Philosophers do not usually conduct empirical research into human motivation, cognition, and behavior, and few philosophers have the training or the resources to conduct such research . This means that philosophical moral psychology isn't empirical psychology; it leaves open, however, a significant role for empirical studies, including psychology and other scientific ones, in the philosophical enterprise. Increasingly, but slowly, philosophers accept the need to go beyond purely "reflective" access to our nature as moral agents. This means that moral psychology must help itself to reliable empirical studies, including those of psychology, anthropology, sociology, and history in exploring human moral capacity (see Flanagan 1991; Glover 2000; and DesAutels and Walker 2004).

Some ambiguity also arises from the "moral" side of moral psychology. Is moral psychology a normative enterprise or a descriptive one? This is a problem moral psychology inherits from ethics itself, and there is no simple answer to it. Moral psychology needs to identify and to understand features of human motivation, cognition, and conduct that explain human capacities for moral evaluation, choice, and behavior, whether these are used well or ill. It needs to describe our basic equipments to be moral agents, to be the kind of beings whose actions it is possible and fair to evaluate morally, and who may be held to account on the basis of those evaluations. Moral psychology here needs assistance not only from empirical methods but from the philosophies of mind and action, and from epistemology and metaphysics. Of course, normative moral theory and meta-ethics also need to presuppose, if not describe, our equipments, and so moral psychology has always formed some part of moral theory. But moral psychology takes a special interest in those tendencies and capacities that support or defeat morally *acceptable* or *admirable* judgment and conduct – what helps people to get it right, instead of wrong. So it needs to take a view about what "getting it right" is; in this, moral psychology is a part of, or borrows from, moral theory itself.

Feminist ethics has made moral psychology a central feature of its critical and constructive theories of morality, agency, and responsibility. Feminist moral philosophers have confronted assumptions in ethics about what people are like, what moves them, and what furnishes our capacities for moral judgment and responsibility. Feminists often argue for a story about self, relationship, and substantive values that contests or rejects claims of many "mainstream" theories – particularly claims about the primacy of self-interest, conceptions of rationality as opposed to emotion, pictures of human agency that ignore or cover over the impact of culture, identity, and social location, or ideals of autonomy that diminish the importance of relationships and social context. Feminists have not found it natural to see our responsiveness to each others' need, suffering, or interest as a "puzzle" to be explained or explained away by an assumption of calculating and basically self-interested behavior. Feminists have been more inclined to see caring responses, shared interests, and attachments as fundamental to continuing human organic, social, and moral life. Emotions have also been a focus of interest for feminists. Being able to form reliable judgments, especially about ourselves and other human beings, requires emotional capacities as well as cognitive ones, if these can even be sharply distinguished. Finally, feminists are critical of theories of mind, action, and emotion that take the individual as an entity or system to be explained independently of interactions with others, and independently of a social setting structured by differing roles, selective distributions of recognition and responsibility, and significant inequalities of power. One might say these themes are characteristic of feminist ethics without being either exclusive to it, or exhaustive of it.

It is on this last point that I will expand in this essay, using the feminist interest in emotion as an illustration. The shift in feminist ethics toward *social moral psychology* is a radical and consequential departure from the individualism – substantive, moral, and methodological – that predominates in the canonized traditions of "western" ethics, but most so in its modern forms. This shift toward a social moral psychology is joined to two defining features of feminist ethics, both of them normative. Feminist ethics examines moral conceptions and theories for unacceptable *gender and other group-based bias*; its informing ethical-political framework aims at *inclusiveness* and asserts the dignity of all human beings. Feminist ethics thus turns attention to the ways in which our cognitive and emotional equipments for moral life are enhanced, deformed, or disabled by the social environments in which they take shape and continue to operate, and how this has morally significant consequences. I will illustrate this feminist focus on the social shaping of our development and behavior as moral agents by featuring feminist work on *emotion*. I will note some of the important developments in this area of feminist philosophy, and sketch a framework of assumptions for future work on the *social moral psychology of the emotions*.

How Feminist Moral Psychology of Emotions Is Social Moral Psychology

Feminist philosophers want to understand the nature, recognition, and expression of emotion. But they want to understand emotions in a way that reveals the emotional impact of conditions of injustice, and makes intelligible the emotional responses and emotionally infused actions of people in unjust social orders. Emotions are shaped by social distinctions and pressures that can work for or against those who are disadvantaged, marginalized, or oppressed in their societies or communities. Feminist studies of emotion reveal that patterns of relationship and social requirements for people's roles and behavior, for example, those created by gender, age, and race privilege, have an impact on what emotions tend be experienced, recognized, expressed, and identified by different individuals. Even if human beings share similar capacities for feeling and a common social and cultural world, significant differences of status, power, recognition, and responsibility in that social world prompt individuals to learn patterns of feeling and patterns of expressing feeling that make sense for those individuals' social places in that world. Although this literature of feminist philosophy of emotions is not vast, it is internally rich and varied enough that I cannot do justice to it in the brief scope of this essay. I will highlight a few illustrative trends, and mark some convergences and disagreements among feminist views of emotion, in order to make clearer how feminist moral psychology of emotions is a social psychology, and why the feminist work makes an important contribution to moral psychology in general.

A number of claims about the social and cultural "shaping" of our emotional lives and emotion vocabularies are commonplace, and by no means unique to feminist moral psychology. Cultures do not share even a limited basic emotion vocabulary, and emotion terms are often not adequately translatable between languages, even though some researchers search for a small number of "basic emotions." (On this claim, see Goldie 2000: chapter 4.) Human beings learn their local concepts for emotion in the context of learning what feeling and action responses are deemed appropriate or normal in the face of certain kinds of situations. We learn how others are likely to respond, or are expected to respond, to the expression of particular emotions, and what forms of emotional display, if any, are acceptable in certain kinds of situations (see Levy 1984; Shweder 1991). Anthropologists tend to be attuned to the importance of the specific cultural setting in shaping the emotional repertory and its expressions, and social psychologists are alert to variations in the eliciting situation and people's possibly varied understanding of it. Philosophers, however, have more often treated the eliciting occasions, experiences, courses, and expressions of emotions in fairly generic ways. A common pattern of analysis is: characteristically, X (an individual, or any individual in a given society) feels emotion E when X believes/perceives the situation to be S (a circumstance of a certain type), has characteristic subjective and somatic feelings of type F, presents tell-tale appearances and expressions E, and is disposed to act/react in way R (for a recent, very subtle analysis in this vein, see Goldie 2000). So, for example, X feels fear when X perceives a situation that X takes to be a danger or a threat, X imagines painful and unwanted consequences and finds his hands cold, his heart pumping, his stomach knotted, his chest tight, etc., and X is disposed to terminate the threatening situation by fleeing or striking out to fend off the source of danger. Of course, the particulars of a description like this might be much more complex and detailed, and the dispositions much less simple to capture, than this example shows.

There is nothing wrong with this rough descriptive template for capturing the complex phenomena we identify with emotion concepts like rage, grief, embarrassment, affection, joy, gratitude, or pride; if we fail to attend to any of these components that identify emotional states and experiences, we will find ourselves with a crudely inadequate understanding. Philosophers have mostly disputed about which of these factors is really essential to or constitutive of the emotion. Yet in filling in the "standard" or "normal" elicitors, feelings, displays, and reactions even for a *given* social and cultural locale, one may fail to consider how much it might matter *who it is* in that social setting whose emotional experience we are describing, and this might affect deeply *what* the emotion is about, features of how it is *felt* and *shown*, how it will be *managed*, whether it will be *expressed, concealed, or encrypted* (Stocker with Hegeman 1996 is a striking exception). While such features might vary idiosyncratically for individuals due to temperaments and distinctive biographies, it is in the ground between individual idiosyncrasies and general culture repertories – in the social field and its power-infused interactions – that feminist moral psychology has found its main material. As Sandra Bartky said in discussing the forms of inchoate shame and diminishment many women express or admit in academic settings, we need "a political phenomenology of the emotions" (Bartky 1990: 98). We also need a social and political understanding of emotional expression and interaction shaped by the similarities and differences of structural location and the similarities and differences of social experience and self-awareness that these produce (on location and experience, see Young 2000: chapter 3). Without this, we might find ourselves complacently generalizing about patterns of emotional salience and emotional reaction of "people" or "human beings," without pausing over the question of whether these emotional valences and responses really make sense for people who have every reason to make different assumptions about what situations mean, what it makes sense to feel in them, and what the consequences will be of expressing certain emotions to, or in the presence of, particular others (see Walker 2003 and 2004).

Some feminists see the *social construction of emotion* as a way to explain not only cultural variability but also the ways social "rules" for emotion and its expression disadvantage those who are socially marginal or subordinate. Thus Alison Jaggar's widely known idea of "outlaw emotions": emotions felt by those on the disadvantaged side of social hierarchies which are conventionally unacceptable for certain kind of situations. Outlaw emotions in many US communities might include, for example, anger instead of amusement at racist humor, resentment rather than gratitude at demeaning "welfare" provisions, or humiliation or anger rather than pleasure in being the object of uninvited sexual approaches. While these reactions make perfect sense to those who are combatting disrespectful and demeaning attitudes and behavior toward some kinds of people, they are disconcerting and unwelcome to others who feel they are entitled to have these attitudes or that it's normal or "just having fun" to do or say what they do. They are likely to label such emotional reactions oversensitive, unbalanced, humorless, paranoid, or "a drag." Since emotions are "outlaw" in a given context because either the majority or those with social power in that context do not share them, outlaw emotions can confuse, embarrass, or isolate those who feel them unless they can find others to share with them these socially unruly feelings and who endorse their expression.

Naomi Scheman takes the social constructionist analysis to its ontological roots. Emotions are, she says, like "constellations" rather than "galaxies," for the configurations of thoughts, feelings, and behavior that we learn to find salient and meaningful are such *only* because socially supported explanatory schemas link them together. There are no causal relations among these elements that give them unity and coherence independently of these socially sustained schemas. The reality of emotions is thus social all the way down. Possibilities of meaningful feeling are constituted, foreclosed, or made deviant by the social rules. Like Jaggar, Scheman believes that new communally shared meanings – and thus new forms of emotional intelligibility – can be co-created. New communities of interpretation shift the boundaries of what it makes sense to feel, as when a feminist consciousness-raising group persuades a member that some of her bad feelings can be understood as anger at oppressive features of her life as a woman (Scheman 1996; see also Scheman 1980).

Sue Campbell believes that social constructionism is too constraining a view of the extraordinarily varied and unstable field of emotional expression (Campbell 1997). Campbell agrees that *standard* emotion categories in a given society are normative, making certain emotions well-defined and their expressions clearly interpretable (and, for the same reasons, concealable). These standard emotion categories and the criteria that govern their application will make only certain occasions for feeling and certain responses in feeling intelligible and legitimate – these will be the things it is "right" and "normal" to feel in "that kind of situation." To see our emotional repertoires as confined to the socially constituted categories, though, is to close the space for "free-style feelings," that is, for a huge and nuanced range of feelings and expressions of feeling which are outside the boxes provided by conventional emotion categories.

Some of these feelings are idiosyncratic, the particular response of a certain individual on a certain occasion – the times where we sometimes say "I can't put it into words," as indeed we can't if the conventional emotion vocabulary does not provide the words we need. Often, though, such feelings outside the conventional categories are shared or at least shareable, even when they are not socially endorsed and conventionally scripted.

Campbell offers us the example of the "white-master's-well-fed-dog" feeling of a black South African woman under apartheid in Miriam Tlali's novel *Between Two Worlds*. The woman, Muriel, is trying to communicate an emotional experience "difficult to understand through the emotion categories with which most of us are familiar," and also the ones with which Muriel is familiar (Campbell 1997: 8). Yet it is a recurrent feeling for Muriel, and one that might well be understood and even shared by others in like situations, as well as difficult to understand for those who are not. But she might have to try to impart the feeling in detail at length, or with concrete examples, to people who share her experience, or by performing a song or making a poem, or by writing a novel (like Miriam Tlali's) and creating in detail the point of view of the character and so our ability to glimpse what she means by "the white-master's-well-fed-dog feeling," which many of us have never felt. Nor should we assume that what Muriel feels is some combination of pride and shame and anger and self-contempt, emotions for which we already possess concepts. Muriel's feeling is not only *in* her specific social situation, it is *about* it, and takes its meaning and complexity precisely from it. Muriel's white supremacist society does not have emotion terms ready for what she feels, and that is not surprising. Social constructionist views, Campbell argues, *limit* our possibilities of quite individual and but also shareable emotional "takes" on our experiences; they make us dependent on some regime of conventionally acknowledged emotional expressions, whether that regime is the dominant culture *or* a subculture of resistance.

Campbell's alternative is an expressive and constructive conception of emotion that is highly *interactive*: emotions are individuated as the particular feelings they are in our expression of them. Successful expression involves uptake in recognition, and recognition often follows socially legitimated scripts. Yet recognition can sometimes be achieved by an observer's ability to track another's responses to an occasion, using her own perhaps very different responses. By this tracking the observer can sometimes grasp both the occasion to which someone else is responding with feeling, and the personal significance of the occasion that the emotion expresses, even outside the boxes of standard emotion categories. The recognition of affective reactions in either case, however, can fail. To make things more precarious, the responses of others to our emotional expression can alter the occasion of our feelings, conventional or free-style, creating instability not only in others' understanding but in our own identification of what we feel. Campbell's model of emotional interpretation explains how our emotional traffic can run smoothly on the socially regimented rails of expression and interpretation, but also how unmarked affective paths can nonetheless be *shareable* by others without instantiating prior norms. We should, Campbell argues, understand feeling as the category through which we experience and express the personal significance of occasions in our lives. We should be able to explain the ample space there remains to confuse, contest, nurture, or distort each other's attempts at expressing this significance. She offers a theory of emotions that "does not already assume that . . . communities are in place and controlling the meanings" of what we feel exhaustively (Campbell 1997: 164). I believe Campbell's interactive view, in which emotions become the emotions they are in the process of their being recognized, and which does not require that all feeling be recognized under some existing emotion category, has superior resources in explaining how new affective vocabularies can emerge, and how new applications of existing vocabularies can come to be shared. This is what the social construction theories seem to assume, but do not explain. Even aside from the idea of free-style feelings and the possibility of intelligible affect outside existing categories, Campbell's interactive view gives a useful picture of the many and diverse maneuvers of expression and concealment that we do and can use. She captures the dynamic interplay of expressions and interpretations that allow us to control or constrain each others' emotional lives. This lays the basis for an "ethics of interpreting the personal" that can identify and distinguish hostile, unsympathetic, and clueless *individual* interpreters, and can target *social practices* of emotional interpretation or dismissal that are politically loaded.

A common theme in much feminist work on emotion is that our emotional responses, and our tutored abilities to understand the responses of others whose social experience we do not share, are indispensable resources for social knowledge and for political solidarity. Uma Narayan examines how "immediate knowledge of everyday life under oppression" and the details of its effects are registered through and in emotional responses of those oppressed to their oppressors (Narayan 1988; see also Jaggar 1989; McFall 1991 and Meyers 1997). Narayan identifies epistemic, moral, and political losses that "outsiders" to a given form of oppression will incur or cause if they fail to adopt a stance of caution and humility, by according "epistemic privilege" to the emotional responses of "insiders," those who experience that oppression. The fine-tuned feelings of insiders are often keenly sensitive to how and where specific practices of oppression actually work and what they do with people and to them. Failure of outsiders to appreciate or honor this epistemic resource foregoes significant understanding of individuals, relationships, and social structures. It betrays the trust necessary for effective political solidarity. It adds insult to the injuries of oppression by disrespecting the authority of those in the best position to identify these injuries, especially in their subtler forms and across different contexts.

In several striking papers, Maria Lugones affirms the importance of the painstaking and often painful process of listening, hearing, and "world-traveling" that outsiders must practice with respect to those who are oppressed, but she also underscores the limits of understanding, and even self-understanding, that result from patterns of oppression, exclusion, and privilege (Lugones 1987; 1991; 1995; collected in Lugones 2003). Anger at other human beings, for example, is commonly understood to embody a perception of being wronged, and the one who expresses anger necessarily claims some credibility as a judge of wrong. Yet the anger of oppression only sometimes communicates the demand that one's judgments of wrong be understood and that one's standing to press them be respected. Sometimes the person expressing the anger of oppression refuses the attempt to communicate, lashing out in resistance against "official worlds of sense" that she cannot and must not join because they deny the intelligibility and agency of people like herself. These "worlds of sense" comprise, at least, the whole set of interlocking norms and practices that assign people to social places, create different expectations of recognition and responsibility for people in their proper places, and govern both the actions and the feelings that are "normal" and "acceptable" for people so assigned. Standard analyses of emotions such as anger are always to some extent normative, suggesting the occasions in which an emotion is apt, makes sense, or is "rational," and sometimes suggesting principles of proportion and appropriate expression (see Jones 2004). Lugones claims that to understand anger one needs to keep in mind "the self who is angry, the worlds of sense that make sense of her and her anger, the worlds of sense in which she makes no sense as angry, and whether the anger has a communicative or an incommunicative intent" (Lugones 1995: 205; also Frye 1983). The intelligibility and proportionality of feelings are not indifferently available regardless of social location, and the expression of feelings (like their concealment or encryption) may be opaque across chasms of social experience. Not to share a world of sense may disqualify one from understanding some others, yet structural differences among groups in social life make sharing worlds of sense – of what is happening, of what it shows and means, of what it feels like to experience it, of what it makes sense to think, feel, or do in response – difficult in the extreme, or simply impossible.

Things are more complicated, however, than understanding emotions or not understanding them. Specific forms or practices of attending to people's emotions, or attending only to some people's emotions, or attending only to some emotions when considering some people, are a revealing study as well. Elizabeth Spelman's remarkable *Fruits of Sorrow: Framing our Attention to Suffering* proposes a "political economy of suffering": a study of the organization of our attention to suffering and its links to social standing. Spelman proposes that "the distribution of compassion . . . is not likely to be neutral with respect to the distribution of other resources in society" (Spelman 1997: 170). What Spelman illustrates, however, goes beyond the fact that some suffering receives too little and other suffering too much attention. Others' suffering can be acknowledged in ways that diminish or erase the one suffering, or allow the suffering of some to be "consumed" by others for their self-dramatization or moral refinement. Slavery becomes the "tragedy" of otherwise noble or good white Americans. Harriet Jacobs, the author of a classic American slave narrative, must skillfully render herself eligible for compassion without making herself a demeaned "object" of it, rather than a dignified moral subject who commands respect, not pity. White suffragists identify their subordination with the condition of slaves, a move poised precariously between subversive solidarity and self-serving illusion.

Emotions show what and whom we take seriously, and calibrations of emotional response expose "what we take to be our responsibilities for others' plights" and our "depth of concern" about them (Spelman 1997: 100, 102). Spelman explores, for example, the differences it makes whether one feels regret, remorse, embarrassment, guilt, or shame in reaction to a racist incident on a college campus. Regret communicates something unfortunate, but not necessarily morally troubling; embarrassment, that one is more concerned with one's appearance than with others' indignity or distress. While guilt implies the transgression of a standard, which may be fairly isolated, shame cuts deeply into a sense of worthiness of a person – or an institution. These feelings encode different moral judgments or the lack thereof; what we do and what we don't feel on an occasion can reveal to us, and, importantly, to others for whom and for what we see ourselves as responsible and accountable. But neither are patterns of caring about and caring for others entirely a matter of individual temperament or discretion. In human societies, emotional labor and the distribution of caring track social roles and social hierarchies. It characteristically "falls to some rather than others to do the work of care and compassion" as much as it falls disproportionately on some to do the material work of caregiving to the vulnerable, the young, the frail, and the dependent. Not only do women and people of color perform a disproportionate share of caring work in US society, but there are correlated expectations about who *ought to feel* concerned or caring when others need not (Spelman 1997: 171; see also Calhoun 1992). There is a division of emotional responsibility that, unsurprisingly, tracks the standard social division of labor.

Our Very Social Emotions: Some Implications

In their now classic survey *The Person and the Situation*, Lee Ross and Richard Nisbett identify three paramount contributions of social psychology (Ross and Nisbett 1991). *Situationism* refers to extensive and surprising empirical findings that features of the immediate situation often overwhelm personal traits in predicting and explaining how people will behave. *Subjectivism* refers to the decisive importance for human actors of how they construe or define the scene of action; the "situation" includes the personal and subjective significance it has for the actor. The *dynamics of tension systems* reminds us that behavior occurs in a dynamic field in which the state of any part depends on the state of others, making much less predictable the relationship between interventions and change in social fields. Small alterations in the social field and people's perceptions of it can trigger massive redirection, while some large changes serve only to fortify factors that keep things in place.

I hope it is fairly easy to see in light of the foregoing that feminist study of emotions strongly embodies the first two of these characterizing themes of a social psychological approach, and suggests the importance of further exploration of the third. Both the environmental and interpersonal situations that confront people and provoke their feelings, and the ways people are apt to construe the nature and meaning of these situations, are affected by social experience conditioned by differences in social location, power, and opportunity. This leaves plenty of room for individual differences, but suggests at least that those who share many or particularly distinctive social experiences are equipped to find each other's emotional responses in certain situations more intelligible, apt, and perhaps more expressively legible than are others who do not share such experience. The impact of this epistemic and affective differential will be most acute in *social* situations, that is, in situations of encountering other people, interacting with them, and being the object of their attitudes and responses. One should not expect to understand feelings and their expressions, whether in theory or in the flow of life, and whether in particular episodes or in the ongoing texture of life, by assuming that there are simply "typical" feelings that make sense in certain "standard" situation-types for "people," and which when expressed in "characteristic" ways can be identified as one of the "familiar" emotions we know how to name.

Much less can we go on straightaway to broach an "ethics of emotion" in which we ask questions such as whether shame (or sympathy, or guilt, or resentment) is morally good, acceptable, or problematic, or what roles kinds of emotion – taken in abstraction from the cultural, social, and situational features of their occurrence and to whom they occur – play in some socially undifferentiated "moral life." This poses significant challenges to those who work on emotion. I suggest in conclusion that three operating assumptions, already put to work in feminist discussion of emotions, be taken consciously as guides to studies of emotion and to critically examining theories of emotion. They help to implement the social psychological insights of situationism, subjectivism, and dynamic tension, and to integrate these with feminism's task of normative political and social critique. We should assume in understanding kinds of emotions and emotional episodes that emotions are *expressive*, *position-sensitive*, and *synergistic*.

Emotions are *expressive*. Not only do they alert us "within" to what certain situations mean for us, but their expressions show others something about how we are experiencing things. It is plausible to see this communicative value of emotions as part of the natural function of our emotional capacities (Damasio 1995: xv). That the complex feeling-expression-action repertories that constitute emotions have communicative roles, sometimes intended and sometimes not, keeps in view questions about the different needs, opportunities, prerogatives, effects, and costs of particular people's sending certain kinds of messages to particular others. Different social positions will affect the likelihood of certain feeling's being expressed, the forms and intensities of their expression, the expressive codes and resources available for their articulation, and the nature of the reception one might expect. And so emotions are in multiple ways *position-sensitive*. There are different stakes in the expression of demanding emotions like anger or indignation for the weak or subordinate; different presumptions about necessary bases of trust between intimates and strangers, and between the dependent and the independent. There can be different occasions that make sense of gratitude or resentment for the superior and subordinate, and differences between what makes sense for each from their own point of view and from the point of view of the other (Card 1996; Walker 2003). The very potential for intelligibility – for being understood as feeling what you are feeling and displaying what you are trying to express – may shift dramatically under the eyes of differently positioned viewers.

Finally, emotions are intensely *synergistic* both within and between persons. William Miller reminds us that "we rarely experience one emotion unaccompanied by others. Emotions flood in upon us as we respond emotionally to our own states. We are guilty about our anger, embarrassed by our grief, disgusted by our own fear" (Miller 1997: 25). But Miller does not pause over the question of *before whom*, other than ourselves, we will feel one way or the other. We need to ask whose gazes we have learned to live under and what we have come to expect, fear, or need to find flows back toward us in the emotional responses of particular others to our displays of feeling. Some emotional synergies between people will have destructive consequences, as in interpersonal spirals of shame and contempt; others may be resources for pulling and keeping each other within bounds of responsibility and relations of moral response (see Calhoun 1989; Houston 1992).

It might seem evident that nothing is more intensely individual and private than what we call our "inner" lives. In fact, though, our emotional lives and the courses of our individual emotions surge through a dynamic field between us which is inescapably structured by objective realities of social power and difference and by the expressive exchanges in which we acknowledge and resist them.

References

Bartky, Sandra Lee (1990) *Femininity and Domination*, New York: Routledge.
Calhoun, Cheshire (1989) "Responsibility and Reproach," *Ethics* 99: 389–406.
—— (1992) "Emotional Work," in *Explorations in Feminist Ethics: Theory and Practice*, eds. Eve Browning Cole and Susan Coultrap-McQuin, Bloomington and Indianapolis: University of Indiana Press.

Campbell, Sue (1997) *Interpreting the Personal: Expression and the Formation of Feelings*, Ithaca, NY: Cornell University Press.

Card, Claudia (1996) *The Unnatural Lottery: Character and Moral Luck*, Philadephia, PA: Temple University Press.

Damasio, Antonio (1995) *Descartes' Error: Emotion, Reason, and the Human Brain*, New York: Avon Books.

DesAutels, Peggy and Walker, Margaret Urban, eds. (2004) *Moral Psychology: Feminist Ethics and Social Theory*, Lanham, MD: Rowman and Littlefield.

Flanagan, Owen (1991) *Varieties of Moral Personality: Ethics and Psychological Realism*, Cambridge, MA: Harvard University Press.

Frye, Marilyn (1983) "A Note in Anger," in *The Politics of Reality*, Trumansberg, NY: The Crossing Press.

Glover, Jonathan (2000) *Humanity: A Moral History of the 20th Century*, New Haven, CT: Yale University Press.

Goldie, Peter (2000) *The Emotions: A Philosophical Exploration*, New York: Oxford University Press.

Houston, Barbara (1992) "In Praise of Blame," *Hypatia: A Journal of Feminist Philosophy* 7: 138–47.

Jaggar, Alison M. (1989) "Love and Knowledge: Emotion in Feminist Epistemology," in *Gender/Body/Knowledge: Feminist Reconstructions of Being and Knowing*, eds. Alison M. Jaggar and Susan R. Bordo, New Brunswick, NJ: Rutgers University Press.

Jones, Karen (2004) "Emotional Rationality as Practical Rationality," in *Setting the Moral Compass: Essays by Women Philosophers*, ed. Cheshire Calhoun, New York: Oxford University Press.

Levy, Robert I. (1984) "Emotion, Knowing, and Culture," in *Culture Theory: Essays on Mind, Self, and Emotion*, eds. Richard A. Shweder and Robert A. LeVine, New York: Cambridge University Press.

Lugones, Maria (1987) "Playfulness, 'World'-Travel, and Loving Perception," *Hypatia: A Journal of Feminist Philosophy* 2: 3–19.

—— (1991) "On the Logic of Pluralist Feminism," in *Feminist Ethics*, ed. Claudia Card, Lawrence: University of Kansas Press.

—— (1995) "Hard-to-handle Anger," in *Overcoming Racism and Sexism*, ed. Linda A. Bell and David Blumenfeld, Lanham, MD: Rowman and Littlefield.

—— (2003) *Pilgrimages/Peregrinajes*, Lanham, MD: Rowman and Littlefield.

McFall, Lynne (1991) "What's Wrong with Bitterness?" in *Feminist Ethics*, ed. Claudia Card, Lawrence: University Press of Kansas.

Meyers, Diana Tietjens (1997) "Emotion and Heterodox Moral Perception: An Essay in Moral Social Psychology," in *Feminists Rethink the Self*, ed. Diana T. Meyers, Boulder, CO: Westview Press.

Miller, William (1997) *The Anatomy of Disgust*, Cambridge, MA: Harvard University Press.

Narayan, Uma (1988) "Working Together Across Difference: Some Considerations on Emotion and Political Practice," *Hypatia: A Journal of Feminist Philosophy* 3: 31–47.

Ross, Lee and Richard E. Nisbett (1991) *The Person and the Situation: Perspectives of Social Psychology*, New York: McGraw-Hill.

Scheman, Naomi (1980) "Anger and the Politics of Naming," in *Women and Language in Literature and Society*, eds. Sally McConnell-Ginet, Ruth Borker, and Nellie Furman, Westport, CT: Praeger.

—— (1996) "Feeling Our Way toward Moral Objectivity," in *Mind and Morals: Essays on*

Cognitive Science and Ethics, ed. Larry May, Marilyn Friedman, and Andy Clark, Cambridge, MA: MIT Press.

Shweder, Richard (1991) "Menstrual Pollution, Soul Loss, and the Comparative Study of Emotions," in *Thinking Through Cultures: Expeditions in Cultural Psychology*, Cambridge, MA: Harvard University Press.

Spelman, Elizabeth (1997) *Fruits of Sorrow: Framing Our Attention to Suffering*, Boston, MA: Beacon Press.

Stocker, Michael with Hegeman, Elizabeth (1996) *Valuing Emotions*, New York: Cambridge University Press.

Walker, Margaret Urban (2003) "Ineluctable Feelings and Moral Recognition," in *Moral Contexts*, Lanham, MD: Rowman and Littlefield. Previously published in Peter A. French, and Howard K. Wettstein, eds. (1998) *Midwest Studies in Philosophy*, vol. XXII, *Philosophy of Emotion*, Notre Dame, IN: University of Notre Dame Press.

—— (2004) "Resentment and Assurance," in *Setting the Moral Compass: Essays by Women Philosophers*, ed. Cheshire Calhoun, New York: Oxford University Press.

Young, Iris (2000) *Inclusion and Democracy*, New York: Oxford University Press.

Further Reading

Baier, Annette (1995) *Moral Prejudices*, Cambridge, MA: Harvard University Press.

—— (1997) *The Commons of the Mind*, Chicago and LaSalle: Open Court Press.

Bartky, Sandra (2002) *Sympathy and Solidarity*, Lanham, MD: Rowman and Littlefield.

Blum, Larry (1994) *Moral Perception and Particularity*, New York: Cambridge University Press.

Brender, Natalie (2001) "Political Care and Humanitarian Response," in *Feminists Doing Ethics*, eds. Peggy DesAutels and Joanne Waugh, Lanham, MD: Rowman and Littlefield.

Brison, Susan (2002) *Aftermath: Violence and the Remaking of a Self*, Princeton, NJ: Princeton University Press.

Calhoun, Cheshire (1984) "Cognitive Emotions?" in *What is an Emotion?* eds. Cheshire Calhoun and Robert Solomon, Oxford: Oxford University Press.

—— (2004) "An Apology for Moral Shame," *The Journal of Political Philosophy* 12: 127–46.

Campbell, Sue (2003) *Relational Remembering: Rethinking the Memory Wars*, Lanham, MD: Rowman and Littlefield.

Dillon, Robin (1995) *Dignity, Character, and Self-Respect*, New York: Routledge.

Govier, Trudy (1997) *Social Trust and Human Communities*, Montreal and Kingston: McGill-Queens University Press.

Jones, Karen (1996) "Trust as an Affective Attitude," *Ethics* 107: 4–25.

Little, Margaret Olivia (1995) "Seeing and Caring: The Role of Affect in Feminist Moral Epistemology," *Hypatia: A Journal of Feminist Philosophy* 10: 117–57.

McGeer, Victoria (2002) "Developing Trust," *Philosophical Explorations* 5: 21–38.

—— (2004) "The Art of Good Hope," *Annals of the American Academy of Political and Social Science* 592: 100–27.

Meyers, Diana (1994) *Subjection and Subjectivity*, New York: Routledge.

——, ed. (1997) *Feminists Rethink The Self*, Boulder, CO: Westview Press.

Mills, Charles (1997) *The Racial Contract*, Ithaca, NY: Cornell University Press.

Nelson, James Lindemann (1999) "Death's Gender," in *Mother Time: Women, Aging and Ethics*, ed. Margaret Urban Walker, Lanham, MD: Rowman and Littlefield.

Nelson, James Lindemann (2001) "Constructing Feelings: Jane Austen and Naomi Scheman on the Moral Role of Emotions," in *Feminists Doing Ethics*, ed. Peggy Des-Autels and Joanne Waugh, Lanham, MD: Rowman and Littlefield.

Noddings, Nel (1984) *Caring*, Berkeley and Los Angeles: University of California Press.

Nussbaum, Martha (2001) *Upheavals of Thought: The Intelligence of Emotions*, New York: Cambridge University Press.

Potter, Nancy (2002) *How Can I Be Trusted?* Lanham, MD: Rowman and Littlefield.

Scheman, Naomi (1983) "Individualism and the Objects of Psychology," in *Discovering Reality: Feminist Perspectives on Epistemology, Metaphysics, Methodology and Philosophy of Science*, eds. Sandra Harding and Merrill B. Hintikka, Dordrecht, Holland: Reidel.

—— (1993) *Engenderings: Constructions of Knowledge: Authority and Privilege*, New York: Routledge.

Thomas, Laurence Mordekhai (1993) *Vessels of Evil: American Slavery and the Holocaust*, Philadelphia, PA: Temple University Press.

Tronto, Joan (1993) *Moral Boundaries*, New York: Routledge.

Walker, Margaret Urban (2006) *Moral Repair: Reconstructing Moral Relations After Wrongdoing*, New York: Cambridge University Press.

Chapter 6

Feminist Bioethics

Where We've Been, Where We're Going

Hilde Lindemann

In Canada and the US, the bioethics movement and second-wave feminism both began in the late 1960s, but the two discourses had little to say to one another for the better part of two decades. It was not until 1989 that the journal of feminist philosophy, *Hypatia*, published two special issues devoted to feminism and medical ethics. The few essays by feminists published up to that time in the premier journal in bioethics, the *Hastings Center Report*, dealt solely with ethical issues surrounding women's reproductive functions.

Where We've Been

All that has changed. The 1990s saw a steady stream of conferences, monographs, anthologies, and essays in learned journals that examine bioethical issues through a feminist lens. Susan Sherwin's groundbreaking *No Longer Patient: Feminist Ethics and Health Care* appeared in 1992, as did Helen Bequaert Holmes and Laura M. Purdy, eds., *Feminist Perspectives in Medical Ethics*, and Rebecca Dresser's *Hastings Center Report* article, "Wanted: Single, White Male for Medical Research." The International Network on Feminist Approaches to Bioethics, begun in 1993 by two US feminists, has some 300 members worldwide and has sponsored several conferences in conjunction with the International Association of Bioethics. The year 1993 also saw the publication of Mary Mahowald's *Women and Children in Health Care: An Unequal Majority*, and Susan Bordo's *Unbearable Weight: Feminism, Western Culture, and the Body*. In 1995 the prestigious Kennedy Institute of Ethics devoted its advanced bioethics course to feminist perspectives on bioethics, and the plenary lectures of that course were then published in a special issue of the *Kennedy Institute of Ethics Journal*, edited by Margaret Olivia Little. In 1996 the *Journal of Clinical Ethics* published special sections in each of its four issues on feminism and bioethics. Laura M. Purdy's *Reproducing Persons* appeared that year as well, as did the much-cited anthology edited by Susan M. Wolf, *Feminism and Bioethics: Beyond Reproduction*. These were followed in 1997 by the publication of Rosemarie Tong's *Feminist Approaches to Bioethics: Theoretical Reflections and Practical Applications*, Dorothy Roberts' influential *Killing the Black Body*, and Elizabeth Haiken's *Venus Envy*, a feminist history of cosmetic surgery. In 1998 the Feminist Health Care Ethics Research Network published *The Politics of Women's Health: Exploring Agency and Autonomy*, while the *Journal of Medicine and Philosophy* devoted an entire issue to the feminist ethic of care. Anne Donchin and Laura M. Purdy's anthology, *Embodying Bioethics: Feminist Advances*, appeared in 1999, along with Eva Feder Kittay's *Love's Labor*. Textbooks and readers in bioethics now routinely include essays written from an explicitly feminist point of view.

The primary contribution of feminism to bioethics is to note how imbalances of power in the sex-gender system play themselves out in medical practice and in the theory surrounding that practice. It follows that one of its tasks is to challenge medicine's androcentrism – its standing assumption that men are the norm for human beings – and to call attention to the ways in which this assumption marks women as either unimportant or pathological. To some extent, feminist bioethicists have done this. They have, for example, pointed out that excluding women from controlled clinical drug trials to avoid the "complications" of hormonal fluctuation or pregnancy must inevitably result in our knowing relatively little about how women respond to these drugs (Dresser 1992). They have pointed out that the tendency of physicians to tailor treatment in ways that advance the physician's goals rather than those of the patient are especially harmful to women (Rorty 1999). They have pointed out that a medical model of anorexia nervosa depoliticizes the condition, since it assumes that there is something the matter with the patients, 90 percent of whom are female, rather than with a socially defined feminine ideal that literally makes some women sick (Mahowald 1992). They have pointed out that because the liberal tradition of political theory conceives of citizens as autonomous, rational, self-interested contractors, it disenfranchises not only chronically ill or badly impaired people, but also their (largely female) primary caregivers (Kittay 1999).

Feminism has more to offer bioethics, however, than this sort of *critique*. It also has the potential to enrich bioethical *theory*. Feminism's unique contribution to moral theory in general has arguably been that of finding gender bias in the preoccupations, assumptions, and perspectives of the dominant theories of Anglo-American ethics. This activity has produced feminist correctives to mainstream Kantian and utilitarian theories, nourished a major smokeless industry in care theory, and challenged the standard philosophical accounts of what moral theories are supposed to do in any case. Attention to gender enriches utilitarian theorizing when it illuminates previously obscured consequences of actions and policies and thus permits a better view of the range of ways in which women have been harmed simply because they were women (Purdy 1996). Attention to gender has also offered possibilities for a richer understanding of what happens to key concepts in Kantian moral philosophy, such as respect for persons, when these are not modeled on moral and intellectual virtues valued most highly by privileged men (Dillon 1994). Attention to differences in adolescents' moral reasoning that fall out roughly along the lines of gender gave rise to care theory (Gilligan 1982; Ruddick 1989; Tronto 1993; Held 2005). And attention to gender has also produced theory that stands clear of Kantian, utilitarian, and virtue theories altogether. Rejecting the role of the ideal ethical reasoner as a solitary and power-ful – read masculine – judge who applies lawlike principles derived from one or several of these theories to the case at hand, some feminists have instead conceived of ethical deliberation as an expressive-collaborative process in which a group of people strive for mutual moral intelligibility, forging shared understandings of who is responsible for what, to whom (Walker 1998).

While feminist ethicists have enriched ethical theory in these many ways, femi-nist *bioethicists* have not yet done the same for bioethical theory. For that matter, they have not yet fully availed themselves of feminist resources for critique of medical practice. For all the growing body of literature that has accumulated since 1990, feminist contributions to bioethics have largely remained focused on one kind of rather narrowly defined critique, and there has been almost no theory-building of any kind.

The vast preponderance of feminist critique in bioethics has been directed at practices surrounding the care of women's bodies, and in particular, the parts of women's bodies that mark them as different from men. There has been a relent-less focus on women's reproductive systems, whether in the form of arguments in defense of abortion, debates about the wisdom of various methods of assisted reproduction, arguments against sustaining postmortem pregnancies, ethical analyses of various sorts of maternal–fetal conflicts, concern about HIV testing of newborns and pregnant women, pleas for better prenatal care for pregnant women, debates about the use and abuse of long-acting contraception, arguments for and against amniocentesis and other genetic testing of fetuses, and discussions about hormone replacement therapy for postmenopausal women. And when femi-nist bioethicists have moved "beyond reproduction," as Susan M. Wolf puts it, they have tended to critique practices of health care for *women* – weighing in, for example, on the debates over the medical management of breast cancer, arguing that tying health care insurance to employment disadvantages elderly women, or protesting the injustice of a health care delivery system that devotes a dis-proportionate amount of high-tech care, such as arterial angioplasty and organ transplantation, to men.

I do not at all mean to underestimate the importance of these critiques, or of the necessity for continuing to make them. A 2001 survey by the Kaiser Family Foun-dation found that only 41 percent of insured employees in the US had coverage for contraceptives, even though virtually all insured employees (98 percent) had coverage for prescription drugs in general (Dailard 2003). This is surely a reason for feminist bioethicists to remain vigilant about women's reproductive health, as is the fact that in 87 percent of counties in the US there is no licensed provider of abortions (Henshaw and Finer 2003). The Drug Policy Alliance reported in 2006 that black women are still ten times more likely than white women to be reported to child welfare agencies for prenatal drug use. It needs no ghost come from the grave to tell us that feminist critique is still required here.

The point I want to make, however, is that the preoccupation with women's bodies, and especially women's reproductive health, tends to reinforce the androcentric social understanding of women as Other. It leaves in place too many of the practices, institutions, and assumptions of a sex-gender system that is biased in favor of men and thus configures women as not only different, but deviant. And this reinforces the idea that women present a special social problem but that men's role in society is somehow normal and unproblematic. Where material conditions and institutions systematically favor men's interests, underplay women's interests, and insist on a strict gender binary, however, gender itself is problematic. So for all the importance of continued critique of the policies and practices surrounding women's wombs and other body parts, there are many other health-care issues requiring an ethical analysis that is sensitive to imbalances of power within the sex-gender system. For example, what might a feminist analysis reveal about the ethical impact of a gendered power system on the care of people with Alzheimer's disease? On the care of the frail elderly? On medical education? On physician-assisted suicide? On medical treatment decision-making? On health-care financing? On health-care rationing? It is particularly odd that feminist bioethicists have paid so little attention to social justice issues, given that feminism emerges from a critique of social institutions that have been unjust toward women. Work on these topics is underway (for example, Nelson and Nelson 1995; Overall 2003, Baylis and Downie 2004), but we have barely made a beginning.

If feminist critique in bioethics has been too narrowly focused, feminist bioethicists' contributions to ethical theory have been practically nonexistent. The major exception has been the work of some feminist bioethicists on the ethic of care (Carse and Nelson 1996; Little and Veatch 1998). Much more needs to be done, however, both to expand care ethics so that it furnishes conceptual tools for social and political analysis, and to use the practice of medicine itself to enrich ethical theory. That so little of this work has been done is not surprising, not only because feminist bioethics is a very young discourse indeed, but also because bioethics in general has failed to produce theory, contenting itself with the pragmatic strategy of agreeing on middle-level ethical principles where it can, and scavenging from the standing political and moral theories when it must. Feminist bioethicists, however, haven't the luxury of that sort of pragmatism, because it is the business of feminism to be deeply suspicious of the standing political and moral theories, on the grounds that they are shot through with gender bias and so must be regarded as untrustworthy. Our task is to come up with new theory, not to refine theories that leave everything exactly as it was.

Why ought feminists to scrutinize *medical* practice as they build moral theory? Why, that is, should there be a feminist bioethics at all? My answer is that medicine ought to be of particular concern to feminists because it is one of the hegemonic discourses of our time, commanding enormous amounts of social prestige and authority. Because it is so powerful that no other discourse except, possibly, that of international capitalism competes with it, it interacts with gender at many levels and in many different ways. Feminists need to *critique* that interaction, but they also need to *learn* from it. They do this by studying it and constructing theory concerning it.

Where We're Going

Where we've been, then, is busily engaged in critique, especially critique of healthcare practices that ignore or undervalue women's interests and favor the interests of powerful men. Where we're going depends to some extent on where the rapid succession of technological innovations takes the field of biomedicine, but it also depends on how we position ourselves with respect to that field. We might, for example, conceive of our role as that of giving good ethical advice to clinical practitioners, patterning ourselves on the consultancy model: when a patient develops a pneumonia, a pulmonologist is summoned to the bedside to offer an expert opinion; when a clinician encounters a moral difficulty, the requisite consultant is a feminist bioethicist. On a rather different model, we might conceive of the clinic as a particularly instructive setting in which to produce feminist scholarship, using an examination of the practice of health care to ground theory that guides political change. Either model has its attractions and many bioethicists adopt some combination of the two. Regardless of which prevails, or whether a new model emerges that differs from them entirely, I can discern two distinct directions in which we might now go. I propose that we pursue them both simultaneously.

First, I should like to see us take on the same cutting-edge topics that are now being addressed by nonfeminist bioethicists, but to use our own methodology, paying careful attention to how gender is installed and reinforced by power as it circulates through our practices of responsibility. Take research ethics – a very hot topic in the US at the moment. One problem that has received a fair amount of attention in this area is the one of "undue inducement." When does an offer of money or other reward for participating in a clinical drug trial become a *coercive* offer, one so tempting that, despite the risk posed to the subject, it's nearly impossible to refuse? Ezekiel Emanuel (2005) has argued that because Institutional Review Boards (IRBs) oversee all protocols for research on human subjects and may approve only studies with a risk–benefit ratio that a reasonable person could accept, the worry about undue inducement is "nonsense on stilts." But just who is the "reasonable person" Emanuel has in mind? IRBs consist mostly of well-educated white men, and a risk that is reasonable for a well educated white man to undertake may not be reasonable at all for a desperately poor, uneducated brown man or a single woman with paraplegia. Surely gender, ethnicity, social class, and ability are crucial considerations here, and these are familiar categories of analysis for feminist bioethicists.

Another cutting-edge topic in bioethics that might be enriched by feminist analysis is neuroethics. With recent advances in neuroscience has come an increased understanding of how the brain works. New neuroimaging technologies developed in the last two decades in particular let us observe the neurobiological processes of what many scientists take to be the mind in action. But does the mind actually reside inside the brain, as scientists seem to think? And do imaging studies really reveal the thinking, feeling, intending self? A number of feminists, drawing on models of dependency and interdependency that reflect the actual lives of many women, children, and marginal men, have done careful, innovative theoretical work on the nature of selves, viewing them as socially constructed, relational entities that are produced by social interaction with other selves. To what extent has the picture of socially unencumbered, self-sufficient, autonomous individuals that represents only some privileged people, for some time in their lives, influenced the assumptions that neuroscientists seem to make about isolated selves that exist entirely inside the head?

Another cutting-edge topic in bioethics that might be enriched by feminist analysis is embryonic stem cell research. To what extent is our understanding of the moral value of the blastocyst from which such cells may be obtained shaped by the abortion debate, and how much, in turn, is that debate a product of gender politics? What would happen if the moral framework we used for thinking about embryos were shifted, so that the question of whether an embryo is or is not a person was taken to be, not a fact that we could discover, but rather a political question about the social construction of personhood? Put another way, what would happen if the moral status of the embryo were something we would have to *confer* rather than discover? And what gendered assumptions lie behind the persistent unwillingness of the parties to the stem cell debate to acknowledge that the embryo has no future whatsoever as a human being if it will never be implanted in a woman's body?

Research ethics, neuroethics, and embryonic stem cell ethics, then, are just three examples of the kinds of issues that point mainstream bioethicists in a new direction and that also point feminist bioethicists in the same new direction. I think we are in fact going in that direction, and that the work we do there will certainly enrich health policy and bioethical reflection. But now I want to propose that we go in another direction as well – to promising areas of theory that mainstream bioethicists have not yet begun to develop. Let me offer two examples of the kind of thing I have in mind. The first builds on work in feminist epistemology, and the second builds on work in feminist narrative ethics. Both suggest new possibilities for how we could do bioethics.

Feminist Epistemology

First, let us consider a clinical case.

> Al Brown is a seventy-three-year-old man with cerebral palsy and severe spastic paraly-
> sis in all four limbs. He was admitted to a dependent care facility forty years ago and

has lived there ever since. Despite his significant physical impairment and need for assistance with basic life functions, he is cognitively intact.

Several years ago, Mr Brown was given phenobarbitol for treatment of a seizure disorder. When the threat of seizures subsided, he continued to receive 60 milligrams of phenobarbitol four times a day. Now, each time a new pharmacist or physician is assigned to his unit, phenobarbitol levels are drawn. These invariably run in the 50s in micrograms per milliliter, suggesting to clinicians that his dosage should be reduced. Mr Brown objects to the reduction, stating that he is doing fine, has not had any seizures, and "always gets messed up when people fool around with my medications."

(Mahowald 1996: 107).

What Mr Brown knows about the amount of phenobarbitol that works best for him is apt not to get registered by the pharmacist and the physician as knowledge at all. The health-care professionals, who know authoritatively what the proper dosage is, will likely discount Mr Brown as an ignorant layman who lacks the scientific training and is unfamiliar with the risks reported in the medical literature. Moreover, if Mr Brown continues to insist on the 60 milligram dose, his physician might begin to pathologize him, explaining away the insistence by supposing that Mr Brown has a psychological need to draw attention to himself, or to exert undue amounts of control over his health-care providers.

As a number of feminist epistemologists have argued, cognitive authority is dependent on social position: it requires a certain standing within one's community (L. Nelson 1990; Potter 1993; Addelson 1994). What a scientist can know, for example, and with whom she can work to advance knowledge, depends crucially on how she is situated vis-à-vis those who know authoritatively (Harding 1986). Nor is social situation relevant only to the production of formally bounded, public bodies of knowledge. A sense of competence regarding what we know about ourselves and our relationships to others, about the world and our personal possibilities for living well in it, also requires social standing within the community of those who know. Those who do not possess the requisite standing – such as women, or, in the case just recounted, patients – have often been ignored, belittled, or dismissed.

Mr Brown lacks cognitive authority. He probably never acquired a college education, let alone medical or pharmaceutical licensure, and from his idiolect we can infer that he is probably not a member of a privileged social class. Moreover, he is a patient, and disabled. But if his physician dismisses what he knows from his own experience about his body's reaction to phenobarbitol, solely because he occupies a lower position than she does in the cognitive hierarchy, she is doing something morally wrong. Thinking one knows more than someone else is not in itself a moral failing; a physician generally *does* have knowledge the patient lacks, and with regard to medical matters the patient would generally prefer to trust the physician's judgment over his own. In the area of medical expertise, the physician rightly commands greater cognitive authority than most patients. When, however, a physician discounts a patient's experiential testimony for no other reason than that the patient is her social inferior, the physician's claim to epistemic legitimacy is no longer warranted. At that point, the doctor–patient relationship stops being merely a hierarchy and becomes an oppressive hierarchy, no different morally from that of patriarchy, which permits powerful men to discredit a woman's judgment just because she is a woman.

By contrast, the physician who begins from the standpoint of the patient, respecting the patient's judgments about his bodily experience, the character of his daily life, what conduces to his happiness, and the other considerations that can be brought to bear on his condition, is then able to enter into a collaboration with her patient. Working together, they can construct an understanding of what the patient is doing and thinking, and what constitutes an optimal medical response.

Counterstories

Feminists have been skeptical of the ideal moral agent posited by impartialist moral theories, pointing out that this unencumbered contractor, self-asserter, or games-man looks suspiciously like a privileged white male. By the same token, impartialist theories' insistence that the moral deliberator is to disregard social context and other particulars of a morally troublesome situation has also prompted feminist skepticism, as inattention to context serves to maintain social hierarchies based on gender. Feminists have therefore been especially interested in developing modes of moral deliberation, such as narrative approaches to ethics, that take social context and other morally salient particularities into account.

It might be thought that bioethics would be particularly hospitable to narrative approaches, whether via feminist theory or some other source, since bioethicists so often work with narratives in the form of case studies. I believe, however, that when bioethicists work with cases they typically do *not* approach them narratively, at least for cases that find their way into print. Case commentators generally act as solitary, powerful judges, applying lawlike principles derived from one or several of the mainstream moral theories to the situation described in the case. The principles produced by the theory then serve as guides to right conduct. Call this the theoretical-juridical model of morality and moral theory (Walker 1998).

Judging skillfully and well on the theoretical-juridical model involves a consideration of the economic, cultural, class, gender, and religious contexts in which the participants operate, as these social contexts might have some bearing on which principles are pertinent and how much relative importance to assign to conflicting principles. However, once the commentator has gotten hold of the correct principles and a rationale for ranking them, context is of no further interest. The commentator can now judge impartially what ought to be done in any similar set of circumstances.

In a *narrative* approach to a case, by contrast, social contexts are important, not because they guide the selection of the principles that will be used to resolve the case, but because of what they reveal about the identities of the participants: the religious, ethnic, gender, and other settings in which a person lives her life contribute to her own and others' sense of who she is. How others see her crucially influences how they will respond to her, so it matters whether they get these contextual features right. While those espousing the theoretical-juridical model could in principle take the same view as narrativists of the moral importance of *social* contexts, only a narrative approach will feature the case's *temporal* context. Because juridical methods center on an ethical analysis of what is going on here, in the present moment, and because the arguments used in the analysis are themselves atemporal, those who employ these methods tend to approach the morally troublesome situation as if it were atemporal as well. But understanding how we got "here" is crucial to the determination of where we might be able to go from here, and this is where narrative is indispensable. The story of how the participants of the case came to their present pass is precisely a story, as is the narrative of the best way to go on in the future. The backward-looking story is explanatory; the forward-looking story is action-guiding. Approaches based on the theoretical-juridical model of morality tend to move only sideways, considering context as it fleshes out the here and now. Because narrative approaches also move backward and forward, they are better suited to ethical reflection than are juridical approaches. They also, as I will explain, make of morality something quite different from what the standing theories have supposed it to be. Because feminists, for reasons I have already given, must call the standing theories into question, a narrative approach to moral deliberation is particularly well suited to a feminist bioethical analysis of a case.

At this point, a demonstration is in order. So let us consider a case:

Mrs Shalev is now eighty-three years old. She was born in Poland and escaped to the United States in the earliest years of the Second World War. She adapted pretty quickly to Brooklyn and raised a family there, but two years ago she suffered a serious stroke. Since then she has spent a good deal of her time in hospitals and nursing homes, always carefully attended by her daughter, Becky Putnam, whose home Mrs Shalev had shared for the five years just before her stroke.

Mrs Shalev is now back in the hospital, with a long list of serious problems. Her physicians regard her situation as "short-term survivable, long-term terminal." But she still has periods of lucidity, and her daughter is still deeply involved in her care.

In the opinion of the team treating Mrs Shalev, her daughter may in fact be too deeply involved. Ms Putnam is particularly concerned about the amount of pain medication that her mother is getting. The analgesics rob her mother of the little capacity she has left – in particular, the ability to recognize her daughter's presence.

At the same time, Mrs Shalev has developed a number of serious pressure sores from being bed-bound so long. Some of these are bad enough that bone tissue shows through. She needs regular changes of dressings on these sores, and this is apparently quite an uncomfortable procedure. How uncomfortable, no one can really tell, but she certainly reacts negatively to them, moaning and trying to pull away.

The treatment team also feels that it's time to start rethinking the goals for Mrs Shalev's care more generally. She is currently undergoing a number of invasive treatments, none of which have any real chance of making her any better; the best they can do is spin out her life just a little longer. Some of the physicians involved in her care have been heard to utter the word "futility," and the nurses in particular are very concerned that the aim of Mrs Shalev's treatment be to keep her as pain free as possible so that she can end her life in dignity and comfort.

Ms Putnam has a very different view of the matter. While she doesn't deny that her mother faces a grim outlook, she does believe that the growing consensus of the treatment team is inappropriate, to put it mildly. She insists that her mother continue to receive aggressive, life-sustaining treatment, and that the analgesics be minimal. During one care conference, she exclaimed, "Where we come from, we find it offensive that you insist on discussing withdrawal of life support – we have never even talked about these things among ourselves!"

This position is rapidly driving the treatment team crazy. The call goes out to the hospital's ethics committee in hopes that some strategy for changing Ms Putnam's mind can be worked out. Failing that, perhaps there's a way of getting her out of the decision making loop. As one nurse puts it, "While I respect the unique perspective of the family, there have to be limits. I feel as though I'm being forced to participate in the abuse of a vulnerable adult."

(Nelson and Nelson 1995: 224–5)

On a standard, theoretical-juridical analysis, it is quite possible that a careful bioethicist would note the importance of the religious and cultural context in which Mrs Shalev has lived her life, assume that she was probably an Orthodox Jew and therefore a vitalist, and, applying the principle of respect for patient autonomy, conclude that she ought to continue to receive intensive treatment in accordance with her religious beliefs. The bioethicist might counsel the caregivers to ask Mrs Shalev in one of her lucid periods if she wishes to continue receiving such treatment. If her wishes cannot be ascertained, the bioethicist would perhaps be somewhat skeptical about the daughter's insistence on full treatment, since her authority as a proxy is supposed to rest on her knowledge of her mother's wishes and she has clearly stated that they have never even talked about these things among themselves. Because of that statement, the bioethicist might well judge that the principle of substituted judgment cannot be applied here, and that the treatment team is therefore obligated to fall back on the best interests principle – which surely means, if nothing else, that Mrs Shalev not be forced to endure treatable pain. If Ms Putnam cannot be brought to see that her demands are abusive, the bioethicist might conclude, then the courts should be asked to appoint a more responsible proxy.

Let me now propose a different way of deliberating about this case, one that involves telling further stories. I contend that by pulling the case apart and retelling it so that it reveals the moral importance of contextual features that were originally played down or ignored, the deliberators can come to a better understanding of who the participants are and what the appropriate moral response to them might be. The backward-looking stories the deliberators tell about the participants have explanatory force: they supply the temporal setting that allows us to make sense of what the various actors are now doing.[1] The sideways stories also broaden our understanding of "now": they exhibit the effect of the various social contexts on the participants' present identities. Both sorts of stories show us more clearly who the participants are.[2]

The first thing to notice is that the original case is told from the professional caregivers' point of view – which is hardly surprising, since they are the ones who brought the case to the ethics committee in the first place. But because it is their story, we do not see much of how things look from Becky Putnam's point of view. The second thing to notice is that the values featured in the original case – in particular, the values of not prolonging dying and of freedom from pain – are also those of the ideology of medicine. In the story we see that the caregivers assume these ought to be universally shared values, but this assumption can be questioned. The third thing to notice is that the treatment team sees the patient and family member not only as two very different individuals, but as pitted against each other, and in this contest, their professional loyalties lie with Mrs Shalev – this too is a part of medical ideology. But this view of the relationship between mother and daughter can also be questioned.

Let us now suppose that there is a feminist physician on the ethics committee and that he takes a narrative approach to ethics. Let us also suppose he has noticed the aforementioned three things about the original case. Taking the story apart at these three seams, he reassembles it, telling it as it might appear from Becky Putnam's point of view and augmenting it where the original story was silent about or underplayed morally relevant features of the situation. Here is the retold story:

> Becky Putnam has always looked up to her mother, admiring the courage it took to flee the Nazis and to build a new life in a foreign land. Theirs has been a close family, and while it hasn't always been easy to get along with this strong-willed woman, especially when Becky was younger, they understand each other very well. Becky's husband and teenage children didn't have to be asked whether they were willing to have Mrs Shalev come and live with them when Mr Shalev died – they took it for granted that their home would be hers. There's no need to discuss what everybody understands.
>
> That observation, by the way, also holds true for stopping treatment. We should discuss this? wonders Becky. Let's discuss whether I should put a gun to my head, while we're at it. What's the matter with these doctors, that they want to discuss this?
>
> Becky also understands that her mother has something better to do than simply to lie there, obtunded by morphine, until death finally takes her. She may be old and tired, but she isn't so tired that she no longer cares about her family, and if she can't know they're there, she might as well be dead. She's put many years of time and energy into raising Becky and loving her son-in-law and grandchildren, and it would be cruel to take her enjoyment of these people away from her by drugging her into a stupor. Becky's lost count of the number of times she's heard her mother say, "Pain, schmain!" Seeing and knowing her family is worth the pain it's costing her.
>
> Becky doesn't think of herself as a very different person from her mother. That's not how family is supposed to be. Their life-stories are tightly twisted together, so that even when her mother gets on her nerves, she's a part of Becky's self. When she was very young her mother took care of her, loved her, and played a large part in forming Becky's identity. Now that her mother is old and ill, it's up to Becky to

return the favor, helping her mother to maintain her sense of who she is by safeguarding the relationships that are central to *her* identity. She wishes the treatment team would let her get on with the job.

This story is a *counterstory* – "counter" because it resists the identity of "abusive family member" that the original story seems to impose on Ms Putnam. The medically imposed identity is arguably oppressive, because it unfairly characterizes Ms Putnam as morally incompetent and thereby poses a threat to the exercise of her moral agency: if she is pushed out of the decision-making loop on the strength of this characterization, she will be unable to help her mother to live well in this final illness. If, with the help of the counterstory, Ms Putnam is reidentified as a morally competent person, she will no longer be oppressed by a system of medical power that discounts what she knows because she is only a family member. Instead, she will be free to act as she judges best.

The moral terms and general rules that can be brought to bear on Ms Putnam's story need not be understood as inflexible laws. Instead, they can be regarded as markers of the moral relevance of certain features of the story: "Shouldn't we *respect* the sanctity of life?" "Don't I *owe* my mother something?" Certain features of the retold story suggest ways of understanding the relevant moral ideas, and these ideas in turn may point to other previously neglected details of the story. The story is finished when the augmented context and its attendant moral concepts are in a state of equilibrium that allows the deliberators to see the situation from Ms Putnam's point of view.

Other counterstories might need to be told – there ought surely to be one from Mrs Shalev's perspective – but when the case has been retold often enough to get a sense of who the participants are and what moral considerations ought to be brought to bear on them, it is time to stop telling the story backward (which lets us see where the participants are coming from) and sideways (which lets us flesh out all the relevant features), and start telling it forward. The deliberators do this by putting into equilibrium the details of all the previously told stories and the moral descriptions that are suggested by them. From their sense of how the narrative pieces shed light on one another they construct, together, the closing story of how best to go on from here.

It should be clear, then, how this narrative mode of moral deliberation makes of morality a rather different sort of thing from what the standard theories have supposed it to be. On the theoretical-juridical model, morality is a matter of applying codified rules derived from comprehensive theories as criteria for assessing wrongdoing and making rational choices. The narrative approach I have been describing sees morality instead as a continual interpersonal task of becoming and remaining mutually intelligible. It is *expressive* of who we are and hope to be; it is *collaborative* in that it posits, not a solitary judge, but a community of inquirers who need to construct ways of living well together. And it is *feminist* because it offers a means of resisting powerful ideologies, whether these be of gender, medicine, race, or all three at once.

This, then, is my overview of feminist bioethics. Where we've been is mostly a matter of feminist critique of medical practice that has asked, "Where are the women in this picture?" or focused on ethical issues surrounding women's health. Where we're going, I hope, is in two general directions – one that looks at the cutting-edge concerns in medicine and health-care policy through the lens of gender, and the other that develops various aspects of feminist theory and brings them to bear on issues in bioethics. We have not yet traveled very far in either direction, but the road beckons.

Acknowledgments

Earlier versions of this essay were published as Hilde Lindemann Nelson, "Resistance and Insubordination: A Feminist Response to Medical Hegemony," in *Proceedings of the 21st International Wittgenstein Symposium: Angewandte Ethik*, ed. Peter Kampits et al. (Vienna: Holder-Pichler-Tempsky, 1999); and Hilde Lindemann Nelson, "Feminist Bioethics: Where We've Been, Where We're Going," *Metaphilosophy* 31 (5) (October 2000): 492–508. My thanks to James Lindemann Nelson for useful comments and suggestions.

Notes

1 Alasdair MacIntyre puts the point this way: "In successfully identifying and understanding what someone else is doing we always move towards placing a particular episode in the context of a set of narrative histories, histories both of the individuals concerned and of the settings in which they act and suffer . . . We render the actions of others intelligible in this way because action itself has a basically historical character" (MacIntyre 1984: 211–12).

2 For arguments about actions requiring the expected responses of other agents for their completion and actions' ability to reveal morally significant things about the agent, see Baier (1997) and Benson (1990).

References

Addelson, Kathryn Pyne (1994) *Moral Passages: Toward a Collectivist Moral Theory*, New York: Routledge.
Baier, Annette (1997) *The Commons of the Mind*, Paul Carus Lecture, Chicago: Open Court Press.
Baylis, Françoise and Downie, Jocelyn (2004) "The Limits of Altruism and Arbitrary Age Limits," *The American Journal of Bioethics* 3 (4): 19–20.
Benson, Paul (1990) "Feminist Second Thoughts about Free Agency," *Hypatia: A Journal of Feminist Philosophy* 5 (3): 47–64.

Bordo, Susan (1993) *Unbearable Weight: Feminism, Western Culture, and the Body*, Berkeley and Los Angeles: University of California Press.

Carse, Alisa, and Nelson, Hilde Lindemann (1996) "Rehabilitating Care," *Kennedy Institute of Ethics Journal* 6 (1): 19–35.

Code, Lorraine (1991) *What Can She Know? Feminist Theory and the Construction of Knowledge*, Ithaca, NY: Cornell University Press.

Dailard, Cynthia (2003) "The Cost of Contraceptive Insurance Coverage," *Guttmacher Report on Public Policy*, March 2003, Alan Guttmacher Institute.

Dillon, Robin (1994) *Dignity, Character, and Self-Respect*, New York: Routledge.

Donchin, Anne and Purdy, Laura M., eds. (1999) *Embodying Bioethics: Feminist Advances*, Lanham, MD: Rowman and Littlefield.

Dresser, Rebecca (1992) "Wanted: Single, White Male for Medical Research," *Hastings Center Report* 22 (1): 24–9.

Emanuel, Ezekiel J. (2005) "Undue Inducement: Nonsense on Stilts," *The American Journal of Bioethics* 5 (5): 9–13.

Feminist Health Care Ethics Research Network (1998) *The Politics of Women's Health: Exploring Agency and Autonomy*, Philadelphia, PA: Temple University Press.

Gilligan, Carol (1982) *In a Different Voice: Psychological Theory and Women's Development*, Cambridge, MA: Harvard University Press.

Haiken, Elizabeth (1997) *Venus Envy: A History of Cosmetic Surgery*, Baltimore, MD: Johns Hopkins University Press.

Harding, Sandra (1986) *The Science Question in Feminism*, Ithaca, NY: Cornell University Press.

Held, Virginia (2005) *The Ethics of Care: Personal, Political, and Global*, New York: Oxford University Press.

Henshaw, S.K. and Finer, L.B. "The Accessibility of Abortion Services in the United States, 2001," *Perspectives on Sexual and Reproductive Health*, 35 (1) (2003): 16–24.

Holmes, Helen Bequaert and Purdy, Laura M., eds. (1992) *Feminist Perspectives in Medical Ethics*, Bloomington: Indiana University Press.

Kittay, Eva Feder (1999) *Love's Labor: Essays on Women, Equality, and Dependency*, New York: Routledge.

Little, Margaret Olivia, ed. (1996) *Kennedy Institute of Ethics Journal* 6 (1), Special Issue: Feminist Perspectives on Bioethics.

Little, Margaret Olivia and Veatch, Robert M., eds. (1998) *Journal of Medicine and Philosophy* 23 (2), Special Issue: The Chaos of Care and Care Theory.

MacIntyre, Alasdair (1984) *After Virtue*, 2nd edn., Notre Dame, IN: University of Notre Dame Press.

Mahowald, Mary Briody (1992) "To Be or Not Be a Woman: Anorexia Nervosa, Normative Gender Roles, and Feminism," *Journal of Medicine and Philosophy* 17 (2): 233–51.

—— (1993) *Women and Children in Health Care: An Unequal Majority*, New York: Oxford University Press.

—— (1996) "On Treatment of Myopia: Feminist Standpoint Theory and Bioethics," in *Feminism and Bioethics: Beyond Reproduction*, ed. Susan Wolf, New York: Oxford.

Nelson, Hilde Lindemann and Nelson, James Lindemann (1995) *The Patient in the Family: An Ethics of Medicine and Families*, New York: Routledge.

Nelson, Lynn Hankinson (1990) *Who Knows? From Quine to a Feminist Empiricism*, Philadelphia, PA: Temple University Press.

Overall, Christine (2003) *Aging, Death, and Human Longevity: A Philosophical Investigation*, Berkeley: University of California Press.

Potter, Elizabeth (1993) "Gender and Epistemic Negotiation," in *Feminist Epistemologies*, eds. Linda Alcoff and Elizabeth Potter, New York: Routledge.

Purdy, Laura M. (1996) *Reproducing Persons: Issues in Feminist Bioethics*, Ithaca, NY: Cornell University Press.

Roberts, Dorothy (1997) *Killing the Black Body: Race, Reproduction, and the Meaning of Liberty*, New York: Vintage.

Rorty, Mary V. (1999) "Feminism and Elective Fetal Reductions," in *Embodying Bioethics: Recent Feminist Advances*, eds. Anne Donchin and Laura M. Purdy, Lanham, MD: Rowman and Littlefield.

Ruddick, Sara (1989) *Maternal Thinking: Toward a Politics of Peace*, Boston: Beacon Press.

Sherwin, Susan (1992) *No Longer Patient: Feminist Ethics and Health Care*, Philadelphia, PA: Temple University Press.

Tong, Rosemarie, ed. (1996) Special section: Feminist Approaches to Bioethics, *Journal of Clinical Ethics* 7, nos. 1, 2, 3, and 4.

—— (1997) *Feminist Approaches to Bioethics: Theoretical Reflections and Practical Applications*, Boulder, CO: Westview.

Tronto, Joan (1993) *Moral Boundaries: A Political Argument for an Ethic of Care*, New York: Routledge.

Walker, Margaret (1998) *Moral Understandings: A Feminist Study in Ethics*, New York: Routledge.

Wolf, Susan M., ed. (1996) *Feminism and Bioethics: Beyond Reproduction*, New York: Oxford.

Chapter 7

Feminism and Disability

Anita Silvers

Looking back over the twentieth century, we can see how feminist philosophy transformed the philosophical climate and stimulated the evolution of philosophy to a high and rare degree. Initially, philosophers who adopted a feminist stance pursued critical analyses of the prevailing philosophical standards, methodologies, and views. They questioned whether the universality to which philosophy aspired extended to women and applied to women's lives. They asked if and why women had been excluded from the philosophical tradition.

Their goal was to remedy the philosophical inadequacies occasioned by philosophy's silence about the way the world looks to women. In doing so, they made interventions that changed the course of philosophy. Illuminating the significance of experiences of limitation is one of feminism's prominent contributions to philosophy. Early feminist philosophers examined the limitations that pervaded their lives, and the lives of women generally, asking whether these resulted from alterable social arrangement or immutable biological destiny. Everywhere in the practice of philosophy women found traces of a bias that disregarded their interests and occluded their views. Subsequent feminist philosophical work has aimed at repairing the imbalances in traditional philosophical positions, paradigms, and methodologies. Feminists also have tried to remedy the narrowness in the usual ways of framing issues that philosophers customarily have considered important enough to deserve philosophical attention and work. To induce change, feminist philosophers craft approaches that draw upon the very limitations they encounter when attempting to pursue women's interests within philosophy. All of this work offers stimulating ideas to philosophers seeking to import the singular insights and different perspectives of other subordinated groups into contemporary philosophy to improve its inclusiveness and extend its scope.

Disabled people's philosophical interests find ready-made conveyances in several of feminist philosophy's signature themes. Women also have been dismayed by traditional metaethical analyses and moral and political theories that inflate typical male behaviors into paradigmatic moral actions and political principles. Although these theories have claimed to embrace everyone alike, feminist critiques show that their presumptions often exclude devalued kinds of people from fulfilling significant ethical, political, and social roles. Consequently, feminist philosophers have pioneered in exploring more inclusive alternative theories centering on the ethics and politics of trust and care, the virtues of dependency, and the establishment of moral interconnectedness among people who, like disabled and nondisabled people, do not occupy similar positions in life (see Mahowald in Silvers et al. 1998: 209–52).

Women have been alienated, unsatisfied, and unconvinced by traditional epistemology's paradigm of the isolated knower and by its detached, universalizing, and controlling approach to knowledge. Dissatisfaction with this kind of view prompts epistemological insights about the advantages of collaborative practices in acquiring knowledge; the importance of situating, contextualizing, and nuancing truths; and the possibilities for achieving objectivity without insisting that cognition works the same way for everyone.

Like women as a group, disabled people as a group have been denied and displaced because they do not comply with biological or social paradigms and therefore are dismissed as nothing more than anomalies. Oppressive practices have been defended with the rationale that "nature" has made women, and disabled people, physically, intellectually, and emotionally frail (Miles 1988). The interplay of biological and social identities – whether these be innate, imposed, or embraced – has become a subject of first-order importance in disability studies as well, and in philosophical ventures into disability studies.

Identities

Feminist philosophers have been by far the most numerous of philosophical writers on the topic of disability identity. They have offered a rich variety of sophisticated approaches to the question of how the sensibilities and histories of people with very different kinds of limitations can be collected into a cohesive philosophical account. Some write with the perspective of lifelong disability identity, others describe their transition into the world of disability, and still others write about disability without having experienced being disabled themselves.

In view of so many differences, feminist disability philosophy faces the challenge of constructing accounts of disability identity in which no one counts or is cited as a normal example. That is to say, no one should claim to speak as, or about, the typical disabled person. The enormous diversity of disabled people, and the overriding importance of reflecting all their differences in formulating disability theory, calls for sensitivity to nuance and context. The resulting scholarship can be of benefit to philosophy generally, and especially to feminist philosophy's efforts to reflect the situations of many different (kinds of) women. Approaches to reformulating feminist theory in response to differences displayed by disabled people may be extrapolated to illuminate the broader issues of difference beyond disability theory.

Unlike traditional ideas of race and sex, disability has always been understood to be a permeable classification. Some people have lifelong disabilities, some are newly so, and others have lived through periods in which they were disabled but now are not so. A large number of us should expect to become disabled later in our lives. And many of us find ourselves intimately involved in the lives of family members or friends who now are disabled or who face a future of disability. Further, as Eva Kittay reminds us, social policies that pertain to disabled people also affect their family members, friends, and professional caregivers (Kittay 1999; 2001). So feminist disability theory should recognize that disability affects the identities of many people beyond the 600 million worldwide who are themselves disabled (Herr, Gostin, and Koh 2003).

The inclusiveness of the various identity theories promoted in feminist philosophy is of preeminent and persistent concern to women with disabilities. Discussing whether women with disabilities can comfortably be feminists, Anita Silvers has asked whether feminism privileges the functional capabilities and social roles characteristic of "normal" women. She has found some feminist theories guilty of "magnifying these [functional capabilities of typical women] until they become standards of womanhood against which disabled women shrink into invisibility" (Silvers 1998).

Not all women are admitted to women's roles. Even in the most progressive contemporary societies, women with disabilities encounter opposition to their maintaining fertility, or accessing reproductive medical technology in achieving fertility, or even retaining custody of the children to whom they have given birth.

Karin Barron, who has engaged in extensive studies of the lives of young women with disabilities, observes that we place great value on the womanly art of caring for dependents, but the traditional dependent position of young women with disabilities prevents them from perfecting this art (Barron 1997). We should be clear that what precluded the young women Barron observed from being homemakers and mothers was not their lack of potential for executing these roles but, instead, their having been assigned to an alternative social position, one defined in terms of such dependence that their capacity to nurture others becomes virtually inconceivable.

Licia Carlson has shown that a gendered process of conceptualization even affects the diagnostic classification of mental retardation (Carlson 1998). Complex interconnections characterize the linked history of cognitive disability and gender oppression. Carlson's analysis should compel feminist philosophers to reconsider their understanding of cognitive disability. They should question whether they privilege their own modes and levels of cognition, just as they once questioned the privileged status of masculine ways of thinking (Carlson 2001).

They should, further, ask whether they have constructed feminist philosophizing in terms that make intellectual endeavor too central an undertaking. Eva Kittay makes this point penetrating, poignant, and personal when she describes the transformative insight occasioned by being told that her child is congenitally mentally retarded:

the worst anticipation was that her handicap involved her intellectual faculties . . . I was committed to a life of the mind . . . How was I to raise a daughter that would have no part of this? If my life took its meaning from thought, what kind of meaning would her life have? . . . [W]e already knew that we had learned something. That which we believed we valued, what we – I – thought was at the center of humanity – the capacity for thought for reason, was not it, not it at all.

(Kittay 1999: 150)

A somewhat similar dilemma may confront people who acquire a cognitive disability later in their lives. Kate Lindemann (Lindemann 2001) and Ann Davis (Davis 2004) both write about such experiences. Lindemann challenges the overspecialization of academic feminism. Her critique points to radical and profound ways in which feminist appreciation of the diverse workings of mind can enlarge philosophical inquiry. Feminist theory stands to gain by paying new attention to philosophical issues that should be rethought to reflect the situation of adults with brain injuries: personal identity, mind–body dualism, conceptions of the self, and philosophical psychology.

Recognizing that some individuals have invisible disabilities should remind us, Davis observes, of the extent to which we always are epistemologically dependent on people's disclosures of their own identities. Davis rejects the presumption that we can clearly separate self-imposed from inadvertent limitations. She proposes to weaken our faith in finding physical correlates of cognitive or psychological functioning, and by doing so constrain demands for public demonstration or third-party confirmation of functional limitations. Many cognitive and psychological differences cannot be documented by reference to physical anomalies. Yet, Davis rightly says, experiences of them are no less real.

These personalized experiences of limitation should not be discounted. Indeed, we need to recalibrate our sensibilities to honor the evidence of other people's senses. People's testimony about their own limitations and disabilities deserves respect even if uncorroborated by biological confirmation. Such experienced limitations may place the individual at activity-impeding, pain-inducing or life-threatening risk. We improperly burden people whose limitations we cannot directly see, and aren't sufficiently knowledgeable to appreciate, by constantly challenging them to prove their disabilities.

Embodiment and Disability

Feminist scholars have especially explored how corporeal or biological distinctiveness mediate daily activities so that self-identification and social experience act on, and become attuned to, each other. Feminist research such as that of Susan Sherwin (Sherwin 1992) shows that medicine has treated women like disabled people, intervening in their bodies to eliminate or discipline (to use Foucault's term) those parts that mark their identification with a purportedly inferior group. Medicine has, in particular, been dismissive of women's emotional lives. The history of how medicine has addressed disabled people is similar. It is a history of the repression and rejection of bodies and minds that diverge from the supposed paradigm or norm.

Enlightened by these parallels with their own history, some early disability studies theorists rejected medical practices directed at altering themselves. They characterized the medical model of disability as oppressive. They saw medicine itself as a coercive instrument that subordinates disabled people, not the least by inducing feelings of inadequacy and self-hate in them.

Just as biological sex, and the division of humans into two sexes, male and female, initially were taken as givens in feminist theory, so early disability studies scholars proposed to treat embodied impairments as givens, and disabilities as social interpretations of impairments. On such accounts, the properties of bodies are supposed to be presocial. Socially constructed interpretations and assessments of neutral corporeal properties consign people with various kinds of bodies to advantageous or detrimental social roles.

Recently, however, enhanced recognition of and reflection on the facts about sex and gender have complicated the picture for both feminist and disability studies. There are, for example, intersexed people, born with the biological markers of both female and male. A socially imposed allegiance to sexual dualism demands they be submitted to medical intervention that (usually through amputation) presses their bodies into one or the other sexual mold. Yet having a woman's body does not necessarily suit a person for feminine roles, nor do all those with men's bodies find themselves fitting comfortably into masculine roles. The materiality of sexual characteristics does not make them unbreachable constants. There are individuals who adapt with facility to gendered roles that are not traditional for their sex.

Others, however, find their sexual characteristics too restricting for the roles they adopt and consequently seek to change these elements of their bodies through surgical and chemical intervention. The way transgendered people see themselves in the world indicates that the body's limitations cannot always be discounted. While some people do not think their corporeal alteration is required to comfortably fit into opposite gendered roles, others seek medical intervention to facilitate their transgendering. Thus, the experiences of transgendered people suggest that there are circumstances in which altering one's body to better execute preferred social roles can be an affirming, rather than a degrading, choice.

These considerations show not only the error in supposing that the natural and social dimensions of embodiment should be cleanly dichotomized, but also the superficiality of thinking that we always should take bodies as they come. Extrapolating this insight to disability helps us to see the oversimplification in condemning medical transformations of the body as being expressions of self-hatred. There is no phenomenological firewall separating our awareness of our biological properties from our social experiences. How our own bodies feel to us is shaped by social discourse.

Our bodies' responses and responsiveness mark the social as well as the solitary aspects of our experiences. Nor is social practice isolated from, or prior to, materiality. An individual's impairments are no more neutral than her sexual characteristics are, for they mediate much of the content of her consciousness of the world with which she interacts. Performing major life functions such as mobilizing, hearing, seeing, communicating, and understanding are such intimate elements of the fabric of our experience that what we view as within our reach in the world around us – and thereby what we take as the objects of our ambition – arises out of the scope and facility of our biological functioning.

Considering whether the experiences of women are sufficiently acknowledged in disability studies, Susan Wendell points to maculinist influences on the field's standard model of disability (Wendell 1989; 1996). Wendell offers a refreshing look at the disability politics of promoting an image of the healthy disabled, which is similar to the feminist politics of excluding disabled women altogether in an effort to advance more appealing and powerful icons. She argues that the social model of disability, which until recently has been the unquestionable paradigm for disability studies, tends to obscure how disability is tied to illness (Wendell 2001).

Opponents of the medical model of disability urged the disentanglement of disability from illness, pointing out that many individuals with disabilities are as strong and capable of productivity as nondisabled people, and therefore should not be consigned to the limitations of the "sick" role (Amundson 1992). This model also promotes self-reliance over dependence and replaces trust with strategies for taking control. The point of such emphasis, Wendell proposes, is to affirm our own bodies by getting our political positions right. Yet it's a mistake to suppose that political correctness will make us feel right about our bodies or make our bodies feel right. Illness is itself disabling, and chronically ill individuals constitute a prominent part of the population considered to be disabled. Making healthy rather than ill disabled people paradigmatic of the disability category may obscure disabled people's differences. Worse, doing so may perpetuate our culture's devaluing of dependency and inflating of the importance of self-sufficiency. Wendell argues for reforming disability studies through a more inclusive feminist approach to disablement (Wendell 1996).

Wendell also proposes that feminist disability politics consider the implications of chronic illnesses that mark the unhealthy disabled's experience of embodiment (Wendell 2001). One such implication concerns the reaction to suffering. Many chronically ill people experience pain, fatigue, feebleness, and disorientation to a degree that forestalls productivity, saps self-sufficiency, and even may alienate them from their own bodies or minds. The social response in both mainstream society and disability circles is to support cures for chronic illnesses, as though the suffering caused by illnesses renders these conditions less important to how disabled individuals form their identities than other disabilities are claimed to be by advocates of disability pride.

A related implication concerns the reaction to emotional or psychiatric suffering. Unlike feminist literary scholars, who have been drawn to studies of madness, feminist philosophers have shown comparatively little interest in addressing the phenomena of neurodiversity.[1] Feminist and disability studies theorists who are undermining the domination of paradigms of youth and health should extend their efforts so as to liberate psychiatrically disabled people from the idealization of the neurotypical mind. Andrea Nicki (Nicki 2001) argues that feminists ordinarily do not think of anger and aggression as being valuable because they are emotions of competition rather than cooperation. But, Nicki thinks, these feelings may serve as morally valuable – because liberating – expressions for some neurodiverse people, especially for emotionally abused individuals.

Disruptive Embodiments

The negative meanings of disability may outweigh any moral respect autonomy or independence commands. Thus, even healthy people with disabilities are stigmatized because their embodied modes of functioning strike others as disruptive, however adeptly adaptive and independent they may be. Feminist and gender studies already have shown that atypical, and thereby transgressive, modes of functioning offer a rich resource for developing more adequate concepts of the materiality of human experience and of our personhood (Clare 1999). Yet, whether in illness or in health, the lives of disabled people largely have been ignored when these concepts are explored, to the detriment of the scholarship.

People who talk or read with their fingers, walk with their hands, recoil from other people's touches, or float through the day on waves of pain, often develop resilient and innovative approaches to fleshly function. Further, disabled people often are the first to incorporate adaptive technology into their lives. From machines that write (typewriters were invented to permit blind people to write) to machines that speak (computerized speech output was invented to permit blind people to read), disabled people have piloted the use of mechanical devices that now are integral to so many lives. Machines combine with fleshly effort to secure their basic capabilities: they hear with amplifiers, breath with respirators, mobilize in wheelchairs that they guard with more concern than the care they give their bodies.

A supportive intimacy of flesh with machine thus is a feature of many disabled people's lives. Although ordinarily considered unfit to participate in competitive schemes, their perceived cyborgian advantages also can lead to disabled people's being shunned. In a case that went to the United States Supreme Court, the Professional Golf Association (PGA) attempted to ban an otherwise qualified individual (professional golfer Casey Martin) because a physical anomaly prevented him from walking for a full eighteen holes. The PGA evoked a Frankensteinian slippery slope: if an anomalous golfer could mobilize with a golf cart while normal golfers walked, what would prevent a future contender, an upper limb amputee, from strapping on a bionic arm that can drive a golf ball more than two miles?

Lower leg amputees used to be banned from competitive running because their prostheses made them run too slowly. Now new materials and designs have created specially springy sports feet that permit their wearers, when very skilled and talented, to run faster than can be done with fleshly feet. A hit-and-run driver's victim, Dory Selinger now bicycles with a cleated peg replacing an amputated foot. Because it does not flex, the peg is more efficient at pedaling than a fleshly foot. Selinger's best time is only four seconds off the longstanding world record for "normal" racers (Squatrighlia 2001).

Given the fight the PGA put up to exclude a golf cart, however, it is hard to imagine that the Olympic Committee will welcome the Games being integrated by individuals whose impairments require machined parts more intimately connected to them than the golf cart is to Martin (Silvers and Wasserman 2001). Arguably, it is unfair to exclude racers with disabilities on the ground that crude prosthetics render them uncompetitive, and then also to exclude them when better prosthetics make them very highly competitive. Such a practice of limiting eligibility to typical competitors narrows social opportunity for whoever does not conform to the conventional rules of embodiment. And it is precisely because of the ease with which such rules of competition can be rigged to favor some modes of functioning over others that feminists rightly have been suspicious of invoking competitive models as the regulative basis of social justice (Pateman 1988).

Exclusions

In general, people with physical and mental disabilities have at least the experience of social exclusion in common. Indeed, experiences of exclusion loom large in many disabled people's lives (see Silvers et al. 1998: 35–53). This is a familiar story in the history of nondominant groups: presumptions about biological fitness often have engendered enforced segregation of parts of the population.

In this vein, courts have endorsed the separation of people identified as being of different races by advancing the rationale that segregating social schemes merely acknowledge "natural" affinities among people of the same race and "natural" antipathies among people of different races (Silvers and Stein 2002a and b). The supposed benefits of biological separatism have often been evoked to deny women employment that would place them in the company of men. For example, on May 29, 2001 a state law denying women the opportunity to be employed as bartenders was adjudged to be in compliance with the US constitution's guarantee of equal protection. The US Supreme Court held that there is no requirement that different kinds of people to be treated the same. The Court declared that women's presence "naturally" incites males to lust and violence, and that women typically do not have the physical ability to impose orderly behavior on the rowdy patrons of a bar (Silvers and Stein 2002a and b).

Similarly, people with disabilities have been characterized as being too biologically inferior to execute the responsibilities and thereby enjoy the privileges of citizenship, to work and play with nondisabled people, and to be permitted reproductive freedom. For example, people with mental retardation, cerebral palsy, and deafness all have had their children removed or have been sterilized by the state, have been denied access to public education on the ground their presence harmed other children, and been institutionalized to remove them from social contact with citizens who function in species-typical ways (as have native people, women, and gays and lesbians regularly during the past two centuries).

Two main approaches to addressing the social exclusion of disabled people have surfaced in philosophical literature that refers to them. Some writers focus first on procedural justice to open up disabled people's opportunities for social participation (Young 1990; Silvers et al. 1998; Anderson 1999). Others take the answer to lie first of all in distributive justice to increase provision of resources to the disabled (Kittay 1999; 2001; Nussbaum 2002). (Neither of these approaches denies the importance of the other's objectives; their differences are in part a matter of practical priorities, but also a matter of whether moral priority lies in agreement about what is right, or instead about what is good.)

Feminist thinkers have questioned the ability of traditional moral theories to take account of the needs and experiences of both care-receivers and caregivers (Kittay and Feder 2003). They have asked whether moral theories about independent individuals contracting freely with one another for mutual benefit give a plausible account of obligations to people who are, temporarily or permanently, profoundly dependent on others for physical, cognitive or emotional support. In her 2002 Tanner Lectures, Martha Nussbaum suggests that the source of political philosophy's ignoring the disabled lies in a foundational assumption of social contract theory. When she criticizes Rawls for casting citizens in the role of rough equals who relate reciprocally because they can benefit each other, Nussbaum pictures a theme found in feminist writers such as Annette Baier (1987) and Eva Kittay (1999). She says, "Instead of picturing one another as rough equals making a bargain, we may be better off thinking of one another as people with varying degrees of capacity and disability, in a variety of different relationships of interdependency with one another" (Nussbaum 2001: B9).

Construing reciprocal bargaining as the foundational and therefore paradigmatic social connection among citizens "effaces the more asymmetrical forms of dependency that human life contains: the need for care in infancy, extreme age, and periods of severe illness or a lifetime of severe disability," Nussbaum observes (Nussbaum 2001: B9).

Women, who do a very large proportion of society's caregiving, have their equality compromised unless the carer role is adequately acknowledged and compensated. They are more likely to remain in relationships with ill or disabled dependents – partners, children, or elders – than are men (Cohen 1996). Possibly, fewer men than women identify with caregiving as a self-affirming role. In this regard, the literature on ethics of care would benefit from recognizing that many disabled people, men as well as women, are caregivers to themselves and therefore are crucially positioned to understand how giving care best connects to receiving it.

The moral dimensions of how caregivers relate to dependent disabled individuals, as well as to disabled people who do not need extraordinary levels of care, deserve the attention of feminist and disability scholars. Joan Tronto finds the power imbalance between caregivers and care-receivers carries with it a potential for oppression. Helping relationships are voluntary, but asymmetrically so (Tronto 1993). Helpgivers choose how they will help, but helptakers cannot choose how they will be helped, for if one's connection to others is as the recipient of help, rejecting others' choice of proffered help leaves one solitary (Silvers 1995). Working out better understanding of the moral, political, and social dimensions of caregiving relationships is of crucial importance not only to disabled people themselves, but also to families who are as dependent on securing care for their dependent members as their dependents are on them.

Nussbaum rightly observes that we must preserve the self-respect of dependents without exploiting caregivers. The British feminist and disability scholar Jenny Morris (Morris 2001) argues that the solution lies in eliminating the presumptions about normate embodiment and normal functioning that now pervade the way caregivers and care-receivers usually are conceptualized by ethics of care. Morris appeals to the feminist principle that "anatomy is not destiny" as a reason for returning to the social model of disability, which she sees as the conceptualization of disability best suited for advocating and protecting disabled people's human rights.

Morris believes the social model makes it possible to talk about impairment in terms of personal experience rather than in a detached and medicalized way. Doing so enables disabled people to define their own bodies and their differences. She thinks that such self-authorization by receivers of care is a much-needed change in the way care ethics is thought about and practiced. The answer for her lies in thinking again about how feminist principles might recommend improvements in the ethics of care.

Conclusion

Morris' is just one of a growing number of calls upon feminist theory to reconsider disability through feminism's own lenses of liberation, self-affirmation, and inclusiveness. For example, Alison Kafer (2004) criticizes ecofeminism for assuming that authentic engagements with nature are possible only through purely natural immersion experiences that preclude using the assistive and prosthetic devices that distinguish some disabled people's embodiment. Ecofeminism remains bound by the traditional dualism of human artifice versus nature, Kafer argues, in part because of mistakenly equating species typical bodies with naturalness. Species typicality remains a presumption of feminism, she says. If she is right, feminist theory may benefit not only from applying its theoretical lenses to better understand disability, but also from polishing those lenses with the cloth of which disabled people's lives are made.

Note

1   "Neurodiverse" is a self-description favored by many of the advocacy and affinity groups organized around autism. Neurodiverse people include individuals with dyslexia, dyscalculia, dysgraphia, and dyspraxia, Asperger syndrome and similar conditions that are grouped under the broad category of "autism," Tourette syndrome and/or ritual or compulsive behavior, and others whose brains or neurotransmitters do not

operate neurotypically. "Neurodiversity" is the idea that such biologically based differences in the ways people perceive, conceptualize, and express themselves is beneficial to the human species. See Kathleen Seidel, http://www.neurodiversity.com/, for a list of famous historical figures who may have been neurodiverse and much other information, and see also "What Is Neurodiversity?" Coventry Neurodiversity Group, http://www.geocities.com/CapitolHill/7138/rights/neurodiversity.htm

Bibliography

Amundson, R. (1992) "Disability, Handicap, and the Environment," *Journal of Social Philosophy* 23 (1): 114–18.

Anderson, E. (1999) "What Is the Point of Equality," *Ethics* 109 (2): 287–337.

Baier, A. (1987) "The Need for More than Justice," in *Science, Morality, and Feminist Theory*, eds. M. Hanen and K. Neilson, Calgary: University of Calgary Press.

Barron, K. (1997) "The Bumpy Road To Womanhood," *Disability and Society* 1 (2): 223–39.

Bordo, S. (1993) *Unbearable Weight: Feminism, Western Culture, and the Body*, Berkeley: University of California Press.

Breslau, N. (1983) "Care of Disabled Children and Women's Time Use," *Medical Care* 216: 620–9.

Carlson, Licia (1998) "Mindful Subjects: Classification and Cognitive Disability," dissertation submitted in partial fulfillment of the requirements for the doctorate in philosophy, Toronto: University of Toronto.

—— (2001) "Cognitive Ableism and Disability Studies: Feminist Reflections on the History of Mental Retardation," *Hypatia: A Journal of Feminist Philosophy* 16 (4): 124–46.

Clare, E. (1999) *Exile and Pride: Disability, Queerness, and Liberation*, Boston, MA: South End Press.

Cohen, M.D. (1996) *Dirty Details: The Days and Nights of a Well Spouse*, Philadelphia, PA: Temple University Press.

Davis, Ann (2004) "Invisible Disability," unpublished manuscript.

Deegan, M.J. and Brooks, N. (1985) *Women and Disability: The Double Handicap*, New Brunswick, NJ: Transaction Press.

Hanna, W.J. and Rogovsky, E. (1991) "Women with Disabilities: Two Handicaps Plus," *Disability, Handicap and Society* 6 (1): 49–63.

Herr, S., Gostin, L., and Koh, H.H. (2003) *The Human Rights of Persons with Intellectual Disabilities*, Oxford: Oxford University Press.

Kafer, A. (2003) "Hiking Boots and Wheelchairs: Ecofeminism, the Body, and Physical Disability," unpublished paper.

Kallianes, V. and Rubenfeld, P. (1997) "Disabled Women and Reproductive Rights," *Disability and Society* 12 (2): 203–21.

Kittay, E. (1999) *Love's Labor: Essays on Women, Equality, and Dependency*, New York: Routledge.

—— (2001) "When Care Is Just and Justice Is Caring: The Case of the Care for the Mentally Retarded," *Public Culture* 13 (3): 557–79.

Kittay, E. and Feder, E. (2003) *The Subject of Care: Feminist Perspectives on Dependency*, Lanham, MD: Rowan and Littlefield.

Lindemann, Kate (2001) "Persons with Adult-Onset Head Injury: A Crucial Resource for Feminist Philosophers," *Hypatia: A Journal of Feminist Philosophy* 16 (4): 105–23.

Meekosha, H. and Pettman, J. (1991) "Beyond Category Politics," *Hecate* 17 (2): 75–92.

Miles, R. (1988) *A Women's History of the World*, London: Michael Joseph.

Morris, J. (1991) *Pride Against Prejudice*, Philadelphia, PA: New Society Publishers.

—— (1992) "Personal and Political: A Feminist Perspective on Researching Physical Disability," *Disability, Handicap and Society* 7 (2): 157–66.

—— (1993) *Independent Lives*, New York: Macmillan.

—— (2001) "Impairment and Disability: Constructing an Ethics of Care that Promotes Human Rights," *Hypatia: A Journal of Feminist Philosophy* 16 (4): 1–16.

Nicki, A. (2001) "The Abused Mind: Feminist Theory, Psychiatric Disability, and Trauma," *Hypatia: A Journal of Feminist Philosophy* 16 (4): 80–104.

Nussbaum, M. (2001) "The Enduring Significance of John Rawls," *The Chronicle of Higher Education* Section 2, B7–B9, July 20.

—— (2002) *Beyond the Social Contract*, Tanner Lectures in Human Values, delivered at Australian National University, Canberra, November 12–14.

Pateman, C. (1988) *The Sexual Contract*, Stanford, CA: Stanford University Press.

Sherwin, S. (1992) *No Longer Patient: Feminist Ethics and Health Care*, Philadelphia, PA: Temple University Press.

Silvers, A. (1995) "Reconciling Equality To Difference: Caring (F)or Justice For People With Disabilities," *Hypatia: A Journal of Feminist Philosophy*, 10 (1): 30–55.

Silvers, A. (1998) "Women and Disability," in *Blackwell's Companion to Feminist Philosophy*, eds. A. Jaggar and I.M. Young Oxford, Basil Blackwell.

Silvers, A. and Stein, M.A. (2002a) "From Plessy (1896) and Goesart (1948) to Cleburne (1986) and Garrett (2001): A Chill Wind From the Past Blows Equal Protection Away," in *Backlash Against the ADA: Interdisciplinary Perspectives*, ed. L. Krieger, Ann Arbor, University of Michigan Press.

—— (2002b) "Disability, Equal Protection, and the Supreme Court: Standing at the Crossroads of Progressive and Retrogressive Logic in Constitutional Classification," *The Michigan Journal of Law Reform*. Available at http://ssrn.com/abstract=307721

Silvers, A., and Wasserman, D. (2001) "Convention and Competence: Disability Rights in Sports," in *Ethics in Sport*, eds. W.J. Morgan, K.V. Meier, and A.J. Schneider, Champaign, IL: Human Kinetics.

Silvers, A., Wasserman, D., and Mahowald, M. (1998) *Disability, Difference, Discrimination: Perspectives on Justice in Bioethics and Public Policy*, Lanham, MD, Rowman and Littlefield.

Squatrighlia, D. (2001) "Triumph Out of Tragedy," *San Francisco Chronicle*, July 1, A19, A22.

Tronto, J. (1987) "Beyond Gender Difference to a Theory of Care," *Signs* 12 (4): 644–61.

—— (1993) *Moral Boundaries: A Political Argument for an Ethic of Care*, London: Routledge.

Wendell, S. (1989) "Toward A Feminist Theory of Disability," *Hypatia: A Journal of Feminist Philosophy* 4 (2): 104–24.

—— (1996) *The Rejected Body: Feminist Philosophical Reflections on Disability*, London: Routledge.

—— (2001) "Unhealthy Disabled: Treating Chronic Illnesses as Disabilities," *Hypatia: A Journal of Feminist Philosophy* 16 (4): 17–33.

Young, I.M. (1990) *Justice and the Politics of Difference*, Princeton, NJ: Princeton University Press.

—— (1997)"Asymmetrical Reciprocity: On Moral Respect, Wonder, and Enlarged Thought," *Constellations* 3 (3): 340–63.

Part III

Political Perspectives

Chapter 8

Feminist Political Philosophy

Nancy J. Hirschmann

Given the fact that one of the key projects of feminism has been to establish that "the personal is the political," it might seem that almost everything can be seen to fall under the term "feminist political philosophy," ranging from Plato to transexuality to domestic violence. As a result, an essay on this topic could take a wide variety of approaches, present a vast diversity of material (some of which has been covered by other essays in this volume), and still be incomplete.

Feminist political theorists and philosophers should, of course, be delighted by this "problem," for it attests to the strong impact that feminism has had on both the academic and the everyday understanding of politics. Whereas traditional political philosophy concerns itself primarily with concepts like justice, equality, and freedom, as well as with theories of the state and the legitimating principles of various forms of government, feminism has revealed the relations of power that pervade almost every social relation in which humans engage. Thus the family, the workplace, reproduction, and even sexual pleasure, are all considered "political" by feminist political philosophers.

Though feminist political philosophy within the academy arguably got its start by considering "women in western political thought," focusing on what canonical figures such as Plato, Aristotle, Rousseau, and Mill had to say about women,[1] feminist political philosophers quickly expanded the scope of their project into analyzing women's relation to the state and their exclusion from key political concepts such as "justice" and "equality" by considering the implications of their role in the family and their relationship to the state and law. Early Marxist, lesbian, and African-American feminist thinkers also considered the politics of women's economic position, sexuality, and racial inequality.[2] Whether having babies is a submission to "barbaric" oppression or a unique power offering a pacifist perspective on social relations;[3] whether working in capitalist society is a way for women to achieve equality to and recognition from men or is rather a sign of complicity in our continued subordination to the needs of capital;[4] whether heterosexuality is a valid expression of sexuality or the ultimate capitulation to patriarchy:[5] all of these questions were raised by early feminist philosophers and political theorists who were deeply affected by a new understanding of politics that included just about all aspects of our social lives.

Thus the topic of "feminist political philosophy" is extremely broad. Moreover, as a field it has much more porous disciplinary boundaries than do other branches of feminist philosophy. Works by feminist political theorists, sociologists, historians, anthropologists, and even psychologists are regularly included under the rubric of feminist political philosophy, are regularly taught in feminist political thought courses, and are found in feminist political philosophy texts. Indeed, it may be testimony to the interdisciplinary nature of this topic that I am the only contributor to this volume not to come from the discipline of philosophy.

Doing Politics with Gender

An early attempt to capture the diverse categories and ideals motivating feminist political philosophers was offered by Alison Jaggar, whose *Feminist Politics and Human Nature* postulated a typology of feminist political philosophers: liberal, radical, Marxist, and socialist.[6] Each of these types of feminism presented a different vision of feminist politics, a different vision of the political goals that feminists should value and pursue. Liberal feminism valued the primacy of individual women and their ability to compete with men, which required the elimination of the kinds of social barriers placed in the way of women's achievement: ending sexual discrimination in hiring and unequal pay for equal work; providing on-site childcare to enable mothers to combine paid work with family responsibilities; ensuring equal access to the legal system. Radical feminists, by contrast, argued that such things would merely shore up the very liberal-capitalist system that was subordinating women, and therefore women's "equality" within that system would never liberate women. Instead, the system itself had to be changed. Radical feminists engaged in a much wider variety of arguments, ranging from Shulamith Firestone's claim that technologized reproduction and the end to biological birth was the only way to end women's oppression, to arguments for matriarchal communities in which competition was abandoned in favor of nurturance and care.[7] But all radical feminists, as their name suggests, argued for a complete overhaul of the dominant political, economic, and social systems; and many take a rereading of women's biology as a fundamental starting point for such a reconstruction of society.[8]

Marxist feminists argued more limitedly for the end of one particular dominant system, namely capitalism. They operate from Engels' claim in "The Origin of Private Property and the Family" that women's oppression would end once capitalist oppression ended, a view endorsed by Rosa Luxemburg. But contemporary Marxist feminists such as Nancy Hartsock inverted that argument, claiming that capitalism could not be destroyed until women were liberated.[9] In other words, whereas Marxists argued that capitalism was the foundation for patriarchy, Marxist feminists argued that patriarchy was the foundation for capitalism. Socialist feminists, according to Jaggar, combined aspects of each of the other three lines of argument, to advocate for some state intervention in "private life," such as federally funded childcare centers, some liberal ideals of equality, and some radical notions of "difference." Starting with a Marxist understanding of human nature as socially produced, socialist feminists go beyond the realm of economics to a broader, more inclusive, and more complex identification of the sources of women's inequality and oppression in the family, culture, and social customs, the workplace, law, and institutions.

Jaggar showed how these four approaches to feminism, taken together, demonstrated that how we engaged in politics was itself political: that how one "did" feminism made a difference for how one understood gender relations and the social relations of reproduction, how one conceptualized what a "woman" was, and how one saw what a feminist world would need to look like. In other words, this diversity among feminist politics made what might roughly be called "methodology" particularly important to feminist political philosophy; because the issue of how one does philosophy, the kinds of questions that are seen as appropriate and legitimate, the way in which one goes about answering those questions, whose perspectives and experiences "count" in looking for evidence on which to base one's answers, are all centrally political for feminists. As feminist philosophers of science such as Sandra Harding argued, methodology is key to "dis-covering reality" and is thereby intensely political: power shapes our knowledge frameworks, what we consider to be "true," how we interpret and evaluate the experiences of different categories of people.[10]

This focus on "methodology" truly opened the floodgates of feminist political thought to include a variety of aspects of social life under the term "politics," including how best to do feminist theory. Jaggar's typology gave way to a different set of divisions in feminist political thought, based on a philosophy of method. Liberal positivist feminism stood by the assessment of women's oppression through the observation of empirical reality. Standpoint feminism problematized such approaches by arguing that women's experiences of oppression and particularly household and reproductive labor provided an epistemological foundation for reinterpreting social relations, that women's experience provided not just a different set of information or knowledge claims, but different ways of understanding reality and of evaluating knowledge claims. Postmodern feminism criticized standpoint theory as positing a new "truth," thereby replicating the Enlightenment ideals that oppressed women, and argued for a feminism that was open-ended and critical, and refused closure. These methodological debates and fissures gave way to an appreciation of new categories of identity that cohered with different ways of conducting feminist argumentation. Transgender and lesbian feminism instantiated this approach by establishing that the term "woman" itself, and the categories of "sex" and "gender" were themselves open-ended, undefinable, fluid, and porous.[11] African-American feminism, and works by other feminists of color, pointed out the racism, latent and overt, in these typologies that failed to attend to the intersections of gender with race, and argued that including race required feminists to understand gender oppression as interlocking and interdependent with other forms of oppression, all of which needed to be considered at the same time.[12] Postcolonial and "third world" feminism pointed out the inadequacy of western feminism of color by illustrating that not just racial categories, but culture and ethnicity needed to be considered along with gender which took on significantly different meanings in different cultural and political contexts.[13] These various approaches radically enlarged what could be counted as "political," to include things such as: how, and with whom, one had sex; who was entitled to call oneself a "woman," and by what criteria; how race and class were gendered, even as gender was raced and classed; how the body was presented and interpreted by medicine, social institutions, and the law. They also highlighted the political character of central issues of mainstream philosophy, such as what "truth" was and whether any claim to truth was itself a function of, or a claim to, power; whether "human nature" was definable or simply a fiction produced for purposes of oppressing women and racial and sexual minorities; the meaning of central categories of knowledge and ethics.

Thus, as I said at the opening of this essay, just about everything could be included under "feminist political thought." Many of these various aspects of feminist political philosophy have been covered by other essays in this book: "women in western political thought" has been dealt with by essays on the history of philosophy and feminist philosophers in history; issues of identity and the "subject" of feminism, namely what constitutes the category of woman, have been discussed in essays on lesbian feminism, race, and intersectionality; issues of difference and global justice have been encountered in essays on internationalism and postcolonialism. So in this essay, I will focus on two aspects that are fairly unique to feminist political philosophy: feminist approaches to political concepts, like justice, equality, freedom, and obligation; and theoretical approaches to practical political issues of particular significance to women, such as welfare reform, domestic violence, abortion, pornography, and sexual assault.

Feminist Concepts

The project of redefining the basic concepts of feminist political philosophy is one that really took off in the 1990s and the first decade of the twenty-first century.[14] But contemporary feminism began in the 1960s and 1970s as a political struggle for equality, and feminist philosophers quickly pointed out that the concept of equality itself needed to be analyzed, that it was a site of political struggle. The early second-wave feminist movement focused on demands for treatment the same as men, particularly in the arena of professional development. But the sexual division of labor in the home did not change very much in response to women's paid employment, resulting in women being burdened with a "double day." This led feminist philosophers to question what "equality" meant in the context of sexual and gender-role difference. Two dominant strains emerged, what was called "difference feminism" and "equity feminism." Equity feminism held to a liberal feminist line of equality as sameness: women were entitled to work in the same jobs as men, at the same pay, under the same conditions. To the extent that these conditions were themselves sexist, they needed to be changed for all workers. Accordingly, changes to the workplace such as on-site childcare, parental leave, and "flex-time" were demanded in the name of equality for women. Equality was conceived in terms of rights and procedures, though the fact that many procedures were biased against women required them to be altered. Difference feminism maintained that such "bias" was an inevitable function of the fact that the world was defined by and for men, and that women's attempt to "fit into" that male-defined framework would only perpetuate the problem of gender subordination; hence, for instance, few businesses actually provided childcare, and in those providing for parental leave, few fathers took advantage of it, because women retained primary responsibility for childcare and the family.[15] Thus difference feminists argued that the notion of equality promoted by equity feminists did not allow for women's differences from men to be considered. In order to recognize women's particularity, equality had to be focused on substance and outcome rather than procedure, and institutions and practices needed to be restructured to include the ideals historically associated with women's work, such as care, nurturance, and relationship. Thus care work needed to be recognized as socially valuable and afforded resources such as financial compensation and social recognition.[16]

The focus on women's difference and their attention to care also influenced arguments over other concepts, such as obligation. Whereas liberal social contract theory created an understanding of obligation based on consent, women's historical exclusion from politics meant that they were not afforded opportunities to consent to governments except indirectly through their husbands or fathers. Yet at the same time, women's obligations to care for children and husbands, to take responsibility for the home, were not ones that they had much choice about: they automatically adhered to their status as women. This led feminists ranging from Mary Astell to Carole Pateman to critique social contract ideology as hypocritical when it came to gender: as Mary Astell caustically asked, "If all men are born free, how is that that all women are born slaves?"[17]

Because of this requirement of caring labor, however, other feminists argued that women developed an understanding of the world that accounted for the needs that they fulfilled every day, of care, connection, and relationship. Carol Gilligan's work on moral psychology in the early 1980s posited that women tend to think about moral issues more in terms of relationships and connection than rules and rights; and this work gave rise to a flood of work in feminist philosophy on an "ethic of care" that implicitly challenged the notion of social contract obligations and asked whether women's historical obligations to care for children, which until the latter half of the twentieth century were often not the result of choice or contract, told us about the "nature" of social life and human relations.[18]

Similar shifts in how we think about the standard concepts in political philosophy occurred in relation to justice, attention to which became keen in the late 1980s to early 1990s. Numerous feminists took up critiques of John Rawls, the premier late-twentieth-century philosopher of justice, in part once again inspired by Gilligan's work on an ethic of care, for the "rights model" that she critiqued held great affinity with Rawls' work.[19] Seyla Benhabib argued that Rawls' focus on "the abstract other" led to an overly formalized theory of justice that ignored the importance of relationship and care, and posited a notion of "the concrete other" as more productive for feminists concerned with justice.[20] Marilyn Friedman critiqued as unrealistic Rawls' assumptions of rationality and impartiality in the original position, where individuals are expected to disregard their own particular needs and concerns, because humans were not capable of meeting the criteria Rawls set. These criteria were themselves unjust because they dismissed differences in values from the very start. Susan Okin's *Justice, Gender, and the Family* took on other "malestream" political philosophers in addition to Rawls, such as Alisdair MacIntyre and Michael Walzer, to argue that dominant understandings of justice ignored women's experiences of economic vulnerability, legal subordination, and social inferiority in the family. In order to have a logically consistent theory of justice, one had to theorize justice within the family as well as between the public and private sphere.[21]

Iris Young soon followed this analysis with *Justice and the Politics of Difference* to recognize that "difference" applies not just to gender but to race and class as well, and that women belonged to a variety of other social categories. Such a complicated understanding of difference demanded an equally complicated notion of justice, which needed to get beyond principles of distribution to understand the workings of domination. The location of differences within various cultural identities meant that justice should be thought of not as something that is owed to others, but as a series of relations between the groups that make up the social landscape. Justice thus required a rethinking of equality and the institution of participatory structures for political decision-making, and needed to be extended not only to the family, but to the workplace, schools, clubs, associations, all of which are considered, like the family, to be "private" and thus exempt from justice considerations.[22] And Eva Kittay critiqued Rawls' failure to recognize the fact that humans are inevitably dependent at various points in their lives; his idealization of the persons in the original position as fully functioning throughout their lives is unrealistic, and formalizes, rather than addresses, vulnerability and inequality not only of dependents, such as the ill, disabled, elderly, and children, but also of those who undertake the labor of caring for such dependents (often women, who perform such labor in families). It similarly fails to account for the asymmetry and inequality of the dependent and the caregiver within care relationships themselves. Dependents and dependency workers are thereby left out of justice considerations. Including them would produce a more comprehensive theory of justice that included considerations of care and dependency, that recognized the particular locations of individuals in relations of inequality and vulnerability, and that served all individuals more completely over the entire span of their lives.[23]

Justice has taken on a new and added dimension for feminists with the advent of "transitional" or "transnational justice" and "restorative justice" in mainstream political philosophy. Transitional justice refers to justice for victims of actions perpetrated by previous, and now overturned, regimes, such as South Africa; restorative justice refers to a goal of making restoration to victims, economically, emotionally, and socially, rather than simply punishing offenders. Though much of the mainstream work on transitional justice fails to acknowledge the ways in which gender factors into such notions, the injustices that have been committed against women throughout the world by overturned regimes have finally been brought to international attention. Issues such as rape being used as an act of war and women's forced impregnation as a weapon of nationalism have raised political philosophical issues of justice, power, and inequality.[24] And restorative justice has been of particular interest to feminist thinkers in the areas of domestic violence and sexual assault, where the traditional notions of retributive justice often fail women because imprisonment does little to address battered women's economic, emotional, health, or psychological needs.[25]

Finally, in the late 1990s and early twenty-first century, feminist philosophers have taken on freedom and autonomy, the most central of concepts to the modern era of political philosophy. Englightenment theory centered itself around a claim that individuals were naturally free, that governments could not intrude upon a zone of privacy within which individuals could order their lives and pursue their preferred goals and desires. Feminists argued that women's basic ability to accomplish this ideal of freedom was compromised by a variety of obvious identifiable obstacles such as laws prohibiting them from attending college or graduate school or owning property, abusive husbands, sexually discriminatory employment policies, and sexual predators. But it was also compromised by less visible obstacles, such as social norms that pressured women to want things that they "should" choose, such as marriage rather than being single, motherhood rather than career, heterosexuality rather than lesbianism. Rejecting the classically liberal "negative liberty" notion of freedom as "the absence of external barriers," feminists recognized that patriarchy has produced desires in women to want the very things that patriarchy needs them to choose. Such "oppressive socialization" caused women to think that they were acting freely and autonomously when in fact they were not thinking critically about their own wants and preferences and goals, and were not making choices self-consciously.[26] As Martha Nussbaum has argued, borrowing from Jon Elster and Amartya Sen, women's preferences have often been forced to adapt to the limited options available to them.[27]

Diana Meyers in particular resolved this by attention to a procedural account of autonomy. For her, autonomy says nothing about what choices we make, but only requires that we are able to, and actually do, reflect critically on our choices. Hence there can be no value judgments about the specific things I choose, there can only be observational judgments about whether I have reached those choices after adequate reflection on them. Similarly, Marilyn Friedman defines autonomy as "acting and living according to one's own choices, values, and identity within the constraints of what one regards as morally permissible." And Jennifer Nedelsky says that autonomy means "we feel that we are following an inner direction rather than merely responding to the pushes and pulls of our environment."[28] But even these procedural criteria are problematically value laden, echoing the essence of Enlightenment rationality of which feminist political philosophers have long been suspicious.[29] Meyers, for instance, says that one must not merely be able to offer reasons, but what guides those reasons must be "firm goals or moral views" rather than "feelings, intuitions, and arguments of the moment," for autonomy "expresses the true self." Meyers notes that "Since one must exercise control over one's life to be autonomous, autonomy is something that a person accomplishes, not something that happens to persons."[30]

The relationship between freedom and autonomy is a close, perhaps interdependent one; if there is such a thing as a "true" self, or "authentic" desire, then in order to determine what that might be, women must be freed from the multiple, intersecting, and overarching barriers that pervade patriarchal society. Yet the individualistic implications of such a move are problematic for feminist political philosophers who have built strong critiques of the masculinist bias of "abstract individualism." Thus, building off the work on obligation and care, feminists developed notions of "relational autonomy" which incorporated a notion of autonomy not as opposed to relations with others, but dependent on them. Arguing that we get the essence of autonomy, our ability to make choices, from relations with others, relational autonomy feminists incorporated a different understanding of what it meant to be a person: not separate and inherently distinct from all others, but connected through networks of relationships, through language, and through physical, material, psychological, and emotional interdependence.[31] Similarly, freedom theorists such as myself, Drucilla Cornell, and Wendy Brown have argued that freedom needs to be understood as a feature of socially situated beings, and that we need to attend to the relationship between the inner forces of desire and will and the external forces of social conditions. For women, this requires a recognition of the ways in which women's desires have both been historically constituted for them by men, "socially constructed" by patriarchal institutions, customs, and practices; and yet have also resisted such constitution and been pursued under conditions hostile to their expression.[32]

Practical Issues

The importance of the philosophical work done to rethink these central concepts of political philosophy stem, of course, from the concrete impact that our concepts have on women's lives. A theory of equality, justice, obligation or freedom that does not account for women's experiences will often result in practices and institutions that perpetuate women's subordination. An important dimension of feminist political philosophy is the connection between philosophical issues and practical issues, between philosophy and lived experience. The feminist phrase "the personal is polit-ical" has led feminist philosophers to take up the ethical and philosophical aspects of a wide variety of practical issues such as domestic violence, pornography, sexual assault, abortion, employment discrimination, sexual harassment, welfare, and a host of others. Consideration of the ethical and normative aspects of practical prob-lems women confront puts a contemporary and concrete face to the issues of power and politics that are discussed by feminist philosophers. I will consider three such issues here, to demonstrate the ways in which feminist political philosophy interacts with practical political issues: domestic violence, welfare, and Islamic veiling.

Domestic violence

For many years, the central question about victims of domestic violence was "Why don't they just leave?" Feminist research and activism on domestic violence in the fields of sociology, law, and political science, however, have revealed that women's choices to leave or stay are seriously constrained by the social circumstances that define the extremely limited options available to battered women: police who do not arrest and courts that do not convict abusers remove effective remedies normally available to men. Sexual discrimination in the workplace makes it more difficult for women to find and hold jobs that pay wages adequate to support single motherhood. When added to women's responsibility for childcare in the family, women's economic dependence on their batterers may make it impractical for women to exit abusive relationships. Social stigma and shame also inhibit women from seeking help. At the same time, the social construction of masculinity, which may push men toward violent behavior and push women to accept such behavior as normal, complicates political philosophical issues of freedom, choice, autonomy, and responsibility.[33]

These issues all raise important questions for feminist philosophy, centering on questions of equality, justice, freedom, and autonomy. For instance, if a battered woman chooses to remain with her abusive partner, should feminists simply assume that her choice is not a free one, and advocate mandatory arrest and prosecution laws? Or should feminists respect the choices that women make, even if those choices are not what we think is optimal? Autonomy philosophers, for instance, sometimes argue that decisions to accept subordination are a result of "oppressive socialization," but does this mean that others should force women to make differ-ent choices?

Legal theorist Martha Mahoney offers a different perspective; that rather than viewing agency as "being without oppression," we should view it as "acting for oneself under conditions of oppression." Under the former definition, the only reasonable option for a battered woman to take is to leave her abuser; otherwise, she is not an agent but a victim. Such a definition denies that she may have tried to leave several times and been thwarted; that she may have no place to go; that she does not trust the legal system to protect her; that she may still be oppressed economically (and racially if she is not white) by conditions that make it difficult, if not equally unattractive, to leave. By contrast, the latter definition would allow us to see the agency she expresses under conditions of coercion, such as when she strategically goes limp when her partner is beating her because doing so will minimize her injury. It would permit us to recognize that women's oppression is not merely caused by intimate assault but by a larger social context that makes such assault possible, even tacitly condoned, in sexist societies.

Other issues are revealed when domestic violence is examined by feminist political philosophers. Do mandatory arrest and prosecution laws take agency away from women, and continue to treat them as inferior, or do they empower women to prosecute their abusers and facilitate equal protection under the law?[34] Is justice served by sending abusers to jail when they are a woman's only means of economic support? Is the model of justice most appropriate to domestic violence the retributive model, or would the restorative model, which might allow for abusers' "reintegrative shaming" back into community, be more effective in ending intimate assault?[35] By engaging these theoretical issues, feminist political philosophers can help feminist activists and policy makers develop policies that are more attentive to the actual needs of domestic violence victims. But they can also help philosophers rethink their approaches to concepts like justice and freedom that can address, rather than perpetuating, masculine privilege and feminine oppression.

Beyond these specifically policy-oriented issues to which feminist political philosophers can contribute are the more complex and abstract notions of the social construction of femininity through the social practice of domestic violence. The ways in which women are "socially constructed" by patriarchy take on particular significance in domestic violence, for women's choices are immediately shaped by patriarchal power, ranging from their partners' violence to tacit endorsement of violence by police who do not arrest and courts that do not convict. This immediate shaping is made possible, however, by the way in which domestic violence manifests a deeper patriarchal construction of gender: the coherence between the personality of many batterers and masculine ideals of the romantic hero, yields the cultural acceptance of violence as a normal dimension of masculinity; the customary expectations that women will take primary responsibility for household and childcare and will not work for an independent income, which is seen as men's responsibility, gives men economic power in the relationship; feminine ideals of women's responsibility for relationships lead to women's internalizing blame for their victimization, and their resultant reluctance to seek assistance. Feminist political philosophy, by identifying the coherence of these psychological, supposedly personal features and the larger political landscape of gendered power reveal the inherently political dimension of domestic violence. The analysis of power can point in new directions for understanding, dealing with, and responding to intimate partner violence.

Welfare reform

Welfare reform in the United States and Europe in the closing decade of the twentieth century raised a variety of issues of particular interest to feminist political philosophers. How was public policy recognizing (or not) the socially necessary work that women did in caring for children and the elderly? What kinds of public policies are needed to address the inequities that the sexual division of labor produces? What do freedom and justice require of welfare policies? Welfare reform in the late twentieth century, feminists have argued, "disciplined" poor women into being certain kinds of people who are more easily managed by the state. Coercive policies such as requiring welfare recipients to work for wages, even if they are mothers of young children, and "bridefare" (paying recipients more if they marry), as well as time limits for receipt of benefits are all promoted under the rubric of "empowering" women by ending their "dependency" on state subsidies. Such rhetoric ignores the reality that women's only alternative is often dependency on an individual man, and that turning to state welfare programs is often a key move for women to gain independence and self-sufficiency, much like Social Security. Subjecting to philosophical scrutiny the ways in which "dependency" and "independence" are defined and used by politicians reveals deep inconsistencies motivated by sexism, racism, and classism. By focusing on the ethical dilemmas that women face every day, feminist philosophers can help create public policies that adhere to ethical standards that recognize women's humanity and the importance of care work to our social and economic landscape.[36]

Some feminists have argued that appreciating the philosophical significance of care and dependency would help us understand its political significance and thereby point to better public policies from a feminist perspective. Eva Kittay's work on nested dependencies, for instance, along with Martha Fineman's argument about "inevitable" and "derivative dependency," demonstrated that dependency is a natural part of the human condition, and that how societies structure their institutions and practices to respond to this need is a political and ethical decision, rather than a function of women's "nature" or "difference."[37] Yet the fact that women have historically tended to perform the labor required by dependency meant that women not only became the people who could see its importance and necessity, but also were thereby excluded from the policy arena. Thus, they were hit doubly hard: recognizing its importance, they could not abandon care work, but by suffering the burdens of its performance, they were de facto excluded from the arenas in which decisions about such activities were made. Including women would not only enable public recognition of the work that women did, and thus result in more humane policies that allowed everyone to be cared for (including the care workers) but could also change our ethical systems to include care as a central moral concept.[38] These feminists urge a social policy that recognizes the importance of women's work raising children, providing direct subsidies to women who are performing this labor, as well as a wider range of resources to provide support for caregivers, such as social security and health care.

All feminists agree that women's responsibilities for childcare puts them at an economic disadvantage: because such work is not financially compensated, mothers must rely on others to support them financially, usually a husband, making them vulnerable to abuse and exploitation within marriage, as well as to poverty if they are abandoned. And all agree that welfare reform, motivated by conservative ideology and politics, has produced bad policies for women by forcing them to take low-wage jobs, sometimes at the cost of foregoing advanced education, and always at the cost of caring for their children. Yet some argue that wage work is nevertheless the answer to single mothers' poverty, even if the conservative agenda of exploitative workfare is not. For instance, Heidi Hartmann has argued that expanding the Earned Income Tax Credit would do more to raise single families out of poverty than any other economic reform. Others argue that provision of greater employment supports, such as high-quality on-site childcare, advanced education and employment training, transportation subsidies, universal health coverage, and increased wages would all make mothers' wage employment a workable solution to poverty. Still others argue for a reconfiguration of public policy's understanding of "the family" to allow for a wider variety of interpersonal and childcare arrangements, moving away from the single-mother model that is a distorted holdover from the patriarchal nuclear family. But all of these feminists believe that any truly coherent welfare policy must require women to combine wage work with care work, and moreover that this is the most consistent feminist position, for it is the only one to challenge the "maternalist presumption," the assumption that women must be the ones to take care of children.[39]

Whether wage work or care work should be the primary focus of welfare, however, feminist political philosophers show that welfare is not merely an issue for public policy scholars, but that it raises central issues of the social construction of gender, class, and race through state institutions, law, and public policy; the coherence between economic and gender inequality; the ways in which the discourse of public and private is inconsistently, even hypocritically, shaped by such inequality; and that the ways in which we understand the human condition, whether isolated and independent or dependent and interconnected, are fundamentally and ineluctably gendered.

Islamic veiling

Islamic veiling might seem to raise central questions of autonomy, if we assume that women who veil are either not free to do otherwise, or have "chosen" the veil in a context of extremely limited options and strong cultural coercion. While casting the issues in such terms reflects a certain reality of the practice in certain cultural contexts, however, it simultaneously raises issues over the west's control of philosophic discourse over what counts as autonomy in the evaluation of social practices. In the wake of September 11, 2001, for instance, Afghan women's burqa became a potent symbol in US political discourse of the supposed "backwardness" and repressiveness of militant Islamic states. Women's freedom was offered as a contributory justification for the attacks on Afghanistan, and their severe form of Islamic veiling was seen as the visible proof of women's oppression. Yet it is arguably the case that the problem was not the burqa itself – a form of dress that some women continue to adopt and defend today – but the lack of women's participation in defining the customs that determine whether to wear it, and more significantly their restrictions from leaving their houses unaccompanied by men. By focusing on the form of dress itself, westerners may misdirect their focus and as a result misinterpret the problems of autonomy faced by Islamic women.

The veil has had a long and varied history in Islam and in east–west relations, and it is often seen as a broad symbol of cultural difference between "east" and "west." Feminist political philosophy can direct our attention less to the policy itself – veiling or not – than to the circumstances leading to the policy, whether women participated in formulating it, and the power that women have in society to participate in an ongoing way in the construction of "culture" and "cultural practices." For instance, the shah of Iran's policy of mandatory deveiling might have been no less coercive than the mandatory reveiling following the Iranian revolution. Similarly, Leila Ahmed argues that the first people in contemporary movements to use the veil as a symbol of resistance were Egyptian university women who viewed their actions as nationalist gestures.[40] Such actions fulfill many political philosophers' criteria of autonomy, such as those of Diana Meyers, discussed earlier in this essay.

To the degree to which they appear to do so, however, western feminists are confronted with a paradoxical dilemma: how to follow a key feminist principle of respecting and supporting women's choice when the substance of that choice is not one that western feminists agree with. In other words, "freedom" and "autonomy" are not about making the choices that cohere with western feminist ideals of what "the good life for women" should be like, but must attend to contextual understandings of choice: the choices that are available, the structural constraints on such availability, the economic, political, and historical reasons for women's choices, the self-understandings of gender and ethnic identity, the role of religion in cultural identity, and the ways in which cultures are defined historically and politically against a backdrop of western colonialism and imperialism.

This does not mean that western feminists cannot engage in cross-cultural critique, though it sometimes seems that way. Cross-cultural "dialogue" has too often involved the west's insistence that things be done "our way," leaving nonwestern women feeling unheard. However, western efforts to be sensitive to such power dimensions have sometimes resulted in an unproductive backlash; in particular, the postmodern emphasis on respecting "cultural difference" has sometimes given way to a helpless relativism that prevents western women from supporting and assisting nonwestern women. It even betrays its own form of racism and ethnocentrism, by exoticizing the other as so different as to be incomprehensible. But this ironically undercuts feminist efforts. As Martha Nussbaum points out, "a community is not a mysterious organic unity by a plurality of people standing in different relations of power to one another;"[41] rather, power is generally defined along lines of gender and class. Hence the "cultures" that western feminists claim they must respect are often defined by and for men at the expense of indigenous women who are denied access to the resources, such as education, that would enable them to challenge and change culture. Philosopher Uma Narayan thus argues that this sort of non-engagement expresses a "cultural essentialism," where nonwestern women take "particular values and practices . . . as central or definitive of a particular 'culture,'" such as when western feminists decry sati as emblematic of Indian culture.[42] Such cultural essentialism is tied, albeit perhaps unintentionally on the part of western feminists, to gender essentialism, for it denies differences among women within specific cultures, a diversity that western feminists insist characterizes women in western society. Such essentialism ironically disables feminist critique of patriarchy, by preventing us from seeing that "culture" is often selectively defined by local patriarchs to include practices most supportive of their own power over women, such as the Taliban's interpretation of the Qur'an to beat women for showing their ankles below the burqa, while at the same time ignoring other equally important aspects of cultural history that balance women's power.[43]

Feminist political philosophy can thereby highlight the complexity of power relations entailed in feminist efforts to confront cultural difference in a world of gender inequality. This in turn can show us that western feminists must engage in the effort to be more fully informed about women's situations in other cultures, to offer their views on women's rights, equality, and freedom with self-critical aware-ness that they may not have a complete understanding of other cultures, and a willingness to listen attentively to the views of women in the indigenous cultures, including those women's views of western cultures. Thus, in terms of veiling, western feminists would need to read the work of Islamic feminists, examine the history of British efforts to associate the veil with eastern barbarism, as well as local efforts to end veiling, the historical role of veiling in nationalist movements, the wide diversity of the practice in different societies in different historical epochs, the critical interpretation various feminists have offered of the Qur'an's position on the veil, and ethnographic accounts of the views of women who wear the veil.[44]

The Future of Feminist Political Philosophy

Future directions that feminist political philosophy may take are as myriad as those it has taken in the past. For instance, there are many more practical issues that feminist political philosophers take up than I have discussed here. Rape and sexual assault, for instance, offer a variety of philosophical issues about power and women's status as human subjects. Issues of bodily integrity and boundaries, the normalization of force in heterosexual relations, and "compulsory heterosexuality" all suggest that rape and sexual assault are not perverse aberrations, but rather on a continuum of "normal" sexual relations. Works on this topic range from feminist jurisprudential arguments about changes in the judicial system of evidentiary requirements and what they suggest about changing understandings of rape victims' status as human subjects, to Susan Brison's attempt to theorize her own sexual assault to develop a philosophical understanding of the self, to Sharon Marcus' theory of a rape "script," as a strategy of intervention into and ending sexual assault.[45]

Pornography is probably the most common topic that people think of when they think of feminism, largely due to the attention garnered by Catharine MacKinnon's writings and legislative efforts to ban pornography, and it is likely to continue to capture feminist attention for some time to come. MacKinnon critiques pornography because it prevents women from defining their own sexuality from their own perspective; in her view pornography is the pinnacle of patriarchal thought that reduces women to body parts and objects of male pleasure, that denies the subjectivity of women, and that justifies violence and brutality against women under the myth that women like it. On the other side, so-called first-amendment feminists like Nadine Strossen argue that censorship of pornography does more harm than good: it leads to the suppression of feminist literature and the closing of feminist bookstores; it infantilizes women by presuming boundaries on the legitimate expression of women's sexuality, denying pornography as a potentially healthy expression of the new forms of women's sexuality; and it dehumanizes men by assuming that men cannot differentiate between a magazine or film and their actual relations with real women. Philosophical questions of autonomy are thereby raised by this issue: what does it mean for women to choose to participate in pornography, or to be consumers of it, for instance? Are they victims of false consciousness, or can pornography help some women achieve their personal sexual fulfillment? The future direction of feminist political philosophy will necessarily include this kind of practice-oriented theorizing and philosophizing, for women's experience holds an apparently endless cache of philosophical problems.[46]

Many more practical issues have been tackled by feminist political philosophers and will continue to be in the future. Similarly, other political concepts, such as democracy, authority, community, and power, are of keen interest to feminist philosophers.[47] And these obviously dovetail with practice-oriented feminist political philosophy. Hence the particular interest in participatory democracy among feminist political philosophers is welcome at a time when the world's apparent fixation on "democratization" in eastern Europe, Africa, and the Middle East echoes uncomfortably with the patriarchal imperialism of the past.[48] Other forward-looking trends in feminist political philosophy reinvoke its past. As interest in the major canonical figures continues to grow, with an entire series in feminist political philosophy devoted to "rereading the canon," feminists are also redefining the canon by rediscovering forgotten females such as Mary Astell, Mary Wollstonecraft, as well as exploring the feminist potential in twentieth-century women such as Hannah Arendt.[49]

The mention of Hannah Arendt, who was hardly what one would call a feminist, as the subject of feminist recuperation raises an issue that current and future feminist political philosophers must confront, namely: how diverse can and should feminist political thought be, and still be "feminist?" For instance, should feminist political philosophy dedicate attention to topics such as "pro-life feminism?" Should – or can – feminism be reconciled with Christian conservativism or Islamic fundamentalism? Since feminism is committed to women's self-determination, then it should be committed to respect for a diversity of views that fall outside the traditional feminist political line. But at the same time, because such views are traditionally at odds with standard feminist ideals, they may contradict and undermine the feminism that supports them. Though some feminists reject such views as self-contradictory, their advocates passionately believe that feminism requires their inclusion. Such claims often hide sexism under the label of feminism, such as the argument that, since feminism is committed to equality, it must oppose abortion on the grounds that it oppresses fetuses; such a position, by presuming what must be proved, namely the humanity of the fetus, gives the fetus unilateral precedence over women's humanity. But that does not mean that "pro-life" arguments cannot be developed that are more plausibly grounded in recognizably feminist ideals – such as the recognition that women are often forced into abortion by poverty or sexist treatment by their sexual partners, leading feminists to support greater resources for indigent pregnant women.[50]

Thus it is clear that the range of feminist political philosophy outstrips any other branch of feminist philosophy in its scope, method, approach, conceptualization, and subject matter. Moreover, the centrality of politics to feminism ensures that the future of feminist political philosophy will confront issues, concerns, and questions that many of today's feminists may not even be able to imagine, just as transgenderism was not imagined by (most) feminist political philosophers of the 1970s. Indeed, if feminist politics succeed in achieving gender equality throughout the world, feminist political philosophy may of necessity "wither away," giving way to a new, unimagined project prophesized by some contemporary "post-feminist" philosophers. That is unlikely to happen in the lifetimes of the readers of this volume, or even of our daughters and granddaughters; but it is a vision that can and should guide feminist political philosophers as we develop arguments, analyses, and projects toward a better future for women.

Notes

1   See Susan Moller Okin, *Women in Western Political Thought* (Princeton, NJ: Princeton University Press, 1979); Lorenne M.G. Clark and Lynda Lange, eds., *The Sexism of Social and Political Theory: Women and Reproduction from Plato to Nietzsche* (Toronto: University of Toronto Press, 1979); Jean Bethke Elshtain, *Public Man, Private Woman: Women in Social and Political Thought* (Princeton, NJ: Princeton University Press, 1981).
2   Lydia Sargent, ed., *Women and Revolution: A Discussion of the Unhappy Marriage of*

Marxism and Feminism (Boston, MA: South End Press, 1981); The Quest Collective, *Building Feminist Theory: Essays from Quest* (New York: Longman Publishers, 1981); bell hooks, *Ain't I a Woman? Black Women and Feminism* (Boston, MA: South End Press, 1981); Audrey Lorde, *Sister Outsider: Essays and Speeches* (Trumansburg, NY: Crossing Press, 1984); Jeffner Allen, ed., *Lesbian Philosophies and Cultures* (Albany: SUNY Press, 1990).

3 Shulamith Firestone, *The Dialectic of Sex* (London: The Women's Press, 1979); Sara Ruddick, *Maternal Thinking: Toward a Politics of Peace* (Boston, MA: Beacon Press, 1989).

4 Jane Mansbridge, *Why We Lost the ERA* (Chicago: University of Chicago Press, 1986); Heidi Hartmann, "The Unhappy Marriage of Marxism and Feminism," in Sargent, *Women and Revolution*; Ann Ferguson, *Blood at the Root: Motherhood, Sexuality and Male Dominance* (London: Pandora, 1989); Catherine A. MacKinnon, *Sexual Harrassment of Working Women: A Case of Sex Discrimination* (New Haven, CT: Yale University Press, 1979).

5 Adrienne Rich, "Compulsory Heterosexuality and Lesbian Existence," *Signs: Journal of Women in Culture and Society* 5 (Summer 1980), pp. 631–60.

6 Alison Jaggar, *Feminist Politics and Human Nature* (Totowa, NJ: Rowman and Allenheld, 1983).

7 Firestone, *Dialectic*; Adrienne Rich, "Notes for a Magazine: What Does Separatism Mean?" *Sinister Wisdom* 18 (Fall 1981), pp. 83–91.

8 Mary Daly, *Gyn/Ecology: The Metaethics of Radical Feminism* (Boston, MA: Beacon Press, 1978).

9 Nancy C.M. Hartsock, *Money, Sex, and Power: Developing a Feminist Historical Materialism* (Boston, MA: Northeastern University Press, 1984); also Sargent, *Women and Revolution*.

10 Sandra Harding and Merrill B. Hintikka, eds., *Discovering Reality: Feminist Perspectives on Epistemology, Metaphysics, Methodology and Philosophy of Science* (Dordrecht: Kluwer Academic Publishers, 1983).

11 Though she would most likely reject being categorized as a lesbian or transgender feminist, that literature has its origins in Judith Butler's, *Gender Trouble: Feminism and the Subversion of Identity* (London: Routledge, 1990). See also Butler's *Bodies that Matter: On the Discursive Limits of "Sex"* (London: Routledge, 1993). Similarly, because of her attraction across the disciplines it is not often recognized that Butler is a philosopher by training, though again I am not sure that she would "own" such an identity. See also Jacqueline Zita, *Body Talk: Philosophical Reflections on Sex and Gender* (New York: Columbia University Press, 1998), Shane Phelan, *Sexual Strangers: Gays, Lesbians, and Dilemmas of Citizenship* (Philadelphia, PA: Temple University Press, 2001), and Claudia Card, ed., *Adventures in Lesbian Philosophy* (Bloomington: Indiana University Press, 1994).

12 Cherríe Moraga and Gloria Anzaldúa, eds., *This Bridge Called My Back: Writings by Radical Women of Color*, foreword by Toni Cade Bambara (Watertown, MA: Persephone Press, 1981); Patricia Hill Collins, *Black Feminist Thought: Knowledge, Consciousness, and the Politics of Empowerment*, 2nd edn (New York: Routledge, 2000); Kimberlé Crenshaw, "Mapping the Margins: Intersectionality, Identity Politics, and Violence Against Women of Color," *Stanford Law Review* 43 (1991), 1241–99.

13 Chandra Talpade Mohanty, Ann Russo, Lourdes Torres, eds., *Third World Women and the Politics of Feminism* (Bloomington: Indiana University Press, 1991).

14 Nancy J. Hirschmann and Christine DiStefano, eds., *Revisioning the Political: Feminist Reconstructions of Traditional Concepts in Western Political Theory* (Boulder, CO: Westview

Press, 1996); Mary Lyndon Shanley and Uma Narayan, *Reconstructing Political Thought: Feminist Perspectives* (University Park: Pennsylvania State University Press, 1996).

15 Arlie Russell Hochschild, *The Time Bind: When Work Becomes Home and Home Becomes Work* (New York: Henry Holt, 2001).

16 Christine Littleton, "Reconstructing Sexual Equality," *California Law Review* 75 (1987), pp. 1279–337; Joan Scott, *Gender and the Politics of History*, 2nd edn (New York: Columbia University Press, 1999); Elizabeth Wolgast, *Equality and the Rights of Women* (Ithaca, NY: Cornell University Press, 1980).

17 Mary Astell, "Reflections upon Marriage," in *Political Writings*, ed. Patricia Springborg (New York: Cambridge University Press, 1996); Carole Pateman, *The Sexual Contract* (Stanford, CA: Stanford University Press, 1988).

18 See for instance Eva Kittay and Diana Meyers, *Women and Moral Theory* (Lanham, MD: Rowman and Littlefield, 1987) for various feminist philosophical discussions of Gilligan and the Gilligan–Kohlberg controversy. On care as a critique of contract theory, see Virginia Held, "Non-contractual Society: A Feminist View," in *Feminism and Community*, eds. Penny Weiss and Marilyn Friedman (Philadelphia, PA: Temple University Press, 1995) and Nancy J. Hirschmann, *Rethinking Obligation: A Feminist Method for Political Theory* (Ithaca, NY: Cornell University Press, 1992).

19 Indeed, Lawrence Kohlberg, whose work was the focus of Gilligan's critique, explicitly allied his theory of moral development with Rawls' theory of justice. See Lawrence Kohlberg, "Justice as Reversibility," in *Philosophy, Politics and Society*, ed. Peter Laslett and James Fishkin, 5th series (Oxford: Blackwell, 1984).

20 Seyla Benhabib, "The Generalized and the Concrete Other: The Kohlberg–Gilligan Controversy and Feminist Theory," in Kittay and Meyers, *Women and Moral Theory*; Marilyn Friedman, *What Are Friends For? Feminist Perspectives on Personal Relationships and Moral Theory* (Ithaca, NY: Cornell University Press, 1993). See also Martha Nussbaum, "Rawls and Feminism," in *The Cambridge Companion to Rawls*, ed. Samuel Freeman (New York: Cambridge University Press, 2003).

21 Susan Moller Okin, *Justice, Gender and the Family* (New York: Basic Books, 1989).

22 Iris Marion Young, *Justice and the Politics of Difference* (Princeton, NJ: Princeton University Press, 1990).

23 Eva Feder Kittay, *Love's Labor: Essays on Women, Equality and Dependency* (New York: Routledge, 1999).

24 Alexandra Stiglmayer, ed., *Mass Rape: The War against Women in Bosnia-Herzegovina*, tr. Marion Faber (Lincoln: University of Nebraska Press 1994); Julie Mostov, "'Our Women/Their Women:' Symbolic Boundaries, Territorial Markers, and Violence in the Balkans," *Peace and Change* 20 (4) (1995), pp. 515–29; Caren Kaplan, Norma Alarcón, and Minoo Moallem, eds., *Between Woman and Nation: Nationalisms, Transnational Feminisms, and the State* (Durham, NC: Duke University Press, 1999).

25 Heather Strang and John Braithwaite, eds., *Restorative Justice and Family Violence* (Cambridge: Cambridge University Press, 2002).

26 Paul Benson, "Autonomy and Oppressive Socialization," *Social Theory and Practice* 17 (13) (1991), pp. 385–408.

27 Martha Nussbaum, *Women and Human Development: The Capabilities Approach* (Cambridge: Cambridge University Press, 2001); Amartya Sen, *Development as Freedom* (New York: Anchor, 2000); Jon Elster, *Sour Grapes: Studies in the Subversion of Rationality* (Cambridge: Cambridge University Press, 1985).

28 Marilyn Friedman, "Autonomy, Social Disruption, and Women," in *Relational*

Autonomy: Feminist Perspectives on Autonomy, Agency, and the Social Self, eds. Catriona Mackenzie and Natalie Stoljar (New York: Oxford University Press, 2000), p. 37; Jennifer Nedelsky, "Reconceiving Autonomy: Sources, Thoughts and Possibilities," *Yale Journal of Law and Feminism* 1 (1) (1989), p. 24. See also Marilyn Friedman, *Autonomy, Gender, Politics* (New York: Oxford University Press, 2002).

29 See for instance Louise M. Antony and Charlotte Witt, eds., *A Mind of One's Own: Feminist Essays on Reason and Objectivity* (Boulder, CO: Westview Press, 1993).

30 Diana T. Meyers, *Self, Society, and Personal Choice* (New York: Columbia University Press, 1989), p. 51; Diana T. Meyers, "Personal Autonomy and the Paradox of Feminine Socialization," *The Journal of Philosophy* 84 (11) (1987), p. 619. Paul Benson makes a similar argument that Meyers' definition of autonomy in terms of "autonomy competence . . . has much in common with the traditional acounts of freedom" ("Feminist Second Thoughts about Free Agency" *Hypatia: A Journal of Feminist Philosophy* 5 (3) (1990), p. 63). However, he himself deploys notions of rationality in his own conception of "critical competence;" see Benson, "Autonomy and Oppressive Socialization," pp. 398–9.

31 See Mackenzie and Stoljar, *Relational Autonomy*; also Susan J. Brison, "Outliving Oneself: Trauma, Memory, and Personal Identity," in *Feminists Rethink the Self*, eds. Diana Tietjens Meyers, Alison Jaggar, and Virginia Held (Boulder, CO: Westview Press, 1997), who argued that her ability to gain autonomy after a violent sexual assault and attempt on her life depended intimately on the help of others.

32 Nancy J. Hirschmann, *The Subject of Liberty: Toward a Feminist Theory of Freedom* (Princeton, NJ: Princeton University Press, 2003); Drucilla Cornell, *At the Heart of Freedom* (Princeton, NJ: Princeton University Press, 1998); Wendy Brown, *States of Injury: Power and Freedom in Late Modernity* (Princeton, NJ: Princeton University Press, 1995).

33 See for instance Lenore Walker, *Battered Women* (New York: Harper, 1980); Kathleen Ferraro, "Cops, Courts, and Woman Battering," in *Violence Against Women: The Bloody Footprints*, eds. Pauline Bart and Elizabeth Moran (Newbury Park, CA: Sage, 1993); Alyce D. LaViolette and Ola W. Barnett, *It Could Happen to Anyone: Why Battered Women Stay* (Newbury Park, CA: Sage, 2000).

34 Alisa Smith, "Its My Decision, Isn't It? A Research Note on Battered Women's Perceptions of Mandatory Intervention Laws," *Violence Against Women* 6 (12) (2000): 1384–1402.

35 Strang and Braithwaite, *Restorative Justice*.

36 Hirschmann, *The Subject of Liberty*, chapter 5.

37 Kittay, *Love's Labor*; Martha Albertson Fineman, *The Autonomy Myth: A Theory of Dependency* (New York: The New Press, 2004). See also Eva Feder Kittay and Ellen K. Feder, eds., *The Subject of Care: Feminist Perspectives on Dependency* (Lanham, MD: Rowman and Littlefield, 2002).

38 On the concept of "doulia," or care for the caregiver, see Kittay, *Love's Labor*, and Eva Feder Kittay, "From Welfare to a Public Ethic of Care," in *Women and Welfare: Theory and Practice in the United States and Europe*, eds. Nancy J. Hirschmann and Ulrike Liebert (New Brunswick, NJ: Rutgers University Press, 2001); for care as a moral and political concept, see Joan Tronto, "Care as a Political Concept," in Hirschmann and DiStefano, *Revisioning the Political*.

39 See Heidi Hartmann and Hsiao-ye Yi, "The Rhetoric and Reality of Welfare Reform," Marcia K. Meyers and Janet C. Gornick, "Gendering Welfare State Variation: Income Transfers, Employment Supports, and Family Poverty," Lisa Dodson, "At the Kitchen

Table: Poor Women Making Social Policy," and Joyce Marie Mushaben, "Challenging the Maternalist Presumption: The Gender Politics of Welfare Reform in Germany and the United States," all in Hirschmann and Liebert, *Women and Welfare.*

40 Leila Ahmed, *Women and Gender in Islam: The Historical Roots of a Modern Debate* (New Haven, CT: Yale University Press, 1992), p. 220. Also, Shahin Gerami, "The Role, Place, and Power of Middle-Class Women in the Islamic Republic," in *Identity Politics and Women: Cultural Reassertions and Feminisms in International Perspective*, ed. Valentine M. Moghadam (Boulder, CO: Westview Press, 1994), p. 332.

41 Martha Nussbaum, "Judging Other Cultures: The Case of Female Genital Mutilation," in *Sex and Social Justice* (New York: Oxford University Press, 1999), p. 126.

42 Uma Narayan, "Essence of Culture and a Sense of History: A Feminist Critique of Cultural Essentialism," *Hypatia: A Journal of Feminist Philosophy* 13 (2) (1998), p. 95.

43 Ibid. See also Schutte, this volume; and Seyla Benhabib, *The Claims of Culture: Equality and Diversity in the Global Era* (Princeton, NJ: Princeton University Press, 2002).

44 See for instance Fatima Mernissi, *The Veil and the Male Elite: A Feminist Interpretation of Women's Rights in Islam* (Reading, MA: Addison-Wesley, 1991); Leila Abu-Lughod, *Veiled Sentiments: Honor and Poetry in a Bedouin Society* (Berkeley: University of California Press, 1986); Ahmed, *Women and Gender in Islam*; Arlene Elowe MacLeod, *Accommodating Protest: Working Women, the New Veiling, and Change in Cairo* (New York: Columbia University Press, 1991).

45 Jennifer Temkin, ed. *Rape and the Criminal Justice System* (Brookfield, VT: Aldershot Publishers, 1995); Susan Brison, *Aftermath: Violence and the Remaking of a Self* (Princeton, NJ: Princeton University Press, 2003); Sharon Marcus, "Fighting Bodies, Fighting Words: A Theory and Politics of Rape Prevention," in *Feminists Theorize the Political*, eds. Judith Butler and Joan W. Scott (New York: Routledge, 1992).

46 Catharine A. MacKinnon, *Feminism Unmodified: Discourses on Life and Law* (Cambridge, MA: Harvard University Press, 1987), and *Only Words* (Cambridge, MA: Harvard University Press 1993); Nadine Strossen, *Defending Pornography: Free Speech, Sex, and the Fight for Women's Rights* (New York: New York University Press, 2000).

47 See, for instance, Anne Phillips, *Engendering Democracy* (University Park: Pennsylvania State University Press, 1991) on democracy; Kathleen B. Jones, *Compassionate Authority: Democracy and the Representation of Women* (New York: Routledge, 1993) on authority; Friedman, *What Are Friends For?* on community; Amy Allen, *The Power of Feminist Theory: Domination, Resistance, Solidarity* (Boulder, CO: Westview Press, 1999) on power.

48 Benhabib, *The Claims of Culture*; Drucilla Cornell, *Defending Ideals: War, Democracy, and Political Struggles* (New York: Routledge, 2004); Zillah Eisenstein, *Against Empire: Feminisms, Racism, and the West* (New York: Zed Books, 2004).

49 Patricia Springborg, *Mary Astell: Theorist of Freedom from Domination* (Cambridge: Cambridge University Press, 2005); Maria J. Falco, ed., *Feminist Interpretations of Mary Wollstonecraft* (University Park: Pennsylvania State University Press, 1996); Bonnie Honig, ed., *Feminist Interpretations of Hannah Arendt* (University Park: Pennsylvania State University Press, 1995); and other volumes in the Re-reading the Canon series (series editor Nancy Tuana).

50 The former argument is made by Jane Thomas Bailey, "Feminism 101: A Primer for Pro-Life Persons," and the latter by Frederica Mathewes-Green, "The Bitter Price of Choice," both in *Prolife Feminism: Yesterday and Today*, eds. Mary Crane Derr, Linda Naranjo-Huebl, and Rachel MacNair (New York: Sulzburger and Graham Publishing, 1995).

Chapter 9

Postcolonial Feminisms
Genealogies and Recent Directions

Ofelia Schutte

This chapter aims at providing a conceptually clear introductory understanding of postcolonial feminisms by (a) analyzing the relationship of postcolonial feminisms to postcolonial studies and (b) reviewing selected contributions by major postcolonial feminist critics.

Defining Postcolonial Feminisms

One way to approach the range of meanings corresponding to the concept of *postcolonial feminism* is to engage in a comparable exercise with respect to the meaning of *postcolonial*. While common sense may have it that the term refers to the state of affairs (or possibly states of mind) denoting something positioned *after* or *beyond colonialism*, such a definition fails to capture the sense of critical resistance to colonialism evoked by a considerable part of postcolonial studies. The condition of something occurring *after* colonialism is better invoked by the term *postcoloniality*. But, as feminist postcolonial critic Gayatri Chakravorty Spivak observes, it does not make sense to speak about postcoloniality without speaking about decolonization (Spivak 1997: 469). She is basically referring to the historically existing conjunction, in the formerly colonized world, of both postcoloniality and what has been variously termed *recolonization* or *neocolonialism*. Similarly, Jacqui Alexander and Chandra Talpade Mohanty document how global capitalism is involved in contemporary "processes of recolonization" of the Third World (Alexander and Mohanty 1997: xxi). Historically and politically, the question cannot be suppressed as to whether the end of the explicitly colonial period in the occupation of colonized countries has indeed resulted in their freedom from the effects of colonizing forces.

Postcolonial studies and theory are born from the awareness of the apparent inability of colonialism to truly exit world history. Historically, some of the political and economic aspects of this problem have been the object of Marxist analysis and its critique of capitalism (after Lenin, the critique of western imperialism). The appearance of new schools of thought in the west such as Foucauldian discourse analysis and Derridean deconstruction provided a fresh approach to the problem of recolonization, although there is no doubt that one of postcolonial theory's points of inspiration was Gramsci's notion of cultural hegemony. With a focus on culture and with access to the tools of poststructuralist analysis, important intellectual work could now be done to expose and deconstruct the codification of colonial discourse and its aftermath throughout the globe.

The object of postcolonial studies is the analysis of colonial(ist) discourses from a critical point of view, with the aim of exposing and disentangling the power such discursive practices may still hold over our thoughts and imaginations, as well as over the legitimation of knowledge and public policy. But it is also the meticulous historical study of colonial periods across the world with special regard for the effects borne by native populations, the forms of struggle and resistance occurring against colonialism, and the local efforts to overcome colonialist legacies in subsequent contexts. In terms of what it includes and excludes (Shohat 1992), within this broad and still strongly contested field postcolonial feminisms highlight both issues pertaining to and affecting women as well as the role of women in leading efforts toward decolonization, e.g., through activist movements. Postcolonial feminists have also used their academic expertise to expose the conceptual frameworks and ideologies used by colonial institutions in the exercise of colonialist-masculinist dominance.

In the United States there appears to be a considerable link between postcolonial feminisms and "women-of-color" feminisms, attributable partly to the fact that there is some overlap in the experiences of women whose intellectual formation is indebted to both groups (Mohanty 1997: 7). "We were not born women of color, but became women of color here [as US immigrants]" (Alexander and Mohanty 1997: xiv). Still, it is important for analytical purposes to maintain a distinction between *women of color*, *Third World feminists*, and *postcolonial feminists*. In general, "women of color" and "Third World women" function as relatively coherent and established categories, even if after the disappearance of the Soviet Union "Third World" is often used tentatively for lack of a better term (Mohanty 1991: 74–5; 1997: 7). No uniform terminology is used by feminists with respect to "Third World," "postcolonial," "transnational," or "global South" feminisms. It is best to check how these terms appear in particular contexts.

As distinct from *Third World*, *postcolonial* is often considered a privileged term insofar as it arises primarily from intellectual debates in the US academy and is thereby removed from the difficulties of living and working in postcolonial societies. Many postcolonial intellectuals in the United States insist, however, that they do have intellectual and literary counterparts in the Third World even though there is no strict parallelism in their respective activities (Spivak 1990: 67; Appiah 1997: 432–6). Regardless of the insufficiently circumscribed nature of the term *postcolonial*, it is a marker that opens up important theoretical and practical questions, at least in the US intellectual milieu, which may then point to the works of Africans, Asians, Latin Americans, and indigenous peoples on issues and problems that previously may have met with indifference, neglect, or intolerance by mainstream scholars. In addition, increasing numbers of people of mixed race and/or hybrid and marginalized cultures offer new perspectives through which postcolonial conditions can be analyzed and assessed. With the increasing globalization of academic knowledge and practices, postcolonial studies acts as a necessary internal critical voice challenging both the imbalance of power existing between north and south, east and west and the representational practices that frame the less powerful of these in the discursive codes of those with the greater power.

Postcolonial feminisms often expand the literary and historical bases of classic postcolonial studies to cover a wider range of topics, including women's activism in Third World and transnational (including migratory) contexts. Some make the case for setting the agenda for postcolonial feminisms also in the Third World (not just in the west) and for including empirically based work in the social sciences (Rajan and Park 2000: 53). Others place the critique of racism at the forefront of the postcolonial feminist agenda (Lewis and Mills 2003: 3). My own approach is to understand feminist postcolonial critique as a practice calling into question cultural, gender, and racial binaries, among others, while keeping the focus of critique on the politics of colonialism and the ethics of interpreting and acting on its consequences.

US-based Postcolonial Theory

By all accounts, Edward Said's *Orientalism* constitutes the founding text of US-based postcolonial studies. Said broke ground when he introduced the concept of Orientalism as a discursive formation framing the representation of east/west issues within the legitimated discourse of Eurocentric knowledge. He used elements from Foucault's analysis of discourse to challenge how the discursive formation of Orientalism reproduces itself from one generation to the next not only to describe what the Orient is supposed to be about but, more importantly, to legitimate such descriptions as conveying "authority over the Orient" (Said 1979: 3). In Said's words, "Orientalism is a style of thought based upon an ontological and epistemological distinction made between 'the Orient' and (most of the time) 'the Occident'" (ibid.: 2). Moreover, the acceptance of this distinction between east and west is used as the "starting point for elaborate theories" and "political accounts concerning the Orient, its people, customs, 'mind,' destiny, and so on" (ibid.: 2–3). It is easy to see why even this most general description of Said's theoretical point of departure would be appealing to feminists from the Third World, particularly those working in the US academy. In a parallel manner, Chandra Talpade Mohanty discloses the colonizing stance taken toward Third World women in some western feminist scholarship. She shifts the primary distinction from west/east (or Occidentalism/Orientalism) to western/non-western in her well-known essay, "Under Western Eyes: Feminist Scholarship and Colonial Discourses," first published in the mid-1980s (Mohanty 1991: 51–80). Similarly, as we will examine below, Uma Narayan (1997) extends Said's and Mohanty's critical frameworks to a specific analysis of one western feminist text insofar as it misrepresents the position of women in India and the incidence of *sati* (widow immolation). More recently, Mohanty criticizes the US women's studies curriculum insofar as it fails to incorporate courses that break with standard notions of center and margin embedded in western national ideologies (Mohanty 2003a: 238–45).

The postcolonial critique is not simply a matter of analyzing how a western text misrepresents an eastern object of knowledge or scientific investigation. Said himself alerted his readers to the applicability of his approach to Third World readers and scholars. "For readers in the so-called Third World," he notes, "my hope is to illustrate the formidable structure of colonial domination and, specifically for formerly colonized peoples, the dangers and temptation of employing this structure upon themselves or upon others" (Said 1979: 25). Spivak takes this consideration one step further. She characterizes as "epistemic violence" the structure of colonial education in India that produced literate subjects (Spivak 1990: 126; for other examples of what she calls "epistemic violence" see Spivak 1988: 280–7). A comparable structure of epistemic dominance – if not violence – affects the global politics of knowledge to this day. For this reason, postcolonial critique is just as relevant in the Third World as it is in the west even if the specific contexts framing such relevance differ. Moreover, Said suggests that "if this stimulates a new kind of dealing with the Orient, indeed if it eliminates the 'Orient' and 'Occident' altogether, then we shall have advanced a little in the process of what Raymond Williams has called the 'unlearning' of 'the inherent dominative mode'" (Said 1979: 28). I emphasize this point because it is a common misunderstanding of postcolonial theory that it relies on an east/west binary or that it is an oppositional anti-western stance precluding its practitioners from engaging constructively with scholarship produced in the west. If such approaches exist in particular cases, they should not be taken to represent postcolonial theory as a whole. A large plurality of postcolonial intellectuals rejects the notion of cultural purity (Appiah 1997: 439; Minh-ha, 1997: 415; Spivak 1997: 478). Moreover, it seems evident that Said's stance involves the deconstruction of the binary rather than its replication. Challenging its replication is precisely one of the motivating factors for the postcolonial critique.

In his 1994 "Afterword" to *Orientalism* Said explicitly states he opposes essentialism and fundamentalism (Said 1994: 347). He sees identities as both unstable and constructed and cultures as "hybrid and heterogeneous" (ibid.: 348). Moreover, he sees cultures and civilizations as "so interrelated and interdependent as to beggar any unitary or simply delineated description of their individuality" (ibid.). "Western civilization," he claims, is largely an "ideological fiction" (ibid.). Addressing the frequent confusion (also prevalent among many western feminists) of identifying postcolonialism with postmodernism, he clarifies that while postmodernism is "still" largely Eurocentric and ahistorical, postcolonialism continues to be engaged in "grand narratives of emancipation" (ibid.: 348–9; cf. Appiah 1997). Here Said asserts postcolonialism's divergence from Lyotard's postmodern approach to knowledge, which Lyotard himself characterized as foregoing such metanarratives of emancipation (Lyotard 1984). Moreover, despite Said's acknowledged debt to Foucault, in *Orientalism* Said had already distanced himself from Foucault with regard to the views on the writer as an individual subject. "I do believe in the determining imprint of individual writers upon the otherwise anonymous collective body of texts constituting a discursive formation like Orientalism" (Said 1979: 23). Similar discrepancies between postmodernism (as generally understood) and postcolonialism involve varying degrees of disagreement among postcolonial critics regarding the acceptance of "humanism" and "universals." Because not all postcolonial theorists agree on a common view, it cannot be assumed that postcolonialism as such involves a rejection of humanism or of the notion of universals. If and when there is an acceptance of such notions, however, the notions will be significantly reformulated and qualified on the basis of a resolute critique of class, racial, sexual, gender, and other forms of dominance, along with a deconstruction of Eurocentrism.

Feminist Postcolonial Criticism

In western feminist philosophy, Uma Narayan's critique of Mary Daly's representation of *sati* in India is a classic example of postcolonial critique. Narayan has drawn important attention to the matter of discourse and representation, in a move toward making western feminist philosophy more aware of how its discourse represents not only Third World women but Third World traditions and cultures. As she explains clearly, the choice of using Daly's treatment of *sati* is motivated by the concern that the colonialist stance uncovered here is not limited to Daly but in fact is quite common in western feminist discourse (Narayan 1997: 43). Moreover, she points to the fact that her critical approach to the colonialist stance is "indebted to the critiques of mainstream western feminism generated by feminists of color" (ibid.: 44). But she shifts the focus of attention from the more usual concern about how women of color have been excluded or marginalized to the discursive modality of how they have been *included* (ibid.: 44–5). This shift of emphasis is very important since colonialism and its descendants operate using a flawed logic of inclusion. Colonized subjects are drawn into the discursive space of colonialism, but on the colonialists' terms, primarily. Changing the criteria that govern the discourses of inclusion and their representation of Third World cultures and traditions is therefore imperative to transforming and overcoming the "colonialist stance." Like Said and Spivak, Narayan points out that such a stance can also affect the discourse of Third World people and is in no sense limited to the repertoire of a western speaker (ibid.: 45). This last point makes plenty of sense, since colonialist education of Third World people and its elite sectors involved acculturation into the colonialist vision of the world. I would note that in a successful colonizing venture there is a simultaneous process both in the home colonizing country and in its colonies to prepare future subjects for a one-world mentality in which the values of the colonizing power are presented as most appealing, reasonable, and universal. As Gauri Viswanathan interestingly shows, the teaching of British literature in nineteenth-century India promoted the notion of an idealized British subject, diverting attention from the realities of local experience (Viswanathan 1997: 121–8).

Narayan defines a "colonialist representation" as "one that replicates problematic aspects of western representations of Third-World nations and communities, aspects that have their roots in the history of colonization" (Narayan 1997: 45). Her perspective is forward-looking, insofar as the purpose of the analysis is to overcome the "obstacles" such representations pose "for feminists to form 'communities of resistance' across boundaries of class, ethnicity, race, and national background" (ibid.). This important point emphasizes the commonalities that may be shared by feminists of different races and backgrounds as a consequence of postcolonial critique. Moreover, Narayan demonstrates that the realities of Third World women and cultures are not homogeneous and in fact that traditions in the Third World both develop across time and respond to a multiplicity of internal as well as external interests. Her analysis, which relies strongly on the expertise of Third World women scholars, clearly undermines any easy racial or ethnic characterization of colonizers and colonized.

In literary studies Said, along with Homi Bhabha and Gayatri Spivak, appear to have produced the most significant theoretical triad in the field. Bhabha is more likely to emphasize, among other things, the presence of the "other" in the west, showing that the construction of the west cannot be disassociated from or understood without the colonizers' relations with their "others" (Bhabha 1994: 46–52). Spivak has built on a deconstructive Derridean framework to address not only literary theory but issues of women in India and in the Third World. She often includes a critique of western feminism as it influences non-western women in elite international agencies. Spivak argues on behalf of identifying a writer's or critic's location in terms of culture, class, politics, and ideology.

Spivak has held persistently that issues of feminism and the so-called Third World are directly relevant to important debates in the west from which they are routinely excluded (Spivak 1993: 384). She adopts a transnational deconstructive feminism as a method for criticizing a global patriarchal capitalism. In *A Critique of Postcolonial Reason* Spivak expands on her notion of "transnational literacy" (Spivak 1999: 357). She means that as educators we must resist dominant and mainstream ideologies, and engage critically with the unjust effects of neoliberal economics. Specifically, she asks that those of us who migrate to the United States from Third World countries point to the unjust effects of the global political economy on our countries of origin and that we resist becoming accomplices of this global order.

Interestingly, despite the feminist use of a Marxist critique of neo-liberal capitalism Spivak does not propose a collectivist ethics. Rather, she advocates a postcolonial ethics of individual responsibility and accountability aimed at addressing and strategically reversing as much as possible our potential or actual complicity with "consolidat[ing] the new unification for international capital" (Spivak 1999: 357, 374, 381, 384).

Spivak's multiple critiques have elicited both support and disagreements. Some Third World women activists openly dispute her earlier claim that the subaltern cannot speak (Spivak 1988) because the hegemonic system of representation is already foreclosed to the subaltern speaker. But subaltern studies theorist John Beverley points out that there can be at least two senses of subalternity (Beverley 1999: 103–4). In one sense, the subaltern could mean the most marginal of people, or those whose political project is to oppose hegemonic power. In another sense, subalternity means precisely that which cannot be represented in discourse insofar as the rules of representation functioning in discourse necessarily exclude it. Beverley claims that Spivak builds her case on the second sense, retaining this sense without contradiction (ibid.) in what one may note is a rather complex and multi-focused discussion. Although considered abstractly the second sense is tautological, Spivak's deconstructive critique is innovative in showing the extent to which both legal and popular gender ideologies, whether foreign or domestic, have failed to represent the female subaltern in India (Spivak 1988: 303–8). As I see it, the second sense sustains Spivak's political strategy of calling attention to the epistemic violence suffered by rural indigenous women and others whose relative separation or independence from dominant cultures either condemns them not to be heard by the dominant culture or to be heard only to the extent that their discourse can be assimilated into it. In the latter case, by her logic, they also fail to be heard insofar as they are subaltern. More recently, Spivak has used the notion of "the new subaltern" (that is, "new" after the post-Soviet capitalist consolidation of the neo-liberal global economy) in order to highlight global capitalism's current interests in appropriating rural indigenous women's labor and knowledge for capitalist profit (Spivak 2000). Spivak argues that we must assume moral responsibility in acknowledging the degree to which any of us is ideologically or materially complicit with the power and goals of neo-liberal global capitalism, even as we claim to deconstruct, criticize, or oppose it. The expectation of accountability should make us more aware of injustices and more motivated to alert others about them.

With regard to the specific project of decolonizing western feminism itself, a "founding" text in the United States is Chandra Talpade Mohanty's "Under Western Eyes," reprinted numerous times since its first publication in the mid-1980s. Mohanty's essay has become canonical in the field of women's studies in the context of teaching Third World feminisms. Its greatest appeal lies in the fact that it shatters the monolithic and ahistorical western construct of "Third World women," much as Said's *Orientalism* shattered the hegemonous discourse on the Orient. In so doing, it validates the voices of Third World women in US universities, one of whose constant challenges is to overcome the cultural stereotypes projected on them not only by the culture at large but also by some western feminist ideology (see also Spivak 1986). Mohanty uses historically specific scholarship to show Third World women as agents resisting colonialism and helping to craft their own futures through collective grass-roots action. Another important strength of her work is to link the critique of colonialism in the academy with knowledge regarding activist feminist projects in the Third World, or what Inderpal Grewal and Caren Kaplan call "transnational feminist practices" (Grewal and Kaplan 1994). In addition Mohanty has collaborated with other Third World feminists and feminists of color, producing path-breaking co-edited anthologies advancing the field of postcolonial feminism in the US (Mohanty et al. 1991; Alexander and Mohanty 1997).

Mohanty has recently published a clarification and revision of views expressed in "Under Western Eyes" (Mohanty 2003a: 221–52; also published in Mohanty 2003b). She clarifies that she is neither a cultural relativist nor a postmodernist. She shifts her critical emphasis to an analysis of the current impact of global capitalism on Third World women (Mohanty 2003a: 222–6, 230). This is not a surprising move for someone committed to the thesis of the recolonizing effects of capitalism. Her terminology also shifts somewhat to the use of First World/North, Third World/South, and One-Third/Two-Thirds World (ibid.: 226–8). She argues that activist movements against the global economy need to align themselves with feminist activism (and conversely) as the top priority for helping Third World women at the beginning of the twenty-first century. Mohanty is optimistic in arguing explicitly for decolonization, as the subtitle of her book, "Decolonizing theory, practicing solidarity," indicates. She asserts her indebtedness both to Fanon and to "feminist anticolonial, anticapitalist struggle," adding that "decolonization . . . can only be achieved through 'self-reflexive collective practice'" (ibid.: 7–8). In contrast, Spivak is skeptical of claims regarding decolonization, pointing out not only the political effects of recolonization in the global economy but the discursive difficulty of speaking of one without the other. But they both target similar problems insofar as they highlight the exploitative effects of global capitalism on the lives of large numbers of Third World women.

The question of integrating the local and the global from an ethical perspective is a crucial feminist issue. Postcolonial studies can help situate local and even national issues in the west within a global transnational context, showing how policies that appear to be only national in scope are in fact transnational, such as the increasing privatization of formerly publicly funded education, health services, and caregiving services such as day care for children of working mothers.

What about Latin American Postcolonialism?

A perplexing aspect of US postcolonial theory is the ambiguous place awarded to Latin America. The relative marginality with which Latin America is treated could be explained in part by the fact that some view the year 1947 (when South Asia becomes independent from the British empire) as the initiating date for the postcolonial period (Schwarz 2000: 1). The problem with this view is that as the British Empire was receding in power, the hegemony of the United States as a world power was on the ascendant. The Spanish–American War of 1898 which included the appropriation of Puerto Rico's territory, among other conquests, demonstrated the United States' exercise of hegemonic power over locations to its south, a situation ongoing up to the present time. To fully come to grips with colonialism, its legacies, and discourses, the north–south axis of dominance should be included along with the west–east axis. Even if the term *postcolonial* is not used to characterize it, there is a significant legacy of political and intellectual movements – among them Latin-American Marxisms, dependency theory, the theology of liberation, the philosophies of liberation, feminist, Afro-Latin, and indigenous movements – throughout twentieth-century Latin America whose point was to resist what was often called *neocolonialism*. These movements and debates, rooted concretely in Latin American political history (not in the US academy), often engaged comparable questions to those highlighted by transnational postcolonial intellectuals (Schutte 1993: 123–91). These grass-roots oriented and liberationist intellectual approaches emphasize solidarity toward the indigenous people of the Americas, North and South, thereby helping to reverse the ideological effects of the European-based conquest of the hemisphere (Schutte 2002b). Moreover, the effects of US continental westward expansion and the long history of south to north migration indicate a link between Latina/o critical studies and border studies in the United States and a Latin American postcolonial perspective (Saldívar 1991; Mignolo 2000; Fusco 2001). Chicana feminist Gloria Anzaldúa depicts the complexity of these issues when she remarks that the once-indigenous land of her ancestors has survived much ill-use by occupying countries, such as Spain and the United States (Anzaldúa 1987: 90–1). Others have called attention to the exploitative conditions under which many Latin American female migrants undertake domestic and care work in the United States (Chang 2000) and the lack of public support and resources provided by neo-liberal capitalist policies with respect to women caught in these or similarly vulnerable conditions whether in their traditional societies or in transnational migratory situations (Schutte 2002a: 148–55).

One outstanding South American critic who does not identify as postcolonial but whose work bears some analogies with Spivak's is the Chilean feminist cultural critic and essayist Nelly Richard. Richard takes up the poststructural path of cultural critique, rooting it in Chile's history from the "post-golpe" (the coup against elected president Salvador Allende in 1973) to the present day. She explicitly assumes a feminist voice, radicalizing both feminist theory and cultural studies – the first by representing feminism as a destabilizing force more or less linked to the concept of an active and subversive "feminine"; the second by defining "cultural critique" as a destabilizing move within/toward the ruling discursive system of "signs" that at any one time obtains hegemony over a given framework of cultural representations (Richard 1993: 11–29). Richard celebrates parody and transgression as ways to destabilize the genders (ibid.: 65–76) and to invert the traditional model/copy and original/translation binaries affecting Eurocentric notions of cultural authenticity (Richard 1995: 219–22). In addition to producing her own theoretical work, Richard edits Chile's *Revista de crítica cultural*, a highly sophisticated journal of avant-garde cultural studies and politics.

Latin American postcolonial critique needs to be recognized if feminist theory and political philosophy are to uphold the vision of an inclusive, ongoing revitalizing process for radically democratizing social change. Current trends in postcolonial feminist theory point to its continuing expansion along new political, geographical, and transdisciplinary boundaries. This means that the study of Latin American women's diverse contributions to knowledge holds in reserve new and important material for the current and future development of postcolonial feminist studies.

References

Alexander, M.J. and Mohanty, C.T., eds. (1997) *Feminist Genealogies, Colonial Legacies, Democratic Futures*, New York: Routledge.

Anzaldúa, G. (1987) *Borderlands/La Frontera: The New Mestiza*, San Francisco: Aunt Lute.

Appiah, K.A. (1997) "Is the 'Post-' in 'postcolonial' the 'Post-' in 'postmodern'?" in *Dangerous Liaisons: Gender, Nation, and Postcolonial Perspectives*, eds. A. McClintock, A. Mufti, and E. Shohat, Minneapolis: University of Minnesota Press, pp. 420–44.

Beverley, J. (1999) *Subalternity and Representation: Arguments in Cultural Theory*, Durham, NC: Duke University Press.

Bhabha, H.K. (1994) *The Location of Culture*, New York: Routledge.

Chang, G. (2000) *Disposable Domestics: Immigrant Women Workers in the Global Economy*, Cambridge, MA: South End Press.

Dirlik, A. (1994) "The Postcolonial Aura: Third World Criticism in the Age of Global Capitalism," *Critical Inquiry* 20: 328–36.

Fusco, C. (2001) *The Bodies that Were not Ours and Other Writings*, New York: Routledge.

Grewal, I. and Kaplan, C., eds. (1994) *Scattered Hegemonies: Postmodernity and Transnational Feminist Practices*, Minneapolis: University of Minnesota Press.

Lewis, R. and Mills, S., eds. (2003) *Feminist Postcolonial Theory: A Reader*, New York: Routledge.

Lyotard, J.-F. (1984) *The Postmodern Condition: A Report on Knowledge*, Minneapolis: University of Minnesota Press.

Mignolo, W. (2000) *Local Histories/Global Designs: Coloniality, Subaltern Knowledges, and Border Thinking*, Princeton, NJ: Princeton University Press.

Minh-ha, T.T. (1997) "Not You/Like You: Postcolonial Women and the Interlocking Questions of Identity and Difference," in *Dangerous Liaisons: Gender, Nation, and Postcolonial Perspectives*, eds. A. McClintock, A. Mufti, and E. Shohat, Minneapolis: University of Minnesota Press, pp. 415–19.

Mohanty, C.T. (1991) "Under Western Eyes: Feminist Scholarship and Colonial Discourses," in *Third World Women and the Politics of Feminism*, eds. C.T. Mohanty, A. Russo and L. Torres, Bloomington: Indiana University Press, pp. 51–80.

—— (1997) "Women Workers and Capitalist Scripts: Ideologies of Domination, Common

Interests, and the Politics of Solidarity," in *Feminist Genealogies, Colonial Legacies, Democratic Futures*, eds. M.J. Alexander and C.T. Mohanty, New York: Routledge, pp. 3–29.

—— (2003a) *Feminism without Borders: Decolonizing Theory, Practicing Solidarity*, Durham, NC: Duke University Press.

—— (2003b) "*Under Western Eyes* Revisited: Feminist Solidarity through Anticapitalist Struggles," *Signs: Journal of Women in Culture and Society* 28: 499–535.

Mohanty, C.T., Russo, A., and Torres, L., eds. (1991) *Third World Women and the Politics of Feminism*, Bloomington: Indiana University Press.

Narayan, U. (1997) *Dislocating Cultures: Identities, Traditions, and Third World Feminism*, New York: Routledge.

Rajan, R.S. and Park, Y. (2000) "Postcolonial Feminism/Postcolonialism and Feminism," in *A Companion to Postcolonial Studies*, eds. H. Schwarz and S. Ray, Malden, MA: Blackwell, pp. 53–71.

Richard, N. (1993) *Masculino/Femenino: Prácticas de la Diferencia y Cultura Democrática*, Santiago, Chile: Francisco Zegers.

—— (1995) "Cultural Peripheries: Latin America and Postmodernist De-centering," in *The Postmodern Debate in Latin America*, eds. J. Beverley, J. Oviedo, and M. Aronna, Durham, NC: Duke University Press, pp. 217–22.

Said, E.W. (1979) *Orientalism*, New York: Pantheon, 1978; New York: Vintage, 1979.

—— (1994) "Afterword," in Edward W. Said, *Orientalism*, New York: Vintage, 1979, pp. 329–52.

Saldívar, J.D. (1991) *The Dialectics of Our America: Genealogy, Cultural Critique, and Literary History*, Durham, NC: Duke University Press.

Schutte, O. (1993) *Cultural Identity and Social Liberation in Latin American Thought*, Albany: SUNY Press.

—— (2002a) "Dependency Work, Women, and the Global Economy," in *The Subject of Care: Feminist Perspectives on Dependency*, eds. E.F. Kittay and E.K. Feder, Lanham, MD: Rowman and Littlefield.

—— (2002b) "Indigenous Issues and the Ethics of Dialogue in LatCrit Theory," *Rutgers Law Review* 54: 1021–9.

Schwarz, H. (2000) "Mission Impossible: Introducing Postcolonial Studies in the US Academy," in *A Companion to Postcolonial Studies*, eds. H. Schwarz and S. Ray, Malden, MA: Blackwell, pp. 1–20.

Shohat, E. (1992) "Notes on the 'Post-colonial'," *Social Text* 31/32: 99–113.

Spivak, G. (1986) "Three Women's Texts and a Critique of Imperialism," in *"Race," Writing and Difference*, ed. H.L. Gates, Jr., Chicago: University of Chicago Press, pp. 262–80.

—— (1988) "Can the Subaltern Speak?" in *Marxism and the Interpretation of Culture*, eds. C. Nelson and L. Grossberg, Urbana: University of Illinois Press, pp. 271–313.

—— (1990) "The Post-Colonial Critic," in *The Post-colonial Critic: Interviews, Strategies, Dialogues*, ed. S. Sarasym, London: Routledge, pp. 67–74.

—— (1993) *Outside in the Teaching Machine*, New York: Routledge.

—— (1997) "Teaching for the Times," in *Dangerous Liaisons: Gender, Nation, and Postcolonial Perspectives*, eds. A. McClintock, A. Mufti and E. Shohat, Minneapolis: University of Minnesota Press, pp. 468–90.

—— (1999) *A Critique of Postcolonial Reason*, Cambridge, MA: Harvard University Press.

—— (2000) "The New Subaltern: A Silent Interview," in *Mapping Subaltern Studies and the Postcolonial*, ed. V. Chaturvedi, New York: Verso and New Left Review, pp. 324–40.

Viswanathan, G. (1997) "Currying Favor: The Politics of British Educational and Cultural Policy in India, 1813–54," in *Dangerous Liaisons: Gender, Nation, and Postcolonial Perspectives*, eds. A. McClintock, A. Mufti, and E. Shohat, Minneapolis: University of Minnesota Press, pp. 113–29.

Further Reading

Emberley, J. (1993) *Thresholds of Difference: Feminist Critique, Native Women's Writings, Postcolonial Theory*, Toronto, Buffalo: University of Toronto Press.
Fanon, F. (1967) *Black Skins, White Masks*, tr. C.L. Markmann, New York: Grove.
—— (1979) *The Wretched of the Earth*, New York: Grove.
Fernández Retamar, R. (1989) *Caliban and Other Essays*, tr. E. Baker, Minneapolis: University of Minnesota Press (original "Caliban" essay published 1971).
Loomba, A. (1998) *Colonialism/Postcolonialism: The New Critical Idiom*, New York: Routledge.
McClintock, A. (1994) "The Angel of Progress: Pitfalls of the Term 'Postcolonialism,'" in *Colonial Discourse/Postcolonial Theory*, eds. F. Barker, P. Hulme, and M. Iversen, New York: Manchester University Press, pp. 253–66.
McClintock, A., Mufti, A., and Shohat, E., eds. (1997) *Dangerous Liaisons: Gender, Nation, and Postcolonial Perspectives*, Minneapolis: University of Minnesota Press.
Mignolo, W. (2000) "Human Understanding and (Latin) American Interests – The Politics and Sensibilities of Geohistorical Locations," in *A Companion to Postcolonial Studies*, eds. H. Schwarz, and S. Ray, Malden, MA: Blackwell, pp. 180–202.
Moore-Gilbert, B. (1997) *Postcolonial Theory: Contexts, Practices, Politics*, London: Verso.
Rodríguez, Ileana (1994) *House/Garden/Nation: Space, Gender, and Ethnicity in Postcolonial Latin American Literatures by Women (Postcontemporary Interventions)*, Durham, NC: Duke University Press.
Schutte, O. (1998) "Cultural Alterity: Cross-cultural Communication and Feminist Thought in North–South Dialogue", *Hypatia: A Journal of Feminist Philosophy* 13: 53–72.
—— (2000) "Continental Philosophy and Postcolonial Subjects," *Philosophy Today* 44 SPEP supplement: 8–17.
—— (2002c) "Feminism and Globalization Processes in Latin America," in *Latin American Perspectives on Globalization: Ethics, Politics, and Alternative Visions*, ed. M. Saenz, Lanham, MD: Rowman and Littlefield, pp. 185–99.
Schwarz, H. and Ray, S. (2000) *A Companion to Postcolonial Studies*, Malden, MA: Blackwell.
Shohat, E., and Stam, R. (1994) *Unthinking Eurocentrism: Multiculturalism and the Media*, London: Routledge.
Spivak, G. (1987) *In Other Worlds*, New York: Methuen.
Young, R.J.C. (2001) *Postcolonialism: An Historical Introduction*, Malden, MA: Blackwell.

Chapter 10

Lesbian Philosophy

Cheshire Calhoun

Relation to Philosophy

Is there a lesbian philosophy? And if so, how should we construe its domain? Philosophers often assume that philosophy is something produced primarily by and for philosophers. If philosophy is written by and for philosophers, then there is not yet a well-established lesbian philosophy. The preponderance of philosophically interesting work on lesbians (and gay men) has either not been written *by* philosophers or has not been written exclusively *for* philosophers. Philosophy has lagged, and continues to lag, behind other disciplines, such as literature, political science, law, and history in the production of scholarship in lesbian and gay studies. Many of the most philosophically interesting issues were originally raised outside of philosophy; and many continue to be pursued primarily outside of philosophy. Many classic texts for philosophical work on lesbians were not written by philosophers; those include Adrienne Rich's "Compulsory Heterosexuality and Lesbian Existence," Gayle Rubin's "Thinking Sex," and Eve Kosofsky Sedgewick's *Epistemology of the Closet*. Of the work produced *by* philosophers, a large portion hasn't been written exclusively (or even primarily) *for* philosophers. Lesbian philosophical work often responds to lesbian needs for self-expression, for dialogue among lesbians, and for setting a group political agenda. Provisionally, then, we might define lesbian philosophy as any critical reflection that enables us to gain greater conceptual clarity about lesbian lives and that, like feminist philosophy, is fundamentally oriented toward liberatory aims.

Lesbian philosophy does not simply apply existing philosophical theories to the subject of lesbians. Doing lesbian philosophy involves rethinking philosophical methods. This is because, in addition to being a branch of philosophy, lesbian philosophy is a branch of three interdisciplinary subject areas: (a) Women's Studies, (b) Lesbian, Gay, Bisexual, and Transgender Studies, and (c) Queer Theory. Lesbian philosophy thus often employs a more interdisciplinary model of good scholarship, a broader conception of the possible content of philosophical work, and a higher estimation of the importance of cross-disciplinary conversations.

Doing lesbian philosophy also involves critically assessing common background assumptions made in philosophy about what problems need to be addressed and which intuitions theories should be tested against. For example, political philosophy typically takes privacy rights to be unquestionably good. From a lesbian and gay standpoint, privacy rights appear more problematic. Unlike heterosexuals, lesbians and gays do not enjoy an extensive social right to make public their identities, sexual attractions, identity-related politics and interests, and partnerships. Thus a right to self-expression behind closed doors may seem less a liberty than an aspect of compulsory closeting. Only a right to privacy coupled with an enforceable right to publicly represent oneself as lesbian or gay would provide adequate liberty of self-expression.

Lesbian philosophy is also a useful critical resource for evaluating the adequacy of feminist theorizing. Although feminist work has, over the past decade, significantly increased its attention to race and class issues, it has been less successful in rupturing the equation of "woman" with "heterosexual woman."

Lesbian Philosophies of Liberation

Like feminist philosophy and African-American philosophy, lesbian philosophy typically aims to illuminate the structure of oppression, to construct theories adequate to understanding and describing human lives lived under oppression, and to envision appropriate political interventions. Lesbian philosophy is unique, however, in being thoroughly divided on the question of *what* the relevant form of oppression is for lesbians. There are at least three candidates: (1) sexism, which oppresses all women, including lesbians; (2) heterosexism, which oppresses lesbians and gay men, where heterosexism is taken to be an axis of oppression distinct from sexism; and (3) regulatory regimes that oppress all sex, sexual, and gender deviants. Radical lesbian feminism, lesbian and gay studies, and queer theory focus on different oppressive systems.

Radical lesbian feminism

Radical lesbian feminism, which emerged in the 1980s and continues to be a lively and important strand of lesbian philosophy, took lesbian oppression to be one instance of a general punitive response to women who diverge from patriarchal gender and sexuality norms (Law 1988; Card 1998). Homophobia is the fear of losing securely differentiated gender roles and the system of male privilege built on them. The threat of homophobic hostility controls both lesbians and heterosexual women. Lesbians must conceal their lesbianism and adopt a heterosexual appearance. Heterosexual women, in order to avoid being accused of lesbianism, must carefully monitor their gender appearance and behavior, and distance themselves from feminist politics.

Patriarchal intolerance of lesbian existence is understandable. Lesbians lead lives centered around women. They do not value male sexualized interest or make themselves sexually and emotionally available to men. Their intimate relationships do not put them in the position of relying on male economic support or of making their labor available to men. Lesbians undermine social schemes built on polarized male–female differences when they refuse to look or act like women or to pursue gender-"appropriate" jobs and pastimes. In short, lesbian existence challenges assumptions, values, and practices that are central to maintaining male supremacy. That challenge is especially threatening if lesbian resistance signals a potential in all women.

On this view, heterosexist oppression of lesbians is a form of sexist oppression of disobedient women. Unlike racism, classism, and sexism, heterosexism is not a separate axis of oppression. Because it is not separate, eliminating women's oppression would automatically entail eliminating heterosexism. By the same token, all women will benefit from ending lesbian oppression. This means that radical lesbian feminists regard heterosexual women as the proper political allies of lesbians. It is unclear to what extent gay men count as genuine political allies on this view. On the one hand, patriarchal societies penalize gay men for their gender deviance, for playing a submissive sexual role, and for not participating in heterosexual power relations (Law 1988). On the other hand, gay male culture has often mirrored patriarchal culture's penis-worshipping, presumption of unrestricted phallic access, and contempt for women (Frye 1983).

Lesbian and gay studies

Work on lesbians conducted within lesbian and gay studies more often proceeds on the assumption that lesbian and gay oppression cannot be reduced to sexism. While sexism and heterosexism intersect in most societies, they are in principle separable. Under heterosexism, heterosexuals on the one hand, and lesbians, gay men, and bisexuals on the other constitute opposing social groups. Heterosexuals' interests are served by multiple social arrangements that reserve a set of privileges for heterosexuals only. Those privileges include the privilege of marriage, of being able to publicly self-identify, of being surrounded by cultural products that reflect their lives, and of having their relationships, parenting relationships, and sexual activity legally protected against intrusion.

On this view, lesbian philosophy's theories and categories of analysis should not be entirely derived from feminist work on women's oppression. One might think this is a good thing. Feminist philosophy has been relatively successful at constructing intersectional analyses that look at gender *and* ethnicity, race, class, and religion. That success is due to its understanding racism, ethnocentricism, classism, and anti-Semitism as separable forms of oppression. What an autonomous lesbian philosophy may hope to supply are comparable tools for an intersectional analysis of gender *and* sexual orientation. In addition, if heterosexism and sexism are, at least in principle, separable systems of oppression, then it will behoove feminist theory to at least raise the question of whether heterosexual women and lesbians necessarily have identical political interests. Some methods of resisting patriarchal culture – for example, eliminating the institution of marriage – might be incompatible with effectively challenging heterosexism – for example, by seeking same-sex marriage rights.

Queer theory

Finally, queer theory provides yet a third option for conceptualizing the relevant oppression. Queer theory attends to normalizing regimes that eliminate or conceal deviant border crossings that might destabilize the cultural status quo. Queer theory draws attention to the fact that sexuality and gender are cultural constructions. Cultures construct distinct categories of acts and actors – for example, masculine men and feminine women, or heterosexual women and lesbians – but the neatness of these categories is artificial. People do not cleanly sort themselves out into heterosexual women and lesbians (Halley 1993). Instead, different bits of one's sexual biography, and sexual acts, fantasies, and desires, may enact different sexual orientation categories. Given their permeability, the apparent discreteness of these categories can be sustained only by concealing and regulating boundary crossings. Liberation is to be sought, then, not in the less oppressive treatment of a distinct social group – women, or lesbians and gay men – but in disruptive practices that call into question these social categories themselves.

Queer theory also draws attention to the socially constructed nature of supposedly natural, normal, nonpathogical, sexuality and gender (Butler 1990; 1991; Foucault 1990; Sedgwick 1990; Rubin 1993). The idea of the normal is constructed through regulatory processes that stigmatize, punish, and attempt to cure some sexualities and genders. Monogamous, heterosexual sex, for example, is established as normal, natural, and healthy through the regulation of adultery, polygamy, lesbianism, and homosexuality. Implicated in this regulatory regime are state laws, psychiatric categories of disease and mental disorder, and religious and moral codes.

On this view, then, the oppression of lesbians and gays is simply one aspect of a more generalized oppression of sexual and gender "minorities," including transsexuals, transvestites, fetishists, sadomasochists, sex workers, boy lovers, bisexuals, and polygamists. Just as radical lesbian feminists assume that ending lesbian oppression depends on resisting women's oppression, so queer theorists assume that ending lesbian oppression depends on resisting the entire regulatory regime surrounding sexuality. Queer theorists would reject any liberatory strategy that tries to normalize lesbianism by insisting that gay people are "just like us." Marriage rights campaigns and campaigns for anti-discrimination protection often take this rhetorical tact; for example, same-sex couples are portrayed as just as loving and committed as opposite-sex couples. Queer theorists criticize such strategies for their failure to challenge the assumption that those who aren't "just like us" deserve to be stigmatized and punished. A genuinely liberatory strategy would resist normalization and underscore the queerness of lesbians.

Heterosexuality and Lesbianism.

The term 'heterosexuality' is used to designate at least five different phenomena.

1 The most common nonphilosophical use of both "heterosexuality" and "lesbianism" is to refer to *sexual orientations*. One's sexual orientation is generally taken to be an unalterable, psychological fact that determines one's sexual and affectional preferences and that grounds judgments of authenticity.

   This popular assumption that sexual orientation is unchosen and unalterable is less likely to be shared within lesbian feminist philosophy. Given how systematically promoted heterosexuality is, and how systematically penalized lesbianism is, it is unclear whether heterosexuality is in fact the "natural" preference for most women (Rich 1983). Moreover, sexual orientation might be better conceived on analogy with tastes in food (Frye 1992). While acquiring a new taste in sexual partners, like acquiring new tastes in food, may take both time and sustained effort, it is possible. Choosing a sexual orientation requires retraining one's perceptual patterns of salience and one's habitual modes of thought, evaluation, and social interaction. Whether women have a real option to choose lesbianism over their early socialization into heterosexuality depends on the institutionalization of lesbian options (Card 1995).

   If sexual orientation is open to choice, then lesbian feminism can reasonably recommend that all women either resist heterosexual relationships entirely or become vastly more selective about their participation in heterosexual relationships. Lesbian feminism can also reasonably insist that feminism become more radical. As Adrienne Rich was the first to point out, feminist criticism stops short of calling into question the assumption that heterosexuality is the natural preference for most women (Rich 1983). Much feminist work still proceeds on the assumption of a natural, near universal heterosexual orientation and thus the reasonableness both of focusing on those political concerns that matter most for heterosexual women (for example, the availability of abortion) and of not aggressively challenging the heterosexual organization of social life (Frye 1992).

2 The term 'heterosexuality' need not refer to a sexual orientation at all. 'Heterosexuality' sometimes refers to *sexualized interactions that take place between males and females*, either voluntarily or under compulsion, irrespective of the participants' sexual orientation. Male purchase of female sexual services is a heterosexual activity even if the prostitute's sexual orientation is lesbian. Male

sexual molestation of female children is also a heterosexual interaction even if the child is too young to be ascribed a sexual orientation. It is in this sense that Adrienne Rich argued that heterosexuality is compulsory for all females.

3 "Heterosexuality" and "lesbianism" can also designate *one's orientation in a social world* (Calhoun 2000). Heterosexuality and lesbianism, in this sense, are similar to gender or ethnic identities. To be lesbian, for example, is to be oriented toward certain cultural productions (music, film, literature that represents lesbians and represents them in a positive light), culturally available activities (women's bars, women's festivals, lesbian and gay political organizations), verbal interactions (*not* participation in homophobic joke telling), and choice of associates (female sexual and domestic partners, female dancing partners, female partners for flirtation). This conception de-emphasizes *sexual* preference and *sexual* activity and treats heterosexuality and lesbianism as complex patterns of socio-cultural preferences and activities. Treating lesbianism as an orientation in the social world makes more evident the magnitude of the restriction imposed by compulsory closeting. Closeting does not simply conceal a sexual orientation or sexual activities. It conceals one's preferred orientation in the social world and requires the enactment of a pretended heterosexual social orientation.

4 Radical lesbian feminism takes "heterosexuality" to refer primarily to a *patriarchal social institution*. "Heterosexuality" is socially institutionalized as a set of social practices – most centrally, marriage – through which women's emotional, sexual, reproductive, and domestic labor are controlled by men for men's benefit (Radicalesbians 1973; Bunch 1987; Wittig 1992). Lesbianism, by contrast, is the refusal to be economically, emotionally, and sexually dependent on men. This view is historically important, because it was the first attempt to understand heterosexuality and lesbianism as something more than private psychological orientations or private sexual behaviors. The personal is political, because personal emotionally and sexually intimate relationships either participate in or resist the patriarchal institution of heterosexuality.

5 Finally 'heterosexuality' sometimes refers to the *social institutionalization of heterosexual privilege*. Heterosexuality comprises the entire set of social arrangements that encourage, support, and reward heterosexual interactions and relationships and discourage, disrupt and penalize same-sex sex-affective interactions and relationships.

Ethics and Politics

There is no one lesbian ethics or lesbian politics. Instead, the different lesbian philosophies take conflicting approaches to ethico-political questions. Radical lesbian feminism, for example, focuses on eliminating patriarchal elements from lesbian practices. Queer theory focuses on disrupting normalizing regimes, especially those that regulate sexual practices and gender performances. Lesbian and gay studies focuses on the unequal distribution of rights and privileges and the problem of enforced closeting.

Lesbian ethics is sometimes equated with radical lesbian feminist ethics, and for good reason. Radical lesbian feminists have been the only ones to take up the question of whether western moral philosophy needs to be replaced with a new approach to ethical reasoning. Sarah Hoagland's classic *Lesbian Ethics* is the best known and sustained argument for an alternative ethical approach. Radical lesbian feminists argue that a lesbian ethics should focus on creating new meaning and value, because lesbians need ways of thinking about their ethical options that are not distorted by patriarchal or heterosexist assumptions (Daly 1978; Frye 1983; 1992; Hoagland 1988; Trebilcot 1994; Card 1995). Creating new meaning sometimes means taking familiar terms, such as "virgin" or "lesbian" and supplying new content and a new evaluative valence. Creating new meaning sometimes necessitates inventing terms – for example, "whiteliness" as a description of stereotypically white, arrogant behavior (Frye 1992) – so that we can see more clearly our lives and actions. Ethics, on this view, is not an individual process of acquiring moral knowledge but a collective process of forging shared social meanings that support lesbian existence. Ethics in this sense is fundamentally liberatory, because it enables lesbians to think about choices that are not readily imaginable within a patriarchal and heterosexist conceptual system. As a result, lesbians are able to disengage from what Hoagland calls "heterosexualism," i.e., dominant–subordinate patterns of interaction.

More so than any other lesbian philosophy, radical lesbian feminism has been willing to make moral judgments about how lesbians ought and ought not to behave. Lesbians ought not to support patriarchal institutions or to enact hetero-patriarchal behaviors in their lesbian relationships. That means, among other things, practicing forms of separatism, not seeking same-sex marriage rights, and possibly not pursuing motherhood. Repudiating hetero-patriarchal behaviors includes rejecting lesbian pornography, lesbian sadomasochism, the equation of having sex with having orgasms, and butch–femme roles. Instead, lesbians should support the creation of female friendships and politically oriented women's communities (Raymond 1986); they should cultivate fully egalitarian intimate relationships that are free from gender-coded roles; and an emotionally rich pan-eroticism should replace preoccupation with genital sexuality.

These are not uncontroversial moral positions. What came to be called the "sex wars" of the 1970s and 1980s resulted from lesbian sex liberals' resistance to condemning consensual sex, including sadomasochism and sex work (Duggan and Hunter 1995). They accused lesbian feminists of being anti-sex and anti women's sexual liberation. Moreover, from the perspective of queer theory, lesbian practices that echo heterosexuality (for example, using a dildo or enacting gendered sexual roles) reveal the nonnaturalness of heterosexual activities and the artificiality of the categories "heterosexuality" versus "lesbian" and "homosexual." In addition, butch gender styles claim masculinity as an equally natural possibility for females, thereby disrupting cultural assumptions that masculinity is natural only for males (Halberstam 1998). Butch–femme enactments also reveal the fundamentally performative nature of gender (Butler 1990). Finally, butch gender styles are one among a variety of ways in which lesbians move outside the category "woman" and become, in Wittig's terms "not-women, not-men" (Wittig 1992). Because gender binarism – the belief that everyone ought to be clearly either a man or a woman – has motivated hostility toward the "third sex," as lesbians and gays were called in the late 1800s, lesbians should resist complying with the expectation (whether patriarchal or feminist) that lesbians ought to behave like women.

While radical lesbian feminism singles out patriarchal practices for critique, other lesbian ethico-political work singles out specifically *heterosexist* practices. By contrast to patriarchy, which works to *subordinate* women by keeping them in socially, economically, and politically inferior places, heterosexism works to *eliminate* lesbians and gay men from being visibly present in any social, economic, or political place. Lethal violence, psychiatric "cures," anti-gay educational policies, and the treatment of gender identity disorder in children aim to prevent the existence of lesbian and gay people.

In addition, compulsory closeting ensures that lesbians and gays will not be visibly present. The threat of loss of employment, assault, and social ostracism moves lesbians and gays to adopt the public appearance of heterosexuality. But doing so is morally problematic. It involves routinely living a lie and acceding to demeaning stereotypes (for example, of lesbians and gays as sexually uncontrolled) that rationalize the closet. It may encourage lesbian and gay "doubling" – dissociating oneself from heterosexist acts that are necessary in order to stay closeted (Card 1995). And it involves complying with a fundamentally unfair social arrangement in which the public sphere is reserved for heterosexuals only (Calhoun 2000).

The fact that lesbians and gays *can* closet their identities complicates advocacy of anti-discrimination policies. Anti-discrimination policies are often thought of as one way of ensuring diversity in social institutions. Not discriminating against women in employment, for example, results in a greater visible female presence. Anti-discrimination policies that cover gay men and lesbians do not necessarily result in a greater visible lesbian and gay presence. That is because anti-discrimination laws may simply forbid discrimination on the basis of sexual orientation *status*. They may not forbid penalizing *conduct* that makes one's lesbianism or homosexuality public. The United States' "don't ask–don't tell" military policy rests on just this status–conduct distinction. Thus, unless carefully worded, anti-discrimination policies do not necessarily have the same diversifying consequence that they do in the case of women and racial minorities.

Same-sex marriage rights have been an especially controversial issue within lesbian philosophy. Against marriage, one might observe that pursuing marriage rights lends support to an institution that has been central to women's oppression (Card 1996a; Robson 1998). Marriage is also a key "normalizing" institution

(Ettelbrick 1993). Sex and intimacy that take place within marriage are culturally taken to be healthy, mature, and normal. Sex and intimacy that escape the terms of heterosexual, monogamous, reproductive marriages are subjected to various social stigmas and legal regulations. To pursue marriage rights is to pursue admission to a repressively normalizing institution. On the other hand, the right to marry is, arguably, a fundamental political right without which equal citizenship is not possible (Koppelman 1994; Pierce 1995; Eskridge 1996; Calhoun 2000). In addition, as the history of anti-miscegenation laws shows, marriage bars serve to preserve existing social group hierarchies. Just as bars on interracial marriage preserved racial distinctions, so too bars on same-sex marriage preserve political distinctions between heterosexuals and non-heterosexuals. Some have also argued that same-sex marriage bars are a form of sex discrimination because they prevent women from doing what men may do (marry a woman) with the goal of preserving gendered sex roles (Koppelman 1994; Eskridge 1996).

Essentialisms and Anti-Essentialisms

Essentialism is the view that it is possible to identify some one trait or set of traits shared by all members of the relevant category. The search for shared, essential traits, however, is always a response to some particular philosophical problem. Different essentialisms, and different lists of essential traits, arise when philosophers have different purposes for identifying commonalities between members of a category. Four different types of essentialism about lesbian identity have played an important role in the development of lesbian philosophy: (1) perspectival essentialism, (2) naturalistic essentialism, (3) cross-cultural/temporal essentialism, and (4) categorial essentialism. All four forms of essentialism are problematic for different reasons and have generated corresponding anti-essentialist positions.

Perspectival essentialism

Perspectival essentialism – the attempt to locate a shared experience or shared perspective – appears in both feminist and lesbian work. Feminist perspectival essentialists hoped to ground talk about a distinctively women's perspective, women's experience, and women's voice. If there were a shared *women's* perspective, then it would be possible to create a distinctive women's culture, to adopt women's epistemic standpoint for the purpose of conducting research and evaluating knowledge claims, and to ground female solidarity in a shared, womanly experience.

Lesbian perspectival essentialists shared a similar purpose: they hoped to ground talk about a distinctively lesbian perspective or experience. Were there a uniquely lesbian perspective, then it would be possible to promote a lesbian culture and ground solidarity among lesbians in a shared experience.

Both feminist and lesbian articulations of this form of essentialism proved vulnerable to the same criticism. This essentialism is insensitive to differences between women or between lesbians. It treats "woman's perspective" or "lesbian perspective" as though one's perspective and experience were uninfluenced by other central features of one's social identity – one's race, class, ethnicity, religion, age, and physical ability. Because these other aspects of one's identity shape one's lesbian experience, there can be no single experience that all lesbians share. In addition, attempting to identify a single lesbian perspective or lesbian experience invites unfortunately normative judgments about who is and who is not thinking, acting, dressing, having sex, etc. like a *real* lesbian.

While both feminist philosophy and lesbian philosophy have aspired to identify a distinctive, shared experience and have rejected that aspiration as insufficiently difference sensitive, the three other essentialisms – naturalistic, cross-cultural/temporal, and categorial – arise (almost) exclusively within lesbian philosophy. The greater complexity of essentialist – and anti-essentialist – positions within lesbian philosophy is a direct result of the fact that placing people into sexual orientation categories is problematic in a way that placing persons into sex/gender categories is not.

Naturalistic essentialism

Sexual orientation is often assumed to be a natural fact about persons. For over a century, scientific studies of lesbianism and homosexuality have typically assumed that sexual orientation is genetically determined – or "congenital" as sexologists of the late 1800s would have said (Ellis 1928). The popular cultural view today is that lesbians and gays are "born that way." What this sort of essentialism enables us to do is offer an explanation of how people come to have one sexual orientation rather than another. Although biological explanations are now particularly popular, naturalistic essentialism also includes psychoanalytic accounts that trace sexual orientations to early childhood experiences. Psychoanalytic accounts are naturalistic because they seek to explain sexual orientation in terms of deterministic causal laws – in this case psychological rather than biological – that apply universally to humans regardless of cultural context (Stein 1999). Naturalistic essentialism does not rule out the possibility that the differences between sexual orientations will also be culturally elaborated. However, because it naturalizes sexual orientation, this form of essentialism makes questions about the material, social, and ideological factors shaping sexual orientations less critical to answer. It is sciences like biology, genetics, and psychology that provide us with the most fundamental and important descriptions of sexual orientations.

Much lesbian and gay philosophy adopts a social constructionist approach instead. Social constructionism is the view that sexual orientations are either wholly a product of culture, or are primarily so. In Gayle Rubin's view "sexuality is as much a human product as are diets, methods of transportation, systems of etiquette, forms of labor, types of entertainment, process of production, and modes of oppression" (Rubin 1993). Sexual orientations are "made up" in much the way we make up other categories of persons. Once sexual orientation categories are "made up," persons come to fit those categories through their intentional action (Hacking 1992). From a social constructionist perspective, the apparent naturalness of sexual categories is an illusion produced by our theorizing, our voluntary attempts to *be* one sexual orientation, and a variety of regulative practices that compel people to enact a single sexual orientation over the course of a lifetime.

Cross-cultural/temporal essentialism

One might be led to naturalistic essentialism not because one wants to causally explain sexual orientations, but because one wants to do lesbian and gay history or anthropology. Historical and anthropological studies of lesbianism are legitimate only if talk about lesbians across time and across cultures is meaningful. If sexual orientation is a natural fact about persons (in the same way that having an infection is a natural fact), then we are licensed to do lesbian history and anthropology.

Cross-cultural/temporal essentialism is the view that sexual orientation categories are culturally and temporally invariant, and thus that it *is* meaningful to talk about lesbians in different cultures and in different time periods. One doesn't have to be a naturalistic essentialist to think that lesbian history and anthropology are legitimate enterprises. One might think instead that "heterosexuality" and "homosexuality" are socially constructed categories, and that cultures *regularly* make up these categories.

This essentialism, which insists that there are lesbians and gays throughout history and across cultures, is controversial. First, unlike the distinction between men and women, which *does* seem to be cross-culturally and cross-temporally drawn, sexual orientations are, arguably, a relatively recent invention. Our contemporary categories of "heterosexual," "lesbian," "bisexual," and "homosexual" originated in sexological and psychoanalytic theorizing of the late 1800s and early 1900s (Foucault 1990). It is not just the terms that are inventions. Earlier time periods in western history lacked the conception of a sexual *orientation* that saturates the entire personality (Halperin 1993). Moreover terms like "female husband" or "tribad" that were used earlier in our history are not equivalent to our category "lesbian" (Halberstam 1998). As a result, applying our category "lesbian" to female husbands and tribads in earlier time periods distorts the historical record.

The problem deepens if one examines the cross-cultural record. Although same-sex sexual activities occur in many cultures and are often socially institutionalized, those same-sex sexual activities are not necessarily organized in a way that opposes heterosexuality. Same-sex sex may be an accepted part of heterosexual practice, as for example the oral sex that adolescent boys have with adult men in New Guinea as part of their preparation for assuming adult male, heterosexual roles. Same-sex sex may also be between partners who would not be viewed in their own cultures as members of the same sex. The Native American female *berdache*, for example, married women but were themselves regarded as members of a third sex. In short, while same-sex sexual activities and same-sex romantic attachments may occur in many cultures and in many time periods, it is controversial whether these are properly described as specifically lesbian or homosexual activities.

Suppose that cross-cultural/temporal essentialism is false – people corresponding to our contemporary conception of lesbians do not appear across cultures and time-periods. How could we still do lesbian history or lesbian anthropology? One option would be to tell the history and do cross-cultural comparisons of women who bear a *family resemblance* to contemporary lesbians. Amazonian independence and rejection of feminine roles, Sapphic erotic relationships, and passionate friendships might serve as three guides for picking out family resemblances (Card 1995). Alternatively, we might include in our lesbian histories and anthropologies everyone who, *if transported to our culture*, would be regarded as a lesbian, acknowledging that they may have a different status in their own culture or time period (Calhoun 2000). What we then do with the term "lesbian" is an open question. We might confine the term "lesbian" to western cultures after the late nineteenth century, using a different culture's or time period's own terminology for lesbian-like women. Or we might think in terms of *lesbianish* activities and relationships in other times and cultures rather than lesbian *persons* (Card 1995).

Categorial essentialism

In addition to giving causal explanations and doing lesbian history and anthropology, there is something else we may want to do that takes us to a fourth essentialism. We might simply want to categorize people around us. And we might want to be able to clearly demarcate who is in and who is outside of the category lesbian because we want to answer a variety of practical questions. How many lesbians are there? Who is entitled to be a member of a lesbian separatist community? What is a lesbian's average income? Categorial essentialism – a type of essentialism that has been central to the philosophical tradition generally – is the view that there is some set of necessary and sufficient conditions for being counted as a member of a category, in this case, the category lesbian. Not only does categorial essentialism treat membership in the category "lesbian" as nonambiguous (because there are clear membership criteria), but it also typically treats one's membership as a stable fact. Being a lesbian is not like being a Democrat – a trait that one might put on or take off at will. It is instead a stable, invariant, defining feature of the self.

Within feminist philosophy, categorial essentialism about *women* has been treated as an unproblematic form of essentialism. Feminist philosophy typically proceeds as though it is obvious who is a woman and who isn't (transsexuals are the notable exception). But for a variety of reasons, categorial essentialism has seemed quite problematic in lesbian philosophy.

Lesbian feminism of the 1980s complicated categorial essentialism by making possible a different kind of lesbian – the political lesbian, who for feminist reasons conducts her erotic and passionate life with women rather than men. Political lesbians lack the continuous sexual biography that categorial essentialism assumes all lesbians have. Instead, their sexual biographies proceed in two phases – an earlier, prefeminist heterosexual stage, and a later feminist lesbian stage. They thus challenge the idea that sexual orientation is a stable identity category and that shift of sexual identity is necessarily a matter of discovering one's true, essential nature.

In the 1990s, postmodern conceptions of identities as fluid and of identity categories as permeable were applied to sexual orientation categories. Sexuality identity is fluid in part because which sexual orientation category one belongs in does not depend on some one fact. A sexual orientation includes ones desires, fantasies, sexual acts, sexual partners, and gendered styles. As a result, one's sexual life might be variously inflected with aspects of heterosexuality and aspects of lesbianism.

Also central to postmodern approaches has been the thought that heterosexual identity is parasitic on homosexual identity. In particular, heterosexuality requires vigilantly excluding from the self aspects of same-sex sexuality. Because bits of lesbian or gay desires, behaviors, fantasies are an ever-present possibility in those claiming heterosexuality, *being* a heterosexual requires a continuous performance; and that performance is always at risk of failure. Moreover, if being a lesbian is at heart a performance or an adopted positionality, then even males might claim to be lesbians (Zita 1998).

Finally categorial essentialism is problematic because "empirico-mosaicism" better describes human sexuality than standard assumptions that persons have one of two sexual orientations (Zita 1998). Sexual mosaicism is the view that the markers of sexual orientation are variable and do not necessarily neatly line up – sexual acts, sexual desire, sexual fantasy, dreams, sexual self-identification, publicly occupied sexual orientation. If one's sexuality is composed of a multiplicity of factors, these may not add up to a single sexual orientation. Thus we may need to abandon the idea the people are monosexual, having one single, coherent, relatively enduring, "true" sexual orientation.

The Future of Lesbian Philosophy

The future directions of lesbian philosophy are likely to be shaped by a number of influences. One is the increasing acceptability of discussions of sexuality within the academic discipline of philosophy itself. This makes it possible to use facts that are especially salient from a lesbian or gay perspective to test the adequacy of accepted views or theories within the various branches of philosophy. In political philosophy, for example, one might test the adequacy of dominant models of discrimination, which were designed with visible identities like race and gender in mind, against the forms that discrimination against invisible identities like sexual orientation take (Calhoun 2000). Or we might use lesbians' and gays' need to politically engage with moral opposition to lesbian and gay rights to critique the adequacy of political theories, like John Rawls', that require moral neutrality in the public use of reason (Ball 2003).

A second influence is the progressive institutionalization of work on sexuality within the academy. Some women's studies programs are now beginning to shift to women's, gender, and sexuality studies so that they can house coursework and programming related to sexual orientation. In other parts of the academy, separate sexuality studies, queer studies, or lesbian, gay, bisexual, and transgendered studies programs are being set up. These institutional frameworks play an important role in determining the directions of intellectual conversations and the parties to those conversations.

Third, global perspectives are becoming increasingly important both inside and outside the academy. One might thus expect lesbian philosophy to participate, for example, in developing human rights frameworks that include sexuality within the scope of human rights (for example, Nussbaum 1999) and in constructing analyses of the relationship between sexual regulations and the formation of national identities. Legal and political developments, both nationally and internationally, especially those related to marriage, family, and employment discrimination, are likely to continue to be a focus of lesbian philosophical work. And finally, the development of an increasingly sophisticated politics of difference within feminist thought will surely motivate continued attention to the interconnections between sexual orientation, gender, race, class, nationality, and religion.

Bibliography

Allen, Jeffner, ed. (1990) *Lesbian Philosophies and Cultures*, Albany, NY: SUNY Press.

Ball, Carlos A. (2003) *The Morality of Gay Rights: An Exploration in Political Philosophy*, New York: Routledge.

Bunch, Charlotte (1987) *Passionate Politics, Essays 1968–1986*, New York: St Martin's Press.

Butler, Judith (1990) *Gender Trouble: Feminism and the Subversion of Identity*, New York: Routledge.

—— (1991) "Imitation and Gender Insubordination," in *Inside/Out: Lesbian Theories, Gay Theories*, ed. Diana Fuss, New York: Routledge.

Calhoun, Cheshire (2000) *Feminism, the Family and the Politics of the Closet: Lesbian and Gay Displacement*, Oxford: Oxford University Press.

Card, Claudia (1995) *Lesbian Choices*, New York: Columbia University Press.

—— (1996a) "Against Marriage and Motherhood," *Hypatia: A Journal of Feminist Philosophy* 11: 1–23.

—— (1996b) "What Lesbians Do," in *The Unnatural Lottery: Character and Moral Luck*, Philadelphia, PA: Temple University Press.

—— (1998) "Radicalesbianfeminist Theory," *Hypatia: A Journal of Feminist Philosophy* 13: 206–13.

Cuomo, Chris J. (1998) "Thoughts on Lesbian Differences," *Hypatia: A Journal of Feminist Philosophy* 13: 198–205.

—— (1999) "Feminist Sex at Century's End: On Justice and Joy," in *On Feminist Ethics and Politics*, ed. Claudia Card, Lawrence: University of Kansas Press.

Daly, Mary (1978) *Gyn/Ecology*, Boston, MA: Beacon Press.

Duggan, Lisa and Hunter, Nan (1995) *Sex Wars: Sexual Dissent and Political Culture*, New York: Routledge.

Ellis, Havelock (1928) *Studies in the Psychology of Sex*, vol. II: *Sexual Inversion*, Philadelphia, PA: F.A. Davis.

Eskridge, William (1996) *The Case for Same-Sex Marriage: From Sexual Liberty to Civilized Commitment*, New York: Free Press.

Ettelbrick, Paula (1993) "Since When Is Marriage a Path to Liberation?" in *Lesbians, Gay Men, and the Law*, ed. William B. Rubenstein, New York: The New Press.

Faderman, Lillian (1992) "The Return of Butch and Femme: A Phenomenon of Lesbian Sexuality of the 1980s and 1990s," *Journal of the History of Sexuality* 2: 578–96.

Ferguson, Ann (1981) "Patriarchy, Sexual Identity, and the Sexual Revolution," in "Viewpoint: On 'Compulsory Heterosexuality and Lesbian Existence': Defining the Issues," by Ann Ferguson, Jacquelyn N. Zita, and Kathryn Pyne Addelson, *Signs* 7: 158–99.

Foucault, Michel (1990) *The History of Sexuality*, vol. I: *An Introduction*, New York: Vintage Books.

Frye, Marilyn (1983) *The Politics of Reality*, Freedom, CA: Crossing Press.

—— (1992) *Willful Virgin: Essays in Feminism 1976–1992*, Freedom, CA: Crossing Press.

Hacking, Ian (1992) "Making Up People," in *Forms of Desire: Sexual Orientation and the Social Constructionist Controversy*, ed. Edward Stein, New York: Routledge.

Halberstam, Judith (1998) *Female Masculinity*, Durham, NC: Duke University Press.

Hale, Jacob (1996) "Are Lesbians Women?" *Hypatia: A Journal of Feminist Philosophy* 11: 94–101.

Halley, Janet E. (1993) "The Construction of Heterosexuality," in *Fear of a Queer Planet: Queer Politics and Social Theory*, ed. Michael Warner, Minneapolis: University of Minnesota Press.

Halperin, David M. (1993) "Is There a History of Sexuality?" in *The Lesbian and Gay Studies Reader*, eds. Henry Abelove, Michele Aina Barale, and David M. Halperin, New York: Routledge.

Hoagland, Sarah Lucia (1988) *Lesbian Ethics: Toward New Value*, Palo Alto, CA: Institute of Lesbian Studies.

Kaplan, Morris (1997) *Sexual Justice: Democratic Citizenship and the Politics of Desire*, New York: Routledge.

Koppelman, Andrew (1994) "Why Discrimination against Lesbians and Gay Men Is Sex Discrimination," *NYU Law Review* 69: 197–287.

Law, Sylvia A. (1988) "Homosexuality and the Social Meaning of Gender," *Wisconsin Law Review*, March–April: 187–235.

Lorde, Audre (1984) "Uses of the Erotic: the Erotic as Power," in *Sister Outsider: Essays and Speeches by Audre Lorde*, Freedom, CA: Crossing Press.

Nestle, Joan (1987) *A Restricted Country*, Ithaca, NY: Firebrand Books.

Newton, Esther (1984) "The Mythic Mannish Lesbian: Radclyffe Hall and the New Woman," *Signs* 9: 557–75.

Nussbaum, Martha (1999) *Sex and Social Justice*, New York: Oxford University Press.

Okin, Susan Moller (1996) "Sexual Orientation and Gender: Dichotomizing Differences," in *Sex, Preference, and Family*, eds. David M. Estlund and Martha C. Nussbaum, New York: Oxford University Press.

Pierce, Christine (1995) "Gay Marriage," *Journal of Social Philosophy* 26: 5–16.

Penelope, Julia (1992) *Call Me Lesbian: Lesbian Lives, Lesbian Theory*, Freedom, CA: Crossing Press.

Phelan, Shane (1989) *Identity Politics: Lesbian Feminism and the Limits of Community*, Philadelphia, PA: Temple University Press.

—— (1994) *Getting Specific: Postmodern Lesbian Politics*, Minneapolis: University of Minnesota Press.

Radicalesbians (1973) "The Woman Identified Woman," in *Radical Feminism*, eds. Anne Koedt et al., New York: Quadrangle.

Raymond, Janice G. (1986) *A Passion for Friends: Toward a Philosophy of Female Affection*, Boston, MA: Beacon Press.

Rich, Adrienne (1983) "Compulsory Heterosexuality and Lesbian Existence," in *The Signs Reader: Women, Gender, and Scholarship*, eds. Elizabeth Abel and Emily K. Abel, Chicago: University of Chicago Press.

Robson, Ruthann (1998) *Sappho Goes to Law School*, New York: Columbia University Press.

Rubin, Gayle (1993) "Thinking Sex: Notes for a Radical Theory of the Politics of Sexuality," in *The Lesbian and Gay Studies Reader*, eds. Henry Abelove, Michele Aina Barale, and David M. Halperin, New York: Routledge.

Sedgwick, Eve Kosofsky (1990) *Epistemology of the Closet*, Berkeley: University of California Press.

Smith-Rosenberg, Caroll (1975) "The Female World of Love and Ritual: Relations between Women in Nineteenth-Century America," *Signs* 1: 1–29.

Stein, Edward (1992) "The Essentials of Constructionism and the Construction of Essentialism," in *Forms of Desire: Sexual Orientation and the Social Constructionist Controversy*, ed. Edward Stein, New York: Routledge.

—— (1999) *The Mismeasure of Desire: The Science, Theory, and Ethics of Sexual Orientation*, New York: Oxford University Press.

Trebilcot, Joyce (1994) *Dyke Ideas: Process, Politics, Daily Life*, Albany: SUNY Press.

Warner, Michael, ed. (1993) *Fear of a Queer Planet: Queer Politics and Social Theory*, Minneapolis: University of Minnesota Press.

Weston, Kath (1991) *Families We Choose: Lesbians, Gays, Kinship*, New York: Columbia University Press.

Wittig, Monique (1992) *The Straight Mind and Other Essays*, Boston, MA: Beacon Press.

Zita, Jacquelyn N. (1998) *Body Talk: Philosophical Reflections on Sex and Gender*, New York: Columbia University Press.

Chapter 11

Can Third Wave Feminism Be Inclusive?

Intersectionality, Its Problems and New Directions[1]

Naomi Zack

Introduction

If a crisis is a time of agitation requiring decision, there has been a crisis in feminism, or more specifically, Second Wave Feminism, since the late 1970s. The crisis revolves around anxieties concerning essentialism in the wake of the realization by United States establishment feminists (who include academic feminists and professionals, as well as those who run large feminist organizations) that their tradition was not inclusive of women of color or poor women. It came to be understood that beginning with Mary Wollstonecraft's 1789 *Vindication of the Rights of Women*, passing through Simone de Beauvoir's 1953 *The Second Sex*, and continuing into the Women's Liberation movement (officially marked by the inclusion of female gender in the anti-discrimination civil rights legislation), feminism was by, about, and for, white middle-class women. From a social science perspective this understanding was accompanied by the claim that particular women experienced differences in social status, material circumstances, and personal identity as a result of *intersections* of race and class in specific historical contexts, so that the *genders* or social identities of non-white and poor women were understood to be different from the genders of white middle class women. The mantra of "race, class, gender" quickly became the new expression of liberatory enlightenment, but the deeper scholarly implications of *intersectionality* are still working their way through the academy. They are evident in the splintering of what used to be thought of as feminism into many different feminisms, and in a highly theoretical postmodern turn within feminism. They are also evident in myriad combinations and permutations of both these sides. These days, everybody has "got a theory for you" (Lugones and Spelman 1990), and it is increasingly likely to be a theory about how theory itself should be "done" given the now-accepted differences among women which in addition to race and class are also currently understood to include sexuality, ethnicity, nationality, religion, ableness, and age.

The multiplication of feminist theories, based on women's differences, has increased employment and career opportunities for women across disciplines in the academy, but unfortunately, this influential subgroup of women remains predominantly white and middle class (Wilson 2002), particularly in the field of philosophy (Zack 2000: 1–22). Except for specific studies within the social sciences, there are few bridges from theories to the real-world problems of actual women.

In this chapter, I sketch the exclusionary feminist history that has led to the idea of intersectionality (part I), describe existing attempts to solve the legacy of exclusion in feminism through the concept of intersectionality (part II), and consider the problems with intersectionality conceptually, and its employment within the field of philosophy (part III). Finally, because it is too soon to give up on the possibility of a coherent, universal, and perhaps even an essentialist theory of women for the "Third Wave," I will propose what such a theory might look like and what its practical benefits would be (part IV).

Before beginning, a note on the meanings of "intersection" and "intersectionality" would be useful. This is easier to promise than to deliver because the feminist social scientists who use these terms often do so in three different senses. The first draws attention to the ways in which women of color have social experiences and identities different from those of white women. In this general sense, discussion of intersections of race with gender often does not go beyond emphases on racial discrimination and exclusion. However, even in this general sense, it is understood that women of color have different social experiences from *both* white women and men of color (Browne and Misra 2003: 488). The second meaning of intersection and the attendant study and methodology of intersectionality goes further, claiming that race and gender are not independent variables that can simply be added or subtracted from one another. Thus, in a recent review article about intersectionality as a methodology applied to studies of race and gender in the labor market, Irene Browne and Joya Misra claim,

> Feminist sociologists call for an alternative theorizing that captures the combination of gender and race. Race is "gendered" and gender is "racialized," so that race and gender fuse to create unique experiences and opportunities for all groups – not just women of color.
>
> (Browne and Misra 2003: 488)

The third meaning of intersection and intersectionality concerns empirical methods used to determine whether in specific social situations, race and gender do fuse. Fusion is the view that race and gender combine to create a new category of race-gender from which neither race nor gender can be separated, not even for theoretical purposes. For example, Browne and Misra are concerned with whether the pay and employment opportunities of women of color in different sectors of the work force can be explained by factors that also appear to affect white women, or by factors that appear to affect male members of their racial groups. That sociologists now test intersections in this way shows that whether or not race and gender do fuse to form uniquely disadvantaged social identities or "sites of multiple oppression" is an empirical question. The answer is that sometimes they do and sometimes they don't. The empirical charge is to specify which social factors determine fused outcomes (Browne and Misra 2003: 504–5).

I The Exclusionary History of Feminism

American women of color have long political and literary traditions opposing both racism and sexism, and a history of activism against economic disadvantage (Hine 1993). However, their distinctive situations, as both objects of oppression and intellectual subjects, did not rivet the attention of white feminist scholars until the late 1970s, nor did women of color have much of a presence in the academy before then. The multifaceted protest of women of color to their exclusion resulted in the perspectives and methods of intersectionality. Some of the critiques that have issued from intersectionality, such as those developed by Native American women (Allen 1986; Jaimes 1995), have not yet been completely absorbed by other feminists. But enough was immediately absorbed to result in broad reexaminations of theoretical foundations. In this regard, the political protest implicit in the writings of bell hooks and Kimberlé Crenshaw was most influential. Hooks pointed out that the nineteenth-century US women's movement was a privileged white women's movement, because its leaders, spokespersons, and writers were white middle-class women. Even on a grass-roots level, suffragettes, temperance advocates, social reformers, and the membership of "women's clubs" were white and middle class. Although there were also women's labor groups during the early twentieth century, white female workers insisted on segregation by race in the workplace. White activists ignored the efforts of women of color toward their own liberation, and it was rare for women of color to be given voice in any forum in which the subject was women's emancipation (hooks 1981, chapters 4, 5).

This invisibility of women of color in practical matters was largely the result of widespread racial segregation in American society, but it became a theoretical flashpoint when advocates for Women's Liberation began to compare themselves to blacks in the 1960s. They did not compare themselves to black women specifically, but to blacks as a generic androgynous group. Overall, such comparisons were insulting to both men and women who were black, because white women's protests that *they* were treated as blacks, did not as such express outrage over how blacks as a whole were treated. Since black women did not participate in the discourse of white feminists (except as an occluded pole of comparison) this discourse symbolically erased their existence *as women*. Among themselves, black women were not silent about the insult, or about their own aspirations, and very clear agendas based on black female identities were drawn up, for internal inspiration, as well as external critique (Combahee River Collective 1977).

Kimberlé Crenshaw explained how even public policy designed to further social justice could in practice erase black women as rights-bearing subjects in the workplace. Newly hired black women were not covered by anti-discrimination laws that protected black men, nor by seniority policies that provided job security for white women. Furthermore when there were cut-backs, black women were often the first to be fired ("last hired, first fired"). However, once unemployed, they could not get legal redress on the basis of a black identity, because blacks were presumed to be already protected by the racial anti-discrimination laws. And neither could they effectively complain as women because women were also presumed to be already protected by the gender component of the laws. The effect was that black women in such situations lost their jobs due to a kind of institutional sexism and racism that worked as though their specific identity *as black women* were the precisely intended target of discrimination (Crenshaw 1989). That kind of an identity, which resulted from more than one kind of oppression, came to be considered the paradigm instance of intersectionality.

Elizabeth Spelman in *Inessential Woman* provided a widely accepted conceptual analysis of how women of color had come to be excluded from what was increasingly acknowledged to be a feminism by, about, and for white women only. In their focus on patriarchal oppression or male domination in western society, feminists had assumed that what they took to be traditional women's roles represented a form of female gender that could be discussed as though it were universally present in all women as a condition of their oppression, regardless of differences in race and class (Spelman 1988). However, this conception of gender, as a universal core of women's identity, ignored the fact that not all women are oppressed through lives spent in traditional roles as wives and mothers within nuclear families with male breadwinners (Zinn and Dill 1994). It ignored the fact that women of color are sometimes oppressed by white women, and that when they are oppressed by men of color they may have good reason to view that oppression as the indirect result of white racism. It ignored the fact that women of color, as well as poor white women, have for centuries worked outside of their homes, in fields, factories, and the homes of other women, and in their own homes as "piece workers." In addition, within their own homes, poor and often middle-class women provided the unpaid labor that reproduced the biological, domestic, and cultural labor of male family members who worked for wages (Hartmann 1997).

II Solutions to Feminist Exclusion

One widely received solution to the ignorance connected with what was increasingly recognized as an exclusively white feminism, was a conception that allowed for multiplicities of women's gender. This was a new conception of gender that was based on varieties of social class and racial categories. That is, there was no longer a universally acceptable notion of a universal women's gender. Women's gender was to be viewed not as a result of only one kind of social construction, but as multiple results of multiple kinds of social constructions. Women had different kinds of identities within their families, and as economic, political, and social subjects. Furthermore, lesbians had problems of oppression different from those experienced by heterosexual women, and the expression of women's sexuality was itself further shaped by race, ethnicity, and social class. This recognized multiplicity was compounded by the realization that even the apparently clear biological division between human males and females was a taxonomy influenced by culture. As a case in point, infants born with ambiguous genitalia come to be culturally identified as male or female (Kessler 1990). All of these multiplicities resulted in an extreme intellectual wariness about any form of essentialism, and in suspicion of any universal feminism, because it might be based on false common essences, either biological or cultural. Questions about what all women could circumstantially have in common or whether there was some attribute that could guarantee their sameness were assumed to be futile. The simple fact of differences among women itself became the leading subject of (proliferating) feminist theor(ies) (Christian 1989; 1994).

The skepticism resulting from intersectionality coincided with a related crisis that might have occurred without awareness of intersectionality among white feminists, a crisis concerning how to define the general term "women." This crisis was in principle present whenever the term "women" was accepted as meaningful within any given intersection. For example, even after it is acknowledged that the problems of white women may not be the same as the problems of black women, within a race-specific study of either white women or black women, it is still necessary to be able to say what is meant by "women." Several theoretical tensions began to make it seem impossible that "women" could be defined. Women's identities had been traditionally connected to their biology but there was growing skepticism about the biological determinism of women's social roles and psychology. However, if women's roles in society and psychology were culturally constructed, it was not clear how women's agency could be mobilized against those constructions. Thus, true ideas of cultural determinism could be as problematic as false ideas of biological determinism. Furthermore, the intuition that women had distinctive subjectivities that could ground liberatory agency was unsettled by deconstructions of many (or any) ideas of pre-formed subjectivity (Alcoff 1989).

The new anti-essentialist feminist polemics that combined awareness of intersectionality with more general problems of defining "woman" often reexpressed established discontents with masculinist intellectual methodologies, particularly in philosophy. Thus, Spelman presented an anti-racist argument that was also anti-essentialist. She claimed that ignored differences among women permitted white feminists to persist in their own practices of domination and she reapplied the older feminist criticism in a further claim that *any* universalist project had the effect of supporting domination:

For the most part, feminists have been eager to postulate a kind of sameness among women that Plato and Aristotle denied existed among humans. We have felt the need to speak of women as in crucial respects constituting a unitary group, sharing something very important in common . . . However, our views can function to assert or express domination without explicitly or consciously intending to justify it. Feminist theory does that whenever it implicitly holds that some women really are more complete examples of "woman" than others are.

(Spelman 1988: 12)

Spelman is speaking of the pitfalls of positing a woman's essence as something that all women share. If overgeneralization from the experience or attributes of those who are dominant is another expression of dominance, it would seem to follow that one way to avoid such injustice is for those dominant to speak only about themselves. This entails that those women less privileged in relevant hierarchies have to speak for themselves as feminists. Although Spelman, a "white/Anglo feminist", in collaboration with Maria Lugones later attempted to construct feminist theory with a "Hispana woman" (Lugones and Spelman 1998). That project suggested that with extreme care and painstaking collaboration, women from different "samples" might be able to generalize together, if each identified her own voice at relevant points of difference. Still, such a project falls short of producing a universal women's voice, because it is impossible for all subgroups of women to construct generalizations, or theory, together, at the same time.

Another caveat against essentialism was expressed by Linda Nicholson when, taking a postmodern perspective, she compared Second Wave feminism to masculinist philosophy:

[M]odern philosophy has been marked not only by its universalizing mode but also by its strong belief in the independence of its pronouncements from the historical context of their genesis . . . Therefore the postmodern critique has come to focus on philosophy and the very idea of a possible theory of knowledge, justice or beauty. The claim is that the pursuit itself of such theories rests upon the modernist conception of a transcendent reason, a reason able to separate itself from the body and from historical time and place. Postmodernists describe modern ideals of science, justice, and art, as merely modern ideals carrying with them specific political agendas and ultimately unable to legitimize themselves as universals (Nicholson 1990: 4) . . . Feminists, too, have uncovered the political power of the academy and of knowledge claims. In general, they have argued against the supposed neutrality and objectivity of the academy, asserting that claims put forth as universally applicable have invariably been valid only for men of a particular culture, class, and race . . . [B]ecause feminist theorists have frequently exhibited a too casual concern toward history and have used categories which have inclined their theories toward essentialism, many feminist theories of the late 1960s to the mid-1980s have been susceptible to the same kinds of criticism as postmodernists make against philosophy.

(Nicholson 1990: 2, 4, 5)

Nicholson's critique of universalism is more general than Spelman's because its subject is an intellectual ambition to discover universal ideals. Nicholson expresses a political skepticism about any human ideals posited by those, in this case academicians, who are in privileged epistemic positions. If the skepticism is well-placed, it would entail that those less privileged in terms of academic credentials, and perhaps even those women who have not been educated (however we are to understand that process), need to construct their own ideals.

The ways in which women of color have themselves gone on from problems of intersected identities to create particular feminisms that speak from their histories and situations are of great importance historically, as well as intellectually. Patricia Hill Collins in *Black Feminist Thought* (1990) first called for black women to create their own knowledge based on their lived experience, and then showed how this could be accomplished in her revised account of sociological theory, *Fighting Words* (1998). Angela Davis has been involved in prison activist projects over the last twenty years or more (Davis 1983; Yancy 2000). Writers such as Gloria Anzulua, Audre Lourde, Chandra Mohanty, Cherie Moraga, Hortense Spillers, and Gayatri Spivak created diverse and contested, inspired, and embittered, accounts of the intersected experience of women of color, both lesbian and heterosexual, Euro-American and postcolonial, historical and contemporary.

III Philosophy and Intersectionality

The exclusion of non-white and poor women from establishment feminism, and in this discussion, philosophy specifically, is partly a legacy and ongoing mechanism of broader social injustice, and within philosophy at this time, partly also an effect of traditional intellectual taxonomies. The idea of intersectionality is a difficult concept for a philosopher to accept, and its use as a principle guiding scholarship poses serious problems for the racial integration of feminist philosophers. Theoretical endorsements of intersectionality as an intellectual project can impose no limits on the numbers or kinds of possible intersected identities. It was noted in part I that black women have been considered a paradigm case of intersected identity, but there is no reason to stop at one dimension of oppression. To race can be added class, age, physical ability, sexual preference, for starters. The only way to limit possible intersected identities is by counting only those whose proponents have managed to give recognized voice to what they are. This requires that feminist theorists who are interested in intersected identities other than their own, maintain a constant solicitude about those who have not yet secured recognition for their voices, and also for those who have not yet been able to voice their intersections. Presumably such interest would not be a desire for information only, but a concern that feminist philosophy be inclusive.

Acceptance of intersectionality thus generates a research methodology which is based on moral principle. So, in addition to its ontological indeterminacy – that is, we cannot know how many relevant intersections there may be before the research is undertaken – intersectionality requires a redirection of philosophy, in method as well as subject matter. This may not count as a problem for feminist philosophers, who are already generally committed to changing philosophy toward greater social relevance. But not all of us who are philosophers, feminists, and liberatory theorists would be prepared to revise and redirect our vocation in this way. Some may wish to hold onto a subject that can be determined in advance, and if they are to keep an open mind about additions to their subject, they may wish to do so on the basis of cognitive, rather than moral or affective criteria.

The practical tension between intersectionality and the field of philosophy plays out in career development. Despite the richness of the intersected counter-traditions within feminism, there has been very little philosophical work by feminist women of color, and indeed very few feminists in philosophy who identify as women of color or write about the intersected experiences of women of color in philosophical ways – less than ten, I would say. There are perhaps ten more women philosophers who identify as women of color and have written about issues of race and ethnicity in recent decades. Indeed, when I began to compile an anthology during the late 1990s, with the confident title, *Women of Color and Philosophy*, I realized that out of about 15,000 professional academic philosophers, less than thirty (30!) were women of color, counting all racial and ethnic groups (Zack 2000: 1–22).

The theoretical caution about universalism in feminism has occurred during the same time in which employment prospects for women entering and moving up in the field have been good, because previously all-male philosophy departments have recognized a need to hire women. But the profession of philosophy, and particularly feminist philosophy, has neither on its own attracted very many women of color as practitioners, nor made the kinds of changes which would attract them. It is usually assumed that such changes would involve philosophy becoming less abstract, universalist, masculinist. However, the abandonment of universal theory in feminism erases women of color as a demographic component of philosophy as the discipline has been traditionally developed, because it encourages women of color to pursue their scholarship in academic disciplines that allow focus on minority groups as subject matter: Africana studies, Asian studies, Hispanic studies, ethnic studies, and so forth. Traditional, which is to say, mainstream and hegemonic, academic philosophy in the United States has thus far included within its canon "foreigners" from only Britian, France, Germany, and ancient Greece (Zack 2003). While philosophy as an American academic field needs to relax an immigration policy that is reminiscent of the United States as a whole before 1965, it is not likely to make such a momentous change during the lifetimes of writers and readers of this volume, and in that meantime, inclusive philosophical feminism is on a collision course with intersectionality. When intersection theory intersects with academic philosophy, it keeps feminist women of color out of the field, as a matter of academic taxonomy, because the thinkers of interest to them who can be studied in disciplines that allow focus on minority and globally subaltern groups, such as Africans and African-Americans, Asians, Hispanics, and Native Americans, are not, because of their national foreignness to philosophy in the US, accepted as philosophers.

Writing as a philosopher and a woman of color, it appears to me that whatever the fate of theories of universal human nature, declaring the death of theories of a universal women's situation is premature. (All that we do know is that some feminists have identified some generalizations as inherently problematic.) While Spelman's caveat that dominant groups may falsely overgeneralize from their own experience should be taken seriously, it is a greater overgeneralization to assert that this must always be the case. We don't yet know that generalization, per se, is inherently unjust. Similarly, Nicholson's postmodern anxiety about "objective" projects is not sufficient to establish that all attempts at neutrality are doomed to bias. If they were, it is not clear how one could then understand the experience of another without having the identical experience oneself. While it is true that many male philosophers have abused notions of objectivity and neutrality by using them to both advance and justify their own interests and social privilege, this does not entail that feminists are incapable of objectivity and neutrality concerning differences among women. Indeed, one would have to be an essentialist about both white and non-white feminist identities to believe that white feminists were incapable of addressing the concerns of non-white women, or that non-white women could not sometimes speak for white women.

Because many men and some women have abused the method of offering definitions of subjects of discourse and politics, it does not follow that the problem lies with the method itself, rather than with the specific distortions inherent in the specific abuses. No definition of women, or of any other group of existent particulars, can capture the diversity within the group, but that is not the purpose of a definition. Definitions are constructed and deployed to emphasize what members of a group have in common. Does anyone think that there is nothing that the referents of the word "women" have in common? The confidence with which individuals are identified as "women" and the continued use of the word in immediately intelligible ways, across cultures and throughout scholarly disciplines, including the multi-discipline of feminism, itself suggests that there must be something that all women have in common. What they do not have in common is an old fashioned physical, cultural, or psychological essence, because there is no evidence that anything like that exists or ever has existed, neither as a necessary and sufficient condition, nor shared same experience. To abandon a search for commonality because essences in this sense are impossible, or because female biology can no longer be viewed as a cause of female social roles or psychology, is to abandon a search before developing a clear understanding of what is being sought.

Feminists still have reason to seek a theoretical commonality among women that will both refer to something real in the world and provide an intellectual basis for political cohesion among women. However, neither nominalism nor idealism can satisfy this search. As a doctrine of meaning, nominalism hales from John Locke in the seventeenth century and it entails that anything posited as an essence comes from the side of social custom and language, rather than from reality or things in themselves. Locke insisted that we do not have the ability to know *real essences*, or what it is in nature that causes distinctive kinds of things, and that our systems of categories and the rules we use to sort things into categories are human inventions. What we can know are thereby *nominal essences* only (Locke 1975, book III, chapter V, §§13–22, pp. 436–51). The problem with applying Lockean nominalism to definitions of women is that it can at best yield a sociological method for studying the identities of different kinds of women, as they have been constructed and practiced under different social conditions. Nominalism cannot by itself connect feminist theory to real women in all their multiplicities in any general or coherent way; nominalism is always on the side of language, and its practices. Thus, Teresa de Lauretis has drawn on Locke's notion of nominal essences to distinguish feminism from other kinds of theories or viewpoints, but with a consistent awareness that a theory of how feminism is to be defined is not a theory about how women are to be defined (de Lauretis 1987: 9–10; Pierce 1999: 246). In a related vein, Cressida Heyes advocates a Wittgensteinian approach to the theoretical fragmentation of intersectionality, with a focus on the interconnected and overlapping ways in which women identify themselves and live out their varied identities. But again – and here, the result is clearly anticipated – hope for a coherent universal theory about women has been abandoned (Heyes 2000).

More extreme than any nominalist proposal is the idealist turn within some postmodern texts, which results in deliberately ignoring the extra-linguistic realness of existing individuals, in favor of concentration on their *signifiers*, the symbols for them in language. For example, Judith Butler advocates an explicit disconnection between the word "women" and existing women (Butler 1993: 67–72). Of course, if everything that previously occupied the attention of feminists now exists and occurs within or through discourse alone, the problem of how any version of feminist discourse serves the needs of those who stubbornly continue to exist outside of discourse is no longer a legitimate subject. It would seem that no matter how free the play of *signifiers*, any system in which signifiers are understood to be free of their otherwise referents, is not a system that can generate one course of action rather than any other, assuming that action occurs outside of discourse. Even if there were a preferred course of action in symbolic terms, we would still need to figure out how to reconnect the signifiers with the women, a problem that could be solved by avoiding the "liberation" or disconnection of signifiers, in the first place.

IV New Directions for Inclusive Feminism

Throughout feminist discussions of difference, as a problem of exclusion and within applications of intersectionality, as well as in consideration of the more abstract question of how "women" can be defined (either across or within intersections), theorists continue to talk about women as existing individuals. Perhaps it is still possible to return to the starting point of a coherent feminist theory and consider what would be required for a feminist definition of "women" to be truly universal, which is to say, inclusive of all the differences that can be disjunctively listed as sites of intersection. First, the definition must apply to all women as we know or can imagine them. Second, the definition should be connected to the goal of feminism as critical theory, which as Toril Moi and others have repeatedly insisted, is theory with the purpose of improving the lives of women (Moi 1999: 9–11; Young 1990c: 7–8, 2000: 10–11; Zack 2005, chapter 4). And third, the definition of women has to be able to link language and theory to the real world and practical problems of existent women. Although feminist theorists do not have sole responsibility for connecting language to the world, it is important that existing women be able to recognize themselves in a feminist definition of them, and that feminist theorists work with an idea of women that keeps them in touch with their subject. This means that we need a *realist* definition of women.

The problems of providing a realist definition of women articulated by anti-essentialists, which include the difficulty of encompassing the multiplicities of intersections (of race, class, sexuality, and so forth), lack of a biological foundation of gender, the dangers to agency of social construction accounts, and the shakiness of the postmodern subject, prove neither that there can be no universal definition of women nor that it is futile to posit one thing shared by all women. What the anti-essentialists have importantly succeeded in establishing, however, is that the thing shared by all women cannot be a substance or a literal thing present in all women. Even if it were agreed that such a substance or essence existed and were biological, it could not be determining of gender, because human female gender is too varied. The variations in gender as cultural construct also preclude a universal cultural condition for all women. However, there is no such biological substance. Some women are born intersexed, and some women, male-to-female transsexuals, were first assigned male sexual identity at birth (or shortly thereafter). The problem with the old essentialisms and the factor that made them so vulnerable to the facts of social differences among women was *substantialism*, an idea there was a thing in women that could constitute them as women. But what if women shared a relation instead, and what if that relation connected them to the very historical realities which have made feminism psychologically, morally, and politically, which is to say, *ideologically*, necessary?

I propose that what all women have in common is a relation to the category of human beings who are: designated female from birth, or biological mothers, or primary sexual choices of (heterosexual) men. Call this the FMP (Females, Mothers, Primary sexual choices) category, which is an historical cultural construction that holds universally across cultures and extends back through all recorded history. It is not necessary that any or all women be any or all of the disjuncts of the FMP category. Even if they are any or all of the disjuncts of FMP, it is not that identity that makes them women from a feminist perspective, but the fact that they have a relation to the FMP category as a whole. This relation of being a woman consists of self-identification with the FMP category and/or assignment to it by others in a dual sex-gender system.

The advantage of defining women relationally is that it avoids all of the problems of substantialism, as well as the old essentialisms, and it also captures the basic structure of how individual women acquire their genders in society. The justification for defining women in terms of their relation to the FMP category is that it captures the historical reality of women in precisely those ways that make feminism necessary. It is because of the ways in which women have been devalued, objectified, obstructed, and exploited as a result of their assignment to and identification with category FMP, that feminism, as advocacy for improving the lives of women, is necessary. However, the FMP category does not exhaust what any existent woman may be or become. To state this is to fulfill a fundamental feminist possibility that particular women may transcend the historical basis of what they are, doing so either as individuals or groups.

The group of women is in reality constituted by individual women who have, do, and will exist. Each individual woman has a date of birth and either has had or will have a time of death. Each individual woman has a proper name and exists in a society that has expectations of her as a member of the FMP category. The relationship of being assigned to and/or identifying with category FMP, but not having an individual (or subgroup) pre-determined subjectivity stemming from that identity and/or identification is what permits women to change their circumstances and improve their lives. Being a woman is thus a relation external to individuals and any individual woman is external to the category that through assignment and identification, defines her as a woman. Any woman shares her relation to category FMP with all other women, although she need be neither designated female from birth, nor a biological mother, nor a primary sexual choice of men (see Zack 2005, chapters 1, 2, 3).

Some further clarifications of the logic of the definition I am proposing might be helpful. The relation to category FMP, once apprehended from the perspective of any individual, may itself enable what we have come to call "women's identities." But it is a mistake to attempt a universal definition of women based on any one or more of such identities. The identities are different, they are constantly changing as history changes (at least, because they also change for individuals over their life times), and future identities of women are, a feminist should hope, undetermined. That is, a feminist theorist does not have to know what all women are, because what women are is a disjunctive set of identities that no one can know in its entirety, any more than all the planets that there are (or ever will be) can be listed. Thus, although women cannot be completely described, they can be defined as those with the relation of identification and/or assigment to category FMP. Even those women who resist assignment to or identification with one or more of the disjuncts of FMP, such as lesbians, women who are not biological mothers, transsexuals, and in the United States, aging and aged women, live out their resistance on the basis of their relation of assignment to or identification with FMP.

As a cultural construction, category FMP is assigned as a whole beginning with female sex assignment at birth, which is when being a women usually begins. Thus, female sex assignment is the beginning of a lifelong process of fulfilling or not fulfilling external gender expectations, and in varying ways making compliance or resistance one's own as a unique individual. There is an active component in this process of women's gender development and enactment, because individuals invariably affirm their versions of the important ways in which others divide the human world. If this results in inward identities, or selves that are distinctively women's selves, then Judith Butler is correct in her Foucauldian insistence that external structures of power preexist the selves or psyches that become gendered persons (Butler 1990). The selves and identities are contingent and even optional collections of energy or dispositions to act in certain ways. Descriptions and theories of how women form their identities or selves are of great interest as shared narratives and psychological accounts. Selves or identities also need to be addressed through rhetoric capable of motivating them toward change. However, the forces of male domination that have formed the historical group of women, as well as the structures that need to be changed in order to improve the lives of particular women, are not identities or selves, but institutions and customs. As Iris Young points out in an analysis of Nancy Chodorow's *object relations* account of female gender formation, a theory of gender formation is not a theory of male dominance in society (Young 1990b: 36–61). To change the world, feminists have to change the world, legally, socially, politically, and economically. That is a different kind of project than changing individual women's identities in a subjective and psychological sense (Zack 2005, chapter 4). Thus, the relational, nonsubstantive, and external definition of women I am calling for is the starting point for a feminist social theory and activism that is capable of addressing oppressive social structures and circumstances. It is also the starting point for feminist psychological theory, phenomenologically understood (Zack 2005, chapter 5).

From this perspective, intersectionality is not wrong (although it may not always result in unique sites of oppression, as noted) but incomplete. It would be a tragedy for feminist aims if the ongoing segregation by race in the American academy were to continue on feminist grounds because no one was able to think coherently about women without positing quaint essences or exclusionary universalisms. But regardless of the contingencies of multiple oppressions and their diverse social consequences, there is a rich and troubled history that all women can in fact relate to, even after their differences have been emphasized. The possibility of such commonality is important in social and institutional contexts where disadvantaged women need the assistance of those less or differently oppressed.

Note

1   This essay is partly an overview of the early chapters of my book, *Inclusive Feminism: A Third Wave Theory of Women's Commonality* (Rowman and Littlefield, 2005) and I wrote it while working on the book. The essay also addresses concerns raised by themes in earlier versions of the book and I thank: the audience at a Symposium on Gender

and Race arranged by the American Philosophical Association Committee on the Status of Women at the March 2003 Pacific Division meeting of the APA in San Francisco; members of the DePaul University Philosophy Department during a Colloquium in April 2003; the audience at the Pacific SWIP meeting at the University of Oregon in November, 2003. I am especially grateful to Eva Kittay and Linda Alcoff as editors of this volume, because they sustained careful and ultimately fruitful conversations with me during the initial process of revision and throughout the editorial process. Each was very patient and thorough and I learned much through working with them.

References

Alcoff, Linda M. (1989) "Cultural Feminism versus Post-Structuralism: The Identity Crisis in Feminist Theory," in *Feminist Theory in Practice and Process*, eds. Micheline R. Malson, Jean F. O'Barr, Sarah Westphal-Wihl, and Mary Wyer, Chicago: University of Chicago Press, pp. 295–326.

Allen, Paula Gunn (1986) *The Sacred Hoop: Recovering the Feminine in American Indian Traditions*, Boston, MA: Beacon Press.

Beauvoir, Simone de (1952) *The Second Sex*, tr. H.M. Parshley, New York: Knopf.

Browne, Irene and Misra, Joya (2003) "The Intersection of Gender and Race in the Labor Market," *Annual Review of Sociology*, 29 (August): 487–513.

Butler, Judith (1990) "Gender Trouble, Feminist Theory and Psychoanalytic Discourse," in *Feminism/Postmodernism*, ed. Linda Nicolson, London: Routledge, pp. 324–40.

—— (1993) *Bodies That Matter: On the Discursive Limits of "Sex"*, New York: Routledge.

Christian, Barbara (1989) "The Race for Theory," *Cultural Critique* (6), reprinted in *Making Face, Making Soul Haciendo Caras: Creative and Critical Perspectives by Women of Color*, ed. Gloria Anzuldua, San Francisco, CA: Aunt Lute Press, 1990, pp. 335–44.

—— (1994) "Diminishing Returns: Can Black Feminism(s) Survive the Academy?"in *Multiculturalism? A Critical Reader*, ed. David Theo Goldberg, Cambridge, MA: Blackwell, pp. 168–77.

Collins, Patricia Hill (1990) *Black Feminist Thought: Knowledge, Power and the Politics of Empowerment*, Boston, MA: Unwin Hyman.

—— (1998) *Fighting Words: Black Women and the Search for Justice*, Minneapolis: University of Minnesota Press.

The Combahee River Collective (1997) "A Black Feminist Statement," in *The Second Wave: A Reader in Feminist Theory*, ed. Linda Nicholson, New York: Routledge, pp. 63–70.

Crenshaw, Kimberlé (1989) "Demarginalizing the Intersection of Race and Sex: A Black Feminist Critique of Antidiscrimination Doctrine, Feminist Theory, and Antiracist Politics," *University of Chicago Legal Forum* 14: 538–54.

Davis, Angela Y. (1983) *Women, Race and Class*, New York: Random House.

De Lauretis, Teresa (1987) *Technologies of Gender: Essays on Theory, Film and Fiction* Bloomington: Indiana University Press.

Hartmann, Heidi (1997) "The Unhappy Marriage of Marxism and Feminism: Toward a More Progressive Union," in *The Second Wave: A Reader in Feminist Theory*, ed. Linda Nicholson, New York: Routledge, pp. 97–122.

Heyes, Cressida, J. (2000) *Line Drawings: Defining Women through Feminist Practice*, Ithaca, NY: Cornell University Press.

Hine, Darlene Clark (1993) *Black Women in America: An Historical Encyclopedia*, 2 vols., Brooklyn, NY: Carlson.

hooks, bell (1981) *Ain't I A Woman?* Boston, MA: South End Press.

Jaimes, M. Annette (1995) "Some Kind of Indian," in *American Mixed Race: The Culture of Microdiversity*, ed. Naomi Zack, Lanham, MD: Rowman and Littlefield, pp. 133–54.

Kessler, Suzanne J. (1990) "The Medical Construction of Gender: Case Management of Intersexed Infants," *Signs* 16 (1) Autumn: 3–26.

Locke, John (1975) *An Essay Concerning Human Understanding*, ed. Peter H. Niddich, Oxford: Oxford University Press.

Lugones, Maria C. and Spelman, Elizabeth V. (1990) "Have We Got A Theory For You," in *Hypatia Reborn: Essays in Feminist Philosophy*, ed. A.Y. al-Hibri and M.A. Simons, Indianapolis: Indiana University Press. Reprinted in Naomi Zack, Laurie Shrage, and Crispin Sartwell eds., *Race, Class, Gender and Sexuality: The Big Questions*, Malden, MA: Blackwell, 1998, pp. 374–88.

Moi, Toril (1999) *What Is A Woman?* New York: Oxford University Press.

Nicholson, Linda J. (1990) *Feminism/Postmodernism*, New York: Routledge.

—— ed. (1997) *The Second Wave: A Reader in Feminist Theory*, New York: Routledge.

Pierce, Christine (1999) "From Postmodernism and Other Skepticism," in *Gender*, ed. Carol C. Gould, Amherst, NY: Humanities Books 1999.

Spelman, Elizabeth V. (1988) *Inessential Woman: Problems of Exclusion in Feminist Thought*, Boston, MA: Beacon Press.

Wilson, Robin (2002) "A Kinder, Less Ambitious Professoriate," *The Chronicle of Higher Education* November 8: 10–11.

Yancy, George (2000) "Interview with Angela Y. Davis," in *Women of Color and Philosophy*, ed. Naomi Zack, Malden, MA: Blackwell, pp. 135–51.

Young, Iris Marion (1990a) *Throwing Like a Girl and Other Essays in Feminist Philosophy and Social Theory*, Bloomington and Indianapolis: Indiana University Press, pp. 141–59. Reprinted from *Human Studies* 3 (1980): 137–56.

—— (1990b) "Is Male Gender Identity the Cause of Male Domination?" in Iris Marion Young, *Throwing Like a Girl and Other Essays in Feminist Philosophy and Social Theory*, Bloomington and Indianapolis: Indiana University Press, pp. 36–61.

—— (1990c) *Justice and the Politics of Difference*, Princeton, NJ: Princeton University Press.

—— (2000) *Inclusion and Democracy*, Oxford: Oxford University Press.

Zack, Naomi, ed. (2000) *Women of Color and Philosophy*, Malden, MA: Blackwell Publishers.

—— (2003) "Philosophies or Philosophy?: The Nationalism of Philosophers," *Newsletter on Hispanic/Latino Issues in Philosophy*, APA Newsletters 2 (2) (Spring): 151–4.

—— (2005) *Inclusive Feminism: A Third Wave Theory of Women's Commonality*, Lanham, MD: Rowman and Littlefield.

Zinn, Maxine Baca and Dill, Bonnie Thornton, eds. (1994) *Women of Color in US Society*, Philadelphia, PA: Temple University Press.

Part IV

Knowing and Representing

Chapter 12

Feminist Epistemologies and Women's Lives

Lorraine Code

Critical Interrogations

For more than two thousand years, since their foreshadowing in Plato's *Republic*, *Meno*, and *Theaetetus*, questions such as "How do we know?" or more stringently "Do we really *know* anything at all?" have pervaded western philosophy. In twentieth-century Anglo-American philosophy, this line of inquiry issued in concerted efforts to determine necessary and sufficient conditions for knowledge in general: conditions that would silence the skeptical challenge while establishing foundational truths and/or normative principles for achieving epistemic certainty. Yet especially since the 1970s, feminist and other postcolonial philosophers have contested the very possibility of such an achievement, submitting its aims to critical scrutiny of a different sort. Perhaps outrageously to those for whom knowledge is no one's and everyone's, they have turned to examine the scope of the "we" named in these questions: the inclusions, exclusions, recognitions, and erasures that determine its membership; the tacit assumptions about who can know and why, not just along lines drawn by gender but along the multiple, often intersecting lines of dominance and subordination, marginalization and difference, that silently legislate matters of epistemic authority, credibility, and trust. Still more radically, some feminist and other postcolonial epistemologists have worked to unsettle the core regulative ideals, methods, and principles of "the epistemological project," exposing the implausibility of references to "knowledge in general," and the hierarchical assumptions implicit even in such seemingly incontestable ideas as reason, objectivity, neutrality, and impartiality. They have shown that a rhetoric of disinterested neutrality integral to hegemonic theories of knowledge has consistently masked operations of power, privilege, and vested interest, where knowledge claims are deliberated within normative conceptions of epistemic subjectivity, and (often tacit) social-political patterns of incredulity and assent, discounting or acknowledging. They have subjected the structural underpinnings of orthodox epistemology to critical scrutiny, thereby exposing a sedimented politics of exclusion and oppression which, in creative successor epistemology projects, they seek to counter.

Philosophical questions about who can know and how are not so recent as my reference to the 1970s implies: this date refers to "feminist epistemology's" appearance on the epistemic terrain. But from its recorded beginnings, white western philosophy has posited evaluative, hierarchical divisions between the rational and the irrational, where only those who can claim – or are accorded – a place within the rational can expect the acknowledgment and respect, and the entitlement to social-political-epistemic authority, that a reason-venerating society confers upon some of its members. Not only have women, generically conceived, been excluded from that group on grounds of putative rational incapacity, but other Others (from a white male norm), both female and male, have been judged variously incapable of the reasoning from which alone valid knowledge is believed to derive. From Genevieve Lloyd's path-breaking (1984) readings of the emblematic status of "the man of reason" in instantiating the positive intellectual character ideals that have infused the western philosophical and social imaginary through historical-cultural variations in conceptions of both manhood and reason, to Michèle Le Dœuff's (2003) exposure of the negative emblematic positioning of the "bluestocking" as recipient of the opprobrium that has awaited women who dared to be rational and sought to be learned, feminists have demonstrated the sex-based effects of entrenched conceptions of reason and knowledge.

With postcolonial and anti-racist theorists, then, feminists interrogate a history of exclusions and unknowings that have installed affluent, educated white men as the principal dispensers of knowledge, rational judgment, and acknowledgment. Hence the disdain in which "the bluestocking" is held, who appears stridently in Le Dœuff's text. The epithet refers to stockings with which she is metonymically identified: coarse, knitted woolen stockings worn by (male) members of Cromwell's Blue-Stocking Parliament who defied propriety by "appearing in the House dressed in the kind of stockings they wore at home instead of the black silk stockings deemed essential for such ceremonial occasions" (2003: 1). The stockings mutate into a derogatory term to refer to "women who like to read and think, and do not hide the fact" (2), and bluestockings become those unsexed, strident female intellectuals who no longer know their place, who fail to "satisfy certain male expectations" (3). The figure of the bluestocking shadows the development of Le Dœuff's argument throughout the text: a persistently cautionary figure who reminds women of the "proper" sex of knowing, thus exposing the tenacity of an imaginary in whose terms they unsex themselves, are "cast-off of men," if they try to know too much. For "an educated woman is a bluestocking with no seductive power whatsoever and it serves her right" (133). The bluestocking stands for the leftovers cast off to women from the feasts of knowledge at which men dine in the House of Solomon; and for women's relegation to places of minimal knowing and cognitive esteem, in a knowledge economy designed by and for men. Hence, knowing is designated male and confined to the masculine by the social imaginary in which it finds its place.

Tracing the development of ideals of Reason internally, within western philosophy, Lloyd shows that throughout diverse historical articulations, these ideals are remarkably consistent in defining themselves by contrast with and exclusion of traits, values, and attributes marked "feminine." In this context, "feminine"/ "female" refers not merely to such derivative qualities embedded in present-day stereotypes of "woman" as delicacy, seductiveness, empty-headedness, or frivolity. In its ancient Greek origins it invokes a metaphysical principle that functions to separate an aggregate of human characteristics into positive masculine qualities and negative feminine ones. In the Pythagorean table of opposites, *maleness*, like limit, light, good, and square is associated with determinate form; *femaleness*, unlimited, dark, bad, and oblong with (inferior) formlessness. Variations on these ancient principles have informed subsequent philosophical beliefs about the relative rational capacities of women and men, to feed ultimately into the popular stereotypes of femininity and masculinity still in common currency. Reason, then, is discursively constructed as an object of descriptive and normative analysis in discourses whose symbols and metaphors shape and are shaped by dominant ideals of masculinity. This reason–masculinity alignment is more than simply about neutral, transparent symbolisms that do not affect the "actual," real-world entities they represent. These exclusions demonstrate that reason is not an independent thing or entity people simply come across in the world. It is symbolically, metaphorically constituted all the way down: its constitution in association with ideal masculinity stakes out a rational domain that is inaccessible, or accessible only uneasily and with difficulty, to people whose conditions of possible experience have not fostered the characteristics by which ideal masculinity has defined itself. Such consequences may be explained by invoking evidence that woman (generically conceived) is "naturally" more emotional, intuitive, unstable, attuned to the concrete and the particular, immersed in the minutiae of the everyday than man (also generically conceived). Historically, as Le Dœuff also shows, intellectual pursuits, hence education in subjects other than those judged "feminine," rarely counted as suitable for women. Excluded from opportunities to exercise their rationality, women remained immersed in immanence, in the trivia of the everyday, confirming the (circular) argument that their naturally limited reasoning powers show this domain to be essentially theirs.

The conceptual-symbolic dichotomies such alignments generate – reason/ emotion, mind/body, objective/subjective, abstract/concrete, are typical samples – align with a male/female dichotomy, both descriptively and evaluatively. They work to establish the features of ideal, universally valid knowledge as a product of strictly rational endeavour, and to separate it from opinion, hearsay, particularity, which are associated with (stereotypical) femininity. Especially efficacious among them is the reason/emotion dichotomy. White western philosophy has persistently associated reason with maleness and emotion/passion with femaleness: associations apparent from folkloric claims that men are "more" rational and women "more" emotional, to philosophical constructions of the nature of reason both in itself as it contrasts with emotion and passion, and as it is enjoined to exclude them. These associations inform gendered divisions of intellectual and domestic labour and hierarchical structurings of the social-epistemic order into private (emotion-governed) female and public (reason-governed) male domains. Representing the emotions/passions as fundamentally irrational, they sustain public disdain of emotion, and of women because of their alleged emotionality. More seriously, they suppress pre-philosophical beliefs about the cognitive salience of emotions and passions, denying any possibility that they might inform knowledgeable responses to situations or even, in some circumstances, generate the most reasonable responses. Thus feminists argue that the style of reasoning the epistemologies of modernity celebrate is neither the best nor the only available one: that dispassionate instrumental rationality serves only a circumscribed range of (morally politically contestable) interests, even as it preserves an exemplary status for traditional white middle-class masculine ways of being.

The feminine/masculine divisions Lloyd and Le Dœuff trace – albeit quite differently – through the history of western (European) philosophy since the Presocratics unify femininity and masculinity along lines other postcolonial critiques might contest. But this homogeneity is a consequence of their chosen domain of analysis: texts that comprise the Eurocentered, white western philosophical canon. Hence these analyses also gesture toward the local character of hegemonic Reason, its constitution through local (albeit historically variant) metaphors within a locally efficacious social imaginary; and its connections with specific practical circumstances. These are exemplary instances of local inquiry, specific to the symbolic events that have shaped western philosophy and their effects in fostering and sustaining social-political arrangements: therein lies their critical salience. Recognition of its contingent local specificity, both synchronic and diachronic, goes some way toward destabilizing Reason's universal pretensions.

Sex and gender are by no means the only factors inflecting dominant conceptions of reason. In a more recent essay, Lloyd again observes that "The *temporalization* of reason and its construction as 'attainment' provide a structure in which it is possible to locate the feminine as a lesser stage of human development" (2000: 33, emphasis added). But she goes on to show how this same construction of reason is mobilized to "rationalize" the exclusion of indigenous Australians from the rational domain. These observations concur with Charles Mills' references to a Racial Contract in which "a basic *in*equality is asserted in the capacity of different human groups to know the world and to detect natural law"(1997: 59); and Patricia Williams' observations that, for black people, an "assimilative tyranny of neutrality" can prompt them to deny the harms of lived racism, while for white people "racial denial tends to engender a profoundly invested disingenuousness, an innocence that amounts to the transgressive refusal to know" (1997: 27).

Ludwig Wittgenstein's *On Certainty* observation that *"Knowledge is in the end based on acknowledgement"* (1971, §378) captures a central issue in these inquiries, through which questions about acknowledgment conferred or withheld, deliberated, refused, negotiated, reconfigured, or enacted run as a guiding thread. Although Wittgenstein was no promulgator of the politics – especially the *gendered* politics – of knowledge, in claiming so fundamental a place for acknowledgment among conditions for the possibility of knowledge he locates epistemic projects within forms of life, in an array of social practices, conventions, customs. He presupposes at least one interlocutor in epistemic deliberations, and likely more than one – a community, a group of interlocutors. Thus, in the language of the late twentieth century, he *socializes* epistemology, opening a space where the question "whose knowledge are we talking about?" can move into focus, thereby unsettling the dislocated, disembodied (Enlightenment and empiricist-positivist) ideals of rational autonomy and solitary epistemic self-sufficiency pivotal to most standard Anglo-American theories of knowledge. Together with his claim that if he were "contradicted on all sides" the foundation of all judging would disappear – the background against which he distinguishes between true and false – his according acknowledgment so central a place, with its attendant refusal to countenance monologic, abstract epistemic individualism, gestures toward conceptions of knowledge, subjectivity, and agency as both social and situated. As Miranda Fricker (2000: 162, n.7) archly observes, "To conceive epistemic subjects as social subjects *is* – for the socially non-myopic – to conceive of them as placed in relations of power." In its effects within such relations, acknowledgment granted or withheld confers or thwarts membership in groups and communities of would-be knowers, grants knowledge claims a hearing or dismisses them out of hand, valorizes or discredits epistemic agency, and much more. The implications of such patterns of incredulity and cognitive marginalization are apparent throughout women's lives and intellectual aspirations in patriarchal, racist, and otherwise hierarchically structured societies.

Yet despite the ongoing, palpable effects of these symbolic associations in epistemic projects and practices, the masculine line is not unbroken: feminists have restored numerous learned women to the historical record, acknowledging and indeed celebrating their intellectual achievements (see Waithe 1987; 1989; Le Dœuff 1991, 2003; McAlister 1996; Schiebinger 1999). But patterns of exclusion or silencing are remarkably intransigent even against such exceptions, who may be invoked only to prove the rule. Margaret Rossiter, for example, writes of Marie Curie's celebrity tour of the United States, intended to "'prove' that women could work in science," that Curie's "glorified image . . . backfire[d] disastrously," prompting faculty members to expect "*every* female aspirant for a faculty position . . . [to] be a budding Marie Curie," and to justify not hiring them "on the unreasonable grounds that they were not as good as she, twice a Nobel Laureate!" (Rossiter 1982: 127). Clearly it takes more than a few exceptions to undo the stereotypes sustaining an epistemic imaginary of masculine scientific reason and men as the only credible knowers. As I will go on to show, this historical and metaphorical distribution of epistemic authority is not merely a social-political problem that would dissolve if social equality were achieved and more women were added to hitherto masculine domains; nor is it a mere embellishment of otherwise neutral epistemological principles and practices. My purpose in showing how deeply it is ingrained in the western epistemic imaginary is to prepare the way for demonstrating how the normative a priori principles governing the epistemological project rely on ideals, methods, and practices that derive from and promote a constitutive androcentricity.

Feminism and Epistemology

Epistemology was a relatively recent arrival on the western feminist agenda. Many early "second wave" feminists remained convinced that knowledge, by (putatively universal) definition, transcends material-cultural-political-historical specificity and experiential diversity. Thus orthodox Anglo-American theories of knowledge have stood stubbornly aloof from claims for the epistemological significance of the hierarchical arrangements in which people live their lives. Risks of relativistic contamination and of perpetuating age-old stereotypes of women (and other Others) as too emotional, too immersed in the concrete to reason objectively or abstractly, initially separated knowledge issues from other contestations of women's ambiguous status in philosophy and its trickle-down effects in the wider world. Thus even as "the woman question" entered moral and social-political philosophy via such presumptively female-specific matters as reproductive freedom, sexual assault, and discrimination in the workplace, epistemology remained secure in its self-proclaimed neutrality which allegedly assured its capacity to transcend particularity, and thus to represent things "as they really are." Nor had feminist philosophers shown how these same female-specific moral-social-political issues work from tacit knowledge claims, and in so doing enact implicit epistemological assumptions. A presumed, rarely articulated or interrogated empiricist-realist stance – almost a *naive* realism – separated moral and epistemic inquiry within professional philosophy, allowing moral and political theory to proceed as though veridical perception were "alike" in moral agents to the extent that they could readily "put themselves in anyone else's shoes," and debate-generating situations would be readily and uniformly *known*. Thus no suggestion either that knowledge of the situation at issue needs to be acquired and assessed for deliberation to be good of its kind, or that knowing, too, is a morally implicated process with attendant responsibilities and duties, claimed a hearing within ethical theory. Since the early 1980s, feminist epistemologists have been engaged in contesting these sedimented beliefs, while exposing the implausible consequences of moral deliberations that proceed from irresponsible knowing, condoned by so implausible an epistemology/ethics separation.

The neutrality assumptions of Anglo-American epistemic (and ethical) orthodoxy are reinforced by an abstract individualism, evident in the presupposition that knowing is an individ*ual* but not an individ*uated* process, and "individuals" are interchangeable, disembodied, hence dispassionate observers, mere place-holders in an S knows that p rubric. Their bodily experiential and circumstantial particularities are of no epistemic consequence, for logical possibility overrides any practical impediments, conceived as merely contingent. Hence epistemological inquiry need not take subjectivity into account: "subjects" are interchangeable within its formal structures. A positivistic philosophy-of-science-derived conviction that the untidy details and material-locational specificities of knowledge production – *of discovery* – must be transcended in *justification, verification,* or *falsification* holds these assumptions in place. Were these procedures neither objective nor uniformly replicable, the conviction is that "knowledge" would reduce to opinion, hearsay, ideology, and chaos would ensue. How could feminists take such risks, yet claim emancipatory salience for their knowledge or resist the age-old stereotypes of irrational femininity? The question functions to render oxymoronic the very idea of *feminist* epistemology.

Yet feminists have shown that collaborative, avowedly engaged, politically committed inquiries can yield knowledge more responsive to human diversity than those derived from presumptions of formal sameness. In the 1980s and early 1990s, such demonstrations were guided by a taxonomy proposed by Sandra Harding (1986) which demarcated three "versions" of feminist epistemology. *Feminist empiricism* offered a reconfigured empiricism committed to unearthing male "bias," and to exposing socially derived, constitutive background assumptions (see Longino 1990) that pervade both the discovery and the justification processes of received knowledge. Through more stringent feminist-informed observational methods, it claimed to be able to capture a more inclusive range of empirical evidence than standard empiricism had done, and hence to expose and counter the androcentricity of secular and scientific knowing. *Feminist standpoint epistemology*, beginning from the material specificities of women's lives, drew analogies between the epistemic positions of women in patriarchal societies and the economic position of the proletariat in capitalist societies. As capitalism "naturalizes" proletarian subordination, so patriarchy "naturalizes" female subordination; and as starting from proletarian lives denaturalizes these assumptions by demonstrating their radical contingency, so starting from women's lives denaturalizes, makes strange, the founding assumptions of the patriarchal order. Engaging with the material-experiential specificities of and differences among women's lives; analysing women's oppressions as structural effects of an unjust social order, standpoint theorists contend that the knowledge the oppressed require for survival can be enlisted as a transformative resource. Yet they do not aim to determine a single, representative or inclusive feminist standpoint: neither reductivism nor a new monolithic analysis has any place here. Diverse standpoints, sometimes united around common issues sometimes not, are possible and indeed necessary. Thus for example, Patricia Hill Collins (1990), showing how knowledge produced by subordinate groups fosters resistance, argues that the "outsider-within" positioning of black feminist standpoints yields an Afro-centered epistemology; and Maria Lugones (1988) advocates "world traveling and loving perception" as strategies for breaking out of the confines of too particular, self-satisfied locations. Alison Wylie (2003: 28) summarizes:

the point of insisting that what we know is structured by the social and material conditions of our lives was to throw into relief the contingent, historical nature of what we count as knowledge and focus attention on the processes by which knowledge is produced.

Such a refocusing, she contends, contributes to a "critical dissociation" (37) from the authoritative knowledge born of, and enlisted to perpetuate, positions of privilege.

Posing questions about the identities and locations of knowers is *postmodern* (Harding's third category) in contesting the master narratives and the universalist, often essentialised, individualist assumptions of modernity. But "postmodern" critique goes further: it is often inimical to the very idea of epistemology in its established articulations; for postmodern anti-foundationalism amounts to an insistence that knowledge in the orthodox, objective, impersonal senses is impossible. According to its detractors, postmodern emphasis on the instability of knowledge and subjectivity erases possibilities of epistemic agency; but its advocates counter that such nihilistic consequences are not inevitable. Many postmodern theorists work from a position that is anti-essentialist on such issues as human nature, knowledge, justice, truth, virtue, to argue that more politically astute and responsible epistemic strategies, sensitive to specificities and differences, become available once the stranglehold of oppressive master narratives is broken and the fiction of a unified, autonomous, dislocated knowing subject (who is tacitly white and male) is displaced. Indebted to the hermeneutics and genealogies of Hans-Georg Gadamer, Friedrich Nietzsche, and Michel Foucault among others, feminists such as Kathy Ferguson (1993) and Joan Scott (1992) have argued that all experience, all knowledge-production is politically constituted and invested, yet open to critical analyses generated out of an anti-imperialist politics of difference. Such analyses may yield no definitive, universal conclusions; but by making strange the basic tenets of post-Enlightenment epistemology, ethics, and politics they can become critical tools for negotiating knowledge that is the prerequisite for action in the interests of justice and fairness. And informed by Freudian and Lacanian psychoanalytic theory, Marxist-derived materialist theories of subjectivity, and Derridean deconstructions of traditional ontologies of the self, feminists such as Denise Riley (1988), Teresa de Lauretis (1987), and Judith Butler (1990) contest post-Enlightenment conceptions of subjectivity as *uniform* in the sense impartiality principles assume, where every subject is substitutable for any other, given their taken-for-granted sameness; as *unified* in the sense that claims for coherent, unconflicted autonomous integrity require; and as *self-transparent* in the sense that there are no hidden corners to its soul, inaccessible to conscious control. These feminists posit a multiplicity of subjectivities, readings, and strategies.

In the years since feminist empiricism and standpoint theory seemed to cover the territory with postmodernism addressing anti-epistemological challenges to both, feminists have worked with these categories as neither mutually exclusive, nor adequate, separately or together, to explicate the sexual politics of knowledge production and circulation. They have moved to blend these strategies and other positionings with analyses of epistemic diversity; to expose the oppressions and exclusions that standard epistemologies enact behind a mask of disinterested neutrality. Thus, critically and creatively interrogating hegemonic conceptions of knowledge and subjectivity together, many feminists have rejected abstract, formal conditions for the possibility of knowledge "in general" to return to the world where people variously and in diverse situations produce and negotiate claims to know, and seek acknowledgment for their knowings.

Whose Knowledge?

It will be evident from what I have said in the previous sections that feminists focus as much on representations of the knowing subject and her/his stance vis-à-vis things or people positioned as "objects" of knowledge as they do on the knowledge of which standard exemplars are made. In early Anglo-American positivist-empiricism, paradigmatic privilege accrues to scientists, or to faceless observers whose simple reports – "The cat is on the mat" – comprise the building blocks from which knowledge is made: on ordinary medium-sized physical objects such as apples, envelopes, coins, sticks, and coloured patches and other items assumed, in a materially replete society, to be commonplace objects in "most people's" experiences. The cultural and class specificity of such "trivial" items rarely evokes comment. Knowers are neutral spectators and objects are separate from them, inert items in an observational knowledge-gathering process. Rarely, even in elaborated theories, does knowing other people figure in accounts of what can be known: such knowing falls below the threshold of epistemic legitimacy, equivocates on the term "knowledge." With reference both to things and to people, it does not matter how such "knowns" figure in anyone's life, nor are the particularities of any life germane to the "nature" or possibility of knowledge. Cognitive and moral agents, in Seyla Benhabib's words, reduce to "an empty mask that is everyone and no one"(1987: 89): thus in S-knows-that-p epistemology ("Sue knows that the box is full"), S is a place-holder for anyone at all, and p an empty container into which anything whatsoever could be inserted. The norms of formal sameness obscure epistemic and moral differences among putative knowers and within the items of their knowledge, with the paradoxical consequence that, because knowledge must transcend experience, a would-be knower hovers behind a "veil of ignorance."

In this conceptual frame, the habits of mind of the "standard knower" bridge the gap between observation and knowledge, just as the intuitions of the "reasonable man" bridge the gap between situation and action in the moral philosophy epitomised, as Margaret Walker argues, in the work of Henry Sidgwick (1998, chapter 2). As I have suggested, tacit experiential-empirical standardization accords a degree of plausibility to the silent commonsensical knowings that inform moral deliberation to the extent that no *negotiation* seems to be required to establish the knowledge from which such deliberation works. And within professional philosophy, a sharp distinction between the interests, purposes, and problems of ethics and epistemology separates questions about the knowledge that, necessarily, informs moral deliberation from the critical domain moral theorists regard as appropriately theirs. A *theoretical-juridical model* of morality and moral theory takes as given a *pure core of knowledge*, whose purity, Walker notes, is "effected by *stipulation* with no obvious rationale"(1998: 35, my emphasis). Methodologically, the very conviction that situations occasioning moral debate lend themselves to one "true" reading which will be obvious from their surface structure, is a function both of the empiricist epistemological assumptions that silently inform moral theory, and of the simplified, self-contained dilemmas that, on this model, exemplify moral conflict. Decisions about whether to keep an appointment or save a drowning child; between an absolute duty not to tell a lie and a particular duty not to reveal a fugitive's hiding place are well known to students of moral philosophy. Sidgwick asserts (plausibly for a certain group of moral agents) that "common sense" will yield clear directives for how "one" must act. But who is "one"? Even in such allegedly everyday conflicts, common sense is "common"only for those of "us" who inhabit a material, social, and moral universe sufficiently like the one the philosopher *him*self inhabits for such situations to be known in the same way by all moral deliberators (see also Code 2002).

In short, an epistemology without the conceptual resources to address experiences in their social-structural-locational specificities occupies a position so remote from the material exigencies of epistemic and moral lives as to be explanatorily impotent. Nonetheless, resistance to particularity has its purpose: it preserves the detached dislocation and impartiality of epistemic and ethical subjects; sustains an illusion of reason purged of emotion, interest, involvement; insulates putative knowers from the responses and responsibilities that concrete particularities demand. It is peculiarly effective for maintaining those willed unknowings that too much particularity evokes from an impassive "knowing subject" (see Code 2001b). But although this model mitigates against knowing well enough to respond adequately to human and situational specificities, shifting the emphasis to pure particularity would be no more viable: *both* subsumption under too-broad generalities *and* deconstruction into too-scattered specificities thwart adequate knowing. Concentration on particularity risks blunting the effectiveness of analysis, rendering it merely episodic, glossing over wide-ranging personal-political-economic structures of power and privilege that produce subjectivities, situations, knowledge, and acknowledgment, even as too remote and abstract an analysis, insufficiently fine-grained to catch the differences and peculiarities that matter, generalizes without sufficient warrant. This is a productive tension, however. It allows no easy resolution, but premature closure is irresponsibly reductive in the possibilities of deliberative acknowledgment it erases.

My purpose in this section so far has been to insist that the ideals of objectivity and value-neutrality at the core of the dominant epistemologies of modernity are best suited to regulate the knowledge of people who are presumed uniformly capable, through the autonomous exercise of reason, of achieving a "view from nowhere" (see Nagel 1986). Yet despite their universalist pretensions, both the ideals of autonomous rationality – of the dislocated, disinterested observer – and the epistemologies they inform are the artifacts of a small, privileged group of educated, usually prosperous, white men whose circumstances convince them of their material and affective autonomy, allowing them to imagine they are nowhere or everywhere even as they occupy unmarked positions of privilege. With an unquestioned belief in the homogeneity of "human nature," these ideals generate what Marguerite La Caze aptly calls "the analytic imaginary" (La Caze 2002). Its principal tenet, with far-reaching consequences for knowledge and subjectivity, is the conviction I have noted: that anyone can put her/himself into anyone else's shoes, and thus can know her or his circumstances and interests just as she or he would know them. Their specificity as *his or her "own"* are epistemologically irrelevant. In their professed disinterestedness, these ideals obscure connections between knowledge and power while reinforcing the conviction that facts, knowings, are as neutral and politically innocent as the processes alleged to produce them. Anyone who cannot see "from nowhere" (= from an ideal observation position that is anywhere and everywhere), cannot take up an epistemic position that mirrors the "original position" of "the moral point of view," cannot *know* anything at all.

Such systematic excisions of "otherness" presume the homogeneity and stability of a social order that the presumers have grounds for assuming they can ensure, for it is they who determine the norms of enquiry and conduct. These convictions, perhaps in spite of themselves, show that ideal objectivity is itself a tacit generalization from the *subjectivity* of a small social group whose positions of power, security, and prestige enable them to believe *their* experiences and normative ideals generalize across the social order to produce a community of like-minded practitioners ("we") that excludes "others" as deviant, aberrant ("they"). These groupings tacitly aggregate a range of generic experiences that are no more "experiential" than the generic "individuals" who allegedly know them are individuated.

Ideal objectivity is thus a vexed issue for feminist epistemologists and moral theorists, even though some form of objectivity seems to be a *sine qua non* for knowledge. Rae Langton, following Catharine MacKinnon, examines one of its particularly vexing facets: "objectivity's" power to *harm* women for, as "the stance of the traditional male knower . . . objectivity objectifies" (Langton 2000: 135) in processes that are neither innocuous nor neutral. The issue, in her view, turns on a neat but complex distinction between beliefs that aim to fit the world and desire that aims to make the world to fit it (p. 137). She illustrates her point with beliefs and desires that make women into objects; where "seeing women as subordinate makes women subordinate" (p. 138). Evidence to the contrary is easily filtered out through the power of a governing imaginary that sustains assumptions about "how things (= women) are." On this view, objectification blocks possibilities of seeing/knowing accurately and well, despite its tacit claims to do just that. One need not be a naive realist to allow that women differ from physical objects and cannot, without distortion, be regarded as manipulable in the ways many physical objects are. Thus objectification yields knowledge claims that are false in a traditionally basic sense. Perhaps more perniciously since less obviously, objectification as Langton glosses it defies the very objectivity it purports to practice; for it conceals its own value-ladenness within a posture of merely observing what is there. The intransigent habits of mind – the imaginary – that inform such "observations" disappear from view.

Phenomenologically, the objectification process is more than a mere looking, which might seem harmless enough. It recalls the "Othering" Simone de Beauvoir analyses in *The Second Sex*, for example in the well-known passage:

> she is simply what man decrees . . . She is defined and differentiated with reference to man and not he with reference to her; she is the incidental, the inessential as opposed to the essential. He is the Subject, he is the Absolute – she is the Other.
>
> (1989: p. xxii)

Alluding to Emmanuel Lévinas' conception of "alterity," Beauvoir observes that when Lévinas "writes that woman is mystery, he implies that she is mystery for man. Thus his description which is intended to be *objective*, is in fact an assertion of masculine privilege" (1989: xxii, fn. 3, emphasis added). The Othering Beauvoir analyses in its structural-experiential minutiae is at once ontological, epistemological, and ethical: it designates what "woman" is, how she can be known, and how she should realize the imperatives of femininity. Nor is such objectification merely a third-person practice for, as Sonia Kruks notes,

> if I am a member of a class of people, such as women, that is deemed to be socially inferior, I may judge myself to be inferior . . . the look may become so integral to the self that it functions in a situation of total privacy.
>
> (2001: 63)

Such sedimented knowings move freely in a social imaginary where assertions of women's "natural" inferiority are such everyday events that no one is surprised or incredulous: "Believing women to be subordinate can make women subordinate: *thinking so can make it so, when it is backed up by power*" (Langton 2000: 139, my emphasis). Such beliefs are kept in circulation by a (Foucauldian) disciplinary, capillary power operative imperceptibly, everywhere and nowhere.

Acknowledgment, then, is no trivial matter simply available for the asking nor is it a matter of individual decision: discrete, seemingly unmediated acts of acknowledgment, where I take your knowledge claims seriously, engage with them, evaluate, corroborate, challenge them, are but moments in larger histories and ecological orderings of social epistemic norms, criteria of reliability, and expectations of testimonial veracity. Patterns of acknowledgment and incredulity pervade the epistemic imaginary as it infuses and is reconfirmed in social-political orders that distribute authority, credibility, respect, expertise on the basis of knowledge claimed. Orthodox epistemologists' protests to the contrary, in practice, social identity *is* often germane, whether negatively or positively, to establishing epistemic credibility. In real-world epistemic negotiations, acknowledgment is routinely conferred and withheld according to the place a putative knower occupies in an established epistemic hierarchy, or with reference to his/her identity *as this or that "kind" of person*. It has more to do than commonly meets an epistemologist's eye with whose "qualifications" and "expertise" allow her/him a hearing as an authoritative, reliable witness, a victim of sexual assault or an appropriate candidate for admission to university (Patricia Williams wonders "what it would take to make my experience verifiable. The testimony of an independent white bystander?" 1991: 7). In short, it functions as one of the factors that make knowledge possible. Such examples have prompted some feminists to urge a reevaluation of modes of reasoning long disparaged as *ad hominem* (*ad feminam*) arguments, or as committing "the genetic fallacy" (see Alcoff 2001; Code 1995), arguing that such lines of reasoning often succeed in revealing aspects of epistemic lives that sanitized, formal accounts suppress; showing that "the same" truth or fact may claim a different place in structures of acknowledgment and incredulity, according to who speaks it. *Ad feminam/ad hominem* claims require evaluation as rigorous as any other knowledge claim; but reasons for dismissing them out of hand rely on implausible assumptions about knowledge and subjectivity, and about the epistemic significance of knowing people responsibly and well. I have proposed (Code 1991; 1993) knowing other people as a contender for exemplary epistemic status because of the marked contrasts it presents with the (often facile) immediacy of punctiform sense-perceptual examples. My suggestion mobilizes the thought that if epistemology started from unfamiliar rather than from settled, habitual situations and examples, the complexity of knowing even the simplest things, the *qualitative* variability of knowledge, would become more apparent. When it is responsibly practiced, knowing other people without objectifying them admits of degree in ways that knowing the book is on the table does not; its interactive relationality differentiates it from stylized, detached propositional knowledge. It requires constant learning: how to be with people, respond, act toward and with them. And although the claim that people are *knowable* may sit uneasily with psychoanalytic decenterings of conscious subjectivity and postmodern critiques of unified humanistic subjectivity, it is evident in practice that people often know each other well enough to judge each other's trustworthiness, reliability or credibility, even through fluctuations and contradictions in subjectivity and circumstance. Knowing other people well is particularly vulnerable to the unknowings the analytic imaginary condones in taking for granted an implausible ease at putting oneself in someone else's shoes. Its vulnerability highlights the imperatives of responsible, interpretive attentiveness in knowing, where too-swift conclusions slide readily into an epistemic imperialism that, recalling Langton, is harmful.

In social-scientific inquiry and in its everyday real-world effects, epistemological veneration of observational "simples" contributes to the reductivism of behaviorist psychology; to parochial impositions of meaning onto the practices of "other cultures"; and to simplistic readings of present-day interpretations into past situations and lives that characterize some historical and archeological practice. But feminist, postcolonial, anti-racist, hermeneutic, and postmodern critiques can claim some success in urging social scientists and secular knowers to have done with adherence to such neo-positivistic hegemony. Writing, for example, of white western anthropology's claims to know the people it studies, Trinh T. Minh-ha (1989: 9.48) cautions: "On one plane, we, I, and he, may speak the same language and even act alike; yet, on the other, we stand miles apart, irreducibly foreign to each other." Three decades earlier, Beauvoir makes an analogous claim. She writes (1962: 67): "It is only as something strange, forbidden, as something free, that the other is revealed as an other. And to love him genuinely is to love him in his otherness and in that freedom by which /he escapes." Responsible knowing preserves yet seeks to know the "strangeness," respects the boundaries between self and other that the "forbiddenness" affirms, does not seek to assimilate or obliterate the "freedom." Projects of knowing other people cognizant of such concerns have the potential to offer a reconstructed interpretive mode of inquiry, liberated from positivistic constraints, and in many respects exemplary for knowledge in different registers and domains (see Alcoff 1996).

But how can knowledge integral to human relationships translate to knowing inanimate objects? The case must be made by analogy, not by requiring knowers to befriend tables and chairs, chemicals, particles, cells, planets, rocks, trees, and insects. An obvious disanalogy is that chairs, cells, and rocks can neither reciprocate nor answer back; there is none of the mutual recognition and affirmation that there is between people. The point of proposing the analogy, nonetheless, is to strengthen the claim that privileging an asymmetrical observer–observed relation is but one possibility among many, and thus to argue that if disinterested, autonomous standards were displaced by collaborative discussions and deliberations about provisional, approximate knowledge claims and hypotheses, knowing other people would not seem so different. Remaining open to (re)interpretation, acknowledging the interlocutor(s) whose participation affirms that people rarely know in monologic isolation and that adequate knowledge requires situational, ecological chartings all become clearer through the "personal" analogy. Although the analogy is imperfect and makes no claims to universalizability, it is no more preposterous to argue that people should try to know physical objects in the nuanced way they know their friends, associates, and foes than to assume they could know people in the unsubtle way they often claim to know physical objects. Because knowing other people requires persistent interplay between opacity and transparency, while eschewing monologic practices of speaking a knowledge claim as if into a void, knowers are kept on their cognitive toes. Hence claims to know other people are negotiable between knower and known, "subject" and "object" positions are often interchangeable, and agency can be more evenly distributed between subject and object than in the spectator epistemologies that objectify. Hence too Donna Haraway's depiction of nature as trickster and Karen Barad's agential realism are illuminating in exposing the agency of the natural-physical world (Haraway 1991;

Barad 1997). Neither the self-conception nor the knower-conception can claim absolute authority, for the limits of self-consciousness constrain the process as closely as the interiority of mental processes and experiential constructs and their unavailability to observation. If the limitations of accumulated factual claims were taken seriously for empirical knowledge more generally, the limitations of an epistemology built from observational simples might be more broadly conceived. The persistent idea that people are opaque to one another may explain why this knowledge has been of minimal epistemic interest: because knowledge, traditionally, is *of* objects, opacity or transparency has not been an issue. Yet as Langton notes, in the analytic resources mainstream epistemology makes available, it is only by assimilating people to objects that one can hope to know them. My claim for the exemplary character of knowing other people challenges this assumption, requiring epistemologists, literally and metaphorically, to look beneath the surface.

Naturalizing, Reconfiguring, Situating

In the late twentieth century, inspired in large part by the work of W.V.O. Quine (1969), a revived naturalistic epistemology proposed a departure from dislocated inquiry focused on what ideal knowers ought to do. It would return epistemic inquiry to the world, to determine its real-world (natural) conditions as demonstrated by experiments in scientific psychology and cognitive science. Insisting that the descriptive character of their project does not simply turn an "is" of epistemic practice into an "ought"of normativity, naturalists take a critical stance toward the practices they examine and those in which they engage: they do not merely record how people know in laboratory conditions. In my readings of naturalistic projects, it is their reflexive, self-critical stance that opens space for interpretive negotiation, indicating a possibility for descriptive analyses to yield normative and evaluative principles more adequate to human epistemic lives than a priori epistemologies can provide. Thus epistemological exhortations would respond more closely to the demonstrated capacities and limitations of real knowers than experience-remote analyses of monologic knowledge claims that are everyone's and no one's.

Nonetheless, the cognitive science to which Quinean naturalists appeal incorporates normative assumptions of its own (see the essays in Kornblith 1994), arrogating to itself the power to denigrate the utterances of "folk psychology," except in "folksy" conversations, and thereby sustaining the hierarchy that elevates scientific above "other" knowledge, even for naturalists. The laboratory, which remains so remote from everyday epistemic lives, still poses as the natural knowledge-making setting, despite its constructed, artificial character. For Quinean naturalism the assumptions, methods, and evaluative practices of cognitive science are in order as they stand, readily translatable across the epistemic terrain, to the extent that issues about the epistemic negotiation human and situational difference generate need not arise. Thus despite naturalism's critical stance toward the a priori aims and claims of more orthodox epistemology, designating physical science-cognitive science "natural" preserves the physical-science-dominant assumptions that govern standard epistemic analyses. Yet nature is neither self-announcing, nor "naturally"distinguishable from culture or artefact. Continuing to privilege this source of natural knowledge, then, risks perpetuating scientistic excesses that maintain a gap between a naturalism intent on relocating itself "down on the ground," and everyday epistemic practices that prompt skepticism about the explanatory potential of entrenched theories of knowledge modeled on the methods and presuppositions of physical science. These are contestable assumptions; they come under scrutiny in feminist and other postcolonial epistemologies, despite impressive feminist work indebted to Quinean naturalism (cf. especially Duran 1991 and Nelson 1990; 1999).

Situating epistemic practices, refusing the mythology of the view from nowhere, the god's eye view (Haraway 1991), is germane to naturalizing epistemology, although not precisely as Quinean naturalism advocates (see Code 1996). In "Situated Knowledges," Donna Haraway names *radical constructivism* and *feminist critical empiricism* as the poles of a dichotomy that tempts and traps feminists, warning that dissolving this tension prematurely would block the feminist goal of producing "faithful accounts of a 'real' world" and critical analyses of the "radical historical contingency" of power-implicated knowledge and subjectivity. She advocates a "feminist objectivity [of] limited location and situated knowledge" (1991: 187, 190) in which objectivity responds to the pull of empiricism, location and situation to the pull of constructivism and diversely enacted subjectivities. Knowledge claims would thus gain or fail to achieve acknowledgment *situationally*, according to the patterns of incredulity, authority, and expertise constitutive of the social order and the "institutions of knowledge production" in which they circulate and in whose praxes they are embedded: situations neither so alike as to permit interchangeable, universal, analyses nor so idiosyncratic as to require radically separate and distinct analyses.

In this reading of Haraway, "situation" is *a place to know* in two senses: a place where knowledge is produced; and a place that itself demands to be known in its political, demographic, and material-physical features that facilitate or thwart democratic knowing. Epistemic mappings of such features highlight the structural intricacies of place and its inhabitants, the genealogies, power relations, and commitments that shape the knowledge and subjectivities enacted there, the locational specificities that resist homogenization, the positionings available or closed to would-be knowing subjects. Situation, then, is not just a place *from which to know*, as "perspectives" talk implies, indifferently available to anyone who chooses to stand there. Practices of *negotiating empiricism* emerge, whose negotiations are less exclusively about addressing everyday scientific or secular debates over what counts as evidence than about how the ongoing commitments of an inquiry – the epistemic imaginary that frames it and informs it – generate questions about the nature of evidence and its relation to "facts." Central to such practices are questions about why a knowledge claim "goes through," carries weight, or fails to gain acknowledgment, where answers are as much about epistemic responsibilities to engage in open democratic debate on matters of knowledge and acknowledgment, to cultivate sensitivity to difference, alterity, and moments of incommensurability, as they are about correspondence or replicability; and where, phenomenologically, the Othering that objectifies gives way to engagements with an alterity that elicits reciprocal respect. Quoting Ofelia Schutte,

> the breakthrough in constructing the concept of *the other* occurs when one combines the notion of the other as different from the self with the acknowledgement of the self's decentering that results from the experience of differences . . . [It] involves acknowledging the positive, potentially ethical dimensions of such a decentering for interpersonal relations.
>
> (2000: 46)

Arguing for respectful attention to incommensurabilities between linguistic and cultural symbolic systems that refuses the imperialism, indeed, the epistemic violence, of superimposing the familiar upon the "strange" and suppressing the leftovers, Schutte writes that

> what we hold to be the nature of knowledge is not culture-free but is determined by the methodologies and data legitimated by dominant cultures . . . [T]he scientific practices of a dominant culture are what determine not only the limits of knowledge but who may legitimately participate in the language of science.
>
> (Ibid.)

Schutte's remarks insist on the sensitivity to, and respect owed to incommensurability. They indicate, by way of contrast, how tacitly presumed androcentricity, Eurocentricity, and other centricities work, in their imperialistic assumptions of human and circumstantial sameness, to standardize and naturalize modalities of incredulity and acknowledgment. Consider, for example, the obliterative power of blank incomprehension. As I have argued, these centricities feed into and are fed by the social-epistemic imaginary of neutrality, objectivity, and replicability, usually imagined to be so impersonal and formal that it "could not possibly be oppressive," while, paradoxically, detached neutrality carries within itself the seeds of oppression, obliteration. Knowledge, in the end, depends upon acknowledgment!

In the approach I advocate, "situated knowledges" critically examined and debated in everyday deliberations and institutionally located praxes, interpretive-hermeneutic practices responsibly engaged, and naturalistic epistemology deflected from its scientific course, become cooperators in charting a way forward for successor epistemologies. Enlisting naturalized epistemology's resources for emancipatory ends, locating the "natural" in places orthodox naturalists might scorn to acknowledge, it contends that "natural" too is a negotiable attribution. Although the position maintains some allegiance to a critical empirical-realism in its accountable (= evidence-reliant) engagement with the natural and social worlds, both found and made, this is no value-neutral spectator epistemology, nor does it rely on propositional atomicity or the monologic, punctiform utterances of abstract epistemic agents. It proposes a conceptual apparatus for negotiating situations in which knowledge *and* subjectivity are variously enacted on complex, institutionally patterned and diversely populated epistemic terrains.

Ecological Naturalism

To show how the epistemic terrain could be remapped, taking naturalistic practices in institutions of knowledge-making as guidelines and geographical markers, I am developing an ecological model of knowledge and subjectivity in which I suggest how these proposals might work both for epistemology in its traditional domains, and for moral epistemology, to displace an entrenched, hegemonic epistemic imaginary (see Code, forthcoming). *Ecological naturalism*, as I call it, which situates inquiry as firmly within real-world knowledge-making practices as Quineans situate it in the laboratory world, effects ongoing rapprochements, whether cooperative or contestatory, between epistemic norms and the imperatives of responsible, trustworthy inquiry. It is dependent upon the engaged praxes of practitioners whose commonalities and differences have always to be taken into account in their projects of producing epistemic environments that are neither oppressive nor exploitative.

The dominant, post-positivist epistemologies of post-Industrial Revolution societies enact a rhetoric of mastery and possession: knowledge "acquired" for manipulation, prediction, and control over nature and human nature; knowledge as a prized commodity that legitimates its possessors' authoritative occupancy of positions of power and recasts "the natural world" as a human resource. The "god-trick" Haraway repudiates is about mastery and possession, as are the self-certainties of Sidgwickian moral theory and the objectifying practices Langton discusses. Aggregating, amalgamating differences is also about mastery – over the wayward, the unfamiliar, the strange – as is resistance to any idea of social-cultural incommensurability: to the idea that any item, idea, theory, place or social group could exceed the cognitive reach of the privileged and powerful.

Metaphorically enlisted in this project, the language of ecology articulates a model of knowledge and subjectivity that takes its point of departure from the – natural – dependence of knowledge claims upon one another, and upon and within sociality and location, to promote situation-sensitive knowledge-making practices that refuse the unimaginative, dislocated levellings-off of the epistemologies of mastery. Because it requires mappings internal to specific projects of knowledge production, and external inter-mappings from region to region, negotiating differences is a principal item on its agenda. Nor, on such a view, could there be a master-mapper or master-negotiator. It envisages democratic, collaborative deliberation as the most desirable, potentially effective method. Negotiations have to be attentive to the politics of difference, to know differences respectfully, imaginatively, and critically, to honour and protect them as deliberative practical wisdom (*phronesis*) deems appropriate; to interrogate and challenge them where necessary; yet neither in stasis nor in isolation. This way of thinking about knowledge amounts to a revisioned *naturalism*. Yet in locating inquiry within practices and institutions where people produce knowledge and enact its effects, it makes no before-the-fact assumptions about "knowledge in general." It is ever wary of the power-infused tendencies of racial-gender-class stereotypes and essentialized conceptions of "science" and "nature" to assume the self-fulfilling, self-perpetuating forms that foster illusions of sameness. It maps (interim) conclusions from region to region, location to location, to inform and enable global emancipatory projects, counting among its resources "bioregional narratives" that expose the incommensurability of emancipatory discourses across regional and demographic diversity (see Cheney 1989; Code 1998), thus learning to refuse the imperialism of reading difference through a template of "the same," with its consequent epistemic violence.

Ecological thinking enlists natural scientific evidence in determining how survival is best enhanced, both qualitatively and quantitatively, while contesting scientific claims to the status of master metanarrative. It establishes its evidence in self-critical reflexivity, where locally, environmentally informed studies of disciplines, their subject matters, and interdisciplinary relations generate an ongoing suspicion of presumptions to theoretical hegemony. Thus in its engagement with natural sciences, ecological thinking concerns itself (in Verena Conley's words, 1997: 42) "with active interrelations among . . . [species] and between them and their habitat in its most diverse biochemical and geophysical properties." It conceives of subjectivity as embodied and materially situated; and locatedness and interdependence as integral to the possibility of being, doing, and knowing. This ecological subject is made by and makes its relations in reciprocity with other subjects and with its (multiply diverse) environments, be these benign, malign, or neutral. Nor is the model itself self-evidently benign. Ecosystems are as competitively, unsentimentally destructive of their less viable members as they are cooperative and mutually sustaining. In consequence, if thinking and acting within this conceptual frame is to avoid replicating the exclusions and silencings endemic to traditional epistemologies, its practitioners require moral-political guidelines for regulating and adjudicating the responsibilities invoked by claims to epistemic authority.

Cognizant of the reductivism of the unity-of-knowledge/unity-of-science assumptions by which inquiries are both homogenized to ensure formal homogeneity in knowledge from one to another in the conditions of its possibility, and kept separate by entrenched border-patrolling assumptions, ecological thinking maps locations of knowledge-production separately and comparatively; interpreting the local specifties of "habitat" conditions as a basis for determining analogies and disanalogies. Epistemic evaluation thus stretches to address the (demonstrable) effects of knowledge, the meanings it makes and sustains, the practices it legitimates, the values it embodies and conveys. Responsibility and accountability requirements join verifiability high on the epistemic agenda as epistemic and moral-political issues coalesce around questions of acknowledgment and incredulity, accountability, and trust.

To make good the claim that scientific knowledge is neither the only nor the most "natural" epistemic focus, I propose feminist legal and medical practice as sites where science is integral to the knowledge that informs and is informed by practice, and scientific method often governs "fact-finding," although it does not yield the only knowledge worthy of the label (I draw here on Code 2001a). In these practices situation is "a place to know" whose governing imaginary is infused with the judgment of "the reasonable man" (in law) of whom a judge is the leading exemplar; and the achievements of empirical science (in medicine) where an objective, science-obedient diagnostician is the epistemic exemplar. Both are power-infused institutions, and analogous in how knowledge functions within them, although any "knowledge in general" presumption would erase salient specificities. In law, recalling Sidgwick, I point to the circulation and sedimentation of "commonsense" beliefs at work in legal judgments ("women don't mean it when they say 'no'") and their constitutive role in judicial decision-making, despite their empirical contestability. In medicine, I note how putatively subjective experiential knowledge, which nonetheless merits the label "knowledge" (this too is integral to the argument), slips through the grid of clinical diagnosis, to remain invisible to all but the maverick, eccentric clinician. Here *situated knowledge* does not just announce "where it (or its articulator) is coming from": it engages critically with the detail of knowledge-making situations populated by particular, fallible human beings. Such sites may be analogically ecologically interconnected, but readings insensitive to their local specificities cannot be applied whole, as though every location could stand in for any other. Meanwhile, the negotiated aspect of situated knowledge ensures that its self-scrutiny reduces neither to monologic introspection nor to individualistic retreat into autobiography.

Although this move to investigating knowledge-making and -circulating in public institutions takes praxes (hence specific, engaged human practices) as primary sites of knowledge-making, it is no simple move from a tainted laboratory setting to situations less tainted, more innocent, or more "natural." Few situations can be presumed innocent or neutral before the fact: they need to be analysed, evaluated in their structure and detail, to expose the historical-material contingencies – hence the negotiability – of the social-political arrangements of authority and expertise enabled and enacted there. Nor is there a neutral, unsituated place for critical inquirers to stand. The task of epistemology becomes more, rather than less, complex in this analysis, but its deliverances should be better able to address epistemic matters that matter.

In this reconfigured conceptual frame, feminist epistemology is a critical and constructive response to ways of being in the world: to the diversity and specificities of the lives of women and other Others. Thus it is at odds with a dominant vision/imaginary for which so much is taken for granted simply because it comes from a position (androcentered, white, educated, affluent, Eurocentered) that carries a tacit entitlement *to* assume so much. The scope of the inquiry shows that questions about knowledge and acknowledgment run through everything, even where they may seem not to arise: moral deliberations, putatively basic fact-finding, how "we" know other people, how "we" inhabit the world and engage our projects within it, from the simplest to the most complex. And knowledge is indeed a thing of this world: it both knows and makes the world, although neither at will nor out of whole cloth, for praxes expose the scope and limits both of the world's malleability to human purposes and of knowers' capacities to engage it, adapt to it, or change it. Because these knowers are not sealed away in the privacy of a study or a club culture where knowing occurs in the pristine purity that positivism promised, these engagements, at their best, would escape the subjectivist dangers of what Sonia Kruks calls "an epistemology of provenance," for which

> knowledge arises from an experiential basis that is so fundamentally group-specific that others, who are outside the group and who lack its immediate experiences, cannot share that knowledge . . . that outsiders have no basis from which they can legitimately evaluate the group's claims . . . [and] only those who live a particular reality can know about it . . . and have the right to speak about it.
>
> (2001: 109)

Although feminist epistemology, which includes feminist moral epistemology, comes at least in part out of a commitment to take women's experiences seriously, Kruks' observation points to the danger of allowing what I have elsewhere called the tyranny of an "experientialism" immune to criticism displace the older tyranny of an impartial expertise that subsumed experiences and identities under predetermined categories and structures of authority and expertise, within which everyone could know women's lives better than women themselves could know them. It is in the tension between these polarities that feminist epistemologies have to chart their course.

Bibliography

Alcoff, Linda (1996) *Real Knowing: New Versions of the Coherence Theory*, Ithaca, NY: Cornell University Press.

—— (2001) "On Judging Epistemic Credibility: Is Social Identity Relevant?" in *Engendering Rationalities*, eds. Nancy Tuana and Sandra Morgen, Albany: SUNY Press.

Barad, Karen (1997) "Meeting the Universe Halfway: Realism and Social Constructivism without Contradiction," in *Feminism, Science, and the Philosophy of Science*, eds. Lynn Hankinson Nelson and Jack Nelson, Dordrecht: Kluwer.

Beauvoir, Simone de (1962) *The Ethics of Ambiguity*, tr. Bernard Frechtman, New York: The Citadel Press.

——([1952] 1989) *The Second Sex*, tr. H.M. Parshley, New York: Knopf. (*Le Deuxième sexe*, Paris: Gallimard, 1949.)

Benhabib, Selya (1987) "The Generalized and the Concrete Other," in *Feminism as Critique*, eds. Selya Benhabib and Drucilla Cornell, Minneapolis: University of Minnesota Press.

Bordo, Susan (1987) *The Flight to Objectivity*, Albany: SUNY Press.

Burt, Sandra and Code, Lorraine, eds. (1995) *Changing Methods: Feminists Transforming Practice*, Peterborough, Ontario: Broadview Press.

Butler, Judith (1990) *Gender Trouble: Feminism and the Subversion of Identity*, New York: Routledge.

Cheney, Jim (1989) "Postmodern Environmental Ethics: Ethics as Bioregional Narrative," *Environmental Ethics* 11 (12): 117–34.

Code, Lorraine (1991) *What Can She Know? Feminist Theory and the Construction of Knowledge*, Ithaca, NY: Cornell University Press.

—— (1993) "Taking Subjectivity into Account," in *Feminist Epistemologies*, eds. Linda Alcoff and Elizabeth Potter, New York: Routledge.

—— (1995) *Rhetorical spaces: Essays on (Gendered) locations*, New York: Routledge, especially chapters 2 and 8.

—— (1996) "What Is Natural about Epistemology Naturalized?" *American Philosophical Quarterly* 33 (1): 1–22.

—— (1998) "How to Think Globally: Stretching the Limits of Imagination," *Hypatia: A Journal of Feminist Philosophy* 13 (2): 73–85.

—— (2001a) "Statements of Fact: Whose? Where? When?" *Canadian Journal of Philosophy* 26, Supplement: Moral Epistemology Naturalized, eds. Richmond Campbell and Bruce Hunter: 175–208.

—— (2001b) "Rational Imaginings, Responsible Knowings: How Far Can You See from Here?" in *Engendering Rationalities*, eds. Nancy Tuana and Sandra Morgen, Albany: SUNY Press.

—— (2002) "Narratives of Responsibility and Agency: Reading Margaret Walker's *Moral Understandings*," *Hypatia: A Journal of Feminist Philosophy* 17 (1): 156–73.

—— (forthcoming) *Ecological Naturalism*, New York: Oxford University Press.

Collins, Patricia Hill (1990) *Black Feminist Thought: Knowledge, Consciousness, and the Politics of Empowerment*, New York: HarperCollins.

Conley, Verena (1997) *Ecopolitics: The Environment in Poststructuralist Thought*, London: Routledge.

de Lauretis, Teresa (1987) *Technologies of Gender*, Bloomington: Indiana University Press.

Duran, Jane (1991) *Toward a Feminist Epistemology*, Savage, MD: Rowman and Littlefield.

Ferguson, Kathy E. (1993) *The Man Question: Visions of Subjectivity in Feminist Theory*, Berkeley: University of California Press.

Fricker, Miranda (2000) "Feminism in Epistemology. Pluralism without Postmodernism," in *The Cambridge Companion to Feminist Epistemology*, ed. Miranda Fricker and Jennifer Hornsby, Cambridge: Cambridge University Press.

Haraway, Donna (1991) "'Situated Knowledges': The Science Question in Feminism and the Privilege of Partial Perspective," in *Simians, Cyborgs, and Women: The Reinvention of Nature*, New York: Routledge.

Harding, Sandra (1986) *The Science Question in Feminism*, Ithaca, NY: Cornell University Press.

Keller, Evelyn Fox (1985) *Reflections on Gender and Science*, New Haven, CT: Yale University Press.

Kornblith, Hilary, ed. (1994) *Naturalizing Epistemology*, 2nd edn., Cambridge, MA: MIT Press.

Kruks, Sonia (2001) *Retrieving Experience: Subjectivity and Recognition in Feminist Politics*, Ithaca, NY: Cornell University Press.

La Caze, Marguerite (2002) *The Analytic Imaginary*, Ithaca, NY: Cornell University Press.

Langton, Rae (2000) "Feminism in Epistemology: Exclusion and Objectification," in *The Cambridge Companion to Feminist Epistemology*, eds. Miranda Fricker and Jennifer Hornsby, Cambridge: Cambridge University Press.

Le Dœuff, Michèle (1991) *Hipparchia's Choice*, tr. Trista Selous, Oxford: Blackwell.

—— (2003) *The Sex of Knowing*, trs. Kathryn Hamer and Lorraine Code, New York: Routledge.

Lloyd, Genevieve (1984) *The Man of Reason: "Male" and "Female" in Western Philosophy*, Minneapolis: University of Minnesota Press, 2nd edn., 1993.

—— (2000) "No One's Land: Australia and the Philosophical Imagination," *Hypatia: A Journal of Feminist Philosophy* 15 (2): 26–58.

Longino, Helen (1990) *Science as Social Knowledge: Values and Objectivity in Scientific Inquiry*, Princeton, NJ: Princeton University Press.

Lugones, Maria (1988) "Playfulness, 'World'-Travelling and Loving Perception," in *Women, Knowledge and Reality*, eds. Ann Garry and Marilyn Pearsall, New York: Unwin Hyman.

McAlister, Linda Lopez, ed. (1996) *Hypatia's Daughters: Fifteen Hundred Years of Women Philosophers*, Bloomington: Indiana University Press.

Mills, Charles. W. (1997) *The Racial Contract*, Ithaca, NY: Cornell University Press.

Minh-ha, Trinh T. (1989) "The Language of Nativism: Anthropology as a Scientific Conversation of Man with Man," in *Woman, Native, Other: Writing Postcoloniality and Feminism*, Bloomington: Indiana University Press.

Nagel, Thomas (1986) *The View from Nowhere*, Oxford: Oxford University Press.

Nelson, Lynn Hankinson (1990) *Who Knows. From Quine to a Feminist Empiricism*, Philadelphia, PA: Temple University Press.

——(1999) "The Very Idea of Feminist Epistemology," in *Is Feminist Philosophy Possible?* ed. Emanuela Bianchi, Chicago: Northwestern University Press.

Quine, W.V.O. (1969) "Epistemology Naturalized," in *Ontological Relativity and Other Essays*, New York: Columbia University Press.

Riley, Denise (1988) *"Am I that Name?" Feminism and the Category of "Women" in History*, Minneapolis: University of Minnesota Press.

Rossiter, Margaret (1982) *Women Scientists in America: Struggles and Strategies to 1940*, Baltimore: Johns Hopkins University Press.

Scheman, Naomi (1993) *Engenderings: Constructions of Knowledge, Authority, and Privilege*, New York: Routledge.

Schiebinger, Londa (1999) *Has Feminism Changed Science?* Cambridge, MA: Harvard University Press.

Schutte, Ofelia (2000) "Cultural Alterity: Cross-Cultural Communication and Feminist Theory in North–South Contexts," in *Women of Color and Philosophy: A Critical Reader*, ed. Naomi Zack, Oxford: Blackwell.

Scott, Joan W. (1992) "'Experience'," in *Feminists Theorize the Political*, eds. Judith Butler and Joan W. Scott, New York: Routledge.

Waithe, Mary Ellen (1987) *A History of Women Philosophers*, vol. 1: *Ancient Women Philosophers*, Dordrecht: Kluwer Academic Publishers.

—— (1989) *A History of Women Philosophers*, vol. 2: *Medieval, Renaissance and Enlightenment Women Philosophers*, Dordrecht: Kluwer Academic Publishers.

Walker, Margaret Urban (1998) *Moral Understandings: A Feminist Study in Ethics*, New York: Routledge.

Williams, Patricia J. (1991) *The Alchemy of Race and Rights: Diary of a Law Professor*. Cambridge, MA: Harvard University Press.

—— (1997) "The Pantomime of Race," in *Seeing a Color-Blind Future*, New York: The Noonday Press.

Wittgenstein, Ludwig (1971) *On Certainty*, eds. G.E.M. Anscombe and G.H. von Wright, trs. Denis Paul and G.E.M. Anscombe, New York: Harper Torchbooks.

Wylie, Alison (2003) "Why Standpoint Matters," in *Science and Other Cultures: Issues in Philosophies of Science and Technology*, eds. Robert Figueroa and Sandra Harding, New York: Routledge.

Chapter 13

Feminist Epistemology and Philosophy of Science

Elizabeth Potter

Feminist epistemologists and philosophers of science have argued that contextual values, that is, moral, social, and political values, influence the work of natural and social scientists not only when the work is considered by scientists to be poor science, but also when it is considered to be good science. Making these arguments has, therefore, led feminist philosophers of science to focus on the justification of knowledge claims by scientists and on ways of understanding contextual values that allow us to see their legitimate role in the justification of scientific knowledge. An examination of current feminist epistemologies and philosophies of science reveals that they are converging on empiricist accounts of the justification of knowledge and empiricist understandings of contextual values.

We will understand empiricism to be an approach to the justification of knowledge; thus, empiricists maintain that knowledge claims, as well as other objects of knowledge such as data, models, and theories, about the natural and social world (as opposed to mathematics or logic) are justified by testing them against sensory experience, or by reasoning from claims, etc. which have been justified by testing them against sensory experience.

This minimal working definition leaves several questions open including, first, whether the objects of knowledge are all tested for truth or whether some are tested for other modes of conformity to experience (see Longino 2002); second, whether the objects of knowledge are justified singly or holistically; third, whether the best model of relations among the objects of knowledge is foundational or non-foundational; fourth, whether the best account of the source or origin of concepts and other objects of knowledge is an empiricist one and if so, whether the account must begin with sense data, the firings of C-fibers, etc. Below we will examine an argument for the role of contextual values in the justification of scientific theories; the argument shows us that empiricism need not assume that contextual values cannot be tested and corrected by sensory experience.

Convergence upon Empiricism in Feminist Accounts of the Justification of Scientific Knowledge

Turning to the many accounts of justification offered by philosophers of science, we find that justification can be understood broadly to cover the evaluation of an object of knowledge, e.g. a claim, account, model, theory, etc., as a "good" one – meeting the purposes of knowledge agents – or one that is poor, bad, useless, false, or otherwise infelicitous for their purposes. These purposes differ, including not only the production of true and/or accurate claims, but also a broad array of purposes, many of which do not include discovering truth. Models and theories can be useful in many ways without being true or even accurate – although most purposes require some degree of conformity to some experiences; however, not all purposes do (see Longino 2002, esp. chapter five). Justification as the epistemic evaluation of knowledge lies at the heart of epistemology and philosophy of science, and our broad understanding of it allows us to see the convergence of feminist epistemologies and philosophies of science upon empiricist solutions to epistemological problems surrounding justification.

There is disagreement among feminist philosophers over the best approach to justification. Standpoint theorist Nancy Hartsock, for example, maintains that better knowledge of the social world, that is, better socio-political accounts or theories, are ones that account for large-scale social forces or macroprocesses and so enable self-conscious change of individuals into resistant collectivities with an achieved standpoint. A good social theory enables social justice. Thus, the achieved standpoint of German National Socialism does not offer a better social theory even though it meets this definition because it is not ethically better; it fails to enable more just social relations (Hartsock 1997).

It is central to my argument that, while Sandra Harding's organization of feminist epistemologies and philosophies of science into three categories, empiricism, standpoint theories and postmodernism (see Harding 1986, for explanation of these categories), has been important and very useful as a way of understanding feminist epistemologies and philosophies of science, we are well served now by a conceptual framework comparing approaches to central issues. I suggest nuanced taxonomies based upon the differentiation of epistemic stances toward particular issues, e.g. justification, epistemic agency, values and objectivity, underdetermination, pluralism, judgmental relativism, etc. Within this framework, we can still divide feminist epistemologies and philosophies of science according to Harding's three categories, but we can also divide them in many different ways, for example, by how naturalizing and how normative they are. In particular, this way of understanding feminist epistemologies and philosophies of science will allow us to see that a feminist philosopher may adopt different approaches to different problems. Clearly, then, I am not arguing that all feminist epistemologies and philosophies of science now fall into only one of three general epistemic stances, viz. empiricism.

Hence, my argument for convergence upon empiricism does not deny that insofar as epistemic agency is central to epistemology and philosophy of science, we find a strong consensus around the view – associated with standpoint theory – of agency as situated, i.e., that social, economic, and many other differences among epistemic agents are epistemically relevant. (We will discuss the situated-ness of epistemic agency below.) A distinctive feature of feminist epistemologies and philosophies of science is the unblinking thoroughness with which feminist philosophers have pursued the situatedness of agency into the domain of justifi-cation. This has its downsides, of course, because, based on the recognition that epistemic agency is situated, most have rejected traditional positivist and post-positivist empiricist accounts of justification and the myth of objectivity as the view from nowhere. These rejections, in turn, have led to charges that feminist episte-mologies and philosophies of science are viciously relativist. I am arguing that in feminist technical responses to the problems arising from the challenge of rela-tivism, most have affirmed recognizable empiricisms and this includes responses offered by some standpoint theorists.

The feminist consensus around epistemic agency rejects traditional assumptions that

1   the epistemic agent's "situation" or "life context" is epistemically irrelevant; this is primarily a rejection of the assumption that the objective epistemic agent must be politically and morally innocent and/or that knowledge requires the use of methods insuring that its production is neutral among socio-political and moral values (see Lloyd 1995); and

2   the agent of knowledge in general and of scientific knowledge in particular is the individual; i.e., the epistemic agent is an autonomous individual, able to produce knowledge without other epistemic agents. (Kathy Addelson and I dubbed this view, "epistemological individualism." See Addelson and Potter 1991.)

We find the rejection of epistemological individualism in most feminist epistem-ologies though certainly not in all (Longino 1990; Nelson 1990 and 1993; Addelson 1991; Collins 1991; Harding 1991 and 1993; Potter 1991 and 1993; Alcoff 1993; Wylie 2003). Antony (1995) argues for epistemic individualism and Grasswick (2004) argues for individuals-in-communities as the agents of knowledge.) There is vibrant disagreement over the nature of the epistemic com-munity which produces knowledge and over whether the production of beliefs is still autonomous, e.g. whether the epistemic community is necessary in principle for the production of beliefs. Feminist scholars arrived at the view that "knowl-edge is situated" in several ways. Most found persuasive the many case studies showing that socio-political, religious, and moral values have played a part in the justification of scientific theories considered good science. These include cases put forward by both mainstream science studies and feminist studies of the impact of gender considerations upon good science (see, for example, Gould 1981; Bloor 1982; Shapin 1982; Longino 1983 and 1990; Bleier 1984; Lewontin et al. 1984;

and Nelson 1990). And many found useful Hegel's insight into the epistemic consequences of the master/slave relationship especially as developed in the Marxian
view that the proletarian's knowledge is like that of Hegel's slave. As Harding
describes it,

> From the perspective of the master's activities, everything the slave does appears to be
> the consequence either of the master's will or of the slave's lazy and brutish nature.
> The slave does not appear fully human. However, from the standpoint of the slave's
> activities, one can see her smiling at the master when she in fact wishes to kill, playing
> lazy as the only form of resistance she can get away with, and scheming with the slave
> community to escape. The slave can be seen as fully human.
>
> (1998: 149)

The master's interests do not require a full, accurate understanding of the master/
slave relationship, but the slave's interests, including life itself, demand a more
accurate understanding of the relationship. In the Marxian view, the proletarian
also has an interest in understanding the social and natural worlds accurately, while
the bourgeoisie has less interest in an accurate account of the world for it is well
served by the dominant ideology, a set of beliefs about social life that misrepresents or distorts the world. Since economic and social conditions produce and
reproduce these beliefs, and the beliefs, in turn, legitimate and make the economic
and social system seem "natural," the distorted beliefs will not change until the
proletariat, which has an interest in understanding the world as it really is, achieves
class consciousness and acts to change economic and social relations (Bakhurst
1992: 192).

Arguments such as Hartsock's, then, have been very useful; she generalized
the Marxian position to include women and other subordinated groups. As the
proletariat is the subordinated group under capitalism, women constitute the
subordinated group under patriarchy and people of color constitute the subordinated group under white supremacy, etc. In each case, dominant "ideologies" or
accounts legitimate, that is, "make seem natural and normal," economic, gender,
and racial hierarchies (Harding 1997: 385). In some versions of this view, any
problem of theory selection is solved by the fact that women, like the proletariat
and, it seemed, proletarian women in particular, have a privileged – more accurate
– understanding.

The view that women have general epistemic privilege has been thoroughly
criticized. At its best, it appears to require a form of essentialism, viz. women
are essentially the same, despite differences of race, ethnicity, caste, class, sexuality, etc., etc. However, the essentialism of "woman" was refuted by excellent
analyses such as Elizabeth Spelman's (see Spelman 1988). The claim catches its
proponents on the horns of a dilemma: it leads to a form of the metonymic fallacy
or to vicious relativism. Any claim that there is one "woman's standpoint" and
that it is epistemically privileged vis-à-vis the standpoint of men quickly runs up
against the fact that women differ by culture, race, ethnicity, class, sexuality, and

other epistemically salient categories; therefore, there is no one "woman's stand-point." Instead, there are many. The claim for one standpoint of all women must, then, commit a form of the metonymic fallacy, taking one standpoint, e.g. the standpoint of middle-class, white feminists, to be the standpoint of all. On the other hand, if each different group of women has its own standpoint and if each is *equally* epistemically privileged, then there is no way to decide among them when they conflict; each is true. This view is viciously relativist (see, for example, Hekman 1997).

Standpoint theorist Sandra Harding's recent work offers a theory of multiple and conflicting agency avoiding essentialism, the metonymic fallacy, and vicious relativism. Her theory is, we find, persuasively melded with an empiricist account of the justification of theory choice. Harding describes a standpoint as "an objective position in social relations as articulated through one or another theory or discourse" (1998: 150). Standpoint theorists make a sharp distinction between standpoint and social location; a social location is defined by structures including (but not limited to) social institutions that systematically structure human roles and the social interactions people have with one another. These structures – particularly those of production and reproduction – create the material conditions of people's lives. And they shape and limit what epistemic agents can know. Currently these structures produce relationships among people as hierarchical and constitute a system of power relations resulting in different material conditions, different relations of production and reproduction, different kinds of wage labor, and different kinds of affective labor for those in different social locations. This means that the experiences and understandings of those in different social locations can differ; they can differ not only in the content of their knowledge, but also in what they take knowledge itself to be (see Wylie 2003: 31).

A standpoint, on the other hand, is an achievement, the result of analysis by more than one person who, in the first instance, occupy a particular social location. When some of the people in a social location work out an account of the conditions of their lives and of their pre-standpoint understanding of the world, they have developed a standpoint. The standpoint will also include an account of the conditions giving rise to their standpoint itself. A standpoint is not a perspective, for any group of people occupying a common social location might unreflectively hold a point of view or perspective. Such a perspective might be typical of people occupying that location but the perspective is not a standpoint. A standpoint is "struggled for," arising when people occupying a subordinate social location engage in political struggle to change the conditions of their lives and so engage in an analysis of these conditions in order to change them.

Harding notes that standpoint theories have been especially useful in accounting for

differences in patterns of knowledge and ignorance created by political relations . . . The dominant groups in such political relations produce conceptual frameworks in public policy and research disciplines that value the local knowledge that their own activities and interests make reasonable to them, while devaluing and conceptually suppressing the patterns of knowledge and competing conceptual frameworks that emerge from the activities and interests of the groups disadvantaged by the power of the dominant groups.

> (1998: 160 and 106 n4, citing Hartsock 1983; Harding 1986 and 1991; Smith 1987 and 1990; Collins 1991)

These competing patterns of knowledge include knowledge of the natural world as well as knowledge of the social world. We see that there are many social locations and many standpoints, all of which may produce not only compatible though different accounts of the social and natural worlds, but also incompatible, conflicting accounts.

Harding has argued that dominant groups want to manage the conflict among competing accounts by comparing their own accounts with the accounts of subordinated groups. This desire, she argues, arises from taking an administrative or managing point of view, in this case, managing knowledge for the purposes of authorizing some of it and disqualifying some of it (1997: 386–7). This is an excellent point, but on occasion, for example, if those inhabiting different standpoints wish to form a strategic coalition, they might need to agree enough in their accounts of the world to act together. Harding rejects judgmental relativism, that is, the view that no one can decide among both or all of the conflicting accounts without presupposing one of them or presupposing yet another account (and thereby begging the question in favor of it). And she does not take up the view that women's standpoints are *epistemically privileged*, i.e. that women's standpoints, or the most oppressed women's standpoints, simply give rise to better hypotheses, accounts, or explanations. She thus faces the question, "How do engaged epistemic agents decide among relevant but conflicting accounts or strategically important parts of accounts?"

To avoid judgmental relativism without recourse to the metonymic fallacy, Harding argues that if research begins with questions/hypotheses arising from the lives and standpoints of subordinate groups, and if research is organized in more democratic ways, the results are likely to be "less false" or "more accurate" (1997: 383). She clearly avoids the metonymic fallacy by admitting multiple agents of knowledge, but we need to understand how she avoids judgmental relativism by saying, for example, that "research that starts out from women's bodies and interactions with nature, too – not just men's – will arrive at more comprehensive and accurate descriptions and explanations of nature's regularities" (1998: 97).

Here Harding cites N. Katherine Hayles, whose view combines aspects of coherence theories of truth and correspondence theories. She makes a four-fold distinction among true, false, not-true and not-false and, following Popper, argues that however much we test a set of beliefs, we can never verify it. Nevertheless, "true" makes sense as a limit; that is, we can conceive of having made all possible tests and having found a theory that passes them all. Such a theory would be *true* or "congruent" with all test results. If these results are conceived as corresponding to "how the world is," then our theory would be "congruent" with the world in the sense that it corresponds to the world. But human scientists will never achieve such a theory; instead, scientists test a theory and find that it is inconsistent with one or more test results, in which case it is *false*. At best, the theory stands up to our tests, in which case it is consistent with our results and is *not-false*. Those theories which have not been tested and those which are "imperfectly tested" Hayles relegates to the category of *not-true*. They are not *false* or *not-false* because they have neither failed nor withstood any tests. In this view, Realists are those who think that theories which are *not-false* – i.e., have stood up to many tests – are *true*, i.e. there is some sense in which they correspond to or represent the way the world is (Hayles 1993).

It follows that one set of beliefs is less false than another if it is more consistent with test results; i.e. it survives more tests than the other. (If we factor in significance, it would survive more of the important tests. Of course, we would have to determine criteria for significance. See, for example, Kitcher 1993; Anderson 1995; Solomon 2001.) Harding agrees with Hayles' Popperian view; she says,

> science never gets us truth . . . Scientific procedures are supposed to get us claims that are less false than those – and only those – against which they have been tested . . . Thus, scientific claims are supposed to be held not as true but, only provisionally, as "least false" until counterevidence or a new conceptual framework no longer provides them with the status of "less false."

> (1997: 387)

To the charge that accounts offered by different standpoints might be incommensurable, using even the same words differently so that it is impossible to compare accounts and find one "less false" than another, Harding argues that science studies show how scientists devise temporary, local strategies, "effective, 'good-enough' translations – pidgin languages – and technical equivalences to get from one conceptual terrain to another and to enable them to work together effectively" (1998: 171). (Peter Galison conceives these overlapping boundary areas as "trading zones" in which scientists from very different fields develop pidgin languages for common communication. See Galison 1996.) Thus, within a standpoint and between standpoints, accounts can be compared and one found less false than another.

Harding's account of theory choice fits well with her account of weak and strong objectivity in which objectivity is meant to ensure that the original choice of hypotheses, models, and theories as well as the processes of justification are more likely to yield less partial and less false results. Choosing research hypotheses that "begin from" or take seriously women's experiences and lives as well as their own understanding of their experiences can lead to new research questions and so to "less partial" knowledge, i.e. knowledge that is more empirically adequate. Weak objectivity characterizes contemporary standards requiring methods to ensure that any individual scientist's interests, prejudices, and personal values do not bias the results. However, feminist and other science scholars have noted that traditional standards of objectivity are too weak to identify beliefs, interests, and values widely shared by members of an epistemic community such as a community of scientists in a field of natural or social science. As Harding points out, "widely held beliefs function as evidence at every stage in scientific inquiry: in the selection of problems, formation of hypotheses, design of research . . . collection of data, interpretation and sorting of data, decisions about when to stop research, the way results of research are reported, etc." (1993: 69). Thus, the sciences need stronger standards of objectivity; in particular, the practices of the sciences need to be strongly reflexive, finding ways to reveal widespread sexist, class-based, racist, and Eurocentric cultural beliefs, interests, and values (ibid.).

If the standpoints of women within marginalized races, ethnicities, classes, and sexualities as well as those of women within dominant groups are used to critique dominant accounts of nature and of the social world, they can reveal hidden androcentric, Eurocentric or class-based assumptions. It is for this reason that Harding argues on behalf of a more inclusive, more democratic, science: the inclusion of women and men who have standpoints other than the dominant one(s) can help insure the strong objectivity of the sciences.

Moreover, the standpoints of women can contribute to strong objectivity in additional ways. Harding takes up two arguments offered by Patricia Hill Collins showing how women's distinctive standpoints can contribute to the strong objectivity of research. First, an "outsider" or "stranger," as these concepts are understood in sociology and anthropology, is one who lives among "natives" but does not "go native." The outsider is both near and remote, both concerned and indifferent, in ways that allow her to "see patterns of belief or behavior that are hard for those immersed in the culture to detect." Women are strangers in this sense because they are treated as such by "dominant social institutions and conceptual schemes." Nevertheless, men can learn to see the social order from this standpoint.

Second, groups of marginalized people are also "outsiders within." Examples include domestic workers, any women working in environments dominated by men, or particular groups of women workers, e.g. social science researchers such as black feminist scholars. Thus, black feminist scholars do "women's work" or "black women's work" and so are not engaged in dominant, i.e. white men's activities. But they also do "ruling work," inasmuch as "ruling work" includes the production and transmission of knowledge in universities. This combination makes them "outsiders within," and can allow them to see the dissonances and consonances between dominant activities and their own "outsider" community's beliefs. When marginalized outsiders within offer their accounts both of themselves and of those in the "center" or dominant culture, and when these accounts are brought together with accounts of the marginalized and of themselves offered by those in the dominant culture, the resulting conflicts and convergences can help to maximize objectivity and to produce less partial and less distorted accounts (Harding 1991: 124–5 and 131–2 and Collins 1986, §15, cited in Harding 1991).

We should note that, to solve the problem of judgmental relativism, Harding sets aside the view that the standpoint of women – or of any marginalized group – has epistemic privilege. "Starting research" from their standpoints is more likely to yield less partial and less false accounts of the social and natural worlds, she argues. But ending the research by simply adopting the account put forward by those with a marginalized standpoint is not likely to do so inasmuch as their views are influenced by constraints brought about through their material conditions having been shaped by the dominant group(s). Nevertheless, "strong objectivity" ensures that any assumptions unnoticed by most researchers have a good chance of being examined when people of different standpoints are included in research processes. Most feminist epistemologists and philosophers of science agree on this point and agree that a marginalized standpoint does not *ipso facto* confer epistemic privilege. But Alison Wylie offers a standpoint epistemology embracing a version of epistemic privilege, viz. some standpoints and/or locations provide epistemic privilege; yet she avoids relativism by limiting epistemic priviledge to some proj- ects in some domains. Wylie is the first naturalizing feminist empiricist to offer an explicitly standpoint epistemology of science, bringing together central elements of feminist standpoint epistemology with feminist empiricist philosophy of science.

Wylie joins the feminist consensus that knowledge is socially situated, that women do not have essential features as women, and that they do not have general epistemic privilege. She also agrees with Harding that in scientific research, the inclusion of people from different social locations and/or with different stand- points can contribute to "strong objectivity," i.e. to uncovering and examining widely held but unexamined assumptions (2003: 31–2). However, in response to the question, "Do social locations and standpoints confer epistemic advantage?" Wylie argues that on one account of objectivity, some social locations and stand- points confer contingent epistemic advantage "with respect to particular epistemic projects" (ibid.: 34).

For purposes of her standpoint epistemology, Wylie treats objectivity as a prop- erty of knowledge claims. With Elisabeth Lloyd, she distinguishes objectivity as a property of epistemic agents, as a property of the objects of knowledge and as a property of knowledge claims. Lloyd notes the traditional views that epistemic agents are objective when "they are neutral, dispassionate with regard to a particu- lar subject of inquiry" and that objects of knowledge such as facts are objective or constitute "objective reality" when they "are contrasted with ephemeral, subjective constructs; they constitute the 'really real', as Lloyd puts it (1995)" (2003: 32–3). Wylie rejects these traditional views (as does Lloyd).

Knowledge claims are objective, Wylie suggests, when they maximize some combination of epistemic virtues. Though they differ over the characteristics that constitute epistemic virtues, most epistemologists and philosophers of science include empirical adequacy as an epistemic virtue. Wylie distinguishes two senses of empirical adequacy, one, as "fidelity to a rich body of localized evidence (empiri- cal depth)," and two, as "a capacity to travel (Haraway 1991) such that the claims in question can extend to a range of domains or applications (empirical breadth)." Though objective knowledge claims must have empirical adequacy, they need only have some combination of other epistemic virtues such as "internal coherence, inferential robustness, and consistency with well established collateral bodies of knowledge, as well as explanatory power and a number of other pragmatic and aesthetic virtues," e.g. simplicity (Wylie 2003: 33). The particular combination of virtues which must be maximized depends on the specific epistemic project. Hence, epistemic advantage in Wylie's account can be understood as follows: depending upon the project, some social locations and standpoints have epistemic advantage inasmuch as they allow an empirical assessment of how likely it is that the knowledge particular knowers produce will not be objective, will fail to maximize the epistemic virtues important for that project.

Although a social location permits knowers in that location to assess the likelihood of objectivity of particular claims in epistemic projects carried out by particular epistemic agents, a standpoint confers two further epistemic advantages:

1   it allows those who hold it to further assess the effects of social location upon the objectivity of particular claims in epistemic projects carried out by particular epistemic agents; and
2   because those holding a standpoint are critically conscious of the effects of power relations, i.e. the effects of socio-political location "on their own understanding and that of (some) others," they have epistemic advantage in assessing "how reliable particular kinds of knowledge are likely to be given the conditions of their production" (Wylie 2003: 34).

We can schematically represent these formulations of epistemic advantage as follows:

> S claims that p.
> S_{St} or S_L claims that p': S's claim that p has likelihood r of failing to be objective with regard to domain D (where D includes p, and p' is an empirical assessment based upon evidence which is salient to S_{St} in virtue of S_{St}'s standpoint and to S_L in virtue of S_L's location).
> Additionally, S_{St} claims that p'': given the conditions of knowledge production by S in D, p has likelihood of objectivity r' (and p'' is an empirical assessment based upon evidence which is salient to S_{St} in virtue of S_{St}'s standpoint).

And, finally,

> S_{St} claims that p''': given the conditions of knowledge production by S_{St} in D_{St}, p'' has likelihood of objectivity r' with regard to domain D_{St} (where D_{St} includes p'), and given the conditions of knowledge production by S_L in D_L, p' has likelihood of objectivity r'' with regard to domain D_L (where D_L includes p' and p''' is an empirical assessment based upon evidence which is salient to S_{St} in virtue of S_{St}'s standpoint).

As opposed to the view that some standpoints have general epistemic privilege or epistemic advantage, Wylie states that, "The question of what standpoints make an epistemic difference and what difference they make cannot be settled in the abstract, in advance; it requires the second order application of our best research tools to the business of knowledge production itself. And this is necessarily a problem-specific and open-ended process" (2003: 40). Thus,

> gender location and/or having a feminist standpoint do not always enhance the objectivity of scientific hypotheses; other locations and/or standpoints, e.g. class and race, might be better suited to do so in some cases.

Finally, Wylie avoids the threat of judgmental relativism by arguing that all parties to a local project agree to the same standard of objectivity – to the same degree that scientists usually do. (See Solomon 2001 on consensus in science.) Objectivity, like knowledge, is local.

In this section, we have seen that even feminist epistemologies and philosophies of science such as standpoint theories have turned to empiricist accounts of the justification of knowledge. They have found empiricist solutions best in answer to problems such as the threat of vicious relativism arising from feminist affirmations of multiple agents of knowledge and democratic approaches to knowledge production.

Convergence upon Empiricism in Treatments of Contextual Values

The second area in which we find convergence upon empiricism is in feminist empiricist treatments of contextual values. One of Lynn Hankinson Nelson's radical breaks from Quine is her suggestion that values are not incorrigible and her argument that they constitute part of the evidence for knowledge claims and theories. Quine argued that values should be categorized as "cognitive" and "non-cognitive." Cognitive values are technical ones to be used by scientists deciding among competing theories. Non-cognitive ones include moral, social, and political values which he assumed were not subject to factual or rational arguments. Nelson, however, says that we must "reconsider the assumption that political beliefs and theories, and values are not subject to empirical control, that there is no way to judge between them" (Quine and Ullian 1978; Nelson 1990: 297). As subject to empirical control, socio-political values can be altered by rational arguments and by experience and so can be seen as legitimate constituents in the justification of knowledge claims. This recognition was captured by Longino's (1990) rejection of the standard distinction between cognitive and non-cognitive values – offering in its place a distinction between constitutive and contextual values and arguing that both can function as assumptions in the justification of claims, theories, and models.

Elizabeth Anderson's Cooperative Model of Theory Justification sets out in detail the legitimate use of contextual values in the production of knowledge, particularly scientific knowledge including hypotheses, theories, accounts, models, etc. And in doing so, she offers an account of what we might call the empirical or cognitive aspect of values, i.e. their corrigibility by experience and by rational consideration of facts, including scientifically established facts. Anderson's Cooperative Model of Justification thus reveals the work of contextual values in justification, making use of an empiricist theorization of contextual values.

Anderson reminds us that merely collecting facts does not add up to good science. Scientists need facts that are relevant to the purposes or aims of their investigations and these purposes are certainly "broader than the bare accumulation of truths." Scientists work to achieve human interests or values – captured in their research questions, e.g. "Is the breakup of helium nuclei an endothermic reaction?" or "Does this gene correlate significantly with breast cancer?" An adequate answer to a research question requires all of the significant facts – those truths that bear on the answer to the question, or as Anderson says, "a representative enough sample of such truths that the addition of the rest would not make the answer turn out differently." The justification of theories thus depends upon these broader aims as well as on other truth-conducive features, which, as she points out, leaves "an opening for moral, social, and political values to enter into theory choice" (1995: 37). Truly "value-neutral" production of knowledge would be without direction, for without values and valued interests, researchers cannot distinguish a significant from an insignificant fact and a biased account from one that is impartial. Hence, contextual value-neutrality is not a good standard for research.

Impartiality, however, is a good standard to employ. Impartiality, Anderson argues, is achieved by "a commitment to pass judgment in relation to a set of evaluative standards that transcends the competing interests of those who advocate rival answers to a question." Thus, impartiality *requires* evaluative standards. These evaluative standards include honesty and fairness in judgment, where fairness is understood to demand attention to all the facts and arguments that support or undermine researchers' working presuppositions. When a research question is motivated by contextual values, the evaluative standard of fairness is particularly salient, for it "demands attention to all the facts and arguments that support or undermine each side's value judgments." Anderson takes as an example of bias and partiality the book, *The Secret Relationship Between Blacks and Jews*, purporting to uncover the role of Jews in the Atlantic slave trade. She points out that the implicit question driving the argument of *The Secret Relationship* is, "Do Jews deserve special moral opprobrium or blame for their roles in the Atlantic slave system or bear special moral responsibility for that system's operations?" To answer this question, an adequate theory would give us all the facts morally relevant to it, "or enough of them that adding the rest would not change the answer." But her detailed treatment of *The Secret Relationship* reveals that it ignores many morally relevant facts, e.g. those showing that "Jews behaved no differently, from a moral point of view, than anyone else who had the opportunity to profit from the slave system." Therefore, the book offers a biased account (1995: 42).

We see immediately that in Anderson's Cooperative Model of Theory Justification, contextual values are treated as cognitive, susceptible to correction by reason and by factual evidence. Anderson's Cooperative Model rejects the view that contextual values cannot be rationally changed by facts and that value judgments are dogmatic and so cannot influence scientific work without making it blind to evidence. In this view, if contextual values enter the context of justification, then the answer to a research question will be biased and will not be impartial. Instead, Anderson argues that if contextual values are properly theorized, we see how and when they can be truth-conducive and make better science. Properly theorizing contextual values as they operate in the production of knowledge includes at least two components: a distinction between the legitimate and illegitimate uses of such values, and an account of their cognitive aspect.

Turning first to the distinction between legitimate and illegitimate uses of contextual values, we find that not all moral and political values have equal epistemic value, nor is it the case that a contextual value which is legitimately used and fruitful in one inquiry is legitimately used and fruitful in all. (It will turn out, then, that feminist values are not always legitimately used in science, and masculinist values are not always illegitimately used.) Contextual values are legitimately used in science if they do not drive research to a predetermined or favored conclusion. When empirical research in the social or natural sciences is addressed to an evaluative question, e.g. "Does divorce help or hurt the people involved?" evaluative presuppositions must not determine the answer to the evaluative question. Evidence determines the answer, but value presuppositions can help uncover evidence relevant to the question.

In Anderson's analysis, the illegitimate use of values in science arises because they produce three sorts of bias in research design:

1   "in relation to the object of inquiry if it (truthfully) reveals only some of its aspects, leaving us ignorant of others." All research designs close off some lines of research, so this sort of bias is inevitable but harmless as long as we do not think the research has covered all aspects of the object of inquiry;
2   in relation to its hypotheses if it is rigged (wittingly or not) to confirm them. A good research design must allow its hypothesis to be disconfirmed by evidence. Value-laden research does not necessarily confirm researchers' evaluative presuppositions; it is not the values guiding the research that cause bias in relation to its hypothesis; rather, this bias is caused by the failure to use proper methods, such as drawing fair samples of evidence or treating controversial results symmetrically, i.e. not stopping research when one makes findings that support one's hypothesis, but putting the hypothesis through further tests;
3   in relation to a controversy if it is more likely to (truthfully) uncover evidence that supports one side rather than all sides.

On the other hand, one "research design is more *fruitful* than another, with respect to a controversy, if it is more likely to uncover evidence supporting (or undermining) all, or a wider range of sides of the controversy." It remains an open question, then, when a research design is just less fruitful than others and when it is biased in relation to a controversy (Anderson 2004: 18–20).

Contextual values legitimately influence science if

1   precautions are taken to avoid these three biases, and
2   the values are epistemically fruitful.

Epistemically fruitful values are those guiding research "toward discovering a wider range of evidence that could potentially support any (or more) sides of a controversy." Thus, a contextual value is more epistemically fruitful than others if it has more power to uncover significant phenomena. (Significant facts or phenomena are those that bear on the answer to the research question.) When a less fruitful value guides research, important evidence can still be uncovered, but we must remember that such research is limited to answering only certain questions or giving only a partial answer to a controversial question (Anderson 2004: 20).

The important question remaining is whether research guided by contextual value(s) is epistemically fruitful *because* of the contextual value(s). The commonly held view is that good scientific theories must be neutral, not presupposing contextual values. This (presupposition) value-neutrality thesis assumes that all the epistemic work is done by factual elements; therefore, if the research is epistemically fruitful, it cannot be on account of contextual value(s). Anderson argues that, assuming we can distinguish the factual and normative components of a thick evaluative judgment, i.e. distinguish the empirical features of the world it picks out from its claim to normative authority, then we can ask whether the epistemic fruitfulness of a thick evaluative judgment is due to its normative authority. (A thick evaluative judgment is one that simultaneously expresses both factual and value judgments, e.g. "S is rude," both describes S's behavior and evaluates it negatively.) Space prohibits our setting out Anderson's excellent case study exhibiting epistemically fruitful results based solely on the normative authority of feminist contextual values. Stewart et al. (1997) took up the question whether divorce helps or hurts the people involved. The primary reason for research on divorce, Anderson notes, is to discover evidence that will inform value judgments and so guide practical recommendations regarding divorce. And as an aid to understanding the several points at which feminist values guided the research of Stewart et al., she offers a "stylized" division of the stages of research: researchers

(a) begin with an orientation to the background interests animating the field
(b) frame a question informed by those interests
(c) articulate a conception of the object of inquiry
(d) decide what types of data to collect
(e) establish and carry out data sampling or generation procedures
(f) analyse their data in accordance with chosen techniques
(g) decide when to stop analysing their data
(h) draw conclusions from their analyses.

Here we will merely summarize Anderson's discussion of (a), (b), and (d).

(a) All researchers in this area have a background interest in uncovering the effect of divorce on the well-being of those affected. Researchers oriented to what Anderson dubs "traditional family values" take a model family to be one in which husband and wife are married for life, live in the same household and raise their biological children; the roles of parent and spouse are understood as inseparable and this is held to be best for children and probably for parents. Thus, divorce "breaks up" the family and harms the children. The feminists were more amibivalent about divorce; it might enable men to leave their wives to the wives' detriment or allow women to escape oppressive marriages. They also questioned whether the "traditional" family should be the norm for evaluating post-divorce relationships (Anderson 2004: 12).

(b) Their different background values led researchers to ask different research questions. Traditionalists often ask whether divorce has negative effects on children and their parents. Thus, they often compare members of divorced and non-divorced families on measures of well-being, especially negative ones such as sickness, poverty, and behavioral problems. They implicitly assume (1) that there is one best way of life for everyone captured by traditional roles and (2) that both groups, divorced and non-divorced families, are internally homogeneous. These assumptions lead to a choice of methodology; traditionalists focus on aggregate differences between the two groups and so do main effects analysis which "accepts the average outcome as representative of the group, discounting individual variation." The feminist team believed that it is virtually impossible to distinguish the effects of divorce from the effects of marital problems that led to divorce, and so believed that they should control for preexisting problems in the marriage. This requires a methodology that reveals interaction effects. Moreover, Stewart et al. "also had normative objections to the traditional research question," viz. the focus on negative outcomes makes it hard to find positive outcomes; the focus on aggregate differences between married and divorced people assumes that findings and evaluations based on group comparisons apply to each person; and the focus on divorce as an event assumes it has a fixed, enduring meaning, and misses whether its meaning changes over time – positively or negatively, but especially positively, e.g. divorce may "recede in significance as individuals cope with it and engage the new experiences that it makes possible" (Stewart et al. 1997: 30). Thus, the feminist team asked "how individuals vary among themselves and over time in the meanings they ascribe to divorce, its effects, and their coping strategies" (Anderson 2004: 12–13 and 17).

(d) Some of the standard measures of well-being bearing on the value of divorce include financial security, children's behavioral problems, physical illness, etc. "Traditionalists" gather data using these measures. But the feminist team included, in addition, individuals' post-divorce feelings and their emotionally colored interpretations of the changes they underwent as evidence of their well-being and the value of divorce. Their background assumption here was that the subjects of study have "normative authority to judge values for themselves." The decision to gather data including subjects' self-assessments allowed the Stewart team to discover (1) that 70% of divorced women judged their personalities to have improved since divorce, and (2) that many divorced women left with lower incomes were nevertheless pleased to have greater decision-making power over their money (Anderson 2004: 15).

Contextual values have been referred to as "non-cognitive" to indicate that nothing could count as evidence for or against them; hence, values are held dogmatically by everyone because our intrinsic values – whatever we value for itself and not because it is a means to reach what we intrinsically value – are determined by our desires. In this view, our desires are not altered by reason or by empirical evidence. Hence, our "non-cognitive" values are "science-free" (Anderson 2004: 6, 8). How can contextual values be subject to empirical evidence? We cannot treat Anderson's rich arguments in detail here, but she notes that emotional experiences are among those that function as evidence for value judgments. Emotional experiences are "affectively colored experiences" and have objects such as persons or events; they are "*appearances* of these objects as *important*" – they "present their objects in a favorable or unfavorable light"; and "they reflect the perspective . . . of subjects who care about themselves or others. Emotions appear to signal the importance of things *for* what their subject cares about." Anderson points out that we tend to take these experiences seriously, judging "what arouses our favorable emotions as good, and what arouses our unfavorable emotions as bad."

Such emotional experiences satisfy the conditions on mental states counting as evidence and so can legitimately function as evidence for values. These emotional experiences usually have cognitive content; they are independent of our desires and ends. In Anderson's example, Diane desires elected office and values a political life. Despite her desires and values, she feels badly about the political life, disillusioned by campaign financing, political backbiting, and small political gains. These emotional experiences do not depend on her desires and values and, in fact, undermine them; and these emotional experiences are defeasible (though not as responsive to the world as beliefs); i.e., we can find out that the cognitive content is erroneous, confused, etc. which might lead us to discount the importance of the feeling, too. In Anderson's example, an ally tries to persuade Diane that her "disappointment with what seems to be a merely symbolic victory reflects an unduly narrow perspective." Taken in isolation this victory achieves little, but "in the long view it can be seen as fundamentally shifting the terms of debate. What seems like a hollow victory is a watershed event. This [factual] judgment could be tested over a longer stretch of experience." The ally argues that Diane should continue to value the political life. This sort of persuasive argument is not uncommon and makes sense only because our emotions are responsive to facts (Anderson 2004: 9–10).

Anderson points out that growing up, having human experiences such as disillusionment, etc. allows most people to learn from experience that some of their values are mistaken. Most people are capable of growing and learning in these ways. Some people are not; *these* people are dogmatic, holding to all or some of their values regardless of the facts. One of the primary reasons that most people can learn from experience that their values are mistaken is because we take our emotional experiences to provide evidence that these people or things or events have value (Anderson 2004: 9). And usually our emotions are reliable, though certainly not infallible, evidence for our value judgments. (The exceptions include emotions affected by drugs, depression, etc.) When it is clear that the representational content of an emotional experience is adequate in the ways set out above, we can trust our emotions. "Indeed, we would be *crazy* not to." And if we do not trust our emotions, if we hold to our values despite the facts and despite our feelings, we *are dogmatic* (ibid.: 9–10).

Anderson's arguments allow us to see that contextual values are corrigible; they are not "science-free" and so can have a legitimate role in the justification of knowledge. Their legitimate role is to make a theory more epistemically fruitful than it would otherwise be – and perhaps more epistemically fruitful than its rivals. And in doing so, they help make better justified theories.

Sections I and II above show that current feminist epistemologies and philosophies of science are converging on empiricist accounts of the justification of knowledge and empiricist understandings of contextual values and of their role in the justification of knowledge. This is not to say that feminist epistemologies and philosophies of science are all empiricist or that empiricism is the wave of the future for feminist philosophy. It does indicate, however, that empiricism as broadly understood in philosophy has been very limited and that limited understandings of it prevent our seeing that "facts and values" are not hermetically sealed off from one another, but rationally interact in the production of scientific as well as general knowledge. This recognition allows us to explore the ways in which feminist values can produce better knowledge.

Bibliography

Addelson, Kathryn Pyne and Potter, Elizabeth (1991) "Making Knowledge," in Kathryn Pyne Addelson, *Impure Thoughts: Essays on Philosophy, Feminism, and Ethics*, Philadelphia, PA: Temple University Press. Reprinted in *(En)Gendering Knowledge: Feminists in Academe*, eds. Joan E. Hartman and Ellen Messer Davidow, Knoxville: University of Tennessee Press, 1991.

Alcoff, Linda (1996) *Real Knowing: New Versions of the Coherence Theory*, Ithaca, NY: Cornell University Press.

Alcoff, Linda and Elizabeth Potter, eds. (1993) *Feminist Epistemologies*, New York and London: Routledge.

Anderson, Elizabeth (1995) "Knowledge, Human Interests, and Objectivity in Feminist Epistemology," *Philosophical Topics* 23 (2): 27–58.

—— (2004) "Uses of Value Judgments in Science: A General Argument, with Lessons from a Case Study of Feminist Research on Divorce," *Hypatia: A Journal of Feminist Philosophy* 19 (1): 1–24.

Antony, Louise (1995) "Sisters, Please, I'd Rather Do It Myself: A Defense of Individualism in Epistemology," *Philosophical Topics* 23 (2): 59–94.

Bakhurst, David (1992) "Ideology," in *A Companion to Epistemology*, eds. J. Dancy and E. Sosa, Oxford and Cambridge, MA: Blackwell, pp. 191–3.

Bleier, Ruth (1984) *Science and Gender*, Elmsford, NY: Pergamon.

Bloor, David (1982) "Durkheim and Mauss Revisited: Classification and the Sociology of Knowledge," *Studies in History and Philosophy of Science* 13: 267–97.

Collins, Patricia Hill (1986) "Learning from the Outsider Within: The Sociological Significance of Black Feminist Thought," *Social Problems* 33 (6): 14–23.

—— (1991) *Black Feminist Thought: Knowledge, Consciousness, and the Politics of Empowerment*, New York: Routledge.

Galison, Peter (1996) "Computer Simulations and the Trading Zone," in *The Disunity of Science*, eds. Peter Galison and David J. Stump, Stanford, CA: Stanford University Press, pp. 118–57.

Gould, Steven J. (1981) *The Mismeasure of Man*, New York: W.W. Norton.

Grasswick, Heidi E. (2004) "Individuals-in-Communities: The Search for a Feminist Model of Epistemic Subjects," *Hypatia: A Journal of Feminist Philosophy* 19 (3): 85–120.

Haraway, Donna (1991) "Situated Knowledges: The Science Question in Feminism and the Privilege of Partial Perspective," in *Simians, Cyborgs, and Women: The Reinvention of Nature*, New York: Routledge, pp. 183–203.

Harding, Sandra (1986) *The Science Question in Feminism*, Ithaca, NY: Cornell University Press.

—— (1991) *Whose Science? Whose Knowledge? Thinking From Women's Lives*, Ithaca, NY: Cornell University Press.

—— (1993) "Rethinking Standpoint Epistemology: What Is 'Strong Objectivity'?" in *Feminist Epistemologies*, eds. Linda Alcoff and Elizabeth Potter, Routledge: New York and London, 49–82.

—— (1997) "Comment on Hekman's 'Truth and Method: Feminist Standpoint Theory Revisited': Whose Standpoint Needs the Regimes of Truth and Reality?" *Signs: Journal of Women in Culture and Society* 22 (2): 382–91.

—— (1998) *Is Science Multicultural? Postcolonialisms, Feminisms, and Epistemologies*, Bloomington and Indianapolis: Indiana University Press.

Hartsock, Nancy (1983) "The Feminist Standpoint: Developing the Ground for a Specifically Feminist Historical Materialism," in *Discovering Reality: Feminist Perspectives on Epistemology, Metaphysics, Methodology, and Philosophy of Science*, eds. Sandra Harding and Merrill Hintikka, Dordrecht: Reidel/Kluwer, pp. 283–310.

—— (1997) "Comment on Hekman's 'Truth and Method: Feminist Standpoint Theory Revisited': Truth or Justice?" *Signs: Journal of Women in Culture and Society* 22 (2): 367–74.

Hayles, N. Katherine (1993) "Constrained Constructivism: Locating Scientific Inquiry in the Theater of Representation," in *Realism and Representation*, ed. George Levine, Madison: University of Wisconsin Press, pp. 27–43.

Hekman, Susan (1997) "Truth and Method: Feminist Standpoint Theory Revisited," *Signs: Journal of Women in Culture and Society* 22 (2): 341–65.

Kitcher, Philip (1993) *The Advancement of Science*, New York: Oxford University Press.

Lewontin, Richard, Rose, Steven, and Kamin, Leon (1984) *Not in Our Genes*, New York: Pantheon.

Lloyd, Elisabeth (1995) "Objectivity and the Double Standard for Feminist Epistemologies," *Synthese* 104: 351–81.

Longino, Helen (1983) "Beyond Bad Science," *Science, Technology and Human Values* 8 (1): 7–17.

—— (1990) *Science as Social Knowledge*, Princeton, NJ: Princeton University Press.

—— (2002) *The Fate of Knowledge*, Princeton, NJ: Princeton University Press.

Nelson, Lynn Hankinson (1990) *Who Knows: From Quine to Feminist Empiricism*, Philadelphia, PA: Temple University Press.

—— (1993) "Epistemological Communities," in *Feminist Epistemologies*, eds. Linda Alcoff and Elizabeth Potter, New York and London: Routledge, pp. 121–59.

Potter, Elizabeth (1993) "Gender and Epistemic Negotiation," in *Feminist Epistemologies*, eds. Linda Alcoff and Elizabeth Potter, New York and London: Routledge, pp. 161–86.

Quine, W.V.O. and Ullian, J.S. (1978) *The Web of Belief*, 2nd edn, New York: Random House.

Shapin, Steven (1982) "History of Science and Its Sociological Reconstruction," *History of Science* 20: 157–211.

Smith, Dorothy (1987) *The Everyday World as Problematic: A Sociology for Women*, Boston, MA: Northeastern University Press.

—— (1990) *The Conceptual Practices of Power: A Feminist Sociology of Knowledge*, Boston, MA: Northeastern University Press.

Solomon, Miriam (2001) *Social Empiricism*, Cambridge, MA: MIT Press.

Spelman, Elizabeth V. (1988) *Inessential Woman: Problems of Exclusion in Feminist Thought*, Boston, MA: Beacon Press.

Stewart, Abigail, Copeland, Anne, Chester, Nia, Malley, Janet, and Barenbaum, Nicole (1997) *Separating Together: How Divorce Transforms Families*, New York: Guilford Press.

Wylie, Alison (2002) *Thinking from Things: Essays in the Philosophy of Archaeology*, Berkeley: University of California Press.

—— (2003) "Why Standpoint Matters," in *Science and Other Cultures: Issues in Philosophies of Science and Technology*, eds. Robert Figueroa and Sandra Harding, New York: Routledge, pp. 26–48.

Chapter 14

Feminism and Aesthetics

Peg Brand

Distinguishing Aesthetics and Philosophy of Art

Aesthetics is sometimes considered synonymous with the philosophy of art (or the arts). However, aesthetics is a field within philosophy – generally regarded as a more recent area of study beginning in the eighteenth century – involving theories of perception that focus on the apprehension of beauty and other qualities of intrinsic value. The objects of such study may or may not be works of art. Indeed, examples from the world of nature as well as mathematic proofs were originally offered as appropriate objects of study in aesthetics, each of which offered its own type of beauty.

The philosophy of art, in contrast, dates back to the theories of Plato and his interest in the nature of creativity and art objects, their value and social role, and their power to form character and convey knowledge, but it can also refer to twentieth-century concerns and debates over art's expressiveness, its emphasis on formalism, its increasingly transgressive nature, the interpretation of artists' intentions, and its evaluation: both within and outside the recognized mainstream US, New York-centered artworld. Not surprisingly, the two areas of aesthetics and philosophy of art can converge, and more recently, have come to overlap with new areas of investigation like critical studies and cultural studies which expand our interests beyond a familiar canon of artifacts to the broader ascription of meaning to all types of cultural products, whether considered art or not.

Since the 1970s, established women artists – as well as women working in creative arenas previously considered crafts – have helped to facilitate a blurring of boundaries between aesthetics and the philosophy of art. Quilts, created to honor families and their histories, along with fabric artworks and painted china plates, helped erode entrenched distinctions between fine art and craft, high art and low, men's art and women's. Responses to artworks previously deemed purely aesthetic were reassessed as containing non-aesthetic components. Moreover, feminists suggested that non-aesthetic qualities – previously demarcated contextual qualities that involved ethics, politics, or history and were considered extraneous to the work of art – were indeed relevant, and perhaps even necessary, to a full and fair interpretation and evaluation. In addition to the elevated status of new and unusual media, women artists redirected the male-defined trajectory of performance art toward their own female bodies to explore issues of sexuality (Carolee Schneeman's nude performance with live snakes comes to mind, exhibiting ties to small sculptures of Minoan snake goddesses from the seventeenth century BCE), organic links to nature (for example, Ana Mendieta's body imprints upon the earth and carved cave walls), gender and racial roles within society (Adrian Piper's public street persona as a black man with Afro), and aesthetic surgery (the numerous aesthetic surgeries of the French performance artist, Orlan, intent on showing the futility of women seeking male-defined ideals of beauty). Although not directly engaged in a dialogue with philosophers, these artists were repeatedly challenging deeply held traditions of the concepts of "art" and "aesthetic experience" as they had been defined by white, European or American, middle- to upper-class, self-proclaimed men of taste; men who considered women's proper role to be restricted to appearing in art, not creators of art.

Bringing Feminist Theory into Aesthetics

Essays citing connections between feminism and aesthetics are relatively few in the larger literature of aesthetics. There are several overviews of the field that encapsulate the interplay of feminist theorizing and aesthetics; for some philosophers, this area of research has come to be known as "feminist aesthetics" while for others, resistant to the phrase, the preferred wording is simply "feminism and aesthetics") (Brand 1998; Worth 1998; Devereaux 2003; Korsmeyer 2004b; Eaton 2005). But there are still many scholarly works and survey texts that contain no reference to feminism at all. Why? Perhaps because the philosophical exploration of the role of women in the history of art, the gendering of historical concepts promoted by figures like Kant, and the crossover of feminist art criticism and theory, have been introduced only recently into analytic aesthetics. Its acceptance into the mainstream has been slow and difficult.

A variety of reasons account for this, not the least of which are ones that are social (there are still far fewer women than men in aesthetics, as in philosophy in general, and women generally author feminist research), conceptual (a resistance to scholarship that focuses on gender, race, or class in favor of a purely aesthetic approach to the discussion of works of art), and ideological (insistence on further exploration and teaching of the well-established canon, or core, of philosophical literature, considered "real" aesthetics). What is the history and current role of feminism and how has it fared within the continually expansive field of philosophical aesthetics and philosophy of the arts?

Consider the fact that the first special issues of academic philosophy journals in

English devoted to feminism were *The Monist* and *Philosophical Forum* (both in 1973). Feminist research in complementary fields to the arts such as art history, criticism, and theory, also began at this time, most notably jump-started with the query posed by Linda Nochlin in her famous 1971 essay, "Why Have There Been No Great Women Artists?" (1988). Many previously unknown women artists of the past five centuries were slowly brought to light by art historians (Tufts 1975; Harris and Nochlin 1976; Peterson and Wilson 1976; Chadwick 2002). The reclamation of artists from obscurity naturally inspired questions about their disappearance and omission from standard art history texts (their omission lasted into the early 1980s), prompting a whole new phase of theoretical inquiry. Marked by intense analysis of the social conditions surrounding the creativity and production of women who were well-known in their day – many with significant patrons, paid commissions, and studios staffed with apprentices – feminist scholars sought to understand the lost stature and obscurity of these accomplished artists. These texts in art history and art theory, along with the experiences and artwork of women artists, were to become the foundation of feminist philosophical inquiry within aesthetics.

Linguistic analyses, sociological hypotheses, and cross-cultural comparisons came into focus as the first collection of feminist art-historical essays, *Feminism and Art History: Questioning the Litany*, sought to distinguish itself from standard catalogues and monographs by examining "Western art history and the extent to which it has been distorted, in every major period, by sexual bias" (Broude and Garrard 1982: 1). New research sought to collapse stereotypes about women artists through texts with such intriguing titles such as, *The Obstacle Race: The Fortunes of Women Painters and Their Work* (Greer 1979), *Old Mistresses: Women, Art and Ideology* (Parker and Pollock 1981), *Get the Message? A Decade of Art For Social Change* (Lippard 1984), and *Art and Sexual Politics: Women's Liberation, Women Artists, and Art History* (Hess and Baker 1973). The feminist critique greatly expanded in the 1970s and 1980s and writers brought nuanced investigation to aspects of gender in the arts that had never been previously considered; for example, Christine Battersby's objection to the notion of exclusively male provenance of "genius" (1989), Naomi Schor's insights into the category of details in art and literature which she argued constituted an aesthetic category typically considered feminine (1987), and – in a more self-reflexive phase of commentary upon the feminist critique itself – Rita Felski's questioning of the use of the concepts "masculine" and "feminine" as a methodology of analysis in isolation from the social conditions of their production and reception (1989).

Similarly, a burgeoning interest in the creative work of women writers, filmmakers, and composers arose and achieved a secure hold within the disciplines of literary theory, film studies, and musicology. Non-American writers, such as Sylvia Bovenschen in West Germany (1985, whose original essay was published in 1976), and French writers Luce Irigaray (1974/1985) and Julia Kristeva (1982), were writing about the unique qualities of the female sex and the way gender affected the explanations of creativity, expression, and interpretation in the arts. This European trend of focusing on the experiences and achievements of women in the arts paralleled feminist scholarship in American philosophical fields such as ethics, social-political philosophy, philosophy of law, the philosophy of science, the history of philosophy, metaphysics, and epistemology. Yet philosophical aesthetics during the 1970s and 1980s remained silent on issues of gender.

Developing Feminist Challenges to Aesthetics

Feminist writing within the field of American academic aesthetics did not appear until nearly twenty years after Nochlin's famous essay, when a special issue on aesthetics entitled, "Feminism and Aesthetics," appeared in *Hypatia: A Journal of Feminist Philosophy* (Hein and Korsmeyer 1990), the same year as a special issue, "Feminism and Traditional Aesthetics," of *The Journal of Aesthetics and Art Criticism* (Brand and Korsmeyer 1990). British co-authors Penny Florence and Nicola Foster presented an overview of the literature in the UK (1998; 2000a; 2000b), noting the absence of feminist research within *The British Journal of Aesthetics* throughout its entire publication history. Thus, in spite of rising international interests in women's artistic creativity and a growing interest in feminist inquiry within American philosophy, the introduction of feminism as a serious topic within American and British aesthetics has lagged far behind their feminist counterparts. One explanation cites the strong resistance by analytic aestheticians to any viewpoint not embodying the complex notion of disinterestedness, i.e., the perceiver's shunning of interests – whether ethical, political, religious, economic, ecological, etc. It is worth examining this legacy from the eighteenth century in some depth since it has had an impact that has been both broad and lasting.

A common five-part structure adopted by empiricist philosophers in Britain set the tone for two centuries of thinking that focused on a person's aesthetic experience, particularly the experience of beauty. The first component was perception: the mode whereby one knows the objects in the world and their characteristics. The second was the faculty of taste, a concept that varied among the members of the group, with Joseph Addison vaguely casting it as imagination and Francis Hutcheson describing it as an internal sense of beauty. This sense – like one's external senses – is automatically triggered within a split second of the act of perception. It is prescribed to be free of interest, i.e., unimpeded by any "feeling to what farther advantage or detriment the use of such objects might tend" (Hutcheson 1977: 573). The third component of the theory of taste is the mental product resulting from the reaction of the faculty of taste, generally understood to be pleasure (free of desire and the will to possess). The fourth structural part is the kind of object (or event, such as a theatrical performance) in the perceived world under consideration that contained certain special characteristics (aesthetic properties) that imbue the object with intrinsic value. For Hutcheson, the object was said to possess uniformity amidst variety; for Edmund Burke, qualities of smoothness and smallness. The fifth and final structural part is one's judgment of taste such as, "This painting is beautiful," which functions as a capstone to the entire process.

Feminist philosophers have been highly skeptical of male art viewers who reported or advocated a neutral response of pleasure – particularly when gazing upon a depiction of a sensuous, erotically charged beautiful woman. Feminists have detected inconsistencies and fallacies in the empiricist proscription for disinterestedness and have challenged the rigid distinction between aesthetic and non-aesthetic qualities by intentionally integrating contextual factors, e.g., social, ethical, and political, into the meaning and appraisal of art. It is worth noting that mainstream philosophers in the late 1990s have come to embrace such connections between aesthetics and ethics, yet with no acknowledgment of feminist writings (Levinson 1998).

In further challenges to canonical writings in aesthetics, feminists have given new readings of traditional theories of taste, beauty, and sublimity that exposed purportedly neutral and universal concepts. They have challenged David Hume's classic standard of taste – possessed solely by white, educated males who were well-practiced in the arts – and have questioned Kant's universal judgments of beauty by delving into basic assumptions about human nature used to legitimize masculine rational faculties and belittle feminine wiles. They have questioned the hierarchy of aesthetic responses by which the empiricists ranked the sublime (considered masculine) over the beautiful (feminine), exposing further bias. Carolyn Korsmeyer has provided an unusual analysis of taste that revisits the empirical notion of the eighteenth century but also expands into previously uncharted territory, namely, that of taste involving the physical senses of smell, sight, and gustatory delights (1999).

Numerous publications have established feminism's fragile foothold within philosophical aesthetics. Two books were published as expanded versions of the two initial 1990 journal publications, *Aesthetics in Feminist Perspective* (Hein and Korsmeyer 1993) and *Feminism and Tradition in Aesthetics* (Brand and Korsmeyer 1995). The first volume grew out of a special issue of a feminist philosophy journal and as such, presupposed an audience familiar with feminist ideas and methodology. It debates (among other things) the question initially posed by Sylvia Bovenschen in 1976, namely, that of a feminine – versus a feminist – aesthetic. In this volume, Hilde Hein issues a call for the study of aesthetics within feminist philosophy. Several authors in the volume seek to undermine philosophy's continuing preference for aesthetic/formalist properties over non-aesthetic. Other authors take on the task of examining the cognitive makeup of the artist within her sociopolitical context, for example, her race or sexuality, and the role such factors play in the assessment of art.

The second volume, *Feminism and Tradition in Aesthetics*, presupposed an audience of philosophers trained in analytic aesthetics with no familiarity with feminist research, methodology, or related fields of feminist inquiry, whether in the arts or feminist philosophy generally. Situating newly arrived feminist scholarship within the broader context of historical philosophical writing about the arts in the analytic tradition, feminism is cast as yet another challenge to the traditions of the past, quite similar, in fact, to the mid-twentieth-century backlash of analytic philosophers who defied the essentialism of their predecessors insistence on defining "art" and upholding past standards of beauty. Essays range from critical analyses of historical concepts to interpretive strategies of various art forms, and incorporate viewpoints atypical of traditional aesthetics, such as that of a black female spectator, a Vietnamese film-maker, a woman with disabilities, and a mother analyzing myths involving mothers and daughters. Given the emphasis on gender and race in the creativity and appreciation of the arts, feminists in this volume mount a dual-pronged challenge to both the canon of esteemed artworks and its unquestioned foundation for philosophical inquiry throughout the centuries. The feminist critique in this collection poses a meta-critical challenge to all that had come before: an acceptance of the art historical canon that sought to explain, without question, the aesthetic value attributed to "great" works of art.

Ongoing research in the fields of feminist art history, art criticism, and theory serve to reinforce feminist philosophers' claims that a new – revisionist – art history is being established, that feminist scholarship has posed difficult questions that need to be answered, and that analytic aesthetics can no longer ignore the cultural and historical context (factors like gender, race, and class) of a work of art.

The Role of Women Artists in Feminist Aesthetics

Women artists of the day, beginning in the early 1970s, have been crucial to the feminist effort to establish women as serious contenders in the highly competitive, male-dominated artworld and as newly established paradigms within feminist philosophy of art. Moving beyond women artists of the past, feminist art critics and theorists highlighted their contemporaries with a focus that coincided with a nationwide surge in new, cooperative women's galleries and published art journals (most of which are no longer with us). The content of feminist art became part of an agenda of women artists and writers to promote a message for social change, subversion of the patriarchy, and more equality for all women, including minorities (Piper 1996; Farris-Dufrene 1997). The writings of Judy Chicago provided insights into an artist's psyche and motivation for over thirty years (Chicago 1996) while the influence of the first decades of women's art began to come more clearly into focus (Broude and Garrard 1994). Feminists across the Atlantic celebrated their own artists, with some authors initiating new forms of feminist art criticism (Deepwell 1995) and others stepping back to assess the big picture and take stock of how far they had come as a separate, though inter-related field of study (Robinson 2001).

As women looked around – at themselves and at their peers still marginalized within the dominant artworld – a growing sense of sarcasm and humor took hold that served to organize and embolden a group of women who organized themselves under the name of Guerilla Girls (Isaak 1996). Beginning in the 1985, artworld inequities have been publicized by means of witty posters freely circulated around New York City that used humor and irreverence to express the sentiments of the self-proclaimed "conscience of culture" (Hoban 2004). Always anonymous and adopting names of deceased women artists like Kathe Kollwitz and Frida Kahlo, the Girls have published books, sold T-shirts, and distributed information on gender and racial inequities in the worlds of art, theater, film, politics, and the culture at large (1998; 2003). The Girls always appear in public wearing gorilla masks (to focus on the issues rather than their personalities) and, according to their website, use humor "to convey information, provoke discussion, and show that feminists can be funny." They book tours and appearances across the country, and proclaim their project of "reinventing the 'F word' – feminism." Comparing themselves to "the mostly male tradition of anonymous do-gooders like Robin Hood, Batman, and the Lone Ranger," they have been known to ask pointed questions that beg for answers, for example, in their latest publication on art museums: "Why do they blow a fortune on a single painting by a white male genius when they could acquire hundreds of great works by women and people of color instead?" (2004)

Feminist Philosophers Reflect on Self-Portraiture and Women as Objects of Beauty

Feminist scholarship affecting philosophical writing has developed in at least two specific areas worth noting here. One is the realm of self-portraiture that typically involves the use of the female body, e.g., in performance art; the second is a tangential interest in the depiction of women as objects of beauty, in defiance of a tradition established by male artists for over two millennia in which women have been cast as passive, available, and willing sources of sexual satisfaction and pleasure. Women have used their own bodies to challenge the historical hold and power of male artists over the female body, taking ownership and control over depictions of themselves, from a profoundly distinct woman's point of view. One might even consider the 1940s flower paintings of Georgia O'Keeffe, often interpreted as visual metaphors of women's sexual organs, as a precursor of this interest. This introspection on the part of women artists, in turn, has refocused feminist critics on women's self-representation (Borzello 1998), with artist Judy Chicago and co-author Edward Lucie-Smith dubbing the volatile subject matter of the female body "contested territory" (1999).

Feminist philosophers have come to direct their attention to these artists and their self-depictions as well, as evidenced by a number of essays appearing in a recent special issue of *Hypatia: A Journal of Feminist Philosophy* entitled, "Women, Art, and Aesthetics" (Brand and Devereaux 2003). This collection is designed as a form of self-study, a review and appraisal of how far feminism had come in

thirteen years in the field of philosophical aesthetics since the initial 1990 publication of *Hypatia*. Gauging the progress in the intervening years, it reflects the tenor
of the times – a new century, a new millennium. A considerable portion of this
publication is devoted to seeing the work of women artists such as Adrian Piper,
Jenny Saville, and Renée Cox in new ways: to highlight women's experiences as
the core of artistic expression and evaluative criticism. In this volume, art critic
Eleanor Heartney uses the prism of the Catholic imagination to understand the
controversial works of Janine Antoni, who mops the floor of a gallery with her hair
doused in paint. Michelle Meager formulates a feminist aesthetics of disgust to
explain the oversized nudes of the amply endowed bodies painted by Jenny Seville.
And Joanna Frueh introduces the radical notion of beauty in vaginal aesthetics
as a means to offset the typical evaluation of the female sex organs as ugly and
repulsive.

The attention women have paid to their own bodies and the artistic depiction
of themselves has helped usher in the resurgence of interest in beauty in the 1990s
by the mainstream artworld, although male critics never acknowledged as much
(Brand 2000). Feminist scholars have concentrated on new uses of the female body
in subverting past conventions of beauty. Wendy Steiner has sought to explain
a phenomenon she dubbed "Venus in exile" – the distortion or submersion of
images of women in the twentieth century consistent with abstract artists' rejection
of beauty (2001), while earlier Francette Pacteau proposed psychoanalytic explanations for the symptom of beauty (1994). Joanna Frueh (herself the artist under
discussion) has undertaken an exploration of "Monster/Beauty" and its relation to
body-building and love (2001). The impact of white standards of beauty impressed
upon artists and writers that African-Americans must negotiate an additional level
of *moral* meaning below the surface level of aesthetic meaning of appearances
and representations (Rooks 1996). Feminist philosophers have quickly joined in
discussions of race and gender that have defined the vanguard of feminist art criticism, thereby adding a unique perspective that has drawn upon their knowledge
and unique philosophical mode of investigation.

For instance, Cynthia Freeland poses the standard philosophical question, "But
is it Art?" by confronting controversial works by women involving beauty and
blood (2001). In *Gender in the Mirror: Cultural Imagery and Women's Agency*,
Diana Meyers probes the crucial roles played by agency and self-knowledge for
women caught within a society of patriarchal imagery, beauty-obsessed advertis-
ing, and pressures – from both sexes – to conform to unrealistic standards of bodily
perfection (2002). Ann Cahill revisits the philosophical proscription on interested
pleasure by reclaiming female pleasures based in community experiences and
rituals of feminine beautification (2003). Richard Shusterman proposes a pragmatist reading of Simone de Beauvoir's view of the body, one in which the body and
its senses are the locus of aesthetics' feelings and pleasures (2003). Sheila Lintott
unleashes the notion of Kant's sublime to explicate the phenomenon of eating
disorders within the context of our society's long-standing cult of thinness that
functions as an ideal of beauty (2003).

Future Developments

Substantially furthering feminist scholarship in philosophical aesthetics, Carolyn Korsmeyer's informative text, *Gender and Aesthetics: An Introduction*, is the first comprehensive introduction to the field. It casts the net of philosophical aesthetics even more widely by probing into new topics like disgust, the abject, and the pernicious realm of "deep gender," which she casts as "gendered thinking operating at its most tenacious and subterranean level" below seemingly innocuous statements that "on the surface" appear to be "innocent and neutral" (Korsmeyer 2004a: 3). A virtual cornucopia of disciplines are covered and brought together under the umbrella of inquiry that places gender first and foremost in the careful analysis of artists, artworks, and artistic reception. Familiar topics are revisited but the approach is new, fresh, and all-encompassing.

What does the future hold? One prescient suggestion was proposed by Estella Lauter in her call for feminists to create a truly interdisciplinary discourse to avert a future "crisis" in aesthetics; her plan involves

> an international conference that invites all interested feminist parties to a philosophical debate with all sorts of aestheticians over the nature of aesthetic experience, political engagement in art, theory, difference, opposition, and many other material or nonmaterial issues that may or may not be related differentially at present.

> (Lauter 2003: 282)

Also looking to the future, Brand and Devereaux (2003) recommend more attention be paid to two important areas still relatively untouched. The first is the history of aesthetics itself. With the observation that feminists have shown little interest in the history of their discipline, they have issued a call for more scholarship on historical figures like Plato and Aristotle as well as neglected topics like medieval theories of beauty, but more importantly, new attention to women writers whose role thus far has been unacknowledged in the history of twentieth-century aesthetics, for example, Susanne Langer, Susan Sontag, Iris Murdoch, Eva Schaper, and Mary Mothersill. (Margaret Macdonald, Helen Knight, Katherine Gilbert, and Isabel Creed Hungerland are also figures about whom little is known; Gilbert and Hungerland each served two-year terms as president of the American Society of Aesthetics, in 1946 and 1965 respectively.) Although few of these thinkers would have identified themselves as feminist, their contributions – as well as those of other women whom we have yet to discover – can shed light upon the predominant mode of thinking within a discipline so dominated by men and the questions of artistic value and aesthetic experience they chose to prioritize.

A second suggestion involves a call to explore the underinvestigated topic of the feminization of aesthetics itself, another inward-looking turn that asks philosophers to reassess themselves in light of a bigger picture. The "feminization of aesthetics" captures the marginalization of aesthetics as a "soft" discipline within the larger, more "male" province of philosophy. Future questions about the role aesthetics plays – or fails to play – within feminist philosophy may also enhance our understanding of women's experiences as a core notion of feminist inquiry.

Finally, the newest explosion of research in cognitive science and individual cognitive "architectural" frameworks provides, perhaps, the most open and urgent avenue of invitation to study factors of gender, race, sexuality, ethnicity, etc. Philosophers crossing disciplines are voraciously interested in the makeup and functions of emotions, psychological studies on perception and resultant value judgments, and the role of imagination in creating fictions: all ways of initiating new debates on some of the most traditional questions in contemporary aesthetics that are rich with opportunities (Currie 2003). The intersections of aesthetics with philosophy of mind, neuro-psychology, and developmental psychology, are ripe with testable hypotheses; surely it is worth the effort to explore whether gender plays a role!

Bibliography

Battersby, C. (1989) *Gender and Genius: Towards a New Feminist Aesthetics*, Bloomington and Indianapolis: Indiana University Press.

Borzello, F. (1998) *Seeing Ourselves: Women's Self-portraits*, New York: Harry N. Abrams.

Bovenschen, S. (1985) "Is There a Feminine Aesthetic?" in *Feminist Aesthetics*, ed. G. Ecker, tr. Harriet Anderson, Boston, MA: Beacon Press, pp. 23–50 (originally published 1976).

Brand, P. (1998) "Feminism: Feminism and Tradition," in *Encyclopedia of Aesthetics*, ed. M. Kelly, New York: Oxford University Press, pp. 167–70.

—— ed. (2000) *Beauty Matters*, Bloomington and Indianapolis: Indiana University Press.

Brand, P. and Devereaux, M., eds. (2003) *Hypatia: A Journal of Feminist Philosophy* 18 (Fall/Winter), Special Issue: Women, Art, and Aesthetics.

Brand, P. and Korsmeyer, C. (eds.) (1990) *The Journal of Aesthetics and Art Criticism* 48 (4), Special Issue: Feminism and Traditional Aesthetics.

—— (eds.) (1995) *Feminism and Tradition in Aesthetics*, University Park: Pennsylvania State University Press.

Broude, N. and Garrard, M.D., eds. (1982) *Feminism and Art History: Questioning the Litany*, New York: Harper and Row.

—— eds. (1994) *The Power of Feminist Art: The American Movement of the 1970s, History and Impact*, New York: Harry N. Abrams.

Cahill, A.J. (2003) "Feminist Pleasure and Feminine Beautification," *Hypatia: A Journal of Feminist Philosophy* 18, Special Issue: Women, Art, and Aesthetics, eds. P. Brand and M. Devereaux: 42–64.

Chadwick, W. (2002) *Women, Art, and Society*, London: Thames and Hudson. (Original work published 1990.)

Chicago, J. (1996) *Beyond the Flower: The Autobiography of a Feminist Artist*, New York: Viking Press.

Chicago, J. and Lucie-Smith, E. (1999) *Women and Art: Contested Territory*, New York: Watson-Guptill Publications.

Cox, Renée (2001) *Renée Cox: American Family*, New York: Robert Miller Gallery.

Currie, G. (2003) "Aesthetics and Cognitive Science," in *The Oxford Handbook of Aesthetics*, ed. J. Levinson, Oxford and New York: Oxford University Press, pp. 706–21.

Deepwell, K., ed. (1995) *New Feminist Art Criticism*, Manchester: Manchester University Press.

Devereaux, M. (2003) "Feminist Aesthetics," in *The Oxford Handbook of Aesthetics*, ed. J. Levinson, Oxford and New York: Oxford University Press, pp. 647–66.

Eaton, A. (2005) "Feminist Aesthetics and Criticism," in *Encyclopedia of Philosophy*, 2nd edn, ed. D. Borchert, Basingstoke: Macmillan.

Farris-Dufrene, P. (1997) *Voices of Color: Art and Society in the Americas*, Atlantic Highlands, NJ: Humanities Press International.

Felski, R. (1989) *Beyond Feminist Aesthetics: Feminist Literature and Social Change*, Cambridge, MA: Harvard University Press.

Florence, P. and Foster, N., eds. (1998) "Review Essay and Call for Papers," *Women's Philosophy Review* 19 (Autumn).

—— eds. (2000a) *Women's Philosophy Review* 25 (Autumn), Special Issue: Aesthetics.

—— eds. (2000b) *Differential Aesthetics: Art Practices, Philosophy and Feminist Understandings*, Aldershot and Burlington VT: Ashgate Publishing.

Freeland, C. (2001) *But Is It Art?* Oxford: Oxford University Press.

Frueh, J. (2001) *Monster/Beauty: Building the Body of Love*, Berkeley, Los Angeles, London: University of California Press.

Greer, G. (1979) *The Obstacle Race: The Fortunes of Women Painters and Their Work*, New York: Farrar Straus Giroux.

Guerilla Girls (1995) *Confessions of the Guerilla Girls*, New York: HarperPerennial.

—— (1998) *The Guerilla Girls' Bedside Companion to the History of Western Art*, New York: Penguin Books.

—— (2003) *Bitches, Bimbos and Ballbreakers: The Guerilla Girls' Illustrated Guide to Female Stereotypes*, New York: Penguin Books.

— (2004) *The Guerilla Girls' Art Museum Activity Book*, New York: Printed Matter.

Harris, A.S. and Nochlin, L. (1976) *Women Artists: 1550–1950*, New York: Alfred A. Knopf and the Los Angeles County Museum of Art.

Hein, H. and Korsmeyer, C., eds. (1990) *Hypatia: A Journal of Feminist Philosophy* 5 (2), Special Issue: Feminism and Aesthetics.

—— eds. (1993) *Aesthetics in Feminist Perspective*, Bloomington and Indianapolis: Indiana University Press.

Hess, T.B. and Baker, E.C., eds. (1973) *Art and Sexual Politics: Women's Liberation, Women Artists, and Art History*, New York and London: Collier Macmillan.

Hoban, P. (2004) "Masks Still in Place but Firmly in the Mainstream," *New York Times*, January 4, AR34, 37.

Hutcheson, F. (1977) *An Inquiry into the Original of Our Ideas of Beauty and Virtue*, in *Aesthetics: A Critical Anthology*, eds. G. Dickie and R.J. Sclafani, New York: St Martin's Press, pp. 569–91.

Irigaray, L. (1974/1985) *Speculum of the Other Woman*, tr. G.C. Gill, Ithaca, NY: Cornell University Press.

Isaak, J.A. (1996) *Feminism and Contemporary Art: The Revolutionary Power of Women's Laughter*, New York: Routledge.

Korsmeyer, C. (1999) *Making Sense of Taste: Food and Philosophy*, London and Ithaca, NY: Cornell University Press.

—— (2004a) *Gender and Aesthetics: An Introduction*, New York and London: Routledge.

—— (2004b) "Feminist Aesthetics," in the *Stanford Encyclopedia of Philosophy*, http:// plato.stanford.edu/entries/feminism-aesthetics/

Kristeva, J. (1982) *The Powers of Horror: An Essay in Abjection*, tr. L.S. Roudiez, New York: Columbia University Press.

Lauter, E. (2003) "Aesthetics in Crisis: Feminist Attempts to Create an Interdisciplinary Discourse," *Hypatia: A Journal of Feminist Philosophy* 18: Special Issue: Women, Art, and Aesthetics: 273–82.

Levinson, J. (ed.) (1998) *Aesthetics and Ethics: Essays at the Intersection*, Cambridge and New York: Cambridge University Press.

Lintott, S. (2003) "Sublime Hunger: A Consideration of Eating Disorders Beyond Beauty," *Hypatia: A Journal of Feminist Philosophy* 18: Special Issue: Women, Art, and Aesthetics: 65–86.

Lippard, L.R. (1984) *Get the Message? A Decade of Art for Social Change*, New York: E.P. Dutton.

Meyers, D.T. (2002) *Gender in the Mirror: Cultural Imagery and Women's Agency*, Oxford and New York: Oxford University Press.

The Monist (1973) Special Issue: Women's Liberation: Ethical, Social, and Political Issues, 57 (1).

Nochlin, L. (1988) "Why Have There Been No Great Women Artists?" in *Women, Art, and Power and Other Essays*, New York: Harper and Row, pp. 1–36.

Pacteau, F. (1994) *The Symptom of Beauty*, Cambridge, MA: Harvard University Press.

Parker, R. and Pollock, G. (1981) *Old Mistresses: Women, Art and Ideology*, New York: Pantheon.

Petersen, K. and Wilson, J.J. (1976) *Women Artists: Recognition and Reappraisal from the Early Middle Ages to the Twentieth Century*, New York: Harper and Row.

The Philosophical Forum 5 (1–2) (1973–4), Special Issue: Women and Philosophy.

Piper, A. (1996) *Out of Order, Out of Sight*, 2 vols., Cambridge, MA: MIT Press.

Robinson, H. (2001) *Feminism – Art – Theory: An Anthology 1968–2000*, Oxford and Malden, MA: Blackwell Publishers.

Rooks, N.M. (1996) *Hair Raising: Beauty, Culture, and African American Women*, New Brunswick, NJ, and London: Rutgers University Press.

Schor, N. (1987) *Reading in Detail: Aesthetics and the Feminine*, New York and London, England: Methuen.

Shusterman, R. (2003) "Somaesthetics and *The Second Sex*: A Pragmatist Reading of a Feminist Classic," *Hypatia: A Journal of Feminist Philosophy* 18, Special Issue: Women, Art, and Aesthetics: 106–36.

Steiner, W. (2001) *Venus in Exile: The Rejection of Beauty in 20th-century Art*, New York: The Free Press.

Tufts, E. (1975) *Our Hidden Heritage: Five Centuries of Women Artists*, New York: Paddington Press.

Worth, S. (1998) "Feminism and Aesthetics," in *The Routledge Companion to Aesthetics*, eds. B. Gaut and D.M. Lopes, London: Routledge.

Chapter 15

Feminism and Poststructuralism

A Deleuzian Approach

Tamsin Lorraine

Introduction

The "problem of difference" – that is, the fact of important differences among women including race, class, ethnicity, sexual preference, and ablism, leading to incommensurate experiences, problems, and invested interests – was pointed out early on in feminist theory of the 1970s and has been an important issue ever since. This problem made a feminism rooted in the consciousness-raising of the 1970s suspect; feminists could no longer assume that simply because certain kinds of experience were shared by some women that they could automatically ground the theoretical truths of a feminist perspective (see, for example, Hull et al. 1982, and hooks 1981). And yet the universalizable norms of a liberal model of justice and citizenship, according to some feminists, was also suspect for excluding from its notion of citizenship the very subjects feminism was meant to address; interests and activities not specific to the standard man (male, white, propertied, hetero-sexual, Christian, able-bodied) were marginalized or rendered invisible, skewing the "norm" toward the interests, rationality, and experiences of a subset of the human race that did not include women (see, for example, Jaggar 1983: 27–50 and Butler 1990). Some feminists turned to poststructuralist thought as a resource for theorizing in a way that could be respectful of women's differences. Although their work rarely took feminist theory into account, feminists eagerly developed the feminist implications of French poststructuralist theory by thinkers like Jacques Lacan, Jacques Derrida, Michel Foucault, Gilles Deleuze, and Emmanuel Levinas (see, for example, Mitchell 1974; Spivak 1988; Sawicki 1991; Braidotti 1994; and Chanter 2001). In addition, French feminists – especially Julia Kristeva, Luce Iri-garay, and Hélène Cixous – developed feminist poststructuralist theories that were highly influential in the development of poststructuralist feminism.

Despite the excitement poststructuralist versions of feminist theory inspired in many, it has been criticized for its theoretical elitism (it can be difficult to follow), as well as for inducing political quietism. Martha Nussbaum, for example, attacks Judith Butler and "feminist thinkers of the new symbolic type" for reducing feminist politics to the subversive use of language: "These symbolic gestures, it is believed, are themselves a form of political resistance; and so one need not engage with messy things such as legislatures and movements in order to act daringly" (Nussbaum 1999: 45). She charges Butler with eschewing the clear language and straightforward arguments of traditional, "rational," debate about matters of public policy, and instead obscuring her views behind an esoteric vocabulary, veiled allusions to difficult theorists, and a "teasing, exasperating" theoretical style. What Nussbaum's criticism fails to recognize or acknowledge is that poststructuralist feminists like Butler are struggling to incorporate into their theoretical style tools and strategies inspired by poststructuralist theories that could help us to theorize the multiple factors complicating women's individual experiences of desire, identity, and reality, without forcing their reduction to a uniform set of experiences. For example, rather than assume that a battered woman is simply irrational for desiring to maintain intimate relations with her batterer, an approach inspired by Foucauldian theory might look at the distinct discursive practices that play into the constitution of an identity invested in maintaining what would seem to be a counterproductive status quo. If a woman's desires, interests, and sense of self are in part constituted through the "discourses" (ways of talking attached to different arenas of social life) in which she finds herself, then becoming more aware of the implicit rules attached to distinct discursive practices illuminates the process through which she has developed her perspective. Feminist analysis of such practices could thus not only lead to contextually specific descriptions of her life, but also shed light on the series of steps required for lasting change. This is not to say that arguments of a more traditional sort could not be made as to why a woman should not remain in such a situation. Or even that one might not find a more traditional explanation for why a woman chooses to stay. But arguments and explanations couched in the paradigms of traditional political theory (for example, "rights" or "rational, self-interest," or "consent") can sometimes be more alienating than illuminating. When such language seems to impose upon women the self they should be rather than resonate with the self they experience themselves to be, then the language so prized by feminists like Nussbaum can come to seem as out of touch with reality as Nussbaum believes Butler's prose to be. Feminist theory inspired by poststructuralist thought attempts to allow for more nuanced readings of specific situations, even though this means its pronouncements regarding general cases cannot always be definitive.

Seyla Benhabib expresses a criticism similar to Nussbaum's in a more constructive fashion when she worries that feminists like Butler emphasize an ethics of nonviolent relation to the concrete other (as depicted, for example, in the theories indebted to Levinas or Derrida and Irigaray or poststructuralist feminists inspired by any of these three theorists) at the expense of universal principles of justice.

Benhabib believes that in addition to such an ethics, feminism must also be able to justify "the norms of universal moral respect and egalitarian reciprocity on rational grounds" (Benhabib 1995: 118). An ethics of nonviolent relation to the other presupposes the universal principle that one should treat all human beings with respect. Furthermore, if the principle itself is not explicitly justified, feminists run the risk of including in their notion of the other only those others "to whom we owe a special obligation in virtue of our membership in this or that community" (117). We need more, in other words, than an open-ended ethics worked out in the context of embodied relations to concrete others; we need overarching principles that can be justified independently of context.

Benhabib also worries that notions like Butler's "performativity" that posit the self as a discursive effect (one is constituted as an "I" through discursive systems that precede one; the I is the effect of "performing" what it means to be a daughter, a student, a citizen) "presupposes a remarkably deterministic view of individuation and socialization processes which falls short of the currently available social-scientific reflections on the subject" (1995: 110). This worry expressed more broadly concerns the status of agency and responsibility for accounts of subjectivity informed by poststructuralist theory. Most poststructuralist theories posit the self as an emergent effect of processes beyond the individual's control. If this is the case, what kind of accountability can an individual have? And what possible grounds for critique or resistance could such an individual provide?

Many feminists, including those interested in poststructuralism, share Benhabib's concern that poststructuralist feminist theory's antifoundationalist wariness of overarching principles does not provide adequate grounding for the kind of social critique necessary for feminist change. Most feminists currently investigating and experimenting with poststructuralist theories take criticisms like Benhabib's seriously and share her belief that feminism should provide theoretical perspectives that can galvanize collective action as well as empower individual women. One could say, although of course this is to oversimplify, that poststructuralist feminism has tended toward two different approaches in achieving these goals. One approach responds to the liberal feminist notion of the universalizable emancipatory ideals of the rational subject with the Foucauldian notion that subjects are constituted within and through a field of social relations – gendered and otherwise – inevitably inflected with power. A Foucauldian analysis of a social field can reveal the vested interests masked by various social practices and locate points of resistance that can lead to liberating change. A second approach responds to the notion of authenticating a feminist perspective through the lived experience of women by refusing to take experience at face value and yet investigating it with psychoanalytic and phenomenological analyses that insist upon the importance of experience to understanding the embodied nature of sex and gender. This approach emphasizes aspects of embodiment that render the self more than the emergent effect of discursive practices. These two approaches have sometimes diverged between political and ethical questions. For example, while theorists like Butler and Chantal Mouffe could be said to be theorizing the agonistic arena of politics, theorists like Kristeva and Irigaray could be said to be more interested in the ethical encounters of embodied individuals. While Butler and Mouffe place more emphasis on discursive positioning that entails specific configurations of power and knowledge, Kristeva and Irigaray place more emphasis on the encounters between individuals that activate drives of the body beyond speech (Laclau and Mouffe 1985; Butler 1990; Mouffe 1992; Kristeva 1984; Irigaray 1993). Foucauldian theory can inspire an illuminating mapping of the social field – one that can put a complicated set of power relations into context; Lacanian psychoanalytic theory can inspire a vocabulary for articulating the feelings and affect so often associated with the body and relegated to the "irrational," "emotional" realm of women. While the former kind of theory can be helpful in putting various forms of domination into context (such as race, sexual preference, and so forth), the latter kind of theory can be helpful in articulating the inchoate feelings of the marginalized subject. Despite the responses given to specific criticisms (see Butler 1995: 127–37, for example, for Butler's response to Benhabib), as well as the ongoing development of poststructuralist feminist thought, feminists invested in either or both of these approaches have continued to grapple with the concern that they lead to political paralysis. On the one hand, in addition to challenging the essentializing norms of metaphysical thought, theories emphasizing discursive positioning as a constitutive feature of subjectivity seem to some to undermine the authority of women's experience as well as their sense of agency and control, thus alienating many feminists from the very passion that give their projects purpose. On the other, theories that make embodiment a crucial theme by emphasizing the maternal body and the notion of an embodied "subject in process" seem to essentialize femininity and do not seem to provide the kind of overview necessary for a feminist vision of social change. Common to all these concerns is a question about the appropriate grounding for a feminist critique. At the same time that most feminists agree that we can no longer assume an essentializing definition of woman as the touchstone for feminist theory, poststructuralist feminist theory (as well as other forms of feminist theory) have not been able to provide feminism with a unifying focus.

If poststructuralist feminism invalidates both overarching principles as well as evidence supporting a feminist perspective produced by women claiming epistemological authority and agency as subjects of their own experience, then what is left? The answer is less black and white than some caricatures of poststructuralist feminism would suggest. Although transcendent principles are suspect from a poststructuralist perspective, this does not mean that generalizations of a more open-ended sort cannot be made. And although lived experience cannot be taken at face value, this does not mean that it cannot play an empowering role in the creation of poststructuralist theory. Some of the most exciting work in poststructuralist feminism at the moment attempts to combine the location of subjects and local struggles within the broader context of social fields of political struggle with accounts of lived experience that attempt to give voice to embodied differences rendered invisible by dominant norms. Ewa Ziarek, for example, in a recent work, elaborates what she calls an "ethics of dissensus" that she hopes moves beyond the opposition of a "local, nontheoretical politics of difference without ethics" and a "grand theory of normative justice transcending conflict" (Ziarek 2001: 107). Like most feminists inspired by poststructuralist theory, rather than restricting herself to poststructuralism, Ziarek combines an eclectic array of voices in order to supplement "the hegemonic articulation of struggle and resistance" with a revised notion of freedom reconceptualized "in relational terms as an engagement in transformative praxis motivated by the obligation for the Other" (2). She thus affirms a theoretical approach committed to avoiding a dogmatic insistence on already articulated principles by conceiving freedom as an open-ended concept that must evolve in and through ongoing, ethical interaction with the other. This other, she insists, needs to be conceived in the context of embodiment and sexuality in order to avoid reifying the other's place in preconceptions of the forms social antagonisms will take (7). Thus, as-yet unarticulated concerns, investments, and desire are invited to emerge into articulation even when the new categories they introduce conflict with theoretical dictates.

> This shift from moral law to the event locates responsibility in the always asymmetrical, embodied relation to the Other and redefines freedom as an engagement in the experimental praxis aiming to surpass historically sedimented identities and to create new modes of life.
>
> (Ziarek 2001: 219)

Shifting from moral law to the event requires shifting our focus from the refinement of theories to the praxis of theory in action as we live our lives. Ziarek's insistence on the embodied relation to the other means that we must allow ruptures in our understanding of reality to occur if we are to integrate an evolving awareness of life in all its sensuous complexity into our attempts to make changes for the better. A poststructuralist notion of an emergent self cannot be a deterministic one when such a self is the effect of a unique interplay of material as well as symbolic influences that include what we could call "feedback loops" of self-conscious awareness as well as a dizzying array of other factors (physiological, environmental, familial, social, cultural, and historical). While life's complexity does not invalidate the theoretical impetus to make generalizations, a theory of experimental praxis recognizes theory itself as a co-participant in the creation (rather than a more or less correct interpretation or representation) of reality. Its generalizations are creative interventions that must be judged as much upon their effects on actual lives as upon their rational consistency. Ziarek's approach suggests that one can ground social critique in ongoing critical reflection upon one's life experience that excludes neither rational argument and investment in generalizations that ring true with one's experience nor passionate engagement. At the same time that poststructuralist feminists like Ziarek (as well as Butler) continue to attempt to open theory to the evolving experiences of a culture in transition, they continue to seek theoretical impetus for inciting and connecting disparate struggles for change under a collective feminist front that is not united through preconceived paradigms of "rational" consensus.

In this essay I draw upon the work of Deleuze, and Deleuze and Guattari, in order to suggest a way in which we might combine a keen attention to the subtleties of lived experience with the conceptual tools needed to connect local struggles into a map for social change. Deleuze's concepts of subjectivity as becoming-other and of theory as an open-ended intervention responsive to both the symbolic and the material forces with which it interacts suggest an alternative to grounding feminist theory either in overarching principles or the authority of lived experience. It may be Deleuze's challenge to personal identity in favor of nonpersonal forces of becoming as well as his failure to articulate anything like the nurturing spaces or the responsibility to the other that emerge in the work of Levinas, Derrida, and Irigaray, as well as feminists like Ziarek and Kelly Oliver, that have made some feminists wary of Deleuze (Oliver 2001). Despite this wariness, there is a growing body of feminist work directly addressing or strongly informed by Deleuze's work and the books he wrote with Guattari (see, for example, Braidotti 1994; Grosz 1994; Diprose 1994; Gatens 1996; Griggers 1997; Lorraine 1999; and Buchanan and Colebrook 2000).

Although Deleuze himself does not elaborate a politics adequate to feminist aspirations, his work opens up ways of thinking about embodiment that invite us to open our experience to processes typically beneath our threshold of awareness and about theory as a vector of force that creatively evolves in its interaction with other forces (Deleuze and Guattari 1987). His emphasis on the power of bodies to affect and be affected by other bodies renders what Ziarek calls his "ethos of becoming" one that is responsive to forces of life that include the natural environment and influences upon our experience beneath the threshold of a reality we can represent, as well as personal others (Ziarek 2001: 7). This enables a conception of the future that defies the constraints of personal identity and collective norms. His characterization of how time and memory are synthesized from the organic and reflective responses of human subjects to their surroundings challenges conceptions of the past and the future that treat them as static inversions of the present (Deleuze 1994). His notion of the individual as a serial unfolding entails an unfolding of specific space-times that only come to be correlated to the space-times of others through a process of collective sharing (Deleuze 1990). His notion of the virtual real conceives the shared reality in which all space-times come together not in terms of the totalized whole of a Newtonian conception of space and time, but rather as a transcendental field of virtual relations (Deleuze 1990, 1994; Deleuze and Guattari 1987, 1994). The latter notion allows us to conceive a reality that cannot be represented from any one perspective out of which emerge the times and spaces represented in cultural systems of meaning.

The notions of time, embodied memory, and a virtual real, out of which emerge the space-times of lived experience lead us to reconsider how our lived experience relates to the lived experience of others and challenge the notion that the pasts of a collective of individuals can be easily correlated through one representable past.

Although there is no one way to represent the reality we share, we can still evaluate the force of different opportunities for experimentation available to us. Considering new forms of being subjects as well as new ways of thinking about what we want our theorizing to achieve can give fresh impetus to connecting our disparate struggles into a collective effort for a better future. In the next section, I develop a Deleuzian description of traumatized individuals as just one example of a whole range of experiences that can remain imperceptible due to a process of collective sharing that denies credence to experiences that defy the norm. If we are to draw upon the creative power of the virtual past informing our present, we must be willing to face a certain degree of disorientation. Applying Deleuze's concepts to the trauma survivor is one example of how this might be done.

Challenging a reality that adheres to socially sanctioned categories of representation means neither to sacrifice a notion of reality nor to suggest that we can construct reality any way we like. We live in a world to which we not only respond but which we shape through our actions. Our conceptions of reality and how our experiences can be shared and correlated are an integral part of our collective response to the world. Deleuze's conception of the events of meaning (the "incorporeal" entities that "frolic" above embodied states of affairs) as vectors of force that co-participate with other vectors of force in the actualization of states of affairs suggests a dynamic view of theory as well as of the past (Deleuze 1990: 5). Responding to the disorientation that comes from unfolding the virtual possibilities that enable enlivening connections does not mean refusing to be "realistic," but rather allowing ourselves to resonate to our present in a way that defies extant representations of ourselves and our past. An emphasis on an alternative form of subjectivity premised upon becoming-other rather than opposing itself to the world which it is not, allows us to respond with greater flexibility and resourcefulness to our encounters with what defies our expectations.

Trauma and a Time Out of Joint

People who have difficulties in living a "normal" life after experiencing severe trauma are just one example of a kind of subject that deviates from the norm. Lawrence Langer in his book, *Holocaust Testimonies: The Ruins of Memory* (1991), comments upon the split subjectivity experienced by survivors of the death camps in giving oral accounts of their experiences; there is a rupture or discontinuity experienced between the "normal" self of life prior to and after the death camp experiences and the "abnormal" self which lived through those experiences. The painful sense of discontinuity emerging from this split subjectivity manifests in the survivors' sense of futility at not being able to communicate their experiences as well as in the failure of traditional forms of narrative to account for their experiences by giving them human significance within a coherent chronology. Instead, their memories are fragmented and disconnected, threatening to overwhelm their "normal" present with the horrors of a past beyond all conventional understanding. This leads to a physical sense of disconnection in the present, the feeling of having, in a certain sense, "died" despite one's survival, and a loss of faith in the coherence of values shared with a human collective.

Judith Herman chronicles similar experiences among rape survivors, battered women, and survivors of sexual abuse, in her book, *Trauma and Recovery*. Women (as well as men) subjected to dehumanizing and often life-threatening betrayal of their bodily and psychic integrity experience ruptures in their self-narratives that can be difficult to resolve, particularly when their attempts to do so are met with silence or belittlement. Jonathan Shay in his book on remembering experiences in the Vietnam war, *Achilles in Vietnam* (1994), as well as Langer, argue that the memories of Vietnam vets and Holocaust survivors present painful difficulties because they are of extreme situations in which survivors were confronted with a disconcerting incapacity to react in keeping with familiar forms of self-representation. Herman corroborates a similar phenomenon for survivors of domestic and sexual abuse who often find it difficult to reconcile their reactions in the extreme situations with which they are confronted with socially sanctioned self-narratives. Without the open – and sometimes "irrational" and disorienting – communication needed to fully support the affectively loaded articulation of experiences that challenge what we believe (or hope) to be true of human beings, such survivors lack the means for fully resolving their trauma.

Deleuzian theory is a useful resource for concepts that help us both describe and foster the process, so important to the evolution of feminist thought, of articulating experiences for which we do not yet have words. Although traumatic experiences of violent and/or sexual abuse may be extreme examples, the problem of articulating one's experience in a way that allows one to feel fully integrated into a community (be it feminist or otherwise), and thus to feel one's humanity fully affirmed is one that deserves careful attention. If feminist theory is to evolve in keeping with the always novel experiences of the people it hopes to support, we need concepts that can allow us to generalize beyond concrete situations without reducing new situations to overly rigid categories. I will briefly elaborate Deleuze's notions of the virtual found throughout his later work, as well as his notions of the syntheses of habit and memory found in *Difference and Repetition* (1994) in order to show how they might be useful to a feminist mapping of individuals as well as cultures that are always in process.

Deleuze's notion of the virtual posits what we experience (from what we sense and feel to the meaning words have for us) as the emergent effect of relations that are "virtual" (that is, implicit relations that never became fully manifest) as well as "actualized" (that is, relations that actually become manifest in specific states of affairs) among what he calls "events" or "singularities." Events are turning points where something happens (for example, the point at which water boils or freezes, or a war becomes a revolution). These turning points may be merely implicit in a concrete state of affairs (it is not cold enough for the water to freeze), or become manifest (water becomes ice). Either way the event is what "hovers" over the concrete state of affairs without ever becoming fully manifest since even when it is actualized it could become actualized in many different ways depending on the specific relations involved. For example, the event of eating ice cream can become manifest in the eating of ice cream on a beach in the sunshine or after coming in from the cold. In contrast to the notion of Platonic forms where what appears is a (bad) copy of the enduring reality of the form, what occurs, for Deleuze, does not resemble the virtual real of all possible (and incompossible) configurations of events. For example, "feminist" as an event of meaning manifests specific meanings actualized in the concrete contexts in which it is uttered. There is no one, univocal meaning for the word "feminist" that can act as the standard for all uses of the word. There are only "zones of indiscernability" among elements ("cares about women," "invested in change") of "feminist" as an event of meaning that "hovers" over its various concrete uses. These elements cross thresholds of meaning together or reach critical thresholds that distinguish them when relations of meanings shift enough to bring about a change in meaning ("your notion of a feminist is not my notion of a feminist"). A human being as a complicated and always becoming-other manifestation of events of meaning, as well as events of material processes is, on Deleuze's view, not a better or worse copy of the perfect form of a human being, but rather the emergent effect of a complicated network of physiological, symbolic, and cultural elements. Shifts in any subset of the relations of these elements will have repercussions on other relations that may or may not push aspects of being human over critical thresholds that bring about a recognizable change in state of an aggregate of elements. For example, the physiological shifts that lead from a state of relaxation to a state of alertness, or the symbolic shifts (related to physiological and cultural shifts) that lead from perceiving oneself as first a girl, and then a woman, occur in increments that produce no recognizable change until they cross the threshold that results in a change of state.

Deleuze's notion, derived from Henri Bergson, of memory as bodily habit or what Bergson calls a "sensory-motor apparatus" suggests that the individual is an aggregate of contracted expectations (stimulus–response patterns) that sustain the individual's continuity. Individuals tend to manifest habitual configurations of physiological, perceptual, and signifying elements. According to Bergson, we screen our perceptions in keeping with what is of concern to us in the world and we tend to develop automatic responses to the world on the basis of past adaptations to our environment. What distinguishes human beings from other creatures is that they have "the power to value the useless" and the "will to dream" necessary to achieve a form of memory different from the memory of bodily habit (Bergson 1991: 83). What Bergson calls "true memory" entails imaging the past drawn from a virtual totality presenting possibilities for creative action in light of a hoped-for future. It is only with the active syntheses of memory and understanding which are superimposed and supported by the passive syntheses of habit, that the past becomes a series of representations upon which the subject can reflect and the future becomes the prediction of various possibilities (Deleuze 1994: 71). We can thus live our past into the present in the form of habitual repetitions of the same configurations of events we have lived in the past (I drive the way I have always driven to the supermarket, despite the shortcut I have just learned about), or we can tap the virtual possibilities of our past (instead of taking the second left, I take the first left I only vaguely remember), thus releasing a creative synthesis of the virtual past and the present.

With the help of the Deleuzian concepts of the event, the virtual real, and the syntheses of habit and memory, we might say that survivors of trauma are confronted with situations that disturb "sensory-motor connections." The repertoire of expectations and responses acquired at an organic as well as a psychic level are challenged, confronting the survivors with a painfully alienating gap between habitual reactions and the unfamiliar forces of a world that defies past understanding. Such experiences produce new habits that cannot be reconciled with old ones. In addition, such experiences defy the familiar narratives through which experiences have been organized in the past. Especially when such experiences challenge the survivor's very conception of what it means to be moral and human, they take a toll on her psychic as well as her physical selves.

Langer and Herman both argue that the difficulty in integration posed by such memories of trauma entail psychic and physical damage to the individuals involved (as well as those around them) and that some form of active and non-judgmental listening or witnessing is crucial to the process of integration. Not only does the integration of experiences that disrupt sensory-motor connections require the suspension of traditional categories of thought, the constitution of new habits of being, and the creation of new forms of representation, but it also requires a collective process of integration. Deleuze's concepts of the syntheses of habit and memory suggest that the collective narratives through which the trauma survivor represents the life she shares with others are no longer supported by the organic syntheses of bodily habit. There are no words that can provide recognizable thresholds of meaning for the traumatic experiences imprinted at an organic level. In his two books, *Cinema 1* (1986) and *Cinema 2* (1989), Deleuze characterizes avant-garde cinema that defies conventional representation as an art-form that deliberately puts the viewer into a situation where she is likely to actualize virtual relations among organic and symbolic events that were previously imperceptible. This brings about a shift in the configuration of events that will in turn shift critical thresholds of perception and meaning. The danger for the viewer – as well as for the trauma survivor – is that the individual is unable to resolve the dilemma of meaning precipitated by her situation. In discussing the political possibilities of modern cinema, Deleuze suggests that art, and especially the art of cinema, must not address a preconceived people, but must contribute to the invention of a people (Deleuze 1989: 217). It is precisely because we can have no automatic response to a film by Godard that we engage in a form of self-questioning that can lead to self-transformation in the process of trying to understand it.

The trauma survivor confronted with extreme situations has lost the ability to act in keeping with familiar sensory-motor schemas. To speak her experience she must address someone who does not yet exist, someone who will, in part, come to be through listening to her story. It is in the process of telling her story to an as-yet-to-be-invented subject that her experience can overturn her old "truths" and introduce what Deleuze calls the "power of the false." That is, it is only by telling her story with its ruptures intact that the virtual relations among elements actualize, thus enabling her to synthesize previously imperceptible and unthinkable aspects of her past into her present. It is through this process that a new truth can be created rather than achieved or reproduced (Deleuze 1989: 147), and a new subject capable of hearing that truth invented. It is through this new truth that the survivor can share the reality of her experience.

Langer and Shay agree that a typical response on the part of those listening to accounts of trauma is to retreat as quickly as possible to a heroic narrative that emphasizes the survivor's dignified ingenuity in the face of adversity. What is often most painful to the survivor, however, is the rupture the trauma causes in such collective narratives. Healing trauma at the individual and the collective levels requires confronting ruptures in meaningful accounts of one's self and what it means to be human. This entails contact with aspects of human existence that were previously beneath the threshold of awareness, the ability to genuinely listen rather than automatically react, and the creation of new truths – new reactions, representations, and narratives – adequate to the always novel joys as well as the horrors of human experience.

Deleuze and Guattari (1986, 1987) invite us to attend not only to the minority other addressing a yet-to-be-invented subject, but to the forces beneath the threshold of awareness of one's personal self. Deleuze is suspicious of an ethics that would locate ethical agency and responsibility in notions of personhood that overlook the material and symbolic forces conditioning conscious thought and action. A recognizable personal self is the effect of habitual patternings of interactions among a complicated array of factors affecting human subjectivity. Minute shifts in such interactions will not produce noticeable change in an individual (or a society) until they reach critical threshold points, and yet such shifts are always occurring in keeping with internal and external changes of various sorts (anything from a change in the weather to new information about how the stock market works). Relatively minor changes (a new theory, or a new invention) could set off what appears to be a sweeping change that affects an individual or an entire culture by pushing a cascade of sub-threshold changes over the critical levels needed to produce radical change. Locating agency and accountability in an identifiable personal self is, for Deleuze, to ignore the virtual possibilities always latent in each and every state of being a subject. A Deleuzian ethics thus asks us to follow our passions as well as logic, bringing together the words and bodies that can release new modes of life that we can affirm. This means paying attention to individuals in the context of the social fields in which they find themselves, "mapping" ebbs and flows in movement, and making experimental interventions in words and actions to see what kind of effects we can produce (Deleuze and Guattari 1987).

Even psychoanalysis with its recognition of the negativity of the body fails, in Deleuze's view, to fully grasp the immersion of embodied life in a flux of elements that strive to maintain their patterns even as they shape and are shaped by other patterns. Deleuze and Guattari charge psychoanalysis with attempting to exert a vector of force upon the subjects it interprets that would constrain the subject's power to affect and be affected in keeping with the hegemonic norms of Oedipalized subjectivity (Deleuze and Guattari 1983). The myriad configurations of multiple kinds of elements that constitute embodied existence can combine with various vectors of social life to produce a personal self able to narrate her life with the help of socially available conventions. Personal identity can then be maintained by sustaining the habitual patterns – patterns of meaning and behavior as well as patterns of physical processes – which allow it to survive. But this, on their view, is to overlook the virtual force of other possibilities always with us. New connections with our environment, with others, with words, can always be made through the rupture and reconfiguration of the patterns forming us – some in defiance of our personal selves. Some of these connections might destroy us or send us into a dead-end (the destruction of the suicide bomber or the numb despair of the drug addict), but others could lead to an enlivening "line of flight" precipitating joyful change across the social field (Deleuze and Guattari 1987).

The work of Deleuze, and Deleuze and Guattari, put forward a view of a self that follows vectors of force in response to the problems it encounters. When the events of a hand landing on my face, seeing my child's face, and conceiving of myself as a "feminist" converge in the actualization of a specific state of affairs, I am presented with the problem of how to respond. Certain becomings converge with other becomings in a configuration that reaches a threshold resulting in a qualitative shift in my situation. These qualitative shifts are intensities that cannot be predicted or located in advance because they entail the convergence of multiple becomings at sub-threshold levels. As one vector of force among others, the sense of language also has thresholds that depend on the accumulating effects of forces that are imperceptible until certain limit points of meaning are reached. Selecting one description over another entails pursuing one vector of force as opposed to another. Pursuing the vector of force leading to leaving a man I cannot help rather than attempting to placate him entails the actualization of specific virtual relations in preference to others that are also available to me.

Deleuze and Guattari's notion of the nomadic subject suggests a response to imperceptible forces that could emerge in a responsiveness to difference in ourselves and others that neither renders difference invisible nor assimilates it to the recognizable (Deleuze and Guattari 1987). They encourage us to revisit our method lived experience not in order to repeat forms of the past already captured in cultural forms of representation, but in order to move with the vectors of force most present to us. Thus the meaning of feminism can shift and yet be continuous with past meanings and still resonate with the enfleshed memories we carry into the present. Their work suggests that we can render difference perceptible only if we are willing to continually transform ourselves in the process. Rather than losing ourselves in this process, however, we can rethink what it means to have a self and celebrate a continual becoming-other that shares in the collective transformation of larger social wholes. This entails conceiving ourselves according to a "differential" logic that locates who we are in a serial unfolding extending over time rather than a set of habitual patterns. As we evolve in our becoming-other, we carry with us the embodied passions of past experiences not simply in the form in which we consciously experienced them, but also in the form of virtual relations that were not then pursued. These virtual relations constitute the implicit force of alternative connections to sensations, feelings, words, things, people, events, and life itself in all its forms and all the elements of those forms in their continual becoming.

Although Deleuze and Guattari's project is motivated by what seems to me to be a basic feminist impulse – the desire to listen and respond to the human need to give truthful expression to one's experience – they do not pursue (beyond some discussion of "becoming-woman" I will not comment upon here) the implications of the event of being woman as a vector of force with specific effects in contemporary western culture. A feminist appropriation of Deleuze, and Deleuze and Guattari, needs to examine and experiment with multiple vectors of force that have special significance for women. Words like "woman," "female," and "feminine" have specific effects in configuration with the lived experience of sexed and sexual bodies in specific cultural contexts. Theorizing these effects in touch with a deeper memory than that of conventional narratives about the past means attending and responding to marginalized others as well as nonpersonal aspects of our lived experience in ways that release virtual forces that can then unfold in the creative evolution of our becoming-other.

Conclusion

On the view presented here, there is no need for one monolithic theory or for the fear that the only alternative to such a theory is a lack of theory. If we abandon the notion that all our feminist perspectives must fit into a totalizable whole, we could unfold our projects out of a virtual notion of feminism that conditions all our projects. Feminist theory as one important vector among many others can track concepts across the social field, providing connections among local struggles that release virtual possibilities and enliven a shared sense of purpose in a continually evolving community. Collective sharing requires opening ourselves and our categories to truths that have not yet been represented. These truths may evolve in various cultural arenas from practices like providing battered women with safehouses to the creation of art and the explorations of science. The grounds for social critique would lie neither in transcendent principles nor in a notion of woman that is considered to be complete. And yet generalizations could relate different situations and the experience gained from multiple experiments in living could be carried into the future. Theory would be evaluated in terms of its capacity to create enlivening connections among a diverse community whose members would, as Oliver would put it, attentively "witness" one another and themselves rather than recognize one another as members of an already defined community (Oliver 2001). Witnessing has connotations of allowing the unthought-of experience to emerge into cultural representation. It also requires what Ziarek calls an "ethics of dissensus" whereby we attend to the virtual force of our own nonpersonal and personal selves as well as that of others, ready to unfold unprecedented possibilities in living (Ziarek 2002).

The work of Deleuze and Guattari suggests that we not only can but also should conceive of the self as a becoming that unfolds in concert with other becomings. Theory as well is a force that actualizes, in concert with the other forces with which it unfolds, some relations rather than others among a field replete with the potential of all the relations of the virtual past. To fully respond to an other or to a situation as we enact our feminist principles, we need to welcome the self-transformations and theoretical evolutions resulting from what is always a unique convergence of forces. On the view developed here, this means disorienting recognizable categories in order to allow the creation of new meaning. If we could become more comfortable with the notion of a self as an individuating series or of a theory that evolves, we might worry less about the "correct" way to define what it means to be a woman or a feminist and become more open to experiencing life in terms of a differential logic. We could then engage such a logic in our theorizing by ourselves enacting an alternative style of subjectivity. Although this means challenging traditional conceptions of identity, truth, and reality, it means neither to do away with those notions entirely nor to undermine passionate engagement in social critique.

A feminist operating according to a differential logic would know that there are truths about women that need articulation and urgent work on behalf of women still to be done. She would evaluate her course of action by attending, insofar as she was able, to imperceptible forces moving toward threshold points that she may or may not choose to foster. This means that she would be not only highly attentive to the unfolding of meanings and passions that condition her present, but that she would have the imagination to implement creative insight in pragmatic ways. She would not constrain her desires and expectations to an inversion of a representable past, but would rather welcome the creative chaos that the actualization of new connections in her present resonant with her past entails. This approach to feminism would demand working with others and working with oneself toward new styles of subjectivity and doing theory. Such alternative styles could be terrifying if left unsupported by a collective process of sharing, but could also provide new strategies in empowering feminists to change their world for the better.

Feminist theory is not right or wrong in how it represents a world "out there." Rather it is a vector of force that opens up a way of doing things. It mutates and changes in keeping with the selves, goals, and situations with which it unfolds. It can and should resonate with the experiences we live with our bodies and hearts as well as our minds. It also can and should defy representations of reality in order to actualize the creative potential of a virtual past never actually lived. The thresholds of meaning for the events of "being a feminist" or "being a woman" may shift in keeping with the other becomings actualizations of those events entail. But if we define ourselves not through a core identity opposed to the world, but rather through the unfolding states of our becoming-other, we could better withstand the disorienting effects of listening to the experiences, narratives, and theories that challenge our reality. This, in turn, would allow us as "feminists," in our multiple actualizations of the event of being a feminist, to create a shared space-time in which we could face together the problems that confront us.

References

Benhabib, S. (1995) "Subjectivity, Historiography, and Politics: Reflections on the 'Feminism/Postmodernism' Exchange," in *Feminist Contentions: A Philosophical Exchange*, eds. S. Benhabib, J. Butler, D. Cornell, and N. Fraser, New York: Routledge, pp. 107–25.

Bergson, H. (1991) *Matter and Memory*, trs. N.M. Paul and W.S. Palmer, New York: Zone Books.

Braidotti, R. (1994) *Nomadic Subjects: Embodiment and Sexual Difference in Contemporary Feminist Theory*, New York: Columbia University Press.

Buchanan, I. and Colebrook, C., eds. (2000) *Deleuze and Feminist Theory*, Edinburgh: Edinburgh University Press.

Butler, J. (1990) *Gender Trouble: Feminism and the Subversion of Identity*, New York: Routledge.

—— (1995) "For a Careful Reading," in *Feminist Contentions: A Philosophical Exchange*, eds. S. Benhabib, J. Butler, D. Cornell, and N. Fraser, New York: Routledge, pp. 127–43.

Chanter, T. (2001) *Time, Death, and the Feminine: Levinas with Heidegger*, Stanford, CA: Stanford University Press.

Deleuze, G. (1986) *Cinema 1: The Movement-Image*, trs. Hugh Tomlinson and Barbara Habberjam, Minneapolis: University of Minnesota Press.

—— (1989) *Cinema 2: The Time-Image*, trs. Hugh Tomlinson and Robert Galeta, Minneapolis: University of Minnesota Press.

—— (1990) *The Logic of Sense*, tr. M. Lester, New York: Columbia University Press.

—— (1994) *Difference and Repetition*, tr. P. Patton, New York: Columbia University Press.

Deleuze, G. and Guattari, F. (1983) *Anti-Oedipus: Capitalism and Schizophrenia*, trs. R. Hurley, M. Seem, and H.R. Lane, Minneapolis: University of Minnesota Press.

—— (1986) *Kafka: Toward a Minor Literature*, tr. D. Polan, Minneapolis: University of Minnesota Press.

—— (1987) *A Thousand Plateaus: Capitalism and Schizophrenia*, tr. B. Massumi, Minneapolis: University of Minnesota Press.

—— (1994) *What Is Philosophy?* trs. H. Tomlinson and G. Burchell, New York: Columbia University Press.

Diprose, R. (1994) *The Bodies of Women: Ethics, Embodiment, and Sexual Difference*, New York: Routledge.

Gatens, M. (1996) *Imaginary Bodies: Ethics, Power, and Corporeality*, New York: Routledge.

Griggers, C. (1997) *Becoming-Woman*, Minneapolis: University of Minnesota Press.

Grosz, E. (1994) *Volatile Bodies: Toward a Corporeal Feminism*, Bloomington: Indiana University Press.

Herman, J.L. (1992) *Trauma and Recovery*, New York: Basic Books.

hooks, b. (1981) *Ain't I a Woman? Black Women and Feminism*, Boston, MA: South End Press.

Hull, G.T., Scott, P.B., and Smith, B., eds. (1982) *All the Women Are White, All the Blacks Are Men, But Some of Us Are Brave: Black Women's Studies*, New York: The Feminist Press.

Irigaray, L. (1993) *An Ethics of Sexual Difference*, trs. C. Burke and G.C. Gill, Ithaca, NY: Cornell University Press.

Jaggar, A.M. (1983) *Feminist Politics and Human Nature*, Totowa, NJ: Rowman and Allanheld.

Kristeva, J. (1984) *Revolution in Poetic Language*, New York: Columbia University Press.

Laclau, E. and Mouffe, C. (1985) *Hegemony and Socialist Strategy: Towards a Radical Democratic Politics*, London: Verso.

Langer, L.L. (1991) *Holocaust Testimonies: The Ruins of Memory*, New Haven, CT: Yale University Press.

Lorraine, T. (1999) *Irigaray and Deleuze: Experiments in Visceral Philosophy*, Ithaca, NY: Cornell University Press.

Mitchell, J. (1974) *Psychoanalysis and Feminism*, New York: Vintage.

Mouffe, C. (1992) "Feminism, Citizenship, and Radical Democratic Politics," in *Feminists Theorize the Political*, eds. J. Butler and J.W. Scott, New York: Routledge.

Nussbaum, M.C. (1999) "The Professor of Parody: The Hip Defeatism of Judith Butler," *New Republic*, February 22.

Oliver, K. (2001) *Witnessing: Beyond Recognition*, Minneapolis: University of Minnesota Press.

Sawicki, J. (1991) *Disciplining Foucault: Feminism, Power, and the Body*, New York: Routledge.

Shay, J. (1994) *Achilles in Vietnam: Combat Trauma and the Undoing of Character*, New York: Simon and Schuster.

Spivak, G.C. (1988) *In Other Worlds: Essays in Cultural Politics*, New York: Routledge.

Ziarek, E.P. (2001) *An Ethics of Dissensus: Postmodernity, Feminism, and the Politics of Radical Democracy*, Stanford, CA: Stanford University Press.

Further Reading

Boundas, C.V. and Olkowski, D., eds. (1994) *Gilles Deleuze and the Theatre of Philosophy*, New York: Routledge.

Braidotti, R. (1994) "Of Bugs and Women: Irigaray and Deleuze on the Becoming-Woman," in *Engaging with Irigaray: Feminist Philosophy and Modern European Thought*, eds. Carolyn Burke, Naomi Schor, and Margaret Whitford, New York: Columbia University Press, pp. 111–37.

Colebrook, C. (2002) *Gilles Deleuze*, New York: Routledge.

Deleuze, G. (1983) *Nietzsche and Philosophy*, tr. H. Tomlinson, New York: Columbia University Press.

Grosz, E. (1989) *Sexual Subversions: Three French Feminists*, Sydney: Allen and Unwin.

—— (1990) "Contemporary Theories of Power and Subjectivity," in *Feminist Knowledge: Critique and Construct*, ed. S. Gunew, New York: Routledge, pp. 59–120.

Holland, E.W. (1999) *Deleuze and Guattari's Anti-Oedipus*, New York: Routledge.

Kaufman, E. and Heller, K.J., eds. (1998) *Deleuze and Guattari: New Mappings in Politics, Philosophy, and Culture*, Minneapolis: University of Minnesota Press.

Massumi, B. (1992) *A User's Guide to Capitalism and Schizophrenia: Deviations from Deleuze and Guattari*, Cambridge, MA: MIT Press.

Nicholson, L.J., ed. (1990) *Feminism/Postmodernism*, New York: Routledge.

Patton, P., ed. (1996) *Deleuze: A Critical Reader*, Cambridge, MA: Blackwell Publishers.

—— (2000) *Deleuze and the Political*, New York: Routledge.

Rodowick, D.N. (1997) *Gilles Deleuze's Time Machine*, Durham, NC: Duke University Press.

—— (1999) "The Memory of Resistance," in *A Deleuzian Century?* ed. I. Buchanan, Durham, NC: Duke University Press, pp. 37–57.

Weedon, C. (1987) *Feminist Practice and Poststructuralist Theory*, New York: Basil Blackwell.

Author Index

Addams, Jane, 64, 65, 66–8, 72, 75
Addelson, Kathy, 237
Addison, Joseph, 257
Agrippa, Henricus Cornelius, 21–2
Ahmed, Leila, 157
Alcoff, Linda Martín, 197, 223, 224
Alexander, Jacqui, 165
Amundson, Ron, 136
Anderson, Elizabeth, 245–51
Antoni, Janine, 261
Anzaldúa, Gloria, 173
Appiah, Kwame Anthony, 166, 168, 169
Arendt, Hannah, 46, 159–60
Aquinas, St Thomas, 30, 31, 50–1
Aristotle, 6, 13n, 24, 32, 33, 43, 44, 47, 48–9, 198, 262
Arnault, Lynne, 94
Astell, Mary, 18, 19, 20, 149, 159
Augustine, St, 28–9, 49–50, 55
Austin, John L., 5

Baier, Annette, 17, 47, 128n, 139
Bakhurst, David, 238
Ball, Carlos A., 190
Barad, Karen, 224
Barenbaum, Nicole, 248–50
Bar On, Bat-Ami, 17
Barron, Karin, 133
Bartky, Sandra, 105–6
Basil, St, 29, 30, 33
Battersby, Christine, 256
Baugh, S. Gayle, 87
Beauvoir, Simone de, 1, 3, 18, 46, 56, 64, 193, 222, 224, 261
Benhabib, Seyla, 91–2, 150, 219, 267, 268
Benson, Paul, 128n, 163n
Bergson, Henri, 73, 274
Beverley, John, 171
Bhabha, Homi, 170
Bijvoet, Maya, 23, 24

Boccaccio, Giovanni, 21
Bolte, Angela, 12, 85
Bovenschen, Sylvia, 256, 258
Brand, Peg, 258, 261, 262
Brison, Susan, 159
Broude, Norma, 256, 259
Brown, Wendy, 152
Browne, Irene, 194–5
Brownmiller, Susan, 86
Burke, Edmund, 257–8
Burnyeat, Myles, 24, 39n
Butler, Judith, 65, 161n, 184, 202, 205, 218, 266, 267, 268, 269, 270

Cahill, Ann, 261
Calhoun, Cheshire, 8, 11, 110, 112, 182, 184, 188
Campbell, Sue, 107–8
Card, Claudia, 82, 85, 97n, 112, 178, 181, 184, 188
Carlson, Licia, 133
Cassin, Barbara, 47
Castiglione, Baldesar, 22, 27, 28, 32
Cheney, Jim, 229
Chester, Nia, 248–50
Chicago, Judy, 259, 260
Chodorow, Nancy, 205
Christian, Barbara, 197
Christina of Sweden, Queen, 19
Cixous, Hélène, 266
Clapp, Elsie Ridley, 64–5
Clare, Eli, 137
Clough, Sharyn, 65
Code, Lorraine, 4–5, 12, 220, 223, 226, 230
Cohen, Jean, 87
Collins, Patricia Hill, 199, 217, 242
Conley, Verena, 229
Conway, Anne, 18
Copeland, Ann, 248–50
Cornell, Drucilla, 152

Subject Index

ableness, 82, 94, 194
abortion, 7, 81, 84–5, 118, 121, 148, 153, 160, 181
absolutism, 71
academic feminism, 75, 81, 93, 95, 134, 145, 166, 172, 190, 193, 194, 195, 198, 199, 205
activism, 153, 167, 172, 195, 205
aesthetic(s), 6, 18, 52, 53, 54; of disgust, 261; feminine, 256, 258, 261; feminism and, 256–63; Philosophy of Art, 254–5; vaginal, 261; *see also* art/artworks
affect, 54, 108, 221, 239, 250, 269, 273; *see also* emotion
affirmative action, 87–8
Afghanistan, 157
Africa, 70, 107, 151, 159, 167, 200
African-American feminism, 147–8
agency, 75, 90, 103, 109, 153–4, 197, 203, 215, 224, 236, 261, 268; agentic skills, 90–1; epistemic, 215, 218, 228, 237, 239, 240, 243–4, 269; moral/ethical, 102–4, 123, 127, 216, 219, 220, 276
alterity, 222, 227
American philosophy, 64–8, 75, 211, 257
Ancient Greece, 3, 200
androcentrism, 6, 117, 215–16, 217
anthropology, 224, 242; anti-discrimination, 87; gender, 193; gender as anthropological interest, 36; law, 184, 196; lesbian, 187–8; marriage, 180–1, 184; *see also* discrimination
anti-miscegenation laws, 185
anti-Semitism, 180
art/artworks: cinema, 275; critique of the canon, 259; female body in, 255, 260–1; feminist critique, 256–61; male viewers, 258; performance, 255, 260; responses to, 254–5; *see also* aesthetics
art history, 18, 256, 259

autonomy, 6, 11, 81, 89–91, 103, 121, 137, 151–9, 163n, 215, 218, 221; care ethics and, 11, 81, 89, 103, 117, 152; epistemic, 218, 221, 224, 237

beauty: aesthetics, 6, 198, 254, 257, 258, 262; ideals/standards, 255, 259; women as object, 260–1
Bible, 31, 41n; interpretation, 21, 24, 29–34, 50
bioethics, 10, 116–28
biology: biological determinism, 131, 186, 197, 201; biological essentialism, 93, 197, 203; biological separatism, 138; disability and, 132, 134–5, 138; gendered, 48–9, 50–1, 135, 197
black feminism, 217, 242; *see also* African-American feminism
black women, 75, 118, 195–6, 197, 199, 242; *see also* women of color
bluestocking, 212
the body, 47, 49, 52, 65, 135, 148, 159, 260–1, 269, 276

capital, 145, 171
capitalism, 146–7, 217, 23; global/international, 119–20, 165–6, 170–2; neo-liberal, 170–2
care, 71, 92, 118, 124–5, 139–40, 146, 149, 150, 152, 155, 163n; dependency and, 155; duty to, 52
care ethics, 10–12, 69, 81–4, 85, 89, 92, 95n, 117, 118, 119, 132, 140, 150; *see also* ethics
care work, 87, 110, 117, 149, 155–6, 173
caregiver(s), 75, 117, 125, 126, 133, 139–40, 150, 156, 163n
Catholicism, 24, 30–1, 40n; fideism, 25, 35, 42n
childcare, 70, 88, 146, 147, 149, 153, 154, 156

epistemic subjectivity, 5, 211, 217, 218, 221, 228, 229

epistemic subjects, 215, 217, 220

epistemic violence, 168, 171, 227, 229

epistemology, 8–9, 10, 11; community and, 12, 71–2, 122, 127, 215, 221, 237, 242; contextual values in, 11, 235, 237–6, 245–51; ecological naturalism, 228–31; emotions and, 213–14, 250; feminist, 121–3, 216–31; feminist empiricism, 217, 218–19, 236, 243; individualism in, 20, 53, 215, 216, 227–8, 237; naturalistic, 225–6; orthodox/traditional, 211, 215–17, 223; postmodern, 218, 236; postmodernist critique of, 218, 223; pragmatist, 71–2; situated knowledge, 226–8, 230; social location and, 244; socialized, 215; standpoint, 91, 93, 123, 147, 185, 217–19, 236, 238–40, 242, 243, 244–5; strong objectivity, 242, 243; weak objectivity, 241; see also knowledge

equality: see gender equality

equity feminism, 149

essentialism, 168, 185, 193, 197–8, 201, 203–4, 238–9, 259; anti-essentialism, 185, 197, 203, 218; categorical, 188–9; cross-cultural/temporal, 187–8; cultural, 158; naturalistic, 186–7; perspectival, 185–6

ethical autonomy, 89–91

ethics, 9, 10; applied, 81, 84–9; bioethics, 116–27; care, 10–12, 69, 81–4, 85, 89, 92, 95n, 117, 118, 119, 132, 140, 150; communicative/discourse, 81, 91–2, 93–4; environmental, 88–9; expressive-collaborative model, 92, 118; individualism in, 93–4; Kantian, 52, 83, 117; lesbian, 182–5; neuroethics, 120–1; pragmatist, 65, 67; utilitarian, 83, 117, 118; virtue ethics/theory, 83, 118

ethnicity, 75, 120, 148, 170, 179, 186, 194, 197, 200, 238, 263, 266

ethnocentrism, 157

family, 156; disability and, 133; gender equality, 86; justice, 150; marriage, 85; as private sphere, 93, 150; traditional, 156, 249

feminist epistemology: see epistemology

feminist historiography, 2–3, 20

feminist philosophy: in the academy, 2, 95, 145, 167, 172, 173, 190, 193, 194, 195, 198, 205; as research program, 8–10; women's experiences and, 5–12, 23, 26–7, 50, 53, 65–7, 72, 74, 75, 84–5, 89, 90, 94, 95, 96n, 104, 105–9, 111, 122–3, 131, 134–6, 137, 139, 140, 147, 150, 152–3, 159, 166, 185–6, 193, 194, 197–201, 218–23, 225, 231, 239, 241, 245–6, 249–51, 255–7, 261–3, 266, 267–3, 275–80

feminist political philosophy: boundaries,

145–6; equality, 148–52; justice and dependency, 150; methodology, 147–8

feminist pragmatism: see pragmatist feminism

feminist voice theory, 90–1

freedom, 6, 68, 126, 145, 148, 151–2, 153, 154, 155, 157, 158, 163n, 224, 270; reproductive, 138, 216; see also autonomy

friendship, 183, 188

gender: intersectionality, 87–8, 148, 152, 179–80, 193–205; justice and, 2, 5, 9–10, 81–4, 148, 150–1, 152, 154; performative nature, 184; in philosophical canon, 2–3, 46–53

gender equality, 4, 11, 145, 152, 153, 156, 158, 160; under capitalism, 145–7, 150; care work and, 139; dependency and, 150; epistemology and, 11, 215–16; equity feminism, 149; family and, 85–6, 145, 147, 150; in the history of philosophy, 3, 20, 22–5, 33–4, 47–51; as political struggle, 148–9

gendered reason, 5, 46, 52, 54–5, 82, 94, 211–15

global capitalism, 165, 170–1, 172

global emancipatory projects, 229

global feminist discourse, 92

global subaltern groups, 200

the good, 6, 9

good life, 92, 157

Guerilla Girls, 260

habit, 273–8

health care, 85, 118–20, 122, 128

hermeneutics, 218, 224, 227

heterosexualism, 183

heterosexuality, 181–2, 183, 188, 189; feigning, 178, 184; heterosexist oppression, 179; heterosexual marriage, 85; postmodern approach, 189; public identity, 178; rape and, 159; social construction, 187

history of philosophy, 2–3, 43–59

homophobia, 178, 182

homosexuality: as artificial category, 183, 187; biological understanding, 186; see also heterosexuality

Hull House, 66–8

human nature, 147, 148, 201, 218, 221, 228, 258

humanism, 169

Hypatia, 18, 64, 116, 257, 260–1

identity, 157; Deleuzean theory, 271–80; disability, 132–4; discursively constituted, 267; in epistemic hierarchy, 223; FMP (Females, Mothers, Primary sexual choices), 203–5; gender identity disorder, 184; intersected, 196, 199; intersubjective, 91; lesbian, 185–9; sexual, 189, 203; social, 12, 223